Teaching Reading:
Language, Letters & Thought
Second Edition

Teaching Reading

Language, Letters & Thought

Second Edition

Sara Brody, EdD

editor

LARC Publishing
Milford, New Hampshire
http://www.LARCPublishing.com/

Teaching Reading: Language, Letters, and Thought, Second Edition.

For information contact LARC Publishing, P.O. Box 801, Milford, NH 03055, (603) 880-7691.
http://www.LARCPublishing.com

ISBN 1-886042-13-6

2nd edition   3 4 5 6 7 8 9 10

*Dedicated to caring professionals and parents
who lovingly persist in bestowing
the gifts of literacy by teaching
their students how to read.*

Contents

List of Tables

List of Figures

I. OVERVIEW

Introduction

Reading with understanding augments our ability to learn and remember, and invites us to engage at our leisure with other people's most complex and cherished thoughts. While reading, we draw on our facility with language, identify and interpret printed symbols, and extend our thoughts beyond the confines of our backgrounds.

Reading is enhanced by good teaching that sensitizes a learner to the nuances of language and the subtleties of print. Effective instructors consider when to teach about letters and when to teach about thought; when to focus on a single component and when to integrate the whole. Skilled teachers know how to demonstrate the steps of a process and how to set up unobtrusive environments that let books and readers' curiosity engage spontaneously.

Given the complexity of reading and its instruction, the education literature is replete with ever-changing recommendations concerning how to teach reading. Although these recommendations often seem to conflict with each other, school systems sometimes shift methods and philosophies to flow with prevailing attitudes and theories. Often, recommendations and approaches are instituted broadly without an understanding of students' diverse needs that vary by individual differences such as maturation, experience, and ability.

When teachers use an approach recommended by an article, workshop, or their school system, the responses of their students often indicate that it works for some but not for others. Further, what works for some children at one time seems to lose its effectiveness, even with these students, when they grow beyond its purpose. At times, this conflict between recommendations and practical results contributes to feelings of dissatisfaction and frustration.

Faced with such experiences, educators often seek a means of teaching effectively that transcends shifts in trends and materials. Teachers wish to clarify their experiential knowledge of how and when to present various components of reading. In essence, educators desire a consistent base from which to provide instruction grounded in what students need to learn, and the sequence in which they need to learn it, as a means of enhancing reading competency and pleasure.

In response to these issues, the first edition of this volume was developed to articulate the basic components of reading—what they are, as well as why, when, and how they are taught. An effort was made to specify the elements that underlie effective reading instruction, whatever the approach in favor, as a base from which to teach confidently while using a variety of methods and materials.

Recently, the National Reading Panel released findings concerning their meta-analysis performed with hundreds of methodologically sound research studies drawn from across the field of reading. Their results parallel our earlier recommendations. Their match with our material further confirmed the soundness of our perspective and strategies. We offer this second edition, with updates, in hopes of further assisting dedicated teachers of reading, both specialists and classroom educators, in making informed choices when planning programs and lessons or selecting resources to foster success and love of reading.

The opening chapter presents an overview of essential reading components and their maturation, along with a discussion of effective teaching practices that encourage vulnerable learners. Next, language, a vital precursor and contributor to reading is reviewed through an exploration of its developmental stages and markers, along with recommendations for home and preschool activities. Then, phonemic awareness is discussed by considering its role as a component that bridges between language and reading abilities. A myriad of strategies for teaching and encouraging it at home, preschool, and school are presented.

Several chapters examine the decoding aspect of reading. First, historical trends in reading instruction are described, followed by discussion of various components of beginning reading—the learning of letter-sound correspondences, word families, and common syllabic patterns—taught in a direct and systematic manner as well as through practice while reading engaging stories. Sample frameworks for classroom instruction and more intensive intervention are offered.

A chapter concerning advanced word recognition and practice explores the role of automatic decoding, along with rapid-naming and recognition of story structures, in developing fluent reading. Spelling instruction is presented as a path to reading proficiency. Discussion includes a view of the stage-like progression in which spelling is generally learned and principles for teaching less-skilled spellers. Instructional recommendations include strategies to reduce spelling problems.

The next chapters investigate the comprehension processes of reading. Specific components include: using textbooks and literature to gather information and construct meaning, increasing background knowledge, learning word meanings to enhance understanding, and solidifying knowledge through writing.

To determine which reading component(s) require instruction for particular students at particular times, the final chapters examine several aspects of formal and informal assessment. Guidelines are offered concerning the selection of tests based on their potential strengths and weaknesses for evaluating particular reading components. In addition, wise and ethical procedures are noted for use during assessment and while reporting results. Finally, the process of forging a link between evaluation findings and appropriate instruction is explored by examining case studies drawn from students with various reading needs and abilities.

The authors of this volume come to their writing with rich backgrounds in both theory and practice. They have engaged seriously with language, reading, and cognitive research, yet they also possess practical understanding acquired through teaching. In each chapter, an author describes one particular component of reading, along with various views concerning its role in reading. Then procedures for teaching the component and integrating it with others are presented.

When any method or material is suggested, the author describes the underlying principles that render it effective for a particular instructional purpose. Often, varied materials are noted that can be used to teach one aspect of reading. In these instances, the effective elements that cross materials are discussed. The writings attempt to support teachers as they draw from a variety of materials that achieve the same end, or assemble their own. Some ideas may confirm what teachers already find working; others may suggest variations that can enhance instructional effectiveness. It is hoped that the suggestions encourage teachers as they continue to nurture confidence and a love of reading among all their students.

6

Chapter 1. Reading with Language, Letters, and Thought: An Overview

Sara Brody, EdD

Reading is a complex cognitive process that unfolds over a long period of time. To support its development, a core constellation of reading components and related automatic processes evolve to ever more sophisticated levels of interactive proficiency. Before reading develops, children generally express their ideas with language. Through experience and instruction, novices learn how letters represent language and thought. As readers mature, they branch out to explore increasingly complex material and learn to comprehend multifaceted issues.

This chapter explores critical literacy components and how they contribute to the maturation of reading. Language, decoding, comprehension, and their interplay are viewed along with their underlying automatic processes. In addition, questions concerning which components need focused instructional attention at particular levels of reading development are considered. The chapter includes a review of practical elements that characterize exemplary reading instruction—with emphasis on the use of scaffolds, models, and confirmation.

Reading—Components and Stages of Maturation

Language, decoding, comprehension, and underlying automatic cognitive processes are components that interact to support many levels of reading ability. One or another of these components often requires greater instructional attention at particular levels of development. At such times, several better-coordinated components may function smoothly while readers engage in learning and practicing a less-familiar component. This, in turn, reinforces the more developed abilities. For example, rich knowledge of word meanings confirms novices as they learn to decode words by their letters and sounds. Later, skilled decoding supports learning of unfamiliar technical words and their meanings.

When mastered and integrated, core components of reading produce the desired outcome of instruction—the ability to read thoughtfully, constructively, and with deep understanding of complex issues. This compelling result may tempt us to focus on teaching the reading process at its highest level, holistically, rather than developmentally selecting specific components to emphasize at particular times. However, instruction and planning need to take into account the gradual maturation of human language, cognition, and physiology. In humans, concrete abilities develop early, then serve as a foundation for more complex and abstract skills that unfold later (Fischer, 1980; Fischer & Rose, 1998; Piaget, 1971).

A maturational interactive-component view of reading coordinates both the interactive and maturational aspects of reading components. Such a perspective is supported by a broad array of cognitive, physiological, and educational research. This material has been reviewed and synthesized in various ways by Chall (1983, 1996), Adams (1994), National Research Council (1998), and the National Reading Panel [NRP] (2000). Chall's synthesis presents a format for viewing reading acquisition as a series of stages that begins with a precursor Stage 0, in which the language component is foremost, and then culminates in the reading of diverse, complex perspectives at Stage 5, in which all components interact skillfully and seamlessly. The NRP meta-analysis, which examined the results of hundreds of recent reading studies, delineates specific reading components that contribute to skilled literacy.

The discussion below draws on the reading components highlighted by the NRP research along with Chall's stages to describe increasing levels of reading ability. At each reading level, proficiency is delineated by how well certain components are mastered and the extent others need instruction. These levels provide a convenient means of discussing which reading components need focused instruction at particular times. Chall's stage terminology is used to label levels of reading development throughout the chapters of this text. The use of stages as labels does not imply that reading matures in a lock-step manner. In fact, movement among these stages varies continually based on a reader's background and abilities in relation to a text's difficulty or familiarity.

MATURATION OF READING COMPONENTS–STAGES 0 through 5

Emphasis on the language component (Stage 0). During their early years, children typically develop great facility with oral language. They learn to communicate using a variety of syntactic structures and a wide range of vocabulary. In addition, children generally recognize thousands of spoken words by the time they enter first grade. Along with the development of oral language, children who are read to from books, and who tell stories from pictures, learn that print is a special code that somehow preserves and transmits language. When given guidance, these children often begin to recognize a few letters, identify some words on road signs or products, and draw messages with letters or scribbles (Chall, 1996). Chapter 2 in this volume provides a detailed description of language development activities.

Attention to phonemic awareness (Transition to Stage 1). In languages with alphabetic writing systems, the speech sounds of language correspond to the print system of reading. As children's oral language becomes well established, they can begin to notice the sound patterns of the words in their language. In a step that leads toward becoming readers of an alphabetic system, beginners start to recognize that the words in the sound stream of oral language separate into syllables, and the syllables into initial, medial, and ending sounds (Goswami, 2000; Liberman, 1987).

Phonemic awareness—sensitivity to the sound patterns of oral language— is a crucial understanding that marks the transition from Stage 0 to Stage 1. As phonemic awareness develops, learners can advance in reading. They progress from creating and interacting with speech to actually transforming printed letters into language. Learners demonstrate their phonemic awareness by separating and combining the sounds of spoken words during word play, poetry reading, and other oral language activities (Williams, 1980; Yopp & Yopp, 2000). Phonemic awareness is an ability that can be taught. Instruction that includes the use of letters to represent their sounds effectively combines phonemic awareness and instruction with learning to read during this transition time (Goswami, 2000). Chapter 3 provides a detailed discussion of phonemic awareness and activities that encourage its development.

Learning to decode letters, words, and simple stories (Stage 1). As phonemic awareness becomes established, novices enter Chall's Stage 1. During this stage, beginners break the barrier of print's secret code. As they extend their knowledge of the relationships between single letters and their sounds, learners begin to recognize letter-cluster/sound patterns such as *bug, rug, hug* (Rath, 2000). As they expand their decoding repertoire, readers increase their opportunities for independent access to the wealth of rich language experiences that are locked in print. In alphabetic systems, learning the code appears to be a crucial developmental step in reading maturation[1]. When students are similar in physical and cognitive abilities, background knowledge, vocabulary breadth, and exposure to reading materials, it is print-to-sound knowledge that separates those who can read unfamiliar words and sentences independently from those who cannot (Blachman, 2000; Lyon, 1998; Rath, 1990).

Much debate surrounds the teaching of decoding. Research repeatedly demonstrates the effectiveness of directly teaching phonological knowledge—letters, letter-clusters, and their associated sounds—an approach commonly referred to as phonics (Adams, 1994; Chall, 1967; Ehri, 1998). Some educators contend that children will have a greater love of reading if they discover the code

---

[1] Reading involves the understanding of thought conveyed by print. To understand written messages, readers draw meaning from text in one of two ways. When approaching text that is written in an alphabetic system, readers often decode letters to their corresponding sounds, and then use those sounds to recognize the word and its meaning. In contrast, readers respond to text written in a logographic (picture) system, such as Chinese, by memorizing the look of a printed word as a "picture," and then connecting it with its meaning.

Even in an alphabetic writing system, beginners sometimes read without attending to letter sounds. However, total reliance on the perceiving of words as logographs (pictures), without making use of letters to represent specific sounds, requires memorization of each word. An alphabetic system, such as English, lets readers use letters as symbols of sounds. Rather than memorizing thousands of words, readers in an alphabetic writing system can learn letter-sound correspondences and thereby use the decoding approach. Decoding is an efficient means of comprehending unfamiliar text—it does not require prior memorization of each word used.

If a reader is interested in a detailed understanding of theoretical reading models, background appears in LaBerge & Samuels (1974), Rummelhart & Ortony (1977), and the synthesis by Samuels & Kamil (1984). For a sense of the type of tasks that establish the role of decoding, see the work of Blachman, (2000), Goswami (2000), Lesch & Pollatsek (1993), Perfetti (1984), or Stanovich, Cunningham, & Feeman (1984). And for insight into meaning processes and their interaction with decoding, refer to the models proposed by Adams (1990), Just & Carpenter (1981, 1987), Kintsch, (1998), Kintsch & vanDijk (1978), or Perfetti & Curtis (1986). Some of this material was discussed in Brody (1994).

of print on their own indirectly (Smith, 1988). Yet, research continues to provide overwhelming evidence indicating the need and effectiveness of direct, systematic instruction in letters and sounds for Stage 1 readers (Moats, 2000; NRP, 2000).

Certainly, an overemphasis on phonics instruction after the secret of code is mastered would be fruitless. However, learners who have developed phonemic awareness tend to respond with delight and excitement when introduced to the link between sounds and letters, shown how those sounded letters form words, and helped to read those words in sentences and short paragraphs.

Since people learn at different rates, readers vary in the amount of instruction and practice needed to learn the alphabetic code. This variation is prompted by factors such as how often the learner practices, whether a learning disability is present, and the extent of reading exposure available outside the school setting (Goswami, 2000; Leslie & Allen, 1999; Stanovich, 1994). Children with learning disabilities, as well as learners from environments that offer few opportunities for practice, encounter great difficulty if expected to learn the code only from indirect exposure.

Instruction in the sounds of letters, letter-clusters, and their blending in words is critical for learners. People who do not receive sufficient instruction cannot assimilate the code from limited, indirect classroom experiences (Adams, 1994; Chall, 1967; Honig, 1998; Juel & Minden-Cupp, 2000; Perfetti, 1984). Chapter 4 offers a detailed analysis of Stage 1 reading instruction—its historical development, crucial elements, and methods of instruction. In addition, Chapter 6 explores the role of spelling in enhancing decoding ability.

Advanced decoding strategies and practice to fluency (Stage 2). As learners practice reading words, sentences, and then familiar stories and passages, they mature to a subsequent reading stage. Stage 2 is a time of developing fluency and automaticity (unconscious speed and accuracy) in decoding connected text. Stage 2 learners develop advanced decoding skills and acquire fluency during repeated reading practice with stories and passages that follow common structures to express familiar experiences (Chall, 1996; NRP, 2000).

As they read, beginners develop confidence in their decoding ability. Familiarity with the language and content of simple reading material confirms to beginners that they have read accurately. As learners repeatedly read words many times in many different sentences, and also on word lists, they develop automaticity in sounding words and retrieving meaning in connected text (Brody,

2001; Chomsky, 1978; Samuels, Schermer, & Reinking, 1992; Wolf, Miller, & Donnelly, 2000).

Stage 2 is differentiated from Stage 1 since it is not minimal knowledge of letter-cluster/sound correspondences that constrains progress. Instead, automaticity and fluency with this, and more advanced, decoding knowledge need to develop before one can read and comprehend more challenging text independently. Although readers entering Stage 2 can decipher stories, much of their attention is absorbed by sounding out words and retrieving their meanings (Wolf, Bowers, & Biddle, 2000; Wolf & Obregon, 1997). Consequently, little attention remains available to comprehend unfamiliar content.

After decoding and retrieving word meaning become automatic, through practice with much oral and silent reading, attention becomes free to engage in comprehending unfamiliar text during independent reading (Pressley, 2000; Perfetti, 1984; Stanovich, 1980). Chapter 5 explores the nature of automaticity, its contribution to reading ability, and strategies that enhance fluency and confidence.

Comprehending unfamiliar text (Stage 3). As students emerge from Stage 2 with confidence in their ability to decode print and understand the messages of familiar stories, reading takes on a new dimension. As Chall (1996) aptly states, rather than "learning to read," students now begin to "read to learn." During this stage, learners spend a great deal of time broadening their knowledge of the world around them.

Among Stage 3 readers, language and reading offer a bridge to extend beyond concrete and personally centered messages to an understanding of the larger world. Students typically enter Stage 3 around 4th grade. At the same time, they encounter more difficult texts in the content areas, as well as more sophisticated literature. They begin the process of gathering extensive knowledge by reading specialized text (Chall & Conard, 1991; NRP, 2000). See Chapter 7 for a discussion of the comprehension aspect of reading.

Stage 3 challenges readers to expand in several ways. These readers need to construct understanding from specialized words and unfamiliar concepts. At the same time, readers need to remember their learnings by incorporating them into a growing collection of background knowledge that will be drawn on in future reading. A great deal of learning in Stage 3 involves the development of a depth and breadth of background knowledge. Students need to enrich their knowledge by internalizing an abundance of word meanings and concepts that reach into a broad array of domains (Biemiller, 2000; Brody, 1989). See Chapter 8 concerning background knowledge and Chapter 9 for a discussion of vocabulary development.

During this time, readers also need to extend their language facility to incorporate familiarity with a wider variety of literary genres and expository structures (Liebling, 1989; NRP, 2000). As instruction focuses on development in a variety of areas shared by reading and language comprehension, writing takes on an important role in clarifying, completing, and generating new understanding. The intertwining of the reading and writing aspects of print encourages agility and thoughtful engagement with the abstract language of reading (Stotsky, 1986; Moats, 2000/1999). See Chapter 10 regarding the role of writing in the development of reading comprehension.

Exploring abstract, complex, varied points of view (Stage 4). When students have developed the ability to learn unfamiliar information from text and comprehend specialized concepts, they enter Stage 4. Typically, it is in high school or later that learners begin to read, with relative ease, materials that present abstract concepts and issues from multiple points of view (Chall, 1996). As they continue to read widely, students seem to develop automaticity in their ability to gather meaning from unfamiliar text—a skill that required attention during Stage 3.

Learners begin to read selectively from an array of sources and select material relevant to their studies. Instruction at this stage draws on reading and writing to integrate complex concepts (Curtis & Longo, 2000). As their automaticity in "learning the new" from unfamiliar texts develops, readers appear to assimilate new concepts and multiple meanings with fluent ease. During the wide reading of this stage, they gather material voraciously from diverse sources and multiple points of view to develop their stock of background knowledge (Chall, 1996). Chapters 7 - 10 briefly discuss extending strategies beyond Stage 3 to the complex materials of Stage 4 reading.

Synthesizing abstract, complex, conflicting concepts (Stage 5). Once readers achieve automaticity in gathering and assimilating knowledge from unfamiliar material, readers may advance to Stage 5, the ultimate stage of reading ability. Generally at the college level, Stage 5 readers create new, complex knowledge by synthesizing the material they are reading with the knowledge and beliefs they have acquired over time (Chall, 1996).

Readers at Stage 5 make use of what is learned from reading but extend their understanding beyond any of their earlier conceptions or viewpoints. This new understanding exceeds what is expressed by its constituent parts. Many of the

14

activities recommended in Chapters 7 - 10 for Stage 3 and 4 reading lay the groundwork for later development of Stage 5 reading.

Variation. Variation occurs in the rate at which learners acquire reading ability. How quickly reading matures at any particular stage is influenced by the way in which reading is taught as well as by a number of additional factors. The amount of time spent practicing affects how quickly reading matures.

Some children come to school from homes that provide extensive exposure to books along with practice in identifying letters and their sounds through activities such as games with magnetic letters, writing little notes, playing "school" with older siblings, conversing about letters and their sounds with parents during bedtime reading, and observations of signs during car trips. When these children enter school, some of them need only cursory instruction in letters and their sounds.

Since early home instruction in letters and sounds, books, and listening is invisible to teachers, some children appear to learn how to read in school simply by sharing books and ideas. Many other children begin 1st grade with limited home exposure to letters, stories, and literary language. These children can become very able readers, but only if school provides appropriate instruction at critical stages (Chall, 1996; Goswami, 2000; Lyon, 2000; Stanovich, 1986).

The extent to which earlier stages are mastered before a later one is introduced also influences development. For example, the extent that a reader masters decoding fluency during Stage 2 influences how much attention can be allocated to the comprehension of unfamiliar text during Stage 3. In addition, the extent that a learner develops rich, accurate vocabulary and background knowledge during Stage 3 determines how effectively background knowledge can support the reading of texts that present varied points of view during Stage 4 (NRP, 2000; Pressley, 2000; Stotsky, 1999; Wilson & Anderson, 1986).

Variation in learners' cognitive abilities also influences rate of reading maturation. Students who experience learning disabilities often require additional time to develop competency in the beginning reading stages (Lerner, 2000; National Research Council, 1998). Even physical factors influence the rate of progress through developmental stages, and a check of eyesight and hearing is wise when reading is not progressing as expected. Further, emotional factors such as unresolved family issues, or fear of failure, influence reading growth.

When using a stage framework, there is a danger of viewing reading maturation too precisely. It is crucial to recognize that readers vary in developmental rate and also experience vacillations in ability. During any one time, some developing readers may need instruction in certain areas at one stage and in other areas at a higher or lower stage. For example, readers who possess rich oral vocabularies in a particular content area as well as many sight words may be able to gather new meaning from content text despite limited decoding skills.

Such students could be considered Stage 3 readers since they use content texts to learn new information in a familiar field. Yet they are also Stage 1 readers since instruction in letter-sound correspondences is needed before they can read texts concerning content from a less common field or texts with fewer sight words to support guessing from context.

A reader's place within the stages varies depending on the abilities the learner has developed, the difficulty of the text under study, and the reader's familiarity with the text's subject matter (Applebee, Langer, & Mullis, 1987; Lyon, 2000; National Research Council, 1998). Even within one piece of writing, a mature reader sometimes gathers complex information carefully, sounds out unfamiliar words slowly, and synthesizes all that is read with previous knowledge to form a new understanding of a complicated issue.

Application of the stages to assessment and instruction.   A developmental view of reading can refine assessment and instructional planning by providing a description of progressive abilities that a learner needs to acquire in order to become a mature reader. Debates concerning whether students need to learn decoding strategies or complex vocabulary meanings are clarified by considering which of these components is underdeveloped and blocking further reading progress for a specific individual at a specific point in development.

Knowledge of developmental reading stages and crucial components of reading helps educators focus on what is needed by learners who possess particular skills and abilities rather than on the sometimes less helpful issue of what should be taught at a particular age. An appreciation of developmental levels can reduce the errors that accompany blanket prescriptives that assume all learners of a certain age or grade possess the same abilities and skills or proceed at the same rate.

This view of reading maturation also enlightens debates concerning whether readers ought to learn through direct or indirect instruction (Chall, 1996, 2000). When students are learning new skills, for which they have little knowledge or experience, direct teaching of the rudiments provides background information needed to make progress (Gagne & Driscoll, 1988). However, as students learn the fundamental workings of new skills and need to develop fluency, teaching indirectly, with an abundance of reading practice, makes sense.

Instruction shifts between direct and indirect within a single lesson as well as over a period of time. For example, students may be taught directly the pronunciation and meanings of several unfamiliar vocabulary words, then develop automatic decoding and understanding through independent reading of texts in which the words appear multiple times. Chapters 11 and 12 discuss formal and informal means of assessing reading ability and planning relevant instruction.

Summary. Essentially, a maturational interactive-components view of reading suggests various stages during which students use focused attention to expand proficiency with a particular reading component while continuing to use other more automatic components to maximize reading ability. During certain stages readers need to expand components and extend their application to more complex reading ventures. In other stages, readers need to increase automaticity with a clearly grasped component. Teachers can use a maturational interactive-components view of reading to determine the nature of their students' learning needs. At times this will suggest that students need to be taught how to use certain components more broadly with direct instruction. Other stages will suggest a need for less structured practice in a leisurely environment, with motivating assignments and materials that encourage extensive reading.

Characteristics of Effective Instruction

At any reading level, sensitive instruction increases the rate at which students progress, and enhances their facility with a repertoire of reading components. Whether students are learning the sound of the letter *t*, the meaning of an unfamiliar word, or a strategy for synthesizing convoluted schemata, they are aided by skillful instruction. Such instruction nurtures students through their fear of failure while avoiding practices that foster apathy (Brody, 1987; Leslie & Allen, 1999).

Well timed support, accompanied by sufficient modeling, encourages students to navigate purposefully through the learning of specialized concepts and unfamiliar processes. Effective reading instruction includes opportunities for students to express their knowledge in written and oral language. The discussion that follows considers several salient instructional characteristics that enrich learning.

SCAFFOLDING

Scaffolding is a means of fostering agility with a complex skill or process while focusing on only one or several of its components at a time. During scaffolded instruction, teachers supply supports that bridge gaps in their students' knowledge, experience, or dexterity. Aided by these supports, students can practice one essential component that contributes to a broader, more complex ability or understanding. At any stage of reading, properly executed scaffolds create learning experiences that ensure success (Case, 1980; Fischer, 1980; Leslie & Allen, 1999).

An illustration. The use of scaffolding is illustrated by the process of learning to ride a two-wheeled bicycle with training wheels. Properly adjusted training wheels barely touch the ground when a rider is balanced. The moment balance is lost, or until balance is gained, the rider can trust the training wheels to offer reliable protection against a painful spill. Even while riding in balance, the novice feels secure that the training wheels are ready to provide support should the sense of balance or the skill of balancing be jarred by uneven pavement.

In addition, when a novice is learning to ride, the feel or sound of training wheels momentarily touching the ground provides a cue to shift weight and regain balance. During responsive teaching, scaffolding, as with training wheels, is provided for precisely the intensity and extent that it is needed. More often than not, learners recognize their need for support yet are glad to accomplish the independence of functioning beyond the scaffolds.

Scaffolds in full contexts. Scaffolds sometimes support a process in its full context by taking care of related activities. For example, students may be learning a strategy for finding details that contribute to main ideas in a science text. While searching for details, unfamiliar vocabulary words may surface. A teacher could scaffold the process by directly stating the meaning of the unfamiliar words.

Such scaffolding would encourage students to proceed with finding details, without interruption. The scaffold would spare students the frustration inherent in a forced shift away from the fragile work of schema construction to the process of defining words. Such a shift would remove attention from the process under study and threaten to dismantle tentative understanding.

At another time, students may be learning to develop meanings of unfamiliar words in text through use of context or a computerized meaning search. In this instance, a teacher would scaffold by stating a brief schema summary each time the developing schema was forgotten during definition activity. Students would experience success with the definition strategy since the word would fit meaningfully into the freshly summarized text. Such scaffolding would enable students to concentrate on the practice of one component while engaging in a broader process.

Scaffolds in constrained contexts. At other times, scaffolds narrow an activity's context to decrease the number of processes vying for attention. For example, novices learning the alphabetic principle may feel overwhelmed and resistant if asked to read a story concerning *mice* without first learning to decode *mice*. A teacher can provide the scaffold of a constrained context by teaching, in isolation, the letter-sounds of *mice* and how they blend into *mice*.

When students are learning the letter *m* and its corresponding sound in isolation, the meaning of a text is not present to provide a contextual cue. When the symbol is presented, a teacher would scaffold the learning of *m* by forming her lips for the sound. When necessary, the teacher would begin to make the sound as well. As students begin to sound the phoneme, the teacher fades the prompt. To acknowledge growth and encourage further development, teachers need to reduce scaffolds gradually and shift toward fuller contexts as students' needs for practice with single components decrease.

Teachers need to determine when practice within a broader context encourages learners by providing intrinsic cues and when a larger context creates overwhelming confusion. When a broad ability involves many unfamiliar components, temporary practice with one or several of the central components, in isolation, reduces distractions and develops confidence. In this instance, the teacher's scaffold provides a replacement context, external reminders or cues that trigger the skill under study.

Teach in segments. At any stage of reading, fluid scaffolding enables a teacher to assist hesitant students by segmenting an instructional component into easily achieved parts. Small segments demand only minimal effort and minor risk while producing noticeable success. Success achieved during nonthreatening exertion motivates students to risk a little more exposure and invest a little more effort. When further investment leads to continued success, students commit to the process of learning, and become actively involved.

For example, a teacher may segment the instructional component of telling the plot of a story into smaller steps by asking the following questions one at a time. "Tell what happened first." "What happened next?" "Then what happened?" "And how did it finally end?" The teacher asks only one of these questions at a time and gives verbal clues or points to clues in the book to remind a student of the answer. By confirming a student's response to the one small question before asking the next small question, the teacher ensures success at a task that would have seemed formidable if presented at once as, "What was the plot of the story?"

At times, a teacher will accidentally provide an activity that is too challenging, with too little scaffolding. If this is acknowledged immediately as a teaching error, and treated as an indicator to break instruction into smaller segments with added scaffolds, students' commitment to learning will remain intact. The smaller, achievable objective initiates a successful experience that overrides a momentary sense of failure.

Immediate adjustments in segment size and degree of scaffolding bolster students' courage to remain committed to the process of learning. For example, if a teacher asks a student to tell the plot of a story and the student is not ready, the teacher could say, "Let me try to ask my question a better way." Next, while pointing to the relevant section of text, the teacher would ask, "What happened here in the story?"

Model. Across reading stages, teachers can convey a concept or process through modeling—demonstrating each segment of a process or concept while describing it. An oral explanation alone may be difficult to understand, particularly when a complex process or intricate concept is explained. Conversely, a graph, picture, or demonstration, without oral or written explanation, may convey a feeling for the concept, but leave students with no language to retrieve or describe necessary details of the concept for later use. For maximum effectiveness, lessons need to employ both linguistic explanation and visual demonstration.

Model and apply. After viewing a model while hearing its explanation, students need to engage with the matter themselves in order to understand it fully. To scaffold for immediate success during these engagements, teachers need to explain and model not only the concept, but how to apply it as well. This explanation and demonstration should include a context similar to the one assigned to the student. For example, if the student is assigned to engage with an unfamiliar vocabulary word by using it in a meaningful sentence, first the teacher would explain its meaning and demonstrate its use in a sentence. This would model how to use the word when speaking or writing.

When beginning to engage with a concept, students may need the scaffold of a highly specific suggestion for application. For example, a student may hesitate to use the word *hectic* in a sentence. A teacher could scaffold the application by suggesting that students tell sentences about a time of day when things are hectic at home. This would assist the student in retrieving an appropriate situation from which to develop a sentence. In another instance, if students are to share a detail found in a paragraph, a teacher can model the application process by pointing out one detail, then asking a student for another. If needed, the teacher may add the scaffold of pointing out a specific sentence in which to locate another detail.

Apply in varied contexts. Learning is enriched by many opportunities to engage successfully with a concept in a variety of contexts. Such opportunities motivate students to practice further so long as sufficient modeling and scaffolding assure success. As automaticity develops through practice, the concept can be used in wider and more varied contexts with less support; then attention can turn to less-practiced components.

As automaticity increases, engagement with a concept in varied contexts offers openings to explore nuances that were not communicated during initial instruction. When nuances surface during students' efforts to use the concept in a specialized application, adjustments and exceptions become meaningful.

Teach the exceptions. Exceptions and complicated details are best taught during practice when varied contexts and decreased scaffolds reveal them. In this way, exceptions are introduced when students are ready to absorb them as specialized cases of a general concept or process. Occasionally, students will raise exceptions early in the learning process. It is generally wise to state that they are specialized cases and focus on a variety of examples that support the common generalization.

For example, in words with double vowels, the first vowel is often long and the second vowel silent as in *boat* or *lean*. When learning this rule, a student may question it since it does not hold for a *piece* of *bread*. In this instance, it is important to acknowledge the difference, but equally important to focus quickly on the many words that follow the rule (such as *bead, soak, neat, rail*) to indicate that it is worth learning and using.

It is necessary to acknowledge a specialized case when it is raised early by a student. This assures the student that the concept was understood even though it contains a contradiction. Study of a general concept, before introducing or exploring exceptions in depth, embeds the central concept or process as the main schema. This assures that exceptions are not assumed to be the general case.

ANTIDOTES TO FEAR OF FAILURE

Some learners exhibit deep hesitation when approaching reading. Students who have tried and failed need particular support and encouragement if they are to develop reading ability and confidence. Models and scaffolds aid thought and memory to assure an abundance of immediate success. They also offer emotional support and encouragement—assuring that success is achievable and that mistakes along the way are acceptable.

Confirm and assure. When students fear failure, their fright lends an added drain to their attentional resources. Since attention is limited, as much of it as possible needs to be free to engage with text during reading. Fearful students will not be able to focus the attention necessary for reading if they feel compelled to continually monitor whether they are carrying out a process correctly.

Even with scaffolding, success needs to be confirmed with immediate feedback. Immediate, continual, low-key confirmations from a teacher decrease self-conscious worry. Sensitive confirmation encourages hesitant students to focus all their attention on reading rather than reserving some of their attention for self-checking at this stage.

Continual confirmatory feedback needs to be very brief and cause minimal disruption to the flow of reading and instruction. For example, when students are beginning to read connected text, they should not need to look up from the print to check for a confirming smile or nod. The confirmation should be communicated by a teacher with a soft *um-hum* or *yeah* that unobtrusively indicates success without drawing attention from the text. When a student errs, a soft restating of the last word read correctly, or pointing to the spot that needs repair, interrupts the flow minimally.

Quietly hearing of their continual success encourages learners to involve themselves a little more in the learning process. As students develop automaticity with introductory components, these begin to serve as self-applied scaffolds during later learning. Consistent and accurate letter-sound-meaning connections serve as internal scaffolds that manifest themselves as confidence. These automatized scaffolds assure that text is read accurately. With successful practice, students slowly replace verbal confirmations from a teacher with self-checking—internal recognition that what they hear and understand through their reading makes sense.

Provide missing background. Learners vary in the extent of their background at each stage of learning. Some develop sufficient mastery and background at one level to generalize the central components to a next level for themselves. Others, who lack background and security, need scaffolds and models that teach the intricate details of an unfamiliar component before they can attempt to try it independently. Teachers can reduce an anxiety or failure cycle by providing models and scaffolds instead of expecting fearful learners to guess. Instead of assuming that hesitant students are timid, teachers need to recognize that these learners lack the background, or the skill of retrieving their background, that enables their peers to seem more daring and confident.

Students with learning disabilities, and learners who come from homes where little reading has occurred, need clear procedures to follow as they encounter unfamiliar reading processes. When teachers provide these supports, students with limited background and experience progress well. Their progress develops the background, retrieval-skill, and confidence that encourage the daring required for later levels of reading.

Model vulnerability. As teachers, we encourage learners to take a variety of risks: to explain what they read, to pronounce unknown words, to use a spelling dictionary, to forge into the unknown and learn from mistakes. We state that no one knows everything, that it is fine to need to learn, acceptable not to know an answer. Many mature adults avoid these self-exposing activities assiduously, and hesitant learners fear them immensely.

Modeling these challenging activities, which often are accompanied by deep feelings of vulnerability, intensifies the effectiveness of good teaching. When teachers publicly look up the spelling of a word, say they need to look for information that they do not know, or pause during oral reading to sound through a long word, they model that it really is all right to be a learner and to use the strategies that are under study.

Expect success. When teachers believe that their students will learn, students have a higher success rate (Rosenthal & Jacobson, 1968). Teachers communicate their expectation that students will learn by offering material in manageable segments with supportive scaffolds and models. They freely re-teach portions of the material in smaller segments when necessary. They also test students on what has been taught, rather than on abstruse applications. Such assessments communicate clearly that expectations are met and develop students' confidence that they will encounter success as they continue to learn.

In contrast, "setting high expectations" is sometimes invoked as an explanation for giving students assignments that are too large, too complicated, and unaccompanied by sufficient support. While done in the name of expecting success, this nearly guarantees failure for students who can learn the material, but not without a teacher who takes the time to teach prerequisite background and to present the assignment in manageable steps.

The expectation of success can be communicated through the simple verbal nuance of asking students *to do* a task rather than asking *whether* they *can* do it. For example, teachers can communicate positive expectations by asking students, "Read this sentence," rather than asking, "Do you think you can read this sentence for me?" We tend to use "will you" or "can you" questions to seem less demanding or threatening. One effect is to communicate an unsureness in students' abilities. By directly asking students to do things that we have taught them or things that we think they can do, and by consistently accompanying such requests with sufficient scaffolds for students to experience success, we communicate that we anticipate success.

Conclusion

Reading is a complex and intricate process involving language, letters, and thought. To enhance readers' progress and enjoyment, instruction needs to take into account variations in learning abilities, text difficulty, readers' background knowledge, and the extent various reading components are mastered. These issues can be viewed with an understanding of how the interactive components of reading mature and how their development can be enhanced by teaching that exhibits characteristics of effective instruction. In the chapters that follow, each component of reading sketched in this overview will be examined in depth. Discussion will include recommendations that engender confidence and security as reading matures.

24

References

Adams, M.J. (1990, 1994). *Beginning to read: Thinking and learning about print.* Cambridge, MA: MIT Press.

Applebee, A.N., Langer, J.A., & Mullis, I.V. (1987). *The nation's report card: Learning to be literate in America.* Princeton, NJ: Educational Testing Service.

Biemiller, A. (2000). Vocabulary: The missing link between phonics and comprehension. *Perspectives,* 26(4), 26-30.

Blachman, B.A. (2000). Phonological awareness. In M.L. Kamil, P.B. Mosenthal, P.D. Pearson, & R. Barr (Eds.), *Handbook of reading research.* Mahwah, NJ: Lawrence Erlbaum Associates.

Brody, S. (1987). *Study skills: Teaching and learning strategies for mainstream and specialized classrooms.* Milford, NH: LARC Publishing.

Brody, S. (1989). Elements of effective reading instruction in grades 4 and 5: Lessons from recent research. Unpublished qualifying paper. Harvard Graduate School of Education.

Brody, S. (1994). Language and reading: An overview. In S. Brody (Ed.), *Teaching reading: language, letters, and thought (1ˢᵗ ed.).* Milford, NH: LARC Publishing.

Brody, S. (2001). *The Brody reading manual: An implementation guide for teachers (2nd ed.).* Milford, NH: LARC Publishing. [http://www.LARCPublishing.com/]

Case, R. (1980). The underlying mechanism of intellectual development. In *Cognition, development, and instruction.* NY: Academic Press.

Chall, J.S. (1967). *Learning to reading: The great debate.* NY: McGraw Hill.

Chall, J.S. (1983). *Stages of reading development.* NY: McGraw-Hill.

Chall, J.S. (1996). *Stages of reading development (2nd ed.).* Orlando, FL: Harcourt Brace.

Chall, J.S. (2000). *The academic achievement challenge: What really works in the classroom?* New York: Guilford Publications.

Chall, J.S., & Conard, S.S. (1991). *Should textbooks challenge students?* NY: Teachers College Press.

Chomsky, C. (1978). When you still can't read in third grade: After decoding what? In S.J. Samuels & A.E. Farstrup (Eds.), *What research has to say about reading instruction (2nd ed.).* Newark, DE: IRA.

Curtis, M.E. & Longo, A.M. (2000). Teaching adolescents with reading difficulties: Lessons learned from Jeanne S. Chall. *Perspectives,* 26(4), 49-50.

Ehri, L.C. (1998). Grapheme-phoneme knowledge is essential for learning to read words in English. In J.L. Metsala & L.C. Ehri (Eds.), *Word recognition in beginning literacy.* Mahwah, NJ. Lawrence Erlbaum, Associates.

Fischer, K.W. (1980). A theory of cognitive development: The control and construction of hierarchies of skills. *Psychological Review,* 87(6), 115-169.

Fischer, K.W. & Rose. S.P. (1998). Growth cycles of brain and mind. *Educational Leadership,* 56(3), 56-60.

Gagne, R.M., & Driscoll, M.P. (1988). *Essentials of learning for instruction (2nd ed.).* Englewood Cliffs, NJ: Prentice Hall.

Goswami, U. (2000). Phonological and lexical processes. . In M.L. Kamil, P.B. Mosenthal, P.D. Pearson, & R. Barr (Eds.), *Handbook of reading research.* Mahwah, NJ: Lawrence Erlbaum Associates.

Honig, B. (1998). Preventing failure in early reading programs: A summary of research and instructional best practices. In W.M. Evers (Ed.), *What's gone wrong in America's classrooms?* Stanford, CA: Hoover Institution Press.

Juel, C., & Minden-Cupp, C. (2000). One down and 80,000 to go: Word recognition instruction in the primary grades. *The Reading Teacher*, 53(4), 332-335.

Just, M.A., & Carpenter, P.A. (1981). Cognitive processes in reading: Models based on readers' eye fixations. In A.M. Lesgold & C.A. Perfetti (Eds.) *Interactive processes in reading*. Hillsdale, NJ: Erlbaum, 177-213.

Just, M.A., & Carpenter, P.A. (1987). *The psychology of reading and language comprehension*. Boston, MA: Allyn and Bacon, Inc.

Kintsch, W. (1998). *Comprehension: A paradigm for cognition*. New York: Cambridge University Press.

Kintsch, W., & vanDijk, T. (1978). Toward a model of text comprehension and production. *Psychological Review*, 85, 363-394.

LaBerge, D., & Samuels, S.J. (1974). Toward a theory of automatic information processing in reading. *Cognitive Psychology*, 6, 293-323.

Lerner, J. (2000). *Learning disabilities: Theories, diagnoses, and teaching strategies (8th ed.)*. Boston: Houghton Mifflin.

Lesch, M.F., & Pollatsek, A. (1993). Automatic access of semantic information by phonological codes in visual word recognition. *Journal of Experimental Psychology: Learning Memory and Cognition*, 19(2), 285-294.

Leslie, L. & Allen, L. (1999). Factors that predict success in an early literacy intervention project. *Reading Research Quarterly*, 34(4), 404-424.

Liberman, I. (1987). Language and literacy: The obligation of the schools of education. In *Intimacy with language: A forgotten basic in teacher education. Conference proceedings*. Baltimore, MD: The Orton Dyslexia Society.

Liebling, C.R. (1989). Inside view and character plans in an original story and its basal adaptation. *Theory into Practice*, 28(2).

Lyon, G.R. (1998). Why reading is not a natural process. *Educational Leadership,* 55(6), 14-18.

Lyon, G.R. (2000). Learning to read: A call from research to action. *NEBIDA Newsletter,* Spring/Summer 15-18.

Moats, L.C. (2000/1999). Teaching reading is rocket science: What expert teachers of reading should know and be able to do. *NEBIDA Newsletter,* Spring/Summer, 10-12. [Original work published in 1999.]

Moats, L.C. (2000). *Whole language lives on: The illusion of "balanced" reading instruction*. Washington, DC: Thomas Fordham Fooundation. [Available at http://www.edexcellence.net.]

National Reading Panel [NRP]. (2000). *Report of the National Reading Panel: Teaching children to read*. Washington, DC: National Institute of Child Health and Human Development. [http://www.nichd.nih.gov/publications/nrp.]

National Research Council. (1998). *Preventing reading difficulties in young children*. Washington, DC: National Academy Press.

Perfetti, C.A. (1984). Reading acquisition and beyond: Decoding includes cognition. *American Journal of Education*, Nov. 93, 40-60.

Perfetti, C.A., & Curtis, M.E. (1986). Reading. In R.F. Dillon & R.J. Sternberg (Eds.), *Cognition and instruction*. NY: Academic Press.

Piaget, J. (1971). The theory of stages in cognitive development. In D.R. Green, M.P. Ford, & G.B. Flamers (Eds.), *Measurement and Piaget*. New York: McGraw-Hill.

26

Pressley, M. (2000). What should comprehension instruction be the instruction of? In M.L. Kamil, P.B. Mosenthal, P.D. Pearson, & R. Barr (Eds.), *Handbook of reading research.* Mahwah, NJ: Lawrence Erlbaum Associates.

Rath, L.K. (1990). Phonemic awareness: Its role in reading development. Unpublished qualifying paper, Harvard Graduate School of Education.

Rath, L.K. (2000). Between the Lions: Using television to promote literacy. *Book Links,* 9(4), 41-45.

Rosenthal, R., & Jacobson, L. (1968). *Pygmalion in the classroom: Teacher expectation and pupils' intellectual development.* New York: Holt, Rinehart and Winston, Inc.

Rummelhart, D.E., & Ortony, A. (1977). The representation of knowledge in memory. In R.C. Anderson, R.J. Spiro, & W.E. Montague (Eds.) *Schooling and the acquisition of knowledge.* Hillsdale, NJ: Erlbaum.

Samuels, S.J., & Kamil, M.L. (1984). Models of the reading process. In P.D. Pearson, (Ed.), *Handbook of Reading Research.* New York: Longman.

Samuels, S.J., Schermer, D.R., & Reinking, D. (1992). Reading fluency: Techniques for making decoding automatic. In S.J. Samuels & A.E. Farstrup (Eds.), *What research has to say about reading instruction (2nd ed.).* Newark, DE: IRA.

Smith, F. (1988). *Understanding reading: A psycholinguistic analysis of reading and learning to read (4th ed.).* Hillsdale, NJ: Erlbaum.

Stanovich, K.E. (1980). Toward an interactive-compensatory model of individual differences in the development of reading fluency. *Reading Research Quarterly,* 16, 32-71.

Stanovich, K.E. (1986). Matthew effects in reading: Some consequences of individual differences in the acquisition of literacy. *Reading Research Quarterly,* 21(4), 360-406.

Stanovich, K.E. (1994). Romance and reality. *The Reading Teacher,* 47(4), 280-291.

Stanovich, K.E., Cunningham, A.E., & Feeman, D.J. (1984). Intelligence, cognitive skills, and early reading progress. *Reading Research Quarterly,* 19(3), 278-303.

Stotsky, S. (1986). Asking questions about ideas: A critical component in critical thinking. *The Leaflet,* Fall, 39-47.

Stotsky, S. (1999). *Losing our language: How multicultural classroom instruction is undermining our children's ability to read, write, and reason.* New York: Free Press.

Williams, J.P. (1980). Teaching decoding with an emphasis on phoneme analysis and phoneme blending. *Journal of Educational Psychology,* 72, 1 - 15.

Wilson, P.T., & Anderson, R.C. (1986). What they don't know will hurt them: The role of prior knowledge in comprehension. In J. Orasanu (Ed.) *Reading comprehension: From research to practice.* Hillsdale, NJ: Lawrence Erlbaum Associates.

Wolf, M., Bowers, P.G., and Biddle, K. (2000). Naming-speed processes, timing, and reading: A conceptual review. . *Journal of Learning Disabilities,* 33(4), 387-407.

Wolf, M., Miller, L., & Donnelly, K. (2000). Retrieval, automaticity, vocabulary elaboration, orthography (RAVE-O): A comprehensive, fluency-based reading intervention program. *Journal of Learning Disabilities,* 33(4), 375-386.

Wolf, M. & Obregon, M. (1997). The "double-deficit" hypothesis: Implications for diagnosis and practice in reading disabilities. In L. Putnam, (Ed.), *Readings of language and literacy.* Cambridge, MA: Brookline Books.

Yopp, H.K. & Yopp, R.H. (2000). Supporting phonemic awareness development in the classroom. *The Reading Teacher,* 54(2), 130-143.

II. LANGUAGE

Chapter 2. Language: Structure and Acquisition

Melissa Farrall, PhD
Reading Foundation

Long ago, in a distant time and place, unknown beings opened their mouths, and through a precisely articulated sequence of sounds, exchanged thoughts. What triggered those first words we will never know. We will also never know whether the significance of that moment was appreciated in any way. Did the two people look at each other knowingly? Was there relief or joy or pride? The advent of language, however inauspicious and modest its beginnings, distinguished the history of the human species by allowing men and women to convey needs, thoughts, and desires to one another, as well as from one generation to the next.

The debate over those first words, and whatever precipitated them, has raged for more than two thousand years. Since that time, philosophers, philologists, psychologists, and a host of others have all engaged in the study of language in an attempt to describe the system by which articulated sounds are used to convey information and carry on the affairs of their society (Francis, 1958). In addition, the study of language involves yet another dimension. Language is seen by some to be a manifestation of the inner workings of the brain. The abstract principles that govern the structure of language may be the product of a unique biological design. Whether language is biological, social, or some combination thereof, the study of language teaches much about humans, how we think and how we learn. We may ultimately even satisfy our curiosity about why it is that we speak and animals do not.

This chapter is about language—its structure and the stages in which it is acquired as well as how to enhance its development. We will review the interrelationships and patterns that make up the intricate structures of language, and examine strategies that promote language development. The chapter will review the terminology of language study, analyze the developmental stages of language acquisition, and offer strategies to aid in its evolution in light of several prominent theories concerned with the nature of cognition and language acquisition.

TERMINOLOGY

Before proceeding with the discussion, we will review the jargon commonly employed by linguistic enthusiasts. **Language** is the communication of thoughts and feelings by means of a formalized system of abstract symbols and rule-governed structures. Such systems may include signs, gestures, speech-sounds, and letters of the alphabet. It is important to note that, with the exception of a small category of words known as onomatopoeias (*buzz, moo*), the relationship between a symbol and its meaning is arbitrary. For example, a table is not called a *table* because its sound has a "tablelike" quality, and it is unlikely that we will ever determine a causal relationship between words and the objects or abstractions that they represent.

Innate and learned aspects of language. Because language is essentially a human creation, all languages share certain common properties. Whether we speak French, Swahili, or Urdu, we have an unlimited vehicle for communication. Any language provides a means to refer to the past, the present, and the future. In addition, all languages include vehicles that assist us in creating new vocabulary, and comprehending infinite sets of well-formed sentences. All of this is made possible by the application of humans' immeasurable cognitive resources to a finite set of discrete sounds or gestures that are then linked together in accordance with the rules of grammar.

Humans have always been intrigued by words and language. Apart from their obvious utility, words have been accorded the power to move boulders from cave entrances, reveal secrets of the soul, explain the meaning of life, and turn princes into frogs. Considering their many, many applications, it is no wonder that the nature of language has been fiercely contested by an endless list of poets, theologians, philosophers, philologists, psychologists, biologists, neurologists and, yes, even grammarians.

At one time or another, various disciplines have staked their claims to the progenitorship of language, resulting in a spectrum of theories that is often referred to collectively as the **nature versus nurture debate**. Over time, theorists who engaged in this debate presented a variety of arguments ranging from pure nature—we are born biologically wired with language through our genetic nature—to pure nurture—language is learned through a painstaking process of stimulus and response nurtured by environment.

For example, Chomsky proposed that the human species is endowed with a unique capacity for language; and this capacity determines the form and the range of human mental activity (1980). In support of his theory, Chomsky put forth three major observations.

1. Only humans are able to speak and understand language.
2. All languages have fundamental features in common.
3. Language is developmental.

Chomsky argued for **language universals**—that language experience is essentially the same for all. Wherever people exist, regardless of culture or race, humans learn to speak by organizing words into grammatical sentence forms. Humans, regardless of their experience or native tongue, have the capacity to generate questions, commands, and negations. They are able to use rules that let them reference the past, present, and future. In Chomsky's view, it is these universal features of grammar that attest to the innateness of language in humans.

According to Chomsky, it is universal grammar that allows children to invoke complex rules of language unconsciously, even rules that are beyond the conscious understanding of most adults. By drawing on a universal grammar, children are able to focus on and master the particular constructs, or idiosyncrasies, of their native tongue. While unconsciously using universal rules, a child can transform a thought from its neurochemical origins into a grammatical string of words, with an efficiency that IBM could envy.

Certain fundamental constraints are inherent in a universal grammar. An example of one such constraint is that all transformational rules must be **structure-dependent** (1975). In order to understand what is meant by **structure-**

dependence and the role it plays in language, consider the following examples of how a question is formed from a declarative sentence:

(1)   The boy is in the room.
        Is the boy in the room?

(2)   The book is on the table
        Is the book on the table?

If we were to write a rule governing the transformation of a declarative sentence into a question, we might propose that the sentence is read from left to right until we reach the first verbal element which we then move to the front of the sentence. If this rule is correct, example (3) would be transformed as follows:

(3)   The boy who is ill is in the room.
        Is the boy who ill is in the room?

According to Chomsky, we understand that the above question is ungrammatical, or ill-formed, because it violates one of the basic constraints of how the human mind organizes bits of information. The universal grammar tells us that before we operate on a string of words, we must analyze the structure of the phrases and always keep the noun phrase intact (1975, pp. 30-32).

However, linguists and cognitive psychologists eventually acknowledged both nature and nurture as linguistic theory expanded to encompass new understandings in the areas of infant cognition and neuropsychology. Here the research of Catherine Snow (1986) and John Locke (1993), 20th century social interactionists, suggests that nature and nurture work together to enable humans to communicate their needs, wants, and desires in order to survive.

Speech is defined as the oral expression of language. It is a complex physical process involving the precise interaction of three main functions of the human vocal apparatus. These functions include: the production of air from the lungs; the constriction of airflow in the larynx; and the modification of airflow by the anatomical structures of the vocal tract (For those wishing to learn about the production of speech, please see Hulit & Howard's [1993] *Born to Talk*).

Linguistics is the science of language and it encompasses a broad range of specialties and interests. **Historical linguists** study the history of written languages in order to document the ways in which they change. **Comparative**

linguists classify language into various groups and families in order to posit an explanation for both the diversity and universality of human speech.

Psycholinguists examine the relationship between language and cognitive processes. Recently, this field has focused considerable attention on the biological and neurological aspects of language by scrutinizing emergent language in the child. Finally, **structural linguists** focus on the study of the system, or the structural components, of language. Winograd (1983) compared structural linguistics to chemistry. In his view, the goal of linguistics, as for chemistry, is to define a set of primitive elements and their rules for combination. In this way, we are able to understand how to generate more complex structures of language.

Structure of language. The structure of human language traditionally is divided into four main branches: phonology, morphology, syntax, and semantics. **Phonology** is the study of the patterns and distribution of speech sounds. Within phonology there are two areas of concentration, **phonetics** and **phonemics**. The distinction between phonetics and phonemics causes endless confusion, which I attempt to clarify below.

Phonetics is the study of speech sounds, called **phones**, and their production, transmission, and reception. Although we speak of speech sounds as discrete bits of acoustic data, this is not really the case. Speech is continuous, and the precise articulation of individual sounds is limited by our physical design and our ability to manipulate our speech organs from one position to another. To most of us, a *t* is just a *t*. To a phonetician, the precise pronunciation of a *t* is dependent upon its phonetic environment. The spoken word, *titillate*, may contain three different *t* phones. The transcription, [t' I t⁻ leit], shows that the first [t'] is aspirated, the second [t⁻] is unreleased, and the third [t] is unaspirated. The specific phones produced vary by individual and are influenced by local accents.

In contrast, **phonemics** is the study of **phonemes**. Phonemes are **consistent** representations, in our brains, of the major sounds of speech. For example, in our brains, the phoneme /t/ represents every *t* in *titillate*. Our ability to translate the phones we hear to phonemes that represent them is apparent when we hear someone speak with an accent. In our minds, we recognize what the speaker is saying despite encountering a set of phones that vary from those we are accustomed to hearing. For example, the phoneme /a/ represents both the phone *a* in *what* pronounced by someone from Britain and the phone *a* in *what* pronounced by someone from Michigan. The fact that we understand each other, even when, on an acoustic level, pronunciation differs considerably, is a testament to the substantial capacity of the brain and its ability to translate phones to phonemes.

As we advance to more complex structures of language, we find that phonemes are organized into meaningful groups called morphemes. **Morphology** is the study of words and word building. **Morphemes**, the smallest units of meaning in a word, are categorized into two classes: free morphemes and bound morphemes. A free morpheme can stand on its own as, for example, the word *house*. Bound morphemes cannot stand alone but must be attached to another morpheme. By adding the morpheme *-s* onto a noun, we signify the plural. If we add the bound morpheme *un* to a verb we can turn the world upside down by undoing whatever has already been done.

Syntax involves the rules for the formation of grammatical sentences. Although as native speakers we may not understand the difference between a noun and a verb, we do know how to generate well-formed sentences. Non-native speakers often apply their own rules of syntax when learning to speak foreign languages. The sentence, "Throw me down the stairs my hat," is an example of how speakers may apply rules of syntax from another language to English.

Finally, **semantics** concerns meaning. Knowledge of semantics allows us to make decisions such as whether to use the adverb *badly* or *awfully*. "It is awfully good" is correct. "It is badly good" is not. Over the years there has been much discussion as to whether meaning should be considered part of language structure. Since meaning is part of the knowledge that a speaker utilizes to communicate verbally, it seems crucial to include meaning as part of the structure of human language. For those wishing to learn more concerning language structure, please see Moats' (2000) *Speech to Print*.

Communication and the Speech Chain

Whether we choose to communicate through speech, writing, or sign, communication is a fragile process requiring the speaker and the listener to perform a series of complex operations in order to come to a common understanding. Denes & Pinson (1973, pp. 1-6) call this process the **speech chain** and they break it down into a series of six steps that are summarized below:

1. The speaker has an idea, a feeling, or a conscious need, and a desire to express it.

2. Within the speaker's mind, the concept is put into language.

3. The language that represents the concept initiates neurological activity that conveys the proper neural impulses from the brain to the organs of speech in order to produce the actual message.

4. The message is a series of pressure patterns in the air called **sound waves**. Sound waves cause air particles to move and collide into one another, creating compression between some particles and spaces between others.

5. The movement of the air particles in sound waves causes a series of vibrations in the listener's eardrums. The ear functions to transform these vibrations into neural impulses that travel along the acoustic nerve to the brain.

6. Finally, these neural impulses are mapped into progressively more abstract representations in the listener's consciousness and they are stored into memory as ideas, feelings, or desires. The speech chain, however, does not end here. In order for comprehension to occur, the listener must actively compare the new information to what is already believed to be true. This is achieved by plugging the new data into the established network of schemata and by noting how they differ or conform. Critical thinking occurs when we, on the basis of our analysis, decide to alter or expand our existing network of thought in order to reflect the larger perspective.

Life would be much simpler if the messages that speakers sent were the messages received. Unfortunately, the nature of the communicative process is such that problems can occur at many points along the way. The speaker may have deficits in cognitive processing or poor articulation. The room may be noisy and distracting. The listener may be hearing impaired, lack focused attention, or have difficulty with cognitive functioning.

Even assuming that all these functions are performed fluently and without disruption, the communicative effort may still be in vain. Comprehension may not occur if the speaker and the listener do not share a common background knowledge to support their communication. The expression, "They don't speak the same language," is used frequently when two individuals are not able to communicate their points of view. The language to which this expression refers is not the oral language, but the language in the head. Perhaps the expression should be rephrased to read, "They don't have the same background knowledge."

To further appreciate the complexities of the communicative process, we must understand that oral language is only part of the message. When human beings speak, we also provide additional information in the form of nonverbal cues such as gestures, facial expression, eye contact, tone of voice, emotion, and even significant pauses. Each of these cues provides a context for the interpretation of language. With them, we are able to distinguish a truthful, "I didn't do it," from its less than honorable counterpart. Being able to discern the communicative intent behind an utterance is as important as the language in and of itself. The study of

pragmatics is the analysis of language in terms of the situational context, including the knowledge and beliefs of the speaker, as well as the relation between the speaker and the listener.

Stages of Speech and Language Development

Many parents feel that an eternity passes before their children articulate their first recognizable words. During this time of waiting, tremendous achievement and cognitive growth occur as all the speech and language related mechanisms are finely tuned to work so precisely that we often forget just how complex the process is. The following briefly describes the most significant features of the stages of language development that lead to and follow children's first utterances (see Table 2.1, following page). For those wishing to delve further into the subject, a more thorough examination can be found in Sharon James's *Normal Language Acquisition* (1990).

Although the stages are presented here with references to specific age spans, it is important to note that these are guidelines and not absolutes. To a certain degree, variation in language acquisition is normal. Some children may enter the one-word stage at twelve months of age and others at fourteen months. We accept these variations as part of the diversity of nature.

There are, however, children whose development, for some reason or other, departs significantly from the norm. These children can be helped, and when there is a question, it is prudent to have a child evaluated by a speech and language pathologist. Federal law mandates that local school districts provide services for the identification of such children, at no cost to the parent, from birth. Remedial services are available beginning with the age of three, when warranted. Assistance in determining whether a child needs remediation can be received by contacting one's elementary school principal.

PREBIRTH STAGE

According to the research conducted by John Locke (1993), an infant in the womb is able to experience and process a wide variety of sensory stimuli that are thought to promote neurological development in the brain. Recent research has determined that beginning at about twenty-six weeks, the fetus is able to respond to the stimulus of the mother's voice, as well as other ex utero voices and sounds, amidst the noise of turbulent blood flow. Of these stimuli, maternal vocalizations are said to be the most apparent, possibly explaining why newborns not only prefer their mother's voice, but also the sounds of their mother's native

Table 2.1. Summary of the Stages of Language Development.

Stages of Language Development

Prebirth Stage
Sensory stimulation promotes neurological development.

Infancy: Setting the Stage for Speech
Prefer human voices and smiling faces. Non-verbal dialogue and turn-taking.

Birth	Vegetative sounds
2 months	Locke's "Goo Stage"
5 months	Marginal babbling
6 months	Babbling
9 - 18 mos	Non-reduplicated babbling, phonetically consistent forms

The One-Word Holophrastic Stage (12 months)
The use of one word to express a thought or concern. Single syllable or doubling of single syllable words such as *wawa*. Over/underextend meaning.

Pragmatics:	Satisfy needs and wants. Control behavior of others.
	Interact with others. Express feelings or attitudes.
	Rudiments of turn-taking.

The Two-Word Telegraphic Stage (Between 18 and 24 Months)
Two-word utterances characterized by elimination of unstressed syllables, deletion of final consonants, and substitution of sounds made in front of mouth (/b/, /p/, /d/, /t/, /m/, /n/, /w/). No prepositions, auxiliary words, or conjunctions. No morphological markers for number, person, or tense. No pronouns. Negation signaled by *no* or *not* in initial position.

Pragmatics:	Language of requests. Provide information.
	Comment, remember, question, and predict.

Preschool Years to Fluency (Ages Two to Five)
Language explosion. Morphemes, pronouns, auxiliary verbs, function words, and phrases appear. Negation develops in stages. Overextension of grammar. Fluency.

Pragmatics:	Question formation. Interrogatives, *why, who,* and *how* appear.
	Sustain turn-taking for one or two turns. Fewer interruptions.
	Mechanics of conversational timing. Semantic softeners.
	Conversational repair to suit the needs of the listener.

The School-Aged Child
Effective use of language. Passives with action verbs. Full use of the passive does not occur until adolescence. Principal of minimum distance. Metalinguistic ability.

Pragmatics:	Maintain conversation for several turns.
	Sustained conversational repair. Artful hints.

tongue. It has been suggested, by Locke, that the fetus learns its first lessons about language when the mother reacts to being kicked.

INFANCY: SETTING THE STAGE FOR SPEECH

As stated above, newborns come into the world with a strong preference for the maternal voice and a distinct predilection for the sounds of their native tongue. According to Locke (1993), from the earliest moments of life in the outside world, infants actively seek out stimulation that they find pleasurable. This stimulation includes melodious humans voices and smiling faces. In particular, the infant's gaze is drawn to the eyes, for their expression reveals much about the nature of our communication.

Locke suggests that early mother-infant interactions are linguistically significant. Through the process of nurturance, infants become closely attuned to all the cues, verbal and nonverbal, that a mother emits concerning her emotional state. The primary reason for this is survival. Mother is the infancy equivalent of meals on wheels, and one must be able to flag down the driver for a delivery.

The attachment between parent and child also provides opportunities to develop many language-related processes, such as turn-taking. Infants, in their quest for nourishment and stimulation, actively solicit attention in the form of a friendly face or a familiar voice through eye contact and manual gestures. They are even able to identify whether a mother is in a nurturing mood and modulate their behavior accordingly. In a similar fashion, mothers are continually evaluating and responding to an infant's signals to gather information about the child's physical and emotional well being.

Through a sequence of prompting, attending, and reassessment, infants participate in a nonverbal dialogue with their parents, and this forms a base for language acquisition and later social expertise. This phenomenon, called **turn-taking**, performs two main functions critical to language instruction. It allows the infant to attend to and reproduce parental speech, and it allows the parent to monitor the quality of the utterance and provide feedback.

Assuming that an infant learns to take turns and specifically attend to verbal input, further speech and language development hinges on the ability to process auditory information. This is by no means a simple process, and difficulty can occur in any one of several areas, all of which are critically important to the development of language and reading skills. In short, speech perception, i.e. the ability to discriminate, sequence, and store speech sounds, provides the mechanisms by which the brain processes linguistic data. For a more detailed discussion of the ability to process auditory information, please see Chapter 3 on phonemic awareness.

Speech production in the infant. With their first cries, infants announce their arrival into the world. Their initial sounds—cries, burps, sneezes, and coughs—are reflexive or what is often called **vegetative**. The term, vegetative, refers to what has traditionally been recognized as the passive condition of the child. As time passes, infant crying becomes less frequent and more specialized. Mothers learn to recognize distinct cries of hunger, pain, and anger.

By the age of about two months, infants begin to coo vowel-like sounds in response to pleasurable attention. Locke refers to this period as the "Goo Stage." By the end of the first five months, these utterances are enriched with consonant-like sounds, as well as squeals, growls, and bilabial trills, more commonly known as 'raspberries.' According to Stark (1979), this versatile vocal repertoire is called **marginal babbling.** This transitional behavior precedes true babbling.

At about the age of six months, the infant begins to **babble**. Cries and gurgles are gradually augmented with a large repertoire of repeated consonant-vowel syllables, beginning most commonly with the sounds that are produced in the front of the mouth (/b/, /p/, /t/, /d/, /m/, and /n/). Locke (1983) notes that no matter what the native language, all children babble the same set of sounds and they all share a passion for auditory stimulation. Locke suggests that these babbled sounds are determined by phonetic, i.e. anatomical, physiological, and aerodynamic, factors. In support of this argument, he notes that the set of sounds produced during the babbling stage does not differ among those with retardation, neonatal brain damage, or congenital deafness. Locke (1993) notes, however, that the onset of babbling is delayed in those with severe hearing impairments.

Gradually, between nine and eighteen months of age, this repertoire expands and children's articulations become more dependent upon linguistic input. It is at this point that deaf children's vocal output begins to stall, while hearing children initiate an activity referred to as **non-reduplicated babbling** (Stark, 1980). Children who engage in non-reduplicated babbling often give the impression, through intonational patterns, stress, rhythm, and phrasing, that they are expressing themselves with adult language. All of the cues are present that we, as adults, interpret to signify communicative intent. Contrary to expectation, however, there are no meaningful words.

In addition to non-reduplicated babbling, children at this age engage in a parrot-like imitation of sounds called **echolalia** in which they imitate speech without understanding. Non-reduplicated babbling and echolalia are signs that infants from an early age are apt observers who are able to witness, remember, and apply knowledge with artistry. They are also indications that children are exploring, enjoying, and fine tuning functions of motor control and sensory feedback while, on a neurological level, the left hemisphere of the brain is being primed to process speech data.

In order for children to advance from babbling to speech, they must develop an understanding of the function of language. This realization generally occurs at about one year of age, but from nine to ten months of age, children begin to use **phonetically consistent forms.** Phonetically consistent forms occur when children use identical patterns of sound in order to reference a particular object or situation. Von Raffler-Engler (1973) described her son's use of /i/ to signify objects he wanted and /u/ for his sign of disapproval. Although we cannot call these utterances language, the use of a phonetically consistent form is a critical step toward using language to accomplish specific goals.

THE ONE-WORD (HOLOPHRASTIC) STAGE
Sometime around the first birthday, child and parent enter a new mode of communication that is based upon language. Language at the one-word stage is used to call attention to objects that capture the interest of the child through motion, noise, and their potential for manual play. To those other than family members, these words may be completely unintelligible. To parents, these words are a source of great pride.

The one-word stage of language development is distinguished by the child's use of recognizable words to refer to familiar people, animals, and objects in the home, as well as simple actions or states (Bloom, 1973). Attempts to classify this vocabulary according to adult standards of grammatical function have determined that words at this stage consist mostly of nouns and verbs. Function words, such as auxiliary verbs, articles, and prepositions, are used rarely (Nelson, 1973).

Classifications of first words. When children speak, we often forget that their first words are not products of adult minds. From a child's perspective, a "doggie" might be any furry animal that walks on four legs. This might include a cow, a camel, or the tomcat next door. On the other hand, the word "doggie" could be restricted to none other than the family pet. Although our considerable linguistic knowledge allows us to draw many conclusions about language, adult grammar is not child grammar. Attempts to classify children's first words into nouns, verbs, and other formal categories of grammar may reveal less about the child's use of language than about our own desire to impose *our* structure in order to see the world in our own reflection. In studying the child's acquisition of language, we must, therefore, exercise caution not to let our adult perspectives detract from appreciating the structure of the child's mind.

What then can be said about children's language at the one-word stage? Children's first recognizable attempts at language are said to be **holophrastic**. This means that children use one word to express a thought or a concern that, at a later stage, will be expressed in a phrase or complete sentence. A child who says the word, "ball," may actually be saying, "Give me the ball," or "Look at the ball," or "That is a pretty ball." We have no way of knowing what nonverbal and perhaps verbal thoughts may be serving as the motivation for the utterance.

There has been much speculation as to how children learn the meanings of words as they are generally understood by adults. Vygotsky (1934/1986) proposed that children develop meaning through the internalization of experience. With each new opportunity, word meanings acquire greater depth to reflect a more mature view of the world. This process may be illustrated as children, with their primitive grasp of meaning, typically **overextend** and **underextend** their words. Overextension occurs when children apply a single word to anything with a similar form or characteristic. "Wawa" might be used to signify water, juice, milk, or a lake. On the other hand, underextension occurs when children restrict the more general meaning of a word to a specific narrow reference. In this case, "doggie" may be used only with respect to the family pet or, the word "mama" jealously guarded for use with one's own.

Vygotsky's groundbreaking work on the relationship of thought, language, and experience was expanded upon by Clark in his research concerning children's acquisition of semantics. According to his **semantic feature hypothesis** (1973), words do not represent an object or action in its entirety but rather a cluster of many bits of information called **semantic features**. Although different words may have features in common, each word, in theory, represents a unique semantic set.

When children learn the meaning of a new word, they focus on one or two of the object's physical semantic features, such as shape, size, movement, texture, or taste, to serve as the basis for understanding. A child, for example, may initially perceive a grandparent to be someone old and wrinkled. Only later, after the child has acquired a broader sampling of semantic features, does a child understand a grandparent by virtue of the blood relation. It is through experience that children broaden their perspective to encompass more of the pertinent semantic features and come to use words as understood by adults.

Pragmatics in the one-word stage. In order to present a complete picture of the one-word stage of language development, we must consider not only the grammatical and semantic aspects of language, but also the **pragmatics.** Pragmatics is the analysis of language in terms of situational context. It takes into consideration the communicative intent of the speaker, as well as the relationship between speaker and listener.

When children learn language, their ability to interact with others acquires new depth and potential. It becomes possible for children to overtly articulate their wishes, needs, and intentions. If only, however, communication were as simple as that! Language always occurs in a context. We, as listeners and speakers, have a prior history of conversations and events that create within us a base of knowledge, expectations, and prejudices. Effective communication depends not only on our ability to generate well formed sentences, but also on our ability to read the many extralinguistic cues, such as facial expression, gesture, and emotion, **and** compare new information to an already established data base of what we believe to be true.

When Halliday (1975) researched the development of pragmatics in his son, Nigel, he found that Nigel's communicative repertoire increased with the advent of the one-word stage. In the stage prior to language, Nigel was able to perform four functions of communicative intent including: satisfying needs and wants, controlling the behavior of others, interacting with others, and expressing feelings or attitude. With language, Nigel was also able to investigate and explore his environment, imagine and pretend, and inform others of his thoughts and experiences.

Other researchers (Greenfield & Smith, 1976) note that children at this stage not only begin to adjust their messages according to their assumptions about the listener's prior knowledge, but that they are also grappling with the rudiments of conversational turn taking (Bloom, Rocissano, & Hood, 1976). From birth, the child has been alternately prompting, reacting, and reassessing his caretakers through nonverbal means. It is the challenge of the one year old to integrate language into this communicative effort and initiate the long road to social ease and proficiency. Children may have the ability to express thoughts, but they may not understand how to use that ability to convey their desires efficiently and with consideration. These are skills that continue to develop well into adulthood.

THE TWO-WORD TELEGRAPHIC STAGE
Language during the two-word stage, which often begins between the ages of eighteen and twenty-four months, is often referred to as **"telegraphic."** During

this stage, children typically put two words together in a style reminiscent of the compact language of the old Western Union telegrams. Utterances such as *cookie gone*, *no go*, and *mommy up*, are all indicative of two-word stage expression. There are no function words such as prepositions, auxiliary verbs, and conjunctions, and there are no morphological markers for person, number, or tense. Pronouns are forgone for the more specific *mommy* and *truck*, and negation is expressed by negative words, such as *no* or *not,* placed at the beginning of the utterance. Telegraphic speech is an important milestone in the development of language, for it signals the child's preliminary grasp of sentence structure or **syntax**.

Grammar in the two-word stage. Although the logic sometimes escapes adults, children appear to use basic rules of syntax when putting two or more words together. There has been much discussion about the nature of these rules.There is some acceptance of Roger Brown's (1973) proposed grammar based on **semantic-relations**. By examining the two-word utterances produced by English, Swedish, Finnish, Samoan, and Spanish children, Brown found that children's utterances could be classified according to their semantic relations as demonstrated in the following examples:

Mommy eat	agent + action
Hit kitty	action + object
My cookie	possessor + object
Dirty car	attribute + object
Daddy car	agent + location

Brown suggests that this analysis is in accord with children's early cognitive development and their acute interest in objects and actions. Even though this may be the case, it is important to remember that the analysis is based upon adult logic. What children at this age actually understand about parts of speech and their different functions has not yet been ascertained.

Pragmatics in the two-word stage. From the perspective of pragmatics, the above examples show that children in the two-word stage are able to perform a variety of communicative acts. They can describe objects and actions, identify locations, and indicate who is performing a given act on what. According to Halliday (1975), these acts now form the basis for three new communicative functions.

The **pragmatic** function, often called the "language of request," allows children to interact with and act upon their environment. In this case, language becomes the vehicle for fulfilling needs and regulating the behavior of others. The **mathetic** function is related to learning or discovery. Children use language to satisfy their curiosity about the world. To this end, they comment, remember, question, and predict. Finally, the **informative** function, which is the last function to emerge, occurs when children use language to provide information. These pragmatic skills, together with an understanding of the basic rules of conversation such as turn-taking, allow children to enter and enjoy the world of the verbal arts.

Comprehension in the two-word stage. The final consideration of the skills that make up the communicative process is comprehension. I have written to some degree about children's early understanding of meaning—their tendency to overextend or underextend by viewing the world through a lens focused on one or two distinct physical features—and the difficulty adults have in perceiving what children actually understand. Their comprehension depends not only on linguistic data, but also on a multitude of nonverbal and contextual clues that accompany verbal information. Children's comprehension is significantly greater than their ability to produce language, yet they often appear to understand much more than, in reality, they do. This perception is often enhanced by children's ability to learn new vocabulary (James, 1990). How often do children learn adult expletives after being exposed to only one unfortunate slip of the tongue!

PRESCHOOL YEARS TO FLUENCY

Generally after the second birthday, children's verbal activity assumes a new intensity that makes some parents wonder why they ever waited so anxiously for that very first word. Children's language explodes into a rich variety of grammatical and conceptual relations. Morphemes, pronouns, auxiliary verbs, function words, and even phrases appear. Children learn how to negate sentences (an apparent favorite), bombard caretakers with questions, and demand action. Sentences become more adult-like and, by the fifth year of life, children converse freely and skillfully. Although it is certainly possible to write extensively about the many milestones of linguistic achievement that occur during the preschool years, the discussion below is limited to some of the more pertinent highlights. (For more detail, see James, 1990).

Grammar in the preschooler. The period from twenty-seven to thirty months is generally distinguished by a process that Brown (1973) refers to as the "**modulation of meaning**." Meaning is modulated, or clarified, when morphemes are introduced into simple sentences in order to make the meaning more precise. For example, when the morpheme -ed is added to a verb, the speaker is able to reference and express thoughts or incidents that occurred in the past. When the morpheme -s is added to a noun, the speaker indicates a quantity of more than one. Similarly, prepositions such as *in* or *on* leave no doubt that ice cream was left *in* the freezer and not *on* it.

As children begin to utilize grammatical morphemes in their speech, they often **overextend** or **overgeneralize** their use without consideration for the many nuances of the English language. We often hear sentences such as, "I eated the cake," or, "There were many mooses." In adult language, these errors are interpreted to be signs of poor grammar, but with young children, these errors are evidence of progress in mastering the many rules of language and their application with some regularity.

During the preschool years, children learn how to substitute pronouns for nouns. Pronoun use is by no means a simple task; its complexities often plague individuals well into adulthood. Note, for example, the incorrect sentence, "They saw him and I," in which the subjective *I* is commonly substituted for the objective *me*. This incorrect usage occurs so often that many assume it to be correct by virtue of having heard it said by friends and personalities in the media.

For adults and children, correct pronoun use requires the ability to make judgments about gender and number, and determine whether they are subjects, objects, or modifiers. Three year olds typically have difficulty with these assessments, as in the example, "His name is Mommy." By the time that children are ready to enter school, however, with the exception of the above inaccurate *him and I,* pronoun use is regular and, for the most part, correct.

Between the ages of two and five, we see the advent of structured language. In order to generate more complex utterances, children must be able to form sophisticated grammatical constructions. The development of these grammatical constructions can be understood best by examining how children acquire the ability to negate and form questions. Negations first appear in one-word utterances such as *allgone* or *no.*

In 1966, Klima and Bellugi determined that negation in multiword utterances develops in three phases. In the first phase, *no* is put at the beginning of the utterance as in the examples, "No sleep," or, "No go bed." In the second stage, *no* is moved to the internal position preceding the verb, "Lucas no take bath." It is at this point that the negative forms *can't* and *don't* appear. These forms are somewhat misleading to adults for the child has no sense that these forms are indeed contractions. They are, in fact, **negative preverbs** that are used interchangeably with *no* and *not.* It is interesting to note that auxiliary verbs, such as *can, do, does,* or *did,* do not appear until later. Finally, according to Klima and Bellugi, it is only in the final stage that the negative particle assumes its proper form as in the sentence, "Daddy is not happy."

A similar process is found in the development of questions. Normally adults form yes-no questions by moving the auxiliary verb to the front of the sentence as in the example, "Was he happy?" In the event, however, that the sentence has no auxiliary verb, then the appropriate form of *do* must be supplied, "Does the kitty bite?" Two-year-old children have not yet acquired auxiliary verbs, and they are not privy to the axioms of movement necessitated by the formation of interrogatives according to adult standards. Yes-no questions, therefore, are marked by rising intonation at the end of the utterance.

In addition to yes-no questions, children's early use of the interrogative forms includes the question words, *what* and *where,* reflecting, perhaps, their acute interest in naming and location. Gradually, by thirty-one to thirty-four months, children learn to create questions by adding the auxiliary verbs and inverting word order according to the adult rules of syntax and grammar. Additional interrogatives, *why*, *who*, and *how* also appear.

Pragmatics in the preschooler. By the time children have reached the age of two and a half, they are capable of sustaining a topic of conversation for one or two turns, and they are actively working on strategies in order to prolong and improve the effectiveness of their interactions with others. One of the most significant signs of this effort is that children talk much, much more—requesting, describing, repeating, and responding. Although this speech is sometimes incomprehensible, the originality is often startling.

Children during this stage are beginning to master some of the more subtle features of conversation. They are able to participate in two- and three-party conversations with fewer and fewer interruptions. Often younger children misinterpret syntactic junctures or pauses as an indication that they may take the floor (Ervin-Tripp, 1979). As their social awareness becomes more finely tuned, they are not only able to perceive the difference between a syntactic juncture and a pause signaling the end of the speaker's turn, but they are better able to maintain the conversational rhythm by shortening their response time to match that of adults. Having mastered the mechanics of conversational timing, the child can then focus more on the quality of the communication itself.

Sometime between the ages of one and two, children recognize that their language is not always understood, and that they now have sufficient vocabulary and pronunciation skills to fix breakdowns in communication (Gallager, 1977). **Conversational repair** is the art of responding to a listener's requests for clarification by revising, and attempting to clarify, the original utterance. Initially these attempts at repair may actually cause more confusion than the original misunderstanding. As children's active vocabulary increases, however, they have more tools with which to accomplish the job, and they become more adept at adjusting their speech to suit the needs of the listener.

Responding to the listener's need for clarification is the first indication that a child is grasping the concept of style and its importance in communication. Eventually, a child comes to understand the importance of the word, "please," and the etiquette of the indirect request. In middle-class, American culture, it is considered more correct to phrase requests with delicacy and a certain degree of uncertainty in order to convey the proper respect and avoid the appearance of assertion and threat.

The subtleties of etiquette require syntactic forms known as **semantic softeners** (Becker, 1984). These indirect forms include hints, pauses reflecting apparent or feigned uncertainty, and modal forms of verbs such as *could*, *would*, or *might*. Four-year-old children who have mastered these forms will still say, "Gimme that toy," but more and more frequently they can be heard to exhibit the proper social deference when requesting assistance from those who are older, larger, or in positions of authority.

THE SCHOOL-AGED CHILD

By the time that children enter school, they can use language effectively to express their wants, needs, and desires, discuss events in the past, present, or future, carry on conversations for several turns, and consider the impact of their speech on the listener. This does not mean, however, that their acquisition of language has come to an end. School-aged children are continually refining their use of syntax, semantics, and pragmatics to incorporate more complex forms of expression and comprehension.

The passive voice and the school-aged child. The development of the passive voice in children is perhaps one of the more difficult challenges of language acquisition. Young children seem to have an understanding of passive sentences long before they can produce them. This may be related to contextual cues rather than to understanding the construction itself. By the age of five, most children are able to understand some forms of passives that are constructed with action verbs, such as, "Nolan was punched by Lucas." Passives with nonaction verbs, "Nolan was loved by Lucas," prove to be more of a challenge. In either case, those passives actually produced by five-year-olds tend to be of the shortened form, "Nolan was punched."[1]

Unfortunately for preschoolers, the action-nonaction issue is not the only complexity that stands in the way of early progress with passive constructions. There is also the question of reversible and nonreversible passive sentences. A passive sentence is considered to be reversible if either of the two nouns can function as the agent. If the sentence, "The dog was chased by the cat," is reversed, the sentence will still make sense.

In the example, "The tomato was eaten by the boy," the reversal would not hold true unless, of course, we were retelling bad science fiction from the 1960s. Horgan (1978) found that reversibility plays an important role in children's ability to comprehend and produce passive constructions. Children under the age of four produce more reversible than nonreversible passive sentences. Due to the difficulty in ascertaining meaning in passive constructions, the production of full passive sentences does not occur for many children until they reach the age of adolescence.

Pragmatics and the school-aged child. Children of school age make considerable progress in their ability to maintain a conversation for several turns and repair conversational breakdowns. Preschoolers often attempt to clarify confusing messages through repetition and revision of the original utterance. This facility, however, is generally limited to one or two attempts. Once they are of school age, children are able to focus their attention and respond to a sequence of at least three requests for clarification by providing additional information

---

[1]Having mastered many of the regular features and rules of language, school-aged children are free to focus on the more subtle aspects of syntax that allow them to understand and produce increasingly complex sentences. Carol Chomsky (1969), investigated the **principle of minimal distance (PMD)** which states that, as a rule, the noun that most directly precedes the verb will be the subject of the sentence. This rule allows us to interpret sentences that might otherwise be unclear. Consider the example, "Mommy told Nolan to clean his room." According to the PMD, the noun (Nolan) immediately preceding the infinitive verb (to clean) acts as the subject of the infinitive, and there should be no doubt in anyone's mind that it is Nolan who is to clean his room. There are, however, exceptions to this rule. In the example, "Mommy promised Nolan to clean his room," the PMD does not apply. It is the mother who has assumed that responsibility. Verbs such as *ask, tell,* and *promise* comprise a small group of verbs that violate the PMD, and are learned as exceptions only when the more generally applicable rules are in place.

(Brinton, Fujiki, Loeb, & Winkler, 1986). As this skill becomes more keen, school-aged children are able to actively assess and determine the original point of misunderstanding and address that point directly.

During this period, school-aged children also expand their facility to prompt responses through artfully crafted hints. By the age of eight, requests are carefully phrased in order to acknowledge the possible inconvenience to the listener and, thereby, curry the necessary favor (Ervin-Tripp & Gordon, 1986). At this time, children not only resort to careful phrasing, but also attempt to manipulate adults through subtle hints. The statement, "My tummy is hungry," is an example of a not-so-veiled request for food that is intended to make the listener think that she thought of the snack idea all by herself.

Between the ages of five and eight, the focus on communicative style is enriched by a growing appreciation for the medium itself. The term, **metalinguistic ability**, applies to the conscious awareness of the phonological, semantic, syntactic, and pragmatic aspects of language. It is this awareness that allows us to determine a well-formed sentence, enjoy a good riddle, and appreciate literature as art.

SUMMARY

Children come into the world actively seeking stimulation and the adoring gaze of their mothers' eyes. They are alert and perceptive, and socially aware. By focusing their attention on nonverbal cues, they learn much about the mechanics that govern conversational interactions. During the first year of life, children, driven by a love for auditory stimulation and assisted by their care-givers, labor to coordinate the many specific mechanisms of motor control and sensory feedback. Bit by bit, they learn to babble. Their speech gradually acquires all the trappings of language—the rhythm and phrasing, the intonation and emotion, and finally, the pronunciation itself. By the time of their first birthdays, they will have achieved a cognitive milestone that is unique to humans. Children understand that specific sequences of sounds can be used to designate meaning. From then on, language is not simply a means for amusement, it becomes a means for communication.

Children's first attempts at language are limited to single words that reflect their interest in the immediate environment. By the age of eighteen months, they will succeed in putting two words together. Almost overnight, this primitive telegraphic speech explodes with a rapidly expanding vocabulary, grammar, and syntax. As children acquire linguistic knowledge, they focus on how to make their communicative efforts more effective by modifying their styles of expression to suit the needs of their listeners.

50

The dawning awareness of the capacity of language to satisfy specific wants and desires accompanies yet another cognitive milestone in the life of human beings. At some time between the ages of five and eight, children become able to focus not only on the message, but on the medium itself. The many nuances of pronunciation and expression that children work so single-mindedly to learn and use in speaking fluently are now called upon to embellish and enrich the communicative process.

Strategies for Promoting Language Development

How do parents and preschool educators teach language or at least promote its development? The work of cognitive and language theorists, as well as studies conducted by researchers and educators, is reflected in the strategies offered below. This section begins with strategies for all children then discusses activities for children at specific levels of language development.

STRATEGIES FOR ALL CHILDREN

Inclusive conversations. Regardless of age, children must be provided with opportunities for conversational interactions that promote their active participation. Children must be made to feel that their presence is welcome and that their words are worthy of attention. Parents need to follow their child's lead and expand their conversational repertoire to comment with enthusiasm on everything from spilled milk to the pile of wash waiting to be done. Any person, place, or thing that captures children's eyes is fair subject for conversation. The subject matter is less important than warm, fuzzy, conversational exchanges.

Eye contact. Parents and caretakers should be careful to maintain positive eye contact, and show with their body language that they are attending to every word. It may help to get down on the floor when speaking with young children. By entering their immediate field of vision in a non-threatening manner, we may reduce distraction and allow children to focus, not only on our words, but on nonverbal facial cues.

Extension. In general, whether children are at the babbling stage or engaged in refining language usage, linguistic development can best be promoted through activities that expand upon children's present level of linguistic achievement. Adults can scaffold children's speech by using repetition, modeling, and prompts to extend the content and the complexity of utterances. Children who are at the one- and two-word stages, for example, are encouraged to develop more expressive and grammatically correct language, *if* parents expand upon their children's original utterances and model the usc of descriptive adjectives and adverbs. Five-year-olds, who have mastered the basics of declarative sentences, may be encouraged to tackle basic etiquette and modal forms of verbs as illustrated below:

Child:	Mommy, I want pickles.
Parent:	(eating toast) What *would* you like?
Child:	Pickles.
Parent:	You *would like* some pickles?
Child:	Yes.
Parent:	Say, "I would like some pickles, please."
Child:	I would like some pickles, please.
Parent:	(Offers the child pickles) I would like some pickles, too. Please.

Requests for clarification.   Let children know when they are not understood. It allows them to confirm their ability to read doubt or confusion signaled by nonverbal aspects of communication, and it offers them an opportunity for conversational repair. Selectively and gently offer responses such as, "I do not understand what you are saying," or, "Try again."   When accompanied by appropriate scaffolding, such a request shows children that we care about their concerns. The results will be clearer pronunciation, larger vocabularies, improved syntax, and perhaps higher self-esteem.

Acknowledge meaning.   Children, like adults, enjoy feeling successful. Children who are constantly rebuked for errors in pronunciation and grammar are reluctant to take risks to express themselves, thereby inhibiting language development. Correcting mistakes in language can be done without implying weakness or fault. For example, in response to the utterance, "I goed to the store," the corrected verb can be modeled with an intonation that acknowledges the meaning of the utterance and not the improper form.   With the acknowledgment, "You went to the store!" the child feels interest and enthusiasm, while hearing the correct usage.

Storytime. Read to children at every opportunity—in bed, in the bath tub, while waiting for the doctor—in order to expose them to new vocabulary, syntactic forms, and sequences of events. Storytime can be fun as parents read slowly and with exaggerated expression. Parents find that storytime not only provides children with oodles of good language, but that it can also serve as a graceful transition between the activities of the day and the quiet of the night. Children delight in hearing the same stories again and again, as it provides them with practice in receptive language, as well as the comfort that comes from knowing what is going to happen. Retelling or discussing the plot of a story offers a wonderful opportunity to activate new vocabulary not typically used in the household.

Create communication opportunities. Speech and communication practice are stimulated by creating opportunities for children to choose, refuse, accept, request, and engage in repetitive turn-taking sequences and routines (Siegel-Causey & Wetherby, 1993). During daily activities, take time to ask children which of two options is preferred such as which shirt to wear or what toy to select. In addition, offer activities or objects that can be refused or accepted without creating a difficulty. Encourage children to request by placing cues for a tempting activity or object within sight but out of reach. Follow repetitive sequences when eating meals, playing games, cleaning, or dressing, and accompany these sequences with repetitive sequences of words. For example, "Pass the butter," at dinner is a common sequence along with "Good-bye; have a nice time," at parting.

Zone of proximal development and scaffolding. Vygotsky's (1934/1986) views on the role of instruction in cognitive development are best understood through two notions: *zone of proximal development* and *scaffolding*. The *zone of proximal development* is the difference between an actual developmental level, as determined by a child's ability to work independently, and the level at which problems can be solved with assistance from more capable peers and adults. It is, in effect, a measure of a child's potential for learning when placed in a supportive instructional atmosphere. This method of assessment differs substantially from Piaget's technique, which required that children be observed independently in their problem-solving efforts (1973, 1974).

Scaffolding refers to the instructional process by which a child is provided with cues in order to ensure successful confrontations and mastery of more challenging tasks. By utilizing the zone of proximal development, together with the technique of scaffolding, instruction becomes a vital component that stretches proficiency.

In Vygotsky's view, education that is adapted to the current level of proficiency maintains the status quo. By failing to utilize the higher range of the zone of proximal development, educators do not fully develop the potential for learning. According to Vygotsky, instruction that aims at a child's present level of proficiency provides opportunities for practice, while tasks within the upper range of the zone of proximal development encourage children to tackle and master even higher levels of skill with support. Both of these types of activities are necessary in order for children to learn, develop confidence, and progress.

Scaffolding with child-directed speech. An example of how we utilize the zone of proximal development and scaffolding occurs very naturally between parents and children. According to research conducted by Catherine Snow (1986), adults engage in a unique form of communication with infants and small children. Snow calls this "child-directed speech." During child-directed speech, adults reduce extraneous information and simplify their language in order to enter a child's zone of proximal development for language. The simplified vocabulary, grammar, and syntax let a child focus on the content of the utterance without being overwhelmed by irrelevant data. With adult scaffolding, children use words or syntactic structures that could not have been uttered independently.

During child-directed speech, scaffolding occurs as parents provide cues in the form of exaggerated intonation, enunciation, and facial expression in order to focus attention on the important information. As parents try to solicit speech from children, they often try to exploit the child's upper range of the zone of proximal development. In the following conversation with a two-year-old, note how the parent is using repetition, modeling, and prompts, to enable the child to articulate the word "red" and to use it in a two-word utterance.

Parent:	What's that?
Child:	An apple
Parent:	What kind of apple?
Child:	An apple
Parent:	Is it a red apple?
Child:	Yes
Parent:	Do you like red apples?
Child:	Yes, good
Parent:	Can I have some red apple?
Child:	Child offers the apple.
Parent:	Mmm. Red apples are good.
	What kind of apples do we like?
Child:	Red apple.
Parent:	Mmmmm.

Optimal levels. The concept of optimal levels of performance is one of the central hypotheses of skill theory (Fischer, 1987). The optimal level is the upper level of achievable performance in a particular domain. It is not a global description of a child's abilities, but rather a description of performance of an individual skill under ideal conditions. Such conditions include: tasks that are familiar and highly practiced, a supportive atmosphere, and children who are healthy and motivated. Without a high degree of environmental support, people ordinarily perform at their **functional level.** (The optimal/functional distinction is equivalent to the upper and lower boundaries of Vygotsky's zone of proximal development.) According to Fischer, in order to independently bridge the gap between these two levels of performance, children must, with exposure and practice, internalize strategies that produce optimal performance without support.

If variation is the norm, and not the exception, then educators must be prepared to accommodate a wide variety of skills and approaches in an environment that encourages active and comfortable participation with the support of direct teaching, demonstration, modeling, repetition, and independent practice. Children who are actively supported and involved in learning can more quickly internalize given strategies in order to progress to more complex challenges and increase their levels of performance.

Evaluate interactions. Videotaping conversations with young children provides a means not only to capture precious moments on tape, but also to assess the effectiveness of adult-child interactions. The lens of the camera allows parents and educators to observe both verbal and nonverbal communication with uncompromised clarity. Questions that should be asked include: Is the adult providing opportunities to extend the child's use of language? Are there opportunities to choose, refuse, accept, request, and engage in repetitive turn-taking sequences and routines? Is the adult providing the child with models, prompts, and opportunities for practice? Is the child being corrected in a gentle, caring manner? Finally, what nonverbal signals are being sent? Many young children are skilled interpreters of nonverbal communication. If words say "yes," and the body says "no," children are faced with understandable confusion and a problem of trust.

STRATEGIES FOR INFANTS
Parental role in child-directed speech. Child-directed speech, otherwise known as "motherese," occurs when parents, caretakers, and older children interact with infants and toddlers (Snow, 1986). Some may do this with more ease and artistic flair than others, but it appears that those with language engage in a special form of communication with young children. This form of communication is specifically designed to capture and sustain attention, and promote comprehension.

When directing speech to children, adults often, by their own standards, lose all sense of decorum. They speak with high-pitched voices and exaggerated intonation, facial expressions, and gestures. Using short, simple sentences, adults contrive conversations based on whatever appears to be of immediate interest of the child. Possible ambiguities are clarified as parents drop the pronoun "I" from their speech in order to model more immediately useful (and rewarding) vocabulary such as "mama" and "papa."

In general, child-directed speech is characterized by simplified vocabulary, abundant repetitions, and numerous invitations to participate in conversation prompted by questions and commands. From the first day of life, there is an assumption on the part of most parents that children are aware and active participants in the social milieu. Unconsciously acting on their assumption, these parents provide their children with natural models and endless occasions to practice.

Shaping child-directed speech. As children acquire language, parents and caretakers adjust their expectations of children's ability to communicate. During each stage of language acquisition, parents are always one step ahead of their children, prompting, encouraging, and otherwise increasing the range of the zone of proximal development. Initially, infant smiles, burps, and other sounds are reinforced just as though children were speaking their minds.

With time, however, parents become more selective in their reinforcement. Children who babble sequences of speech sounds vaguely identifiable as "mama" or "papa" experience effusive approval of their command of expression. Less recognizable utterances are now ignored. As children advance to the stage of telegraphic speech, they are encouraged to expand upon their utterances and include adjectives and adverbs. Trucks are no longer just trucks, they are now blue, or big, or noisy.

Parents do not set out to teach their children language. Language occurs as a result of the intense desire on the part of the caretakers and the child to bond and communicate. Even though many caretakers may not be specialists in linguistic transformations, all human beings have significant experience in the area of communication that they gladly and capably pass on to their children.

Innate abilities. One of the arguments in support of the innateness of language is that linguistic rules and their numerous exceptions simply could not be mastered without some innate sense of the acceptable forms of language. According to Locke (1993), an infant innately seeks out and actively prompts the particular kinds of stimulation that it enjoys and that foster the development of the brain. Yet, instruction plays a role as well, since variation in responses of parents and others affects the depth and breadth of language development.

Compared to all other stimuli, the human face, particularly that of the mother, compels the child to attend to facial movements, expression, and voice. This attentiveness initiates the child into the social community. Locke (1993) believes that as social beings, infants use strategies for language acquisition that are commonly attributed to nonnative speakers attempting to socialize with those who are fluent. He describes these strategies as the infantile equivalents of:

- Participating in group activities and pretending to know what is going on.

- Choosing words carefully to give the impression that one can speak the language.

- Counting on friends for assistance.

Infants also utilize certain cognitive strategies. They actively solicit attention by using their available talents effectively. Eye contact, smiling, laughing, kicking, and speech sounds, all serve to attract notice and provide a much-desired opportunity for social intercourse. Verbal and nonverbal cues are all taken into consideration along with an implicit assumption that a conversation is relevant to its immediate surroundings. Infants seek patterns of what is already known, and they focus on the larger event allowing the details to fill in later. Finally, children learn new means of expression and they practice them actively.

Respond and acknowledge. Higher expectations improve performance. Adults can assume that infants are ready, from the day of their birth, to actively socialize and learn about the world. We can be sensitive to children's moods and to their ability to make eye contact. Talk to them using exaggerated facial expressions, enunciation, and intonation, offer direct and tender eye contact, and employ a simplified vocabulary and syntax. Let infants know, through the use of questions, commands, and appropriate pauses, that their comments are anxiously awaited. Acknowledge any and all sounds, such as coos, babbles, smiles, and whimpers, as valuable contributions to the conversation.

Word play. Exploit infants' natural love of speech-sounds by repeating syllables in a rhythmic fashion ("Tum dee, tum dee," has always been a personal favorite). Help them enjoy rhythm through the kinesthetics of clapping and bouncing games. Word play and nursery rhymes promote phonological awareness and provide opportunities for practice in listening and comprehension. For a more detailed discussion, see Chapter 3 concerning phonemic awareness.

Consistent responses to repeated sounds. Listen carefully for early utterances and intonational patterns that are used consistently. The utterance, "bah," may be an early attempt at the request, "Bottle, please." Success is a great motivator. Help infants make that leap into the world of verbal communication by responding to certain sounds or gestures with consistent efforts to meet their apparent need, whether for food, hugs, or comforting words.

Singing. Infants' love of music can help them learn simple words and phrases. Songs modified to have just one word, such as "The Mommy Song," "The Car Song," and "The Kitty Song," allow children under the age of two to participate in music and enjoy the pleasure that it brings, as well as to increase their vocabulary with intensive practice.

Ritual actions and phrases. Model rituals of etiquette, such as greetings, good-byes, and introductions in which speakers commonly engage. Include infants in these rituals to make them feel as though they are part of the social fabric of home and community.

STRATEGIES FOR PRESCHOOLERS

Answer questions. Language proficiency requires practice. It is a credit to our design that we learn language as preschoolers, for there is no other stage of life in which we would have the physical stamina to pursue language in the manner required by mother nature. Preschoolers require a tremendous amount of attention as they delight in their new communicative ability and explore the world verbally. This period can be very trying for parents who are bombarded unceasingly with questions and observations. However, it takes no more energy on the part of the parent to answer their questions and then redirect their interest to less demanding pursuits than it does to tell children to be quiet.

Shared stories. Make story telling an interactive experience. The activity, "Story Soup," allows everyone to add something to the pot and contribute to the fun. Children are asked to pick various story elements, such as character, setting, and conflict. Parents and caretakers are charged with calling upon all their imaginative talents in order to weave these elements into a fairly believable plot. Although suggestions may stretch creative limits, adults enjoy challenges, and children love to hear their ideas incorporated into a tale that may become a family favorite.

Personalize stories. Make up and tell stories in which children play the roles of the heroes and protagonists, and use their creativity to resolve problems. In addition to developing familiarity with plot structure and the roles that characters play, these stories enable children to visualize themselves as heroes who have much to offer the world. Storytime can offer a forum for working out family dilemmas, such as children who will not pick up toys, or who are afraid of the dark.

STRATEGIES FOR SCHOOL-AGED CHILDREN

Preschoolers and children of school age with speech and language difficulties may require direct instruction and opportunities for practice beyond what typical conversations normally offer. Some educators, in an attempt to recreate a normal conversational environment, inadvertently lessen the amount of practice that children actually receive. Classroom language instruction should be designed to maximize speech as much as possible per instructional period without sacrificing either the pragmatic aspects of language or entertainment value of such lessons.

Children with speech and language disabilities may benefit from techniques commonly used in foreign language instruction. These involve songs, memorized dialogues, dictation, choral responses, and repetitive practice of clearly routinized activities such as greeting, shopping, or eating in a restaurant.

Word play. Jokes and riddles are an ideal opportunity to promote metalinguistic awareness in five- and six-year-old children. Many five-year-olds reach the stage of language awareness in which they want to understand the humor behind the joke and not just laugh along with the crowd. To many in the five-year-old crowd, the humor in the following joke is not readily apparent unless they understand that the word "ball" can have two meanings:

Question: Why would Cinderella not make a good football player?
Response: Because she ran away from the ball.

By directly teaching that words can have more than one meaning, and by explaining what in particular makes a joke funny, we help children come to appreciate a whole new world of play with language.

Awareness of style. According to Rath (1987), older siblings often become interested in the speech of their younger brothers and sisters. They may engage in their own form of child-directed speech by experimenting with their words. While it is not necessary, or fruitful, to treat older children to an in-depth analysis of their siblings' language, it is an opportunity to convey the idea that people speak in different styles. This basic understanding of style is the first step to appreciating artistic forms of language.

Role play. As five- and six-year-olds expand their contact with the world, they may come home with inappropriate forms of language. At these times, parents and educators need to remember that such vocabulary, however distressing, is evidence of children's remarkable ability to acquire language and perceive meaning. There is, after all, no doubt that five- and six-year-old children understand the emotional impact of such words.

The pragmatics of language require much time, effort, and direct explanation. Five- and six-year-olds, as they continually refine their language efforts, are ready to work on their social skills and focus on the niceties of social interaction. Role playing to model the etiquette of language usage capitalizes on children's love of theater, and allows them to practice their newly acquired social expertise.

LANGUAGE FACILITATION IN THE CLASSROOM

Language usage in the classroom is much more formal than the language used at home. It requires that students be able understand the individual communication style of the teacher, to recall and sequence ideas in a logical fashion, and express themselves succinctly. Without these particular skills, success in class activities or on the playground is unlikely. In addition, facility with language provides a rich background that enhances the process of learning to read.

A thorough assessment of children experiencing speech and/or language difficulties in school should include an assessment of the teacher's language usage in the classroom. Tape-recorded or videotaped sessions allow teachers and specialists to examine the whole communicative process between speaker and listener. Hallahan and Kauffman suggest that "learning how to be clear, relevant, and informative, and how to hold listeners' attention are not only problems for students with language disorders, but also problems for their teachers" (1993, p.273). They point out that the teacher's role is not merely to instruct about language, but also to model its use. If their students are to succeed, teachers need to express themselves clearly, provide proper feedback to students, and ask questions that are within the linguistic and cognitive abilities of children.

Conclusion

Much research in the areas of language and cognition, and their development in children, has contributed to clarification of our understanding of the stages of language development and the nature of effective interactions to support that development. Familiarity with the stages of language acquisition allow parents and educators to keep a watchful eye on children's progress and promote its advancement.

Critical components of effective language teaching in the home or in school encourage children to take risks and reach for their potential. This is accomplished through the modeling and scaffolding of language usage in social and academic environments, and by providing opportunities for practice and feedback coupled with high expectations, affection, and respect. Such activities further language development and foster language facility, and, in turn enhance learners' progress as they make the transition to learning to read.

References

Akmajian, A. and Demers, R. (1984). *Linguistics*. Cambridge, MA: MIT Press.

Becker, J. (1984). Implications of ethology for the study of pragmatic development. In S. Kuczaj, II (Ed.), *Discourse development: Progress in cognitive development research*. New York: Springer-Verlag.

Bloom, L. (1970). *Language development: Form and function of emerging grammars*. Cambridge, MA: MIT Press.

Bloom, L. (1973). *One word at a time: The use of single-word utterances before syntax*. The Hague: Mouton.

Bloom, L., Rocissano, L., & Hood, L. (1976). Adult-child discourse: Developmental interaction between information processing and linguistic interaction. *Cognitive Psychology*, 8, 521-552.

Braine, M. (1963). The ontology of English phrase structure: The first phrase. *Language*. 39, 1-13.

Brinton, B., Fujiki, M., Loeb, D., & Winkler, E. (1986). Development of conversational repair strategies in response to requests for clarification. *Journal of Speech and Hearing Research, 29*, 75-81.

Brown, R. (1973). *A first language: The early stages*. Cambridge, MA: Harvard University Press.

Chomsky, C. (1969). *The acquisition of syntax in children from 5 to 10*. Cambridge, MA: MIT Press.

Chomsky, N. (1957). *Syntactic structures*. The Hague: Mounton.

Chomsky, N. (1965). *Aspects of the theory of syntax*. Cambridge, MA: MIT Press.

Chomsky, N. (1968). *Language and mind*. New York: Harcourt, Brace & World.

Chomsky, N. (1975). *Reflections on language*. San Diego, CA: Pantheon.

Chomsky, N. (1980). *Rules and Representations*. New York: Columbia University Press.

Clark, E. (1973). What's in a word? On the child's acquisition of semantics in his first language. In T. Moore (Ed.), *Cognitive development and the acquisition of language*. New York: Academic Press.

Crain, W. (1992). *Theories of development: Concepts and applications*. Englewood Cliffs, NJ: Prentice Hall.

Damasio, A. and Damasio, H. (1992). Brain and language. *Scientific American, 267* (3), 88-111.

Deese, J. (1970). *Psycholinguistics*. Boston: Allyn & Bacon, Inc.

Denes, P. and Pinson, E. (1973). *The speech chain*. New York: Doubleday.

Ervin-Tripp, S. (1979). Children's verbal turn-taking. In E. Ochs & B. Schieffelin (Eds.), *Developmental pragmatics*. New York: Academic Press.

Ervin-Tripp, S. & Gordon, D. (1986). The development of requests. In R. Schiefelbusch (Ed.), *Language competence: Assessment and intervention*. San Diego, CA: College-Hill Press.

Fischer, K.W. (1987). *Cognitive development in real children: Levels and variations*. Paper presented at the Conference on Teaching Thinking and At-risk Students, November, Philadelphia, PA.

Francis, W.N. (1958). *The structure of English*. New York: The Ronald Press Company.

Gallager, T. (1977). Revision behaviors in the speech of normal children developing language. *Journal of Speech and Hearing Research, 20*, 303-318.

62

Greenfield, P. & Smith, J. (1976). *The structure of communication in early language development.* New York: Academic Press.

Hallahan, D.P., & Kauffman, J.M. (1993). *Exceptional children: Introduction to special education.* Boston: Allyn and Bacon.

Halliday, M. (1975). *Learning how to mean: Explorations in the development of language.* New York: Edward Arnold.

Hockett, C. (1968). *The state of the art.* Paris: Mouton.

Horgan, D. (1978). The development of the full passive. *Journal of Child Language, 5,* 65-80.

Hulit, L. and Howard, M. (1993). *Born to talk: An introduction to speech and language development.* New York: Macmillan Publishing Company.

James, S. (1990). *Normal language acquisition.* Austin, TX: Pro-Ed.

Klima E. & Bellugi, U. (1966). Syntactic regularities in the speech of children. In J. Lyons & R. Wales (Eds.), *Psycholinguistic Papers.* Edinburgh: Edinburgh University Press.

Lennenberg, E. (1967). *Biological foundations of language.* New York: Wiley.

Locke, J.L. (1983). *Phonological acquisition and change.* New York: Academic Press.

Locke, J.L. (1993). *The child's path to spoken language.* Cambridge:Harvard University Press.

Moats, L.C. (2000). *Speech to print: Language essentials for teachers.* Baltimore, MD: Paul H. Brookes Publishing Co..

Nelson, K. (1973). Structure and strategy in learning to talk. *Monographs of the Society for Research in Child Development, 38.*

Ornstein, R. (1986). *Multimind: A new way of looking at human behavior.* New York: Anchor Books.

Piaget, J. (1973). *The child and reality.* (A. Rosen, Trans.). New York: Grossman Publishers. (Original work published 1972.).

Piaget, J. (1974). *The language and thought of the child.* (M. Gabain, Trans.). New York: Meridian. (Original work published 1923.).

Rath, L. (1987). *Child language and education.* Unpublished manuscript.

Siegel-Causey, E., & Wetherby, A. (1993). Nonsymbolic communication. In M.E. Snell (Ed.), *Instruction of students with severe disabilities 4th ed.* New York: Merrill.

Skinner, B.F. (1948). *Walden Two.* New York: Macmillan.

Slobin, D.I. (1979). *Psycholinguistics (2nd ed.).* Glenville, IL: Scott, Foresman and Company.

Snow, C. (1986). Conversations with children. In P. Fletcher & M. Garman (Eds.), *Language acquisition: Studies in first language development.* Cambridge: Cambridge University Press.

Stark, R. (1979). Prespeech segmental feature development. In P. Fletcher & M. Garman (Eds.), *Language Acquisition.* New York: Cambridge University Press.

Stark, R. (1980). Stages of speech development in the first years of life. In G.H. Yeni-Komshian, J.F. Kavanagh, and C.A. Ferguson (Eds.), *Child phonology: Vol. 1. Production.* New York: Academic Press.

von Raffler-Engel, W. (1973). The development from sound to phoneme in child language. In C. Ferguson & D. Slobin (Eds.), *Studies of child language development*. New York: Holt, Rinehart & Winston.

Vygotsky, L.S. (1986). *Thought and language* (A. Kosulin, Trans.). Cambridge, MA: MIT Press. (Original work published 1934.)

Winograd, T. (1983). *Language as a cognitive process: Vol. 1. Syntax*. Reading, MA: Addison-Wesley Publishing Company.

Chapter 3. Phonemic Awareness: Segmenting and Blending the Sounds of Language

Linda K. Rath, EdD
Curriculum Advisor, WGBH Educational Foundation

Phonemic awareness is acknowledged to be the *sine qua non* of reading acquisition for an alphabetic language and a major source of individual variation in reading and spelling performance for students of all ages (Liberman & Shankweiler, 1979; Stanovich, 1986). Findings related to phonemic awareness suggest practical ways to predict reading achievement, promote reading success, and prevent reading failure. This chapter provides an overview of these findings and presents a set of suggestions for implementing them in the classroom and clinic.

The term "phonemic awareness" was adopted in the 1980s by linguists and cognitive psychologists in an effort to explain one of the many complex processes involved in literacy acquisition. **Phonemic awareness** is an understanding that spoken words can be decomposed structurally into sound units, called phonemes. This awareness allows one to analyze a spoken word into phoneme segments and to blend or manipulate the segments to form a new word. Phonemic awareness plays a key role in literacy acquisition. When learners realize that speech is composed of discrete sound units, they can then begin to learn how to associate speech sounds with the letters they see in print.

Although the term **phonemic awareness** is relatively new, the concept is not. In decades past, numerous educators examined these issues under other names. Describing similar findings, earlier researchers called the underlying processes **auditory perception, blending,** or **analysis** (Chall et al., 1963; Monroe, 1932; Rosner, 1974; Vernon, 1957), and even **ear-training** or **reading readiness** (Dolch & Bloomster, 1937; Gates & Bond, 1937).

The 1980s heard the optimistic claims of many researchers who agreed that in **phonemic awareness** they had isolated a key to reading acquisition. Research findings on the subject were hailed as "the single most powerful advance in the science and pedagogy of reading this century" (Adams et al., 1991, p. 392). Meanwhile, national assessments over the same decade reflected declining scores on tests of reading achievement. National Assessment of Educational Progress (NAEP) data indicated a leveling off in scores among 9-year-olds from 1980-1984, a steep decline between 1984 and 1986, especially among the lowest achievers, and further slippage in subsequent years (Mullis & Jenkins, 1990; NAEP, 1985; Learning First Alliance, 1998). Increasing numbers of public school students in primary grades are commonly labeled "learning disabled" because they have problems with reading acquisition.

In recent years, experts have recommended that we pay close attention to beginning readers and to programs that prepare children to succeed in the primary grades (National Research Council, 1998). Therefore, the purpose of this chapter is to highlight recent discoveries and old truths about phonemic awareness and its potential role in the prevention of reading failure. We examine this component of reading ability in an effort to synthesize and present important evidence that can be used to inform and improve instructional practice.

What Is Phonemic Awareness?

Phonemic awareness refers to an individual's knowledge that spoken words are composed of discrete sound units. Changing one of these phoneme units will create a new and different word. For example, in the words "bit" and "pit" only the initial phonemes are different, /b/ and /p/, and this leads to two different words. Phonemes vary considerably based on the context in which they occur, and they are "coarticulated" with other sounds in words—overlapping so as to be hard to distinguish as individual units. This abstract and elusive quality of phonemes makes them difficult for young children to grasp (Liberman & Shankweiler, 1979; Read, 1978).

While five-year-olds may not be aware of specific phonemic distinctions, their implicit phonemic understanding enables them to comprehend spoken language. In fact, most humans are adept at **implicit** phonemic processing— perceiving the difference between *pin* and *pen*, or *wet* and *went*, especially in the context of a meaningful utterance. However, as individuals, we are strikingly diverse in our ability to segment, analyze, and synthesize these sounds consciously, in order to perform deliberate phoneme manipulations (Rozin & Gleitman, 1977).

Speaking and listening seem to be performed with relative consistency from person to person and are thought to be biologically determined; as humans we are born with this capacity to communicate by speaking and listening (Mattingly, 1972). In contrast, other linguistic activities or skills are thought to be secondary, and not necessarily natural for humans. Reading, writing, or even speaking Pig Latin, are such secondary linguistic behaviors. They rely on one's awareness of and ability to **process** language, controlling and manipulating it as a medium. In this more abstract behavior, individual variation can be far ranging.

Variation in language awareness. To demonstrate phonemic awareness in particular, one must pay attention to the sounds of words rather than to their meanings. This requires a shift in attention from an automatic focus on the message to a more deliberate, analytic focus on the words as objects in and of themselves (Lundberg, 1978). These and similar concerns for the forms of language are called *meta*linguistic behaviors. Tasks that are used to assess phonemic awareness are often called *meta*phonology tasks. They require that the sound units of words be recognized, identified, segmented, blended, manipulated, and the like.

Language awareness might be thought of as a broad continuum that has very skillful metalinguistic performers at one end and poor performers at the other. The most metalinguistically adept individuals demonstrate extraordinary keenness for language forms and the subtle possibilities of sound and sense. For example, author Natalie Babbitt writes:

> The alphabet is still a miracle to me—how those twenty-six funny shapes can group themselves in endlessly different ways to make words with endlessly different meanings. I still play alphabet games with myself, games like trying to think of five words that are exactly the same except for the vowels, like bAg, bEg, bIg, bOg and bUg. Just by changing the vowels, you can utterly change the meaning (1986, p. 43).

While this exquisite delight in our written language system may be common among poets and linguists, it is not something that the typical reader or speaker of English ordinarily celebrates.

In order to become competent at reading and writing English, a learner must possess enough awareness to be able to note how phonemic elements are represented in our alphabetic writing system. Those who experience reading disability are often unable to make this connection and generally tend to be at the low end of the language awareness continuum. Along with a reading disability, they are likely to have difficulty with other complex language processing skills.

Researchers studying disabled readers have found that they often misunderstand spoken sentences containing embedded clauses, arc unaware of morphological connections between words, and have a hard time detecting ambiguity and analyzing syntactic structure (Bialystok & Mitterer, 1987; Crain, 1989; Menyuk & Flood, 1981). In a study of reading disabled young adults, one subject's insight summed up their experience: "I know I talk it alright, but I just don't know language" (Blalock, 1982, p. 608).

ACQUIRING KNOWLEDGE OF SOUNDS AND SYMBOLS
A learner with an awareness of the phonemic structure of spoken language has gained an underlying ability crucial to the acquisition of literacy. Once a learner develops phonemic awareness, the correspondences between phonemes and graphemes (letter symbols) in written English can be mastered. Phonemic awareness is the insight upon which spelling knowledge depends. The task is then to learn how the forty-four phonemes of English are represented by the twenty-six letters of the alphabet.

Acquiring a general knowledge of sound/symbol correspondence is a special challenge in English because of the complexities of the English spelling system (*orthography*). Ours is a "morpho-phonemic" system, one that sacrifices the simplicity of one-to-one sound-symbol relationships in order to reflect meaning-based connections (Chomsky, 1970). For example, in the words "nation" and its derivative "national," the letter "a" is preserved even though it represents a different sound. In the word "sign," a silent "g" remains as a trace to make the connection to "signature" more apparent.

If our spelling system had perfect one-to-one correspondence, the word pairs "nation" and "national" or "sign" and "signature" would look very different from one another. Our alphabet symbols are able to map phonemes, one by one, while at the same time preserving morphemes (units of **meaning**, like "sign").

Flexible and sophisticated enough to include words from many languages, the English spelling system, alas, is not user-friendly for beginning readers and writers.

PHONEMIC PROCESSING SKILL

In addition to phonemic awareness and knowledge of English spellings, a learner's **phonemic processing skill** is a factor in reading and spelling performance. One must possess the ability to perform segmental speech acts, to hold the segments in short-term memory, and to blend sounds to form words (or blend words to form larger units of meaning). For example, imagine a first grader who encounters the following sentence while reading independently: *Suddenly, it started to rain.*

Many young readers will substitute the more familiar *Sunday* for *suddenly*. Their understanding of the sentence, then, may be somewhat different from what the author intended. Learners who are more successful can segment "sud-den-ly" into chunks, try out different sounds while maintaining the letter sequence, reblend the word, and crosscheck to make sure that it makes sense in context. This is an extremely complicated process, requiring several precise and controlled steps. It is an impossible task to accomplish for a young learner without phonemic awareness and/or with a language-processing disorder.

PHONEMIC AWARENESS AND LEARNING 'PHONICS'

Phonics instruction for beginning readers aims to present the correspondences between letters and the speech sounds they commonly represent. With its emphasis on *decoding* the symbols of written language, phonics as a method of instruction was once thought to be successful only when children had achieved a certain "mental age" or "readiness" for reading (Dolch & Bloomster, 1937). But earlier researchers also noted that children who easily learned to read noticed the separate sounds in spoken words (Durrell & Murphy, 1953). For decades, perhaps even centuries, educators have recommended activities that focus on rhyme, alliteration, and within-word sound patterns to provide the "ear-training" necessary as a foundation for instruction in the principles of phonics.

Now, it is widely acknowledged that **phonemic awareness**, rather than mental age, is the pre-requisite that enables instruction in phonics to be effective. Moreover, phonemic awareness and phonics instruction seem to interact. Direct instruction in spelling and decoding of printed letters (phonics instruction) serves to foster phonemic awareness. Thus, the phonic method may be a vehicle for teaching phonemic awareness, which, in turn, enables the acquisition of reading skill.

Whereas experts in prior decades spoke more globally of the optimum mental age and "readiness" for reading, more recent studies explore the specific understandings and misunderstandings of children and the cognitive demands of each particular task. For example, many researchers have found that preschool children are frequently confused about what is meant by "word" or "sound." When asked, "Which word is longer, 'snake' or 'butterfly'?" preschool children commonly say "snake," because they all know that snakes are long and skinny. When asked, "What is the first sound in 'cat'?" they are likely to say "MEOW!" For these children, conventional phonics instruction is sure to be confusing at first. As they gain more experience with language **forms** in books and environmental print, as they learn to rhyme, match words and sounds, note letters, etc., such children stand a better chance of understanding how language is represented by the features of print.

In general, the emphasis of current research represents a continued movement away from a global notion of "readiness." Investigators of literacy acquisition are offering more specific delineations of the numerous interactive processes needed for learning to read and of the various abilities and understandings required for the execution of each process.

How Phonemic Awareness Relates to Reading and Spelling Achievement

Dozens of studies have been conducted in recent years to "operationalize" the concept of phonemic awareness and to explore its importance as a predictor of subsequent reading achievement, an enabler of literacy progress, and a marker of reading disability. The following section presents a brief summary of the research on phonemic awareness as a predictor and an enabler. A discussion of phonemic awareness as a marker of reading disability will be presented later in the chapter.

PHONEMIC AWARENESS AS A PREDICTOR

Researchers have found that children in kindergarten display a broad range of individual variation when asked to perform tasks that require attention to words as objects containing sounds. In some of these tasks, kindergartners match and produce rhyming words or words that begin with the same sound. In another task they blend together familiar words that are made from segments slowly spoken by the examiner (e.g. /f/.../æ/.../t/ = fat). More difficult tasks ask kindergartners to count sound segments as they speak words slowly, or to isolate each sound as they pronounce a word. The strength of a child's performance is likely to predict later achievement on measures such as standardized reading and spelling tests (Stanovich, Cunningham, & Cramer, 1984).

In one extensive study, for example, researchers administered a phoneme segmentation task to 534 children at the beginning of kindergarten. Twenty months later, at the end of first grade, the same students took a reading achievement test battery. Their rankings on the summed achievement tests closely mirrored the rankings they had achieved on the phoneme segmentation task (Share, Jorm, Maclean, & Matthews, 1984).

Other researchers have found that encouraging "invented spelling" on a writing task can provide a simple way to evaluate kindergartners' phonemic awareness (Tangel & Blachman, 1992). When young children are urged to spell out the sounds they hear in words, they very clearly demonstrate their different levels of phonemic awareness and phonics knowledge. Their performance in kindergarten is highly predictive of reading achievement scores at the end of first grade and beyond (Mann, Tobin, & Wilson, 1984; Morris & Perney, 1984; Zifcak, 1981).

In the intervening years since the studies described above, evidence from research has continued to mount: a child's "performance on measures of phonological awareness is a powerful predictor of future reading achievement" (Blachman, 2000). It is, in fact, the best predictor we know of success in learning to read in the primary grades, surpassing other factors such as IQ, general language proficiency, socioeconomic background, and knowledge of alphabet letters (Adams, 1990; Griffith & Olson, 1992).

Clearly, kindergartners with a high level of phonemic awareness will have a head start in first grade. This superior preparedness enables them to out-perform agemates on all aspects of reading, from spelling, to word reading, to reading comprehension. Of course, comprehension of contextual materials in the lower grades is rarely a conceptual challenge; if the words can be decoded, the simple stories with familiar vocabulary can be understood (Chall, 1983).

When such a strong correlation is found between variables in education, the next question is often: "Is this a **causal** connection?" In other words, does phonemic awareness **cause** growth in literacy, or does it, perhaps, represent some other underlying factor, such as exposure to print or experience with books? To answer this question, researchers have conducted numerous experimental studies in which some groups of children receive special phonemic awareness training and are compared to untrained "control groups" who come from similar backgrounds with similar educational profiles.

PHONEMIC AWARENESS AS AN ENABLER

In these experimental studies, a variety of interventions that foster phonemic awareness were found to enhance student achievement on subsequent phonemic awareness tasks and on reading and spelling achievement tests (Goswami, 2000). Children who receive specific training consistently and significantly out-perform their control-group peers (National Reading Panel, 2000). Interventions have proven to be successful with kindergartners in whole-class instruction, before they are even introduced to formal reading instruction (Blackman, Ball, Black, & Tangel, 1994).

Other successful interventions have included phonemic awareness as an important component in early reading instruction, linking phonemic awareness to letter knowledge and the analysis of spoken words to printed word analysis. Using concrete objects, like blocks or moveable letters, researchers have helped children, individually and in small groups, by demonstrating the match between within-word sounds and the letters we use to represent them (Blachman, 1987; Bradley & Bryant, 1985; Ehri & Wilce, 1987; Elkonin, 1973; Goswami & Bryant, 1990; Williams, 1979).

A few interventions have been conducted with older students, underachievers or Special Education students. In these studies as well, activities that required phoneme segmentation and blending improved student performance on subsequent phonemic awareness tasks and on follow-up tests of word and passage reading (Lovett et al., 1994; Torneus, 1984; Vellutino & Scanlon, 1987; Williams, 1980).

Because of this strong evidence from experimental studies, researchers are confident that there is a **causal** connection between variables. Phonemic awareness **enables** progress in literacy development, at least in terms of promoting skills such as decoding and encoding with accuracy. Without intervention, children who lack phonemic awareness at the beginning of first grade are likely to fall behind their peers in reading and spelling achievement.

This was the case for a group of ten first graders who were studied by Fox and Routh (1983). At the end of grade one, these students performed poorly on a phoneme segmentation task. Their average word-reading achievement scores fell two years behind the average scores of their classmates. The same students were tested again at age ten. At this point, they could perform well on the phoneme-segmentation task, but they had **all** repeated a grade in school, and their reading and spelling test scores were still falling below the class average. Predictably, without some type of intervention, lack of phonemic awareness becomes a reading disability. This is what has become known as "Matthew Effects" in reading: the poor keep getting poorer while the rich are getting richer (Stanovich, 1986).

What about those students who are "rich" in phonemic awareness when they come to school? What might be the source of this awareness? What type of developmental course does it follow?

Stages and Sequence in Phonemic Awareness Development

Normally, many children demonstrate implicit or tacit phonemic awareness in the preschool years. They engage in play with rhyming and nonsense words (sometimes endlessly and to the exasperation of their parents). By age five they can usually recognize rhyming words and tell when words begin with the same sound (Chomsky, 1979; Goswami, 2000). This early stage of knowledge is often referred to as phonological awareness (International Reading Association, 1998).

Explicit language awareness comes later, usually by age six or seven, and often by virtue of formal instruction. It is the focused, guided attention to the details of written language, which gives rise to a more analytic, systematic awareness of language forms, that is crucial for the development of competence as a reader and writer.

Numerous researchers have designed studies to suggest a predictable sequence of development that leads to increasing refinement of phonemic awareness (Goswami, 2000; Lewkowicz, 1980; Stanovich, Cunningham, & Cramer, 1984; Yopp, 1988). Taken together, these studies provide a fairly consistent picture of developing skill, which confirms earlier studies by Chall et al. (1963), Bruce (1964), and Rosner & Simon (1971). The sequence appears to be unvarying, systematic, and perhaps developmentally determined. Below, I have synthesized this research into a description of the sequence in which phonemic awareness is likely to develop for a typical, English-speaking child.

By age five, many children demonstrate:

    1. ...awareness of the word as a discrete unit.

2. ...awareness of the syllable as a discrete unit. For example, they can segment multi-syllable words into syllables and tap or count the syllables. They can delete a syllable, giving an appropriate response when asked to "say cowboy without the cow."

Somewhat later, as kindergartners, many children are able to perform:

3. ...rhyme identification, particularly if they are given examples to judge.

4. ...initial consonant matching. They can identify words with the same beginning consonant and may be able to produce initial consonant matches. These partial segmentation tasks are an early form of explicit phonemic awareness. It is at this point in development that some children begin to produce invented spelling, if their knowledge of letter names is strong.

5. ...partial phoneme segmentation. Having mastered steps 1-4, a child is next able to segment a spoken syllable into two parts (C-V; V-C; or C-VC). This skill of splitting a syllable into an **onset** and **rime** is described at length by Adams (1990).

...phoneme synthesis (blending) can often be achieved at this stage, particularly with two spoken segments to be blended into one (V-C more easily than C-V).

By age six, many children are able to perform:

6. ...final sound matching and segmenting of simple spoken words (CV-C).

...blending together of two more complex segments (first CV-C, then C-VC or CC-VC).

Somewhat later, many children have learned to perform:

7. ...blending of three spoken phoneme segments (C-V-C or CC-V-C). While this task is difficult for kindergartners and for many first graders, it can be learned. Helfgott (1976) found that blending (C-V-C) was generally simpler than segmenting for her kindergarten sample, and Yopp's data (1988) confirm this order.

...complete phoneme segmentation: saying, tapping, counting, and marking phonemes. At this stage, children can be encouraged to use invented spelling to represent phoneme segments. This depends on knowledge of letter names and their sounds, which adds additional demands to the task.

By age 8, many children can perform:

8. ...advanced phoneme segmentation. However, peeling apart consonant clusters into individual phonemes continues to be difficult for some subjects through the elementary years and even into adulthood (Rath, 1994).

9. ...phoneme manipulation tasks. These comprise Yopp's "compound" category, for they require segmentation plus deletion, reversal, or substitution, and then re-blending of a word. Most kindergarten children and many first graders are unable to perform these compound phonemic awareness tasks, which prove to be more appropriate measures for older students. Rosner & Simon's *Auditory Analysis Test* (1971) is organized according to their predictions of rank order of difficulty in deleting spoken sounds—syllables and phonemes. From kindergarten to grade six, individuals progress quite systematically through the test levels, deleting initial consonants, final consonants, then medial consonants (e.g. "Say 'man' without the /m/"; "say 'steak' without the /k/"; "say 'desk' without the /s/.").

Although the **sequence** of development appears to be unvarying, the **rate** of development varies widely and depends upon many interacting factors related to nature (constitution/neurophysiology/heredity) and nurture (environment/ instruction/experience).

With regard to "nurture," it appears that phonemic awareness only develops under certain conditions. Unlike verbal communication, it does not simply "emerge" in all individuals at a specific point in development, regardless of culture and experience. For example, illiterate adults who have not learned to read the alphabetic language that they speak also do not demonstrate phonemic awareness (Morais et al., 1979). Expert readers in a non-alphabetic language, such as Chinese, also tend to perform poorly on phonemic awareness tasks (Read et al., 1986). From this evidence, we can gather that phonemic awareness development depends on successful experiences with the written features of an alphabetic language.

Even among able students learning to use an alphabetic writing system, the phonemic properties of the language often need to be demonstrated explicitly and concretely. Insight into the phonemic structure of English rarely occurs without some formal or informal instruction that highlights within-word sounds (Byrne, 1984; Gough & Hillinger, 1980).

However, some preschoolers seem to be remarkably sensitive to language sounds and adept at tasks that require phonemic awareness. Others are just as insensitive and oblivious. The source of this individual variation has been a topic of interest to researchers in the 1980s, particularly because it has **not** proven to be correlated as strongly with "mental age" as had been previously supposed. While standard IQ measures generally account for a small portion of the variation in performance, other factors play an even stronger role.

NORMAL VARIATION

Several correlational studies have explored the factors that might explain variation in phonemic awareness. Some investigators hypothesize that a child must be able to engage in concrete operational thought as a correlate of phonemic awareness, since a focus on form, rather than meaning, is required. They find that there is a moderate, but statistically significant, relationship among a child's performance on a battery of Piagetian conservation tasks, a phoneme-tapping task, and a syntactic awareness task (Tunmer et al., 1988).

Another study of first graders also documents a significant relationship between phonemic awareness and comprehension of complex spoken sentences (Mann et al., 1987). Researchers in England have found that the mother's education and a child's knowledge of common nursery rhymes account for considerable variation in the phonemic awareness of preschoolers (Maclean et al., 1987).

A vast body of ethnographic research has been building steadily as well, presenting "naturalistic" examples of how literacy-related activities foster reading acquisition. Researchers have tried to describe how and why children begin, before receiving formal instruction in school, to learn to read. (See, for example, Durkin, 1966; Mason, 1980.) The term "emergent literacy" is used to describe those literacy-related behaviors that are the explorations of novices into the domain of written language. (See Anderson et al., 1985; Teale, 1986.)

Some studies describe family and cultural environments that foster or inhibit early literacy (Heath, 1986; Taylor, 1983). Specific, scaffolded interactions between child and adult are reported in great detail (Bissex, 1980; Snow 1983). In many of these descriptions, a storybook is used as an opportunity to teach a child about the conventions of literacy, including sign-symbol relations (Snow & Ninio, 1986). The story does not merely get read, but adult and child collaborate to build the knowledge of code and convention that will lead to independent reading. The "big books" included in a "Whole Language" approach are meant to replicate this literacy experience, giving children a chance to interact with good books and adults who know how to present them interactively (Holdaway, 1979).

In addition to frequent storybook-reading events, writing and spelling activities are prominent in the lives of emergent readers. Ferreiro (1986) documented the discoveries of two precocious preschoolers as they explored the letter-sounds in their own names and the names of family members. Others have shown how systematically inventive spellers make progress from early stages of scribbling to increasingly phonetic spelling as their phonemic awareness becomes more sophisticated (Bissex, 1980; Chomsky, 1979; Read, 1971).

While some stress that it is the desire to communicate that drives inventive spellers, that making meaning is critical (Sulzby, 1986; Wells, 1986), others note that inventive spellers are often unconcerned with audience and product; it is the **process** of representing sounds with letters that engages their attention (Read, 1978). Families that foster preschool inventive spellers have a number of things in common: storybook reading is frequent, adults spend time reading and writing for their own purposes, alphabet learning has been valued and advanced through playful as well as rote behavior, and environmental tolerance for spelling errors is high (Read, 1971).

While invented spellings may serve as one window into the development of phonemic awareness (Mann et al., 1987), this behavior does not always lead to an easy entry into reading. Bissex (1980) documents her son's frustrations in learning how to **de**code conventional spellings. Having learned how to map sounds onto plausible symbols, he had to accommodate his logical system to the more complex and less predictable patterns of English orthography.

Schickedanz (1990) records her son's journey through the creative literacy playground of his kindergarten year and into the obstacle course of first grade. She provides the scaffolding he needs to scale these obstacles, leaving the reader to wonder why such assistance is not provided by the teacher. These case studies of individual learners show how many tricky little steps there are in the literacy-acquisition process. They describe confusions and difficulties encountered by even the brightest and most phonemically aware. More than demonstrating how "natural" it is to learn to read, these studies reveal that children need a great deal of guidance along the way from responsive, perceptive, well-informed adults.

Our English spelling system is complex, and, unfortunately, many high-frequency words are not spelled as they sound. Even the simplest storybooks for young children contain words that contradict the patterns and principles that children need to learn at the early stages. For this reason, some researchers argue that **writing** (phonetic encoding) is the simpler, more accessible skill for young children and can serve as useful preparation for a guided entry into reading. Many years ago, Montessori (1912) was convinced by her observations of preschoolers that spelling/sounding activities should precede reading efforts, as a self-generative and active way for children to use their knowledge and curiosity. Her argument has been taken up more recently by Bissex (1980), Chomsky (1971), Frith (1986), and Read (1981).

SUMMARY

Much work has been done to explain the development of phonemic awareness, its correlates, and the conditions that promote its growth. Exposure to nursery rhymes during storytime and focused attention to print on signs in the environment appear to be important experiences for stimulating phonemic awareness. Scaffolded interaction between adult and child, through sharing an interest in letters, signs, words, messages, and stories, is central in early literacy development. Clearly, interest has grown in the writing-and-reading connection and in the constructive process of mapping sounds with letters to develop an awareness that will enable reading in the early stages.

While there has been some consensus in the field, arguments and debates continue. On the one hand, many would like to think that literacy is a natural, developing process that will emerge in environments that emphasize and celebrate the communicative purposes of print. On the other hand, one must ask about those children who do **not** acquire the conventions of literacy in a print-rich, book-loving, story-writing environment. The following section surveys the studies of children with severe reading and spelling difficulties and highlights the role of phonemic awareness in their problematic literacy development.

Phonemic Awareness and Reading Disabilities

An abundance of research has examined the symptoms, causes, and correlates of extreme individual variation in literacy acquisition. In general, a theory of dyslexia as a language-based disorder has gained wide-spread acceptance. In particular, a lack of phonemic awareness has emerged as one of a number of reliable markers of developmental dyslexia. According to researchers at the Yale Center for the Study of Learning and Attention, dyslexia is "An unexpected difficulty learning to read despite intelligence, motivation, and education" (Shaywitz, 1996). "Dyslexics have difficulty with phonological processing: recognizing, manipulating, and learning how speech sounds correspond to the letters in words" (Hall & Moats, 1999). This is often referred to as "a phonological core deficit."

The constitutional origin of dyslexia is currently thought to be traceable to disorders in language processing mechanisms (Vellutino, 1978). One (or several) of these mechanisms affect the development of linguistic awareness in general and phonemic awareness in particular. In addition to this, or, perhaps, as a cause or consequence, a deficit in short-term memory for verbal information contributes to a slow rate in storing the precisely sequenced sound segments of spoken words (Byrne & Shea, 1979; Goswami, 2000; Katz, 1986; Vellutino & Scanlon, 1987).

Children with rapid-automatized-naming-speed (RAN) deficits in addition to low levels of phonemic awareness are likely to need much more training and instruction (Torgesen & Davis, 1996). This double deficit is now hypothesized to be the source of disruption for the most serious forms of reading disability (Wolf, Bowers, & Biddle, 2000).

NEUROLOGICAL ASPECTS

Neuroscientists have tried to locate the cause(s) of developmental dyslexia by examining brain cell structure (autopsy studies), EEGs, and computer images of the working brain as it responds to different tasks. They have found that some dyslexics have an atypical brain structure, with a hemispheric symmetry that is not found in most brains (Galaburda, 1985). It may be that delays in neuronal migration during fetal life result in unusual patterns of neural circuitry that make particular language-processing tasks difficult for dyslexics (Geschwind, 1986). Some dyslexics have been found to project unusual left parietal waveforms in CAT scans (Hynd & Semrud-Clikeman, 1989). The neurological anomalies that may be sources of reading dysfunction, and their effects on reading, are discussed in further detail below. See Wolf, Bowers, and Biddle (2000) for a more detailed discussion.

Phonemic sequencing disorder. The difficulty dyslexics have with segmenting and analyzing speech sounds is currently hypothesized to be part of a broader dysfunction in executing sequential motor programs in general. Dyslexics often display what are called "soft signs" of neuropathology: their finger-tapping responses are awkward, eye-movement patterns are agitated, and nonsense syllable repetitions are halting and inaccurate. These individuals often have difficulty with other fine motor tasks such as handwriting, dancing, or piano playing. In fact, the same nervous system pathways that subserve sequenced motor behavior are those that subserve speech production (Wolff, 1989). Evidence suggests that a single mechanism, such as precise timing, is the common denominator for both fine-motor performance and sequential speech acts (Ojemann cited in Gibson, 1988; Wolf, 1991). This same timing deficit may, in fact, underlie the poor performance of dyslexics on RAN tasks (Wolf, Bowers, & Biddle, 2000).

A motor organization/timing theory is one promising explanation for the severity of the problem some individuals have with processing and producing speech sounds sequentially. Adult poor readers consistently have difficulty when asked to remember and repeat numbers, letters, or words (Read & Ruyter 1985). It seems to be the **production** of sounds in sequence rather than **discrimination** that is difficult for many with a reading disorder (Catts, 1986). Since the fine-motor pathway for speech is located in the peri-Sylvian language region of the left hemisphere (Rudel, 1988), it may be that the Galaburda/Geschwind focus on structural anomalies located on the left side of the brain is the apt locus of causality for this particular syndrome.

Selective attention dysfunction.   Another theory implicates "control processing," also called "executive function," as the mechanism at fault in dyslexic subjects (Bialystok & Mitterer, 1987). Dyslexics have difficulty "changing horses in midstream" (Denckla, 1983), as in shifting attention from meaning to form, or from bottom-up to top-down processing. An interaction between information processing strategies is a crucial part of fluent reading (Lesgold & Perfetti, 1982).

Dyslexics appear to be more single-minded than normal readers and less able to switch focus to integrate processes at the appropriate time, or to exhibit an organized, planful approach. Denckla (1983) notes dyslexics' inability to "pull back" from language meanings and focus on language forms. She questions a "missing link" in their efforts to learn to read—a lack of awareness about the phonemic structure of words.

Other neurologists have observed signs in dyslexics of "a lack of appropriate cortical arousal that may signal problems in the capacity for selective focused attention" (Kirk, 1989, p. 24). Denckla (1983) also noted an "underactivation of frontal contribution" in the brains of dyslexics that might be responsible for a dyslexic's "disorganization and misallocation of cerebral resources" (p. 40).

Clearly, the issues of phonemic processing and awareness have emerged as central in the profile of dyslexia, if not its cause. Dyslexia is commonly referred to as a "specific aptitude deficit, leading to underachievement in reading by children of otherwise normal intelligence" (Rosenberger, 1992). The aptitude that appears to be lacking in dyslexics is that aptitude for *meta*linguistics, for grasping the distinctive features of words and for analyzing their sounds in sequence.

Again, the cause of such a deficit may be a disorder in the motor system for speech, which causes difficulties and delays in sequential processing of linguistic elements. Alternatively (or in addition), it may be that a disorder in the pre-frontal cortex causes a selective-attention problem that impedes fluent switching between meaning and form. This might delay the dawn of phonemic awareness for some affected subjects. Perhaps further research will clarify these two factors and explain the ways in which they are differentiated and interrelated.

DEFICIT OR DELAY?

Progress has been made in resolving the question of dyslexia's status as a deficit or a developmental delay. The majority of the evidence points toward an existing deficit that holds back performance and knowledge acquisition.

Evidence for deficit among dyslexics. Dyslexics are significantly less adept than their "reading-age mates" (younger, normal readers who are matched on achievement test scores) on a number of oral tasks: in segmenting and manipulating speech sounds, particularly in segmenting consonant blends (Morais, et al., 1984) and Pig-Latin production (Olson et al., 1989); in repeating nonsense words (Snowling, et al., 1986); in producing rhymes (Bradley & Bryant, 1985; Read & Ruyter, 1985); and in naming speed on RAN (rapid automatized naming) tasks (Wolf & Segal, 1999).

Snowling et al. suggest that dyslexics have a systemic difficulty in establishing "a new articulatory-motor programme" (p. 80), and that this causes their poor performance on nonword repetition tasks. They further argue:

> If they find the repetition of nonwords difficult, then new word learning will
> be compromised. It follows that dyslexics may take longer to establish lexical
> representations for words which they encounter auditorily than age-matched
> normal readers (1986, p. 515).

In other words, a systemic difficulty/deficit within an individual's naming/speech production system interferes with literacy development. This dysfunction limits their ability to build word knowledge, so that many dyslexics are slower to expand their meaning vocabulary as well as their recognition of infrequent words in print. They need considerably more time and practice than most in learning new words. Hence, Wolf's "double-deficit" hypothesis to explain the performance of students with phonological-core deficits *and* naming-speed deficits (Wolf & Obregon, 1997).

Predictably, dyslexics need more time for learning and applying the alphabetic principle. Researchers have shown that dyslexics are consistently less able to induce and/or use rules and patterns for solving verbal tasks, especially those involving reading and spelling (DiBenedetto, Richardson, & Korchnower, 1983; Manis, et al., 1987; Morrison, 1984; Snowling, 1981).

Once again, this could be a consequence of a selective attention dysfunction. Alternatively, it may be that because of the difficulties experienced with phoneme analysis and production, dyslexics are impeded in their ability to store accurate phonemic representations in memory (Byrne & Shea, 1979). In order to compensate for this deficiency, some may adopt a meaning-based reading strategy, which is initially less difficult. Perhaps they try to store words holistically, as isolated pictures to be remembered.

This strategy of reading words as logographic wholes may further hold back spelling and reading development, as it may distract the student from seeing the more productive phonetic connections among words. While able readers may be recognizing patterns and learning the principles to apply in spelling or reading independently, disabled readers may be memorizing individual words, a practice that becomes unmanageable once many words have been introduced.

Evidence for delay in non-dyslexics. Some researchers object to the deficit theory and offer evidence in favor of a developmental lag theory. They present findings from subjects who are more broadly drawn from the school, and not the more severely affected clinical population. These students are often referred to as "garden variety" poor readers, for their difficulties may be neither constitutional, nor neurological, in origin. Their low achievement in reading may be more related to instruction, motivation, or experience (e.g. lack of exposure to books at home, health problems that have led to school absences, emotional issues that interfere with academic growth). For these students, performance on tasks of speech segmentation, digit span, rhyme production, etc., is only slightly, and not significantly, worse than the performance of younger, normal readers, matched for reading age (Beech & Harding, 1984; Siegel & Ryan, 1988; Treiman 1984).

Evidence influenced by research design. The question of deficit versus developmental lag is answered differently depending on the nature of the research studies used to examine the issue. Using a strict definition of "dyslexia" and considering studies based on the performance of children who are of average intelligence or above consistently leads to a conclusion for a deficit. Using a more liberal definition of dyslexia that includes "garden variety" poor readers leads to a conclusion for delay in development as an underlying condition (Olson et al., 1989; Shaywitz et al., 1992). The answer varies with: the number of readers studied; whether severe dyslexics or "garden variety" poor readers were examined; and whether readers with rich or limited educational experiences were studied.

In many instances, authors comment on the "generally impoverished phonemic-processing skills" (Beech & Harding, 1984, p. 359) of all poor readers and their weak knowledge of phonological information (Bruck, 1988). However, this symptom does not always suggest dyslexia. In some cases this could result from lack of instruction or from instruction that has not been effective (Lyon, 1998). Very little instructional background information is included in these comparative studies, and so the reader is left to wonder whether the poor performance indicates a neurological anomaly, a lack of effective instruction, or a combination of the two.

Historical evidence for deficit among dyslexics. Over fifty years ago, neurologist Samuel Torrey Orton published his findings with regard to reading disability (1937). Although his theory of causation—lack of established cerebral dominance—has not been substantiated (Chall, 1967), he was very close to today's mark in connecting reading problems with a developmental language disorder. He was aware of the cluster of subskills that generally mark the dyslexic population, noting "...a difficulty in repicturing or rebuilding in the order of presentation, sequences of letters, of sounds or units of movement" (p. 145).

> It is this process of synthesizing the word as a spoken unit from its component sounds that often makes much more difficulty for the strephosymbolic child than do the static reversals and letter confusions (p. 162).

He argued that the only way for students with this speech/motor deficit to achieve reading skill is to engage in intensive, systematic practice with letters and sounds.

Similarly, Marion Monroe's experience with poor readers more than sixty years ago (1932) convinced her that the links connecting motor organization, language, and reading are strong. She found that, for children with reading deficits, an emphasis on overt motor responses (particularly in articulation) could serve as an aid in sound discrimination and maintaining attentional focus.

M.D. Vernon accurately anticipated today's focus on phonemic awareness as a factor in the nature and origin of "backwardness in reading" (1957). Having reviewed the reading research conducted from 1920 to 1958, she recognized that:

> The word was so deeply embedded in the sentence, and so impregnated with its meaning, that it could hardly be thought of in isolation....Thus the child has to learn that: (a) each word and its sound pattern are separate entities, with their peculiar, invariable, and universal characteristics; (b) each word's sound pattern can be analyzed into a succession of sounds, with a characteristic and invariable sequence; (c) these unitary sounds can be generalized, in the sense that they occur, in approximately the same form, but in different sequences in different words; (d) the sounds correspond to different letter shapes, visually perceived; but (e) unfortunately in the English language the relationship between sounds and visual percepts vary considerably from word to word (p. 39).

She wrote that reading disability involves the "mechanisms by which linguistic tasks are carried out, rather than the understanding and use of words as such" (p. 191). She also noted the link to "slow speech development" and "motor incoordination" (p. 190) and suspected that these signs are congenital and related to cortical function or dysfunction.

SUMMARY OF DISABILITY RESEARCH

Researchers have arrived at some agreement on the subject of developmental dyslexia. It is generally thought to be a language-related disorder that is connected to verbal processing difficulties, which may be traced to neuro-motor disorders. Alternatively, or in addition, a selective attention dysfunction may result in metalinguistic disability.

Some researchers hypothesize that extreme individual variation in reading and language performance results from hereditary or pre-natal factors that cause neurological anomalies. Affected individuals are not merely developmentally delayed but constitutionally different, just as each of us is unique and yet similar to others. Some educators do not subscribe to the theories presented above, objecting to the medical or deficit model of reading difficulty. However, evidence continues to build in support of the theories that were once put forth by Orton and Vernon.

Fostering Phonemic Awareness: Teaching Strategies

The research literature on phonemic awareness contains a host of suggestions for parents of young children as well as for teachers. Not surprisingly, many of the ideas are specific examples of the type of instruction recommended and implemented by Vernon in the 1950s. She favored varied and engaging reading methods, with an emphasis on rhymes and word games, spelling, story-writing, and opportunities to practice phonetic analysis and blending.

In this section I will describe specific games and activities that focus attention on language elements, particularly word and sound units. For the most part, I will confine my recommendations to activities that have been tested by educational research. The first group includes listening-speaking-movement games, with no reference to print or letters. The second group emphasizes sound-to-print mapping (encoding). The third group emphasizes print-to-sound mapping (decoding). These games and activities may be viewed as preventive measures and used with young children, on an individual or whole-class basis, to call attention to details that are often overlooked. Finally, I will mention briefly several intensive and systematic instructional programs that we know can be effective for students with persistent phonemic processing disabilities.

LISTENING-SPEAKING-MOVEMENT GAMES
The following games/activities provide a place to begin focusing attention on the elements of spoken language: sentences, words, syllables, and sounds. A playful approach is recommended, one that encourages creativity and curiosity. In attempting these activities and games, remember to appreciate and examine children's errors and misconceptions, for they are the best guide to the next step in instruction.

A preschool program. Lundberg (1987) describes the preschool training program he developed and implemented with fellow researchers in Sweden. Daily "sessions" included the whole group (15-20 children), and the program was on-going for six months. The slow but steady nature of the program was purposeful, to give those with limited metalinguistic talent a chance to catch on and perform with the others. The sequence was as follows:

...*weeks 1 and 2*:   listening games, nursery rhymes, and action
songs (e.g., games like "Bear Hunt," "Duck, Duck, Goose"; songs
like "If You're Happy and You Know It," "My Hat It Has Three
Corners," "Chester").

...*week 3*: sentences and words are introduced as concepts...games that focus on segmenting spoken sentences into word units (e.g., clap or march to each word in "Humpty Dumpty sat on a wall...")...games comparing word length (e.g., "Whose name is longer, Sam or Melissa?").

...*month 2*: syllables are introduced...children clap hands to the syllables (introduced as "beats" in their names) then to other multisyllable words in the classroom...marching, walking, dancing with syllabic intonation...plastic markers used to represent syllables...rhyming games, sorting words that rhyme (pictures or objects).

...*month 3*: phonemes are introduced, but only those in initial position...*vowels* and *continuant consonants* are the ones to focus on at this stage, because they can be exaggerated without distortion. (E.g. in "S...am" or "M...ary" or "A...dam," it is easy to elongate the initial phoneme without distorting it. In "T...om" the initial sound is a *stop consonant*, which cannot be elongated without distorting it by adding a vowel.) When including stop consonants, use a repetition technique: "T-t-t-t-om," or "P-p-p-p-amela," and apply to games of matching words (or objects, or pictures) that contain the same initial phoneme.

...*month 5*: phonemes within words are introduced, beginning with words with two sounds (e.g. "m...e", "ea...t") and progressing slowly to more complex words....guessing games where teacher says word in segments and students blend the word together.

It is essential that teachers focus on *sounds* without considering or introducing any information on letters at this stage. (This can be confusing; for example, "face" is "/f/.../e/.../s/"; "arm" is '/a/.../r/.../m/'; and "floor" is "/f/.../l/.../o/.../r/.")

Adams, Foorman, and Beeler (1998) have translated and expanded Lundberg's program into a kindergarten phonemic awareness curriculum. While this type of session is preferred by many teachers who like the structure of a set time for such activities, other teachers may favor a more integrated approach, where the same kinds of activities are performed in the context of other pursuits. It is important to remember that phonemic awareness requires attention to sounds *in the speech stream*, so these games can and should be played along with songs, stories, nursery rhymes—in short, whenever an opportunity for language play arises.

Songs and rhymes. Yopp (1992) presents a host of songs and rhymes that have been developed to highlight phonemes in *spoken* language and have been field-tested in preschool and kindergarten classrooms. She categorizes the recommended activities into the following groups: sound-matching activities, sound-isolation activities, blending activities, sound-addition or -substitution activities, and segmentation activities. One example, in the sound-substitution category, takes the "Fe-Fi-Fiddly-i-o" chorus of "I've Been Workin' on the Railroad" and creates new versions: Ze-Zi-Ziddly-i-o, Me-Mi-Middly-i-o, etc. A sound-segmenting game can be sung to the tune of "Twinkle, Twinkle, Little Star:"

> Listen, listen to my word.
> Then tell me all the sounds you heard: *mice*
> /m/ is one sound
> /i/ is two
> /s/ is last in *mice*, it's true.

Yopp urges teachers to maintain an informal and fanciful tone in these games and to encourage social interaction, for this is what inspires language play. More suggestions can be found in the *Phonological Awareness Handbook* (Ericson & Juliebo, 1998).

For kindergarten children, nursery **rhymes** should be an important part of the curriculum. Children should recite them, act them out, sing them, clap to them, rap to them. Revising the rhymes can be fun:

> There was an old woman who lived in a ...tent.
> She had so many children she never knew where they ...went.

Words in sentences and nursery rhymes can be counted by moving tokens, taking baby steps, passing or bouncing balls. A good rhyming game called "Head or Feet" asks children to point to the body part that rhymes with each word spoken: bed...seat...sled...heat, etc. Other words might rhyme with *hand* or *knee,* or *nose* or *ear* (Cunningham, 1990a).

Of course, many books besides nursery rhymes play with speech sounds. Several examples are *Fox in Socks* (Seuss, 1965), *Green Eggs and Ham* (Seuss,

1960), and *Sheep in a Jeep* (Shaw, 1986). Alphabet books, particularly those like *Animalia* (Base, 1986) that present multiple words beginning with the same sound (e.g., "Lazy lions lounging in the local library"), can be extremely useful as listening exercises. A more complete list of books that play with language sounds can be found in Griffith & Olson (1992).

Name games. Name games can be played at line-up times, e.g., "If your name has /s/ (the sound, not the letter) in it, you can get in line." (Cindy should line up along with Jason and even Max!) "If your name has /v/ in it...," etc. When helpers are needed their names can be announced in segmented form (S-a-m and K-i-t) and blended together by the class. Name games can be a good way to sort into random groups, e.g. "Those with one-beat names stand here"; "those with two-beat names stand here," etc.

Word games. For older students, language play can continue on a more sophisticated level. Word games like "*A* My Name is *A*lice," knock-knock jokes, tongue-twisters, and secret codes all encourage children to monitor and manipulate language, building sensitivity and skill as they do. The mastery of Pig Latin or "Op-Talk" can be a rewarding challenge for elementary school linguists. Such metalinguistic activity seems to train children for other linguistic challenges, giving them an advantage over less playful language-users (Cazden, 1974).

Television. A new PBS series provides a national audience with a daily dose of many of the activities described above. ***Between the Lions*** is designed specifically to foster the phonemic awareness of its viewers, while it exuberantly demonstrates the joys of reading. Co-produced by WGBH Boston and Sirius Thinking, Ltd., of New York, it aims to give 4-7 year olds the background and motivation they need in order to become successful readers. The creators of the series (former talent from *Sesame Street*, *The Electric Company*, and *The Muppets*) surveyed the research evidence and turned its recommendations for practice into a child-friendly half-hour broadcast, loaded with songs, rhymes, dynamic print on screen, name games, and other forms of wordplay. The advisors for the series (Marilyn Adams, myself, and the late Jeanne Chall among them) helped to give the curriculum a systematic focus, with Key Words that permit direct instruction of short-vowel sounds in common word families. Segments demonstrate blending of onsets and rimes, careful decoding and encoding, letter-sound manipulations, and multisyllable word-attack strategies. The alphabetic principle is portrayed in lively fashion, and the dynamic use of the medium makes the process clear, with no need for teachers to use the obscure terminology that often confuses students. For a more thorough discussion of the ***Between the Lions*** curriculum, see Rath (2000).

Before airing its first-season episodes, the creators of **Between the Lions** commissioned two research studies to test the effects of viewing the show. In both studies (Flagg, 1999; Linebarger, 2000), kindergartners demonstrated significant and dramatic gains in the skills required for beginning reading, particularly in phonemic awareness (segmenting words into sounds) and letter-sound matching (reading nonsense words). Moreover, viewers consistently affirmed the strong appeal of the show and its characters.

Between the Lions has also created an award-winning Web site (http://pbskids.org/lions), which provides an "adventure" for each episode, including stories to be printed out and interactive recommendations for the whole family, a variety of printable illustrations and activities, and a veritable jukebox of favorite songs from the show.

ACTIVITIES THAT EMPHASIZE SOUND-TO-PRINT MAPPING

Modeling. The most obvious and productive way to emphasize sound-to-print mapping is to demonstrate just how print becomes the representation of sounds spoken in sequence. Whenever written communication is required during the day, when words are written on the board, when messages are sent home to parents, a teacher can make the process very explicit. She can say the sounds in sequence (slowly pronouncing each *phoneme,* not naming the letters) as she writes the correct letters that map each sound. If the teacher engages students in "interactive writing," she provides a valuable scaffold. See Pinnell & Fountas (1998) for a description of how to conduct an interactive writing session as a whole-class activity.

Guided writing and spelling. In other instructional programs, a guided writing component supports and extends the individual child's level of spelling and writing development. One-to-one writing/spelling support from an adult is an important component of the *Success for All* program, *Reading Recovery*, and *Book Buddies* (Invernizzi, Juel, & Rosemary, 1997), to name a few. In these programs, first graders are encouraged to "write for sounds," using the letters they think should logically represent the phonemes they hear. Conventional spellings are also introduced and practiced, but the emphasis is on slowing down language and listening to the sequence of sounds in words. For techniques that help young learners move from inventive to conventional spelling, Cunningham (1999) and Gentry & Gillet (1993) are helpful.

Most experts recommend including spelling and dictation activities for beginners to give them an opportunity to apply phonemic awareness and phonics knowledge. This can be done as part of a step-by-step, direct instruction process, as is the case in *Project Read* and *Wilson Reading*. A less direct approach, based on the five stages of spelling development, is described in *Words Their Way* (Bear, Templeton, Invernizzi, & Johnston, 1996) and suggested for small-group instruction in the classroom.

ACTIVITIES THAT EMPHASIZE PRINT-TO-SOUND MAPPING

As noted in an earlier section, researchers have found that the development of phonemic awareness is enhanced when children see how the sounds we speak relate directly to letters and letter clusters. In interventions to foster phonemic awareness, researchers have shown that using moveable letters in careful manipulations has helped young children and older special education students gain a more concrete understanding of an abstract system (Blachman, 1987; Cunningham, 1991; Ehri & Wilce, 1987; Williams 1980).

Another way to make the sounds within words *visible* to children is attempted with *Words in Color* charts (Gattegno, 1968). Each of the forty-four phonemes of English is assigned a color, and these colors indicate the sounds one hears in a word. For example, "eight" and "ate" are shown with the same colors; the colors in "kiss" match the colors in the middle syllable of "or**ches**tra." The use of color allows for a kind of one-to-one correspondence that is otherwise lacking in English, giving extra guidance to children in their efforts to map sounds onto print.

This is not the place to go into great detail concerning the many programs that assist learners in discovering and mastering print-to-sound correspondence, since the process of learning to decode is covered in detail in Chapter 4. I will mention just one specific, well-documented program and note the components that numerous others share.

In the model first-grade reading program developed by Blachman (1987), children learn to identify sounds represented by letters on small cards. Then they blend them to form words, reversing and substituting sounds as they go: 'nap,' 'pan,' 'pin,' etc. The children write these words and read them back. They find and read them in little paperbacks that serve as "transitional" readers, books with vocabulary that is controlled so as to be decodable for beginners (e.g., *A Pig Can Jig,* Rasmussen & Goldberg, 1976; *Six Kids*, Modern Curriculum Press, 1978; and *Ready Readers*, a series of code-based paperbacks from Modern Curriculum Press, 1996). These activities are just one component of an overall reading program that also includes literature, some basals, and creative writing.

In general, comprehensive programs for teaching reading in first grade seem to yield greater gains, on average, when they contain a systematic phonics component (Adams, 1990; Chall, 1967; 1983; National Reading Panel, 2000). The more successful programs are those that introduce individual sound elements (letters and the sounds they usually represent) to be blended into words and sentences. Chall called this "synthetic" phonics and recommended it as less confusing than "analytic" phonics.

Another important component for beginning readers is that they have access to short, simple books written with consistency in letter-sound correspondence. These books reward children who are struggling to practice letter-sound mapping; they enable success. Like invented/phonetic spelling, they serve a purpose for a short time, to help children understand one particular strategy used in reading and writing. Decodable books are an important feature of *Success for All*, and first graders make their way through a sequence of 48 little books. The research on materials of this kind shows that first graders who use these books develop stronger skills and more independence at word analysis and spelling than those who have used only texts written to introduce high frequency "sight" words (Beck & Block, 1979; Juel & Roper-Schneider, 1985; Slavin et al., 1990).

If the above strategies are implemented by well-informed, attentive teachers, we might substantially improve the quality of instruction offered to beginning readers. It has been estimated that 80% of kindergartners with limited awareness of phonemes go on to become "reading disabled" (Fox & Routh, 1983). In this we have a fairly accurate marker to which efforts at prevention can be directed. For some, however, the disability may persist. Many of the awareness games described above would be inappropriate for older readers, who would need instruction in phonemic awareness but with content that is sensitive to their maturity. In particular, their instruction could include working with repetitive poetry that expresses mature themes and with activities directly tied to printed letters and words.

INSTRUCTIONAL PROGRAMS FOR READERS WITH DISABILITIES

Research indicates that effective instructional techniques are those that help older dyslexics attend to sounds by presenting an organized, step-by-step system for processing written language. Clark and Uhry (1995) present a thorough discussion of these different programs and a review of the research base that supports their effectiveness. Her basic recommendation underscores the need for explicit phonics instruction for most dyslexic students.

Many code-emphasis reading programs are available, and those that emphasize individual phonemes and the blending of these into words provide the focus that dyslexics seem constitutionally inclined to overlook. For example, the *Auditory Discrimination in Depth* program, designed by Charles and Patricia Lindamood (described in Clark and Uhry, 1995), trains teachers to tackle the phonemic awareness "aptitude deficit" by providing clear and persistent instruction in speech analysis. Such programs demand a great deal of teacher direction and focused time on task. They are highly structured and time consuming. There simply is no quick fix.

Programs to bypass the disability and rely on other strengths have been unconvincing for those with the "specific aptitude deficit" that results in dyslexia. Without the ability to focus on phonemes in sequence, a student predictably will have great difficulty with spelling, accurate oral reading, and decoding new words. Devices such as tape recorders, talking computers, and spell checkers will help students to compensate for this disability so as to function in a literate world. However, students without equal access to this technology, or students who want to become more self-reliant, will need to gain phonemic awareness and to be shown how to use it in learning to encode and decode written language.

Considering that dyslexia may be the linguistic reflection of a motor-organization difficulty, it makes sense to break the reading process down into a series of skills and to teach these skills step-by-step, from simple to more complex. Once a step is "over-learned" it can become automatic, and a new step can be attempted. This is the strategy of the Orton-Gillingham approach, where decoding is taught letter-by-letter, sound-by-sound, with multi-sensory practice. Proponents of this method—teachers, students, and their grateful parents—are convinced of its benefits. The method works best when used consistently, on a daily basis. One-to-one tutorial support is usually recommended, and phonetically regular texts are used so that students can practice applying the rules and generalizations learned to decodable words in context. Over the decades, the *Let's Read* series (Bloomfield, Barnhart, & Barnhart, 1965) also has been used for this purpose.

There are many variations on the Orton-Gillingham prototype: *Alphabetic Phonics, Project Read, Total Reading, Won Way, Wilson Reading System*, and even IBM's *Writing to Read* program, to name but a few in current use. Full descriptions of these programs can be found in Clark and Uhry (1995) or at Educators Publishing Service in Cambridge, MA. With all of the above programs, learners are not permitted to bypass their phonemic processing difficulties. They must master phonemic processing, over time, and with a great deal of practice.

New possibilities have emerged for building and reinforcing phonemic awareness with the use of computer technology. Several projects report good results when students with reading difficulties use a computer-based program like *Daisy Quest* (Erickson et al., 1992), the Orton-Gillingham-based *Lexia* software (Garside, Hook, & Marsh, late 1990s), or modified tape-recorded speech segments, slowed down for focused attention to individual sounds (Tallal et al., 1996). The National Reading Panel (2000) notes that more research is needed to evaluate the effectiveness of computer technology as an instructional tool.

Considering that dyslexia may signal a timing deficit or a failure in selective-attention mechanisms, the focused, systematic approach seems sensible. However, there may be a problem in integrating the various component processes involved in reading. Perhaps a focus on the smallest elements of language alone is not sufficient to help students make meaningful connections based on context and general knowledge.

One program is specifically designed to help children with reading difficulties master a variety of strategies and interactive processes. The RAVE-O program uses a multifaceted focus on retrieval, automaticity, vocabulary, elaboration, and orthography, to help students compensate for difficulties with decoding and word retrieval (Wolf, Miller, & Donnelly, 2000). Students practice common spelling patterns, learn multiple meanings for words, and try out various tricks that will help them become "word detectives." In addtion, they regularly read and write connected text that builds fluency, triggers comprehension, and reinforces discrete skills. Systematic decoding practice is part of each session, and students use Engelmann & Bruner's *Reading Mastery* storybooks (1988) for practice in applying decoding skills.

Having surveyed the accumulated evidence from scientific studies on early reading, the National Reading Panel recently completed a Congressionally mandated report (2000) on early reading. It found that the data consistently confirm the critical importance of instruction in phonemic awareness for young children. The Panel sees this focus as a necessary component of instruction for preschool and kindergarten students. For kindergarten and first grade, reading programs should combine activities that foster phonemic awareness with systematic, direct instruction in letter-sound correspondence (phonics). These foundational skills lay the groundwork for developing fluency and comprehension and should of course be applied and practiced in the context of meaningful tasks: reading and writing for real and satisfying purposes.

Assessment of Phonemic Awareness

Many different tests have been used in research exploring phonemic awareness. Often, the researchers design and administer experimental tasks that have not been validated with a broad population. However, the four tests listed below are commonly used today as comparison measures. They provide norm-referenced information, suggesting age- or grade-level expectations. (See also, Tests of Phonemic Awareness, in Chapter 11, Appendix E, p. 337.)

1. Test of Phonological Awareness (TOPA). (Torgesen & Bryant, 1994)

2. Rosner's *Test of Auditory Analysis Skills* (TAAS). (Rosner, 1979)

3. *Roswell-Chall Auditory Blending Test* (Roswell & Chall, 1987)

4. Test for Assessing Phonemic Awareness in Young Children (Yopp, 1995)

A less formal approach can be useful for assessing phonemic awareness in the context of a writing activity. Clay's *An Observation Survey* (1993) describes how to administer and evaluate a simple sentence dictation task for first graders. Another researcher recommends using nursery rhymes to assess kindergartners' phonemic awareness as it develops over time (Hall, 1985). If these rhymes have been committed to memory, it is easier for children to focus on sounds one at a time, and rereading what they have written becomes a snap. In January, one kindergarten class produced the following range in renditions of "Jack and Jill":

child #1: +L+<V↑_OO>TT+...

child #2: J N J N OP O L...

child #3: JAK N JL YAT UP THE HEL....

It is easy to use this information to gauge the status of each child's phonemic awareness development. A well-informed and sensitive teacher can then use her knowledge of sound-symbol relations and the stages of spelling development to determine where to aim instruction that meets each child's needs. Child #3, for example, is using "Y" to represent the /w/ sound. This is common among young children, since the name of the letter "Y" begins with the /w/ sound, whereas the name of the letter "W" begins with the /d/ sound. There is some logic behind this error. A few re-readings of *Mrs. Wishy-washy* (Cowley, 1980), along with some reminders from the teacher, and this confusion is likely to be corrected.

A highly predictive spelling list to be used at the beginning of first grade is suggested by Morris & Perney (1984), and two separate spelling inventories, one for elementary students, and one for middle school students are included in Bear et al. (1996). A quick check to assess decoding ability can be implemented via "The Names Test" (Cunningham, 1990b), which comprises 25 unusual but phonetic first and last names to be decoded (e.g. "Vance Middleton"). Grade-level means and suggestions for qualitative interpretation are included.

A more comprehensive battery of tests is recommended for older students whose difficulties with reading may **not** stem from a phonemic awareness deficit. At the Harvard Reading Laboratory we found that many of our students were accurate at decoding and spelling but still scored below grade level expectations on tests of vocabulary and comprehension. For these students, of course, the activities described above would not be necessary.

A broad scale assessment of the separate (but interacting) components of reading ability to establish how different strengths and weaknesses might affect a student's performance is certainly recommended. This can be accomplished with a battery of written and oral tests, or with a composite measure such as the *Diagnostic Assessment of Reading* included in the *DARTTS* assessment kit recently developed by Roswell & Chall (1991). Designed to be administered to a student in 20-30 minutes, the assessment instrument has been validated with children in grades 1-12 and includes *Trial Teaching Strategies* to guide the teaching process.

The Phonemic Awareness of Reading Teachers

A word of caution to teachers, especially to those who may be new to the teaching of reading: Teachers cannot assume that their expert reading ability is matched by an equally high level of phonemic awareness. Many excellent reading teachers have difficulty performing the tasks used to assess this factor (Rath, 1994). When asked to count the phonemes in the word *question*, for example, only 19% of the 117 reading teachers sampled were accurate in their count. *Test yourself:* How many individual sounds do you hear when you say the word *question* out loud?

Many teachers indicate that *question* has 4 sounds: *qu e s tion*, presumably because they are thinking about patterns learned and taught in phonics. In the Orton-Gillingham approach, these combinations of letters that reliably represent sound patterns are called "phonograms."

However, when counting phonemes, **each speech sound that requires a different mouth position is counted alone**. Therefore, to pronounce *question*, we form our mouths in 7 different positions: */k/ /w/ /e/ /s/ /ch/ /ə/ /n/*, in order to articulate seven discrete phonemes. The dictionary is a reliable guide in these matters; its phonetic spellings with diacritical markings accurately map the sequence of sounds in all cases. Young inventive spellers, so focused on sounds and so innocent with regard to English spelling patterns, come close to these dictionary representations in their own attempts to spell words like *question*.

Other researchers have noted that there are gaps in teachers' content knowledge and expertise with regard to phonemic awareness and other important aspects of language structure (Lindamood, Bell, & Lindamood, 1992; Moats, 1995). Misconceptions and confusion about subject matter do not serve our students well; professionals must become better informed if they are to support students' language and literacy development. Teachers who would like to assess or improve their own phonemic awareness can try their skill at the short quiz included in Appendix A at the end of this chapter. If the quiz indicates gaps or confusion, enrolling in a course on language structure, applied linguistics, or speech and language disorders would provide useful information.

Summary and Conclusion

Phonemic awareness plays a critical role in literacy development. Educators and researchers have recognized for decades that a young child who focuses on the sound units in spoken words is likely to learn to read with ease and early success. Today's experts continue to recognize the key role of phonemic awareness as a gateway to literacy acquisition; without this awareness, children have difficulty learning to read and spell English accurately. Findings from the research on this subject can be used to inform the practice of professionals in classrooms and clinics, as they suggest a variety of strategies for assessing phonemic awareness, fostering it, and connecting it with reading and spelling instruction.

In learning more about the subject of phonemic awareness, teachers may become more attentive, themselves, to the phonemic structure of English. Such a focus has the potential to broaden teachers' knowledge of spelling—its underlying patterns and principles as well as its many challenges. Teachers with knowledge and confidence in this area will have a better chance of ensuring that students gain the understanding that is crucial for successful literacy development.

Appendix A

A Phonemic Awareness Quiz for Reading Teachers
(Answers appear at end of quiz.)

In order to make the task of focusing on phonemes simpler for students, teachers should begin by selecting examples of words that contain all *continuant* sounds. These are easier to say at a slow speed, lingering on each sound. For example, all the phonemes in **fan** are *continuants*. Try saying this word very slowly, pronouncing each separate sound for a second or two: /f/.../æ/.../n/.

Now try saying **top** in the same exaggerated way. Do you see how hard it is to hold the sounds in **top**? That is because the two consonants in **top** are *stop* sounds. They stop the stream of air in the oral cavity when we say them. In English, the letters that usually represent *stops* are: **p, t, d, b, k, g,** and sometimes **ng**. It is more difficult to hear each phoneme in words that contain *stops*.

I. Continuants and Stops
Look at the words in each numbered set below. Say them aloud very slowly. Decide which word contains *stops*, and cross it out.

1. fish, dish, wish
2. zoom, moon, root
3. live, love, give
4. slow, crow, throw
5. trees, freeze, sneeze
6. clear, here, there
7. books, lines, waves
8. twin, swim, flies
9. mother, father, sister
10. enough, tough, through

Teachers may want to present words in this slowed-down way and ask children to blend them together and say them fast. Another exercise asks children to produce slow pronunciations, noting or marking each discrete phoneme. It is handy to have a pack of cards with illustrations that represent words to be analyzed.

Try to think of at least **10** all-*continuant* words that are easily illustrated. Examples: **nose**, but not **lips**; **shoe**, but not **sock**; **mouse**, but not **cat**.

II. Word Reversals
Say one of the following words out loud. Then *reverse the order of the sounds*, and say the new English word that results. Write the new word with its conventional English spelling. (Hint: It helps to close your eyes as you say each of the numbered words, trying to pay attention to the *phonemes*. Don't worry about existing *letters* or resulting spelling changes. Just reverse the *sounds, not* the letters.)

1. pin _____
2. tub _____
3. sick _____
4. time _____
5. judge _____
6. cuts _____
7. face _____
8. easy _____
9. teach _____
10. talk _____
11. ice _____
12. checks _____
13. votes _____
14. chance _____
15. enough _____

III. Phoneme Counting

Count the number of phonemes you hear in each of the words below. It may help if you circle the letter or letter cluster that represents each sound. (Remember, each time you change the position of your mouth—including lips and tongue—you are forming a new phoneme.)

number:
_____ 1. sun
_____ 2. grass
_____ 3. deeply
_____ 4. thought

number:
_____ 5. laughed
_____ 6. quickly
_____ 7. started
_____ 8. people

number:
_____ 9. station
_____ 10. everything
_____ 11. Christmas
_____ 12. psychology

IV. Phoneme Discrimination

Read the first word (in boldface) in each line, and note the sound that is represented by the underlined letter or letter cluster. Then select the word or words on the line that contain **the same sound**. Circle the word or words you have selected.

1. **paper**   a. village   b. survey   c. contain   d. sleigh
2. **rose**   a. dazzle   b. anxiety   c. azure   d. tissue
3. **push**   a. overlook   b. jump   c. should   d. soup
4. **return**   a. smashed   b. two   c. listen   d. castle
5. **salad**   a. physician   b. usual   c. reception   d. has
6. **this**   a. both   b. their   c. thunder   d. mother
7. **factor**   a. similar   b. restore   c. never   d. create
8. **Stephen**   a. of   b. soften   c. phrase   d. several
9. **nurse**   a. prefer   b. percent   c. journey   d. cure
10. **thin**   a. there   b. gather   c. sympathy   d. thousand

Answers:

I. Continuants and Stops. These words contain stops: 1. dish, 2. root, 3. give, 4. crow, 5. trees, 6. clear, 7. books, 8. twin, 9. sister, 10. tough.

II. Word Reversals. 1. nip, 2. but, 3. kiss, 4. might, 5. judge, 6. stuck, 7. safe, 8. easy, 9. cheat, 10. caught, 11. sigh, 12. sketch, 13. stove, 14. snatch, 15. funny.

III. Phoneme Counting. 1. 3 (s-u-n), 2. 4 (g-r-a-ss), 3. 5 (d-ee-p-l-y), 4. 3 (th-ough-t), 5. 4 (l-au-gh-ed), 6. 6 (k-w-i-ck-l-y), 7. 7 (s-t-a-r-t-e-d), 8. 5 (p-eo-p-ə-l), 9. 6 (s-t-a-t-io-n), 10. 7 (e-ve-r-y-th-i-ng), 11. 7 (Ch-r-i-st-m-a-s), 12. 8 (ps-y-ch-o-l-o-g-y).

IV. Phoneme Discrimination. 1. b,c,d; 2. a,b; 3. a,c; 4. a,b; 5. c; 6. b, d; 7. a,c; 8. a,d; 9.a,c; 10. c,d.

Author's note: The above exercise is *meant* to be challenging, so please don't be discouraged if your accuracy rate is low. I am used to encountering experienced, competent teachers who answer only 50% of the above quiz correctly. We all have room for improvement in areas of knowledge and expertise. If you are confused about any of the above examples, you are encouraged to consult dictionaries and linguistic texts for reference (e.g., Fromkin, V., & Rodman, R. [1988]. *An Introduction to Language, Fourth Edition.* Orlando, FL: Holt, Rinehart, and Winston). Or, contact me with questions *via* this publisher.

98

References

Adams, M.J. (1990). *Beginning to read: Thinking and learning about print*. Cambridge, MA: The MIT Press.

Adams, M.J., et al. (1991). Beginning to read: A critique of literacy professionals and a response by Marilyn Jager Adams. *The Reading Teacher, 44*, 370-395.

Adams, M.J., Foorman, B.R., Lundberg, I., & Beeler, J. (1998). *Phonemic awareness in young children: A classroom curriculum*. Baltimore, MD: Paul H. Brooks Publishing Co.

Alegria, J., Pignot, E., & Morais, J. (1982). Phonetic analysis of speech and memory codes in beginning readers. *Memory and Cognition, 10*, 451-456.

Anderson, R. C., Hiebert, E.H., Scott, J.A., & Wilkinson, A.G. (1985). *Becoming a nation of readers*. Washington, DC: National Academy of Education.

Babbitt, N. (1986). My love affair with the alphabet. In Reading is Fundamental, *Once upon a time....* NY: G.P. Putnam's Sons, 42- 45.

Base, G. (1986). *Animalia*. NY: Abrams.

Bear, D.R., Invernizzi, M., Templeton, S., & Johnston, F. (1996). *Words their way*. Upper Saddle River, NJ: Prentice-Hall.

Beck, I.L., & Block, K.K. (1979). An analysis of two beginning reading programs: Some facts and some opinions. In L.B. Resnick & P.A. Weaver (Eds.), *Theory and practice of early reading (Vol.1)*, Hillsdale, NJ: Erlbaum, 279-318.

Beech, J.R., & Harding, L.M. (1984) Phonemic processing and the poor reader from a developmental lag viewpoint. *Reading Research Quarterly, 19*, 357-366.

Bialystok, E., & Mitterer, J. (1987). Metalinguistic differences among three kinds of readers. *Journal of Educational Psychology, 79*, 147-153.

Bissex, G. (1980). *GNYS AT WORK*. Cambridge, MA.: Harvard University Press.

Blachman, B.A. (1987). An alternative classroom reading program for learning disabled and other low-achieving children. In R. Bowler (Ed.), *Intimacy with language: A forgotten basic in teacher education*. Baltimore, MD: Orton Dyslexia Society, 49-55.

Blachman, B.A., Ball, E.W., Black, R., & Tangel, D. (1994). Kindergarten teachers develop phoneme awareness in low-income, inner-city classrooms: Does it make a difference? *Reading and Writing: An Interdisciplinary Journal, 6*, 1-17.

Blachman, B.A. (2000). Phonological awareness. In M.L. Kamil, P.B. Mosenthal, P.D. Pearson, & R. Barr (Eds.), *Handbook of reading research*. Mahwah, NJ: Lawrence Erlbaum Associates.

Blalock, J.W. (1982). Persistent auditory language deficits in adults with learning disabilities. *Journal of Learning Disabilities, 15*, 604-609.

Bloomfield, L., Barnhart, C.L., & Barnhart R.K. et al (1965). *Let's Read*. Cambridge, MA: Educators Publishing Service.

Bradley, L., & Bryant, P. (1985). *Rhyme and reason in reading and spelling*. Ann Arbor: University of Michigan Press.

Bruce, D. J. (1964). The analysis of word sounds by young children. *British Journal of Educational Psychology, 34*, 158-170.

Bruck, M. (1988). The word recognition and spelling of dyslexic children. *Reading Research Quarterly, 23*, 51-69.

Byrne, B. (1984). On teaching articulatory phonetics via an orthography. *Memory and Cognition, 12,* 181-189.

Byrne, B., & Shea, P., (1979). Semantic and phonetic memory codes in beginning readers. *Memory and Cognition, 7,* 333-338.

Catts, H.W. (1986). Speech production/ phonological deficits in reading disordered children. *Journal of Learning Disabilities, 19,* 504-508.

Cazden, C. (1974). Play with language and metalinguistics: One dimension of language awareness experience. *The Urban Review, 7,* 28-39.

Chall, J. S. (1967). *Learning to read: The great debate.* NY: McGraw Hill.

Chall, J. S. (1983). *Stages of reading development.* NY: McGraw-Hill.

Chall, J. S., Roswell, F. G., & Blumenthal, S. H. (1963). Auditory blending ability: A factor in success in beginning reading. *The Reading Teacher, 17,* 113-118.

Chomsky, C. (1970). Reading, writing, and phonology. *Harvard Educational Review, 40,* 287-309.

Chomsky, C. (1971). Write first, read later. *Childhood Education,* March, 296-299.

Chomsky, C. (1979). Approaching reading through invented spelling. In L.B. Resnick & P.A. Weaver (Eds.), *Theory and practice of early reading (Vol. 2).* Hillsdale, NJ: Erlbaum, 43-65.

Clark, D.B., & Uhry, J.K. (1995). *Dyslexia: Theory and practice of remedial instruction.* Timonium, MD: York Press, Inc.

Clay, M. (1993). *An observation survey.* Portsmouth, NH: Heinemann.

Cowley, J. (1980). *Mrs. Wishy-washy.* Bothell, WA: The Wright Group.

Crain, S. (1989). Why poor readers misunderstand spoken sentences. In D. Shankweiler & I.Y. Liberman (Eds.), *Phonology and reading disability,* 133-165. Ann Arbor: Univ. of Michigan Press.

Cunningham, P.M. (1999). *Phonics they use, 3rd Ed.* NY: Addison Wesley.

Cunningham, P.M. (1990). The names test: A quick assessment of decoding ability. *The Reading Teacher, 44,* 124-129.

Cunningham, P. M. (1991). Research directions: Multimethod, multilevel literacy instruction in first grade. *Language Arts, 68,* 578-584.

Denckla, M.B. (1983). Learning for language and language for learning. In U. Kirk (Ed.), *Neuropsychology of language, reading and spelling,* 33-43. NY: Academic Press.

DiBenedetto, B., Richardson, E., & Kochnower, J. (1983). Vowel generalization in normal and learning disabled readers. *Journal of Educational Psychology, 75,* 576-582.

Dolch, E.W., & Bloomster, M. (1937). Phonic readiness. *Elementary School Journal, 38,* 201-205.

Durkin, D. (1966). *Children who read early.* NY: Teachers College Press.

Durrell, D.D., & Murphy, H.A. (1953). The auditory discrimination factor in reading readiness and reading disability. *Education, 73,* 556-560.

100

Ehri, L.C., & Wilce, L.S. (1987). Does learning to spell help beginners learn to read words? *Reading Research Quarterly, 22*, 47-65.

Elkonin, D.B. (1973). USSR. In J. Downing (Ed.), *Comparative reading*. NY: Macmillan.

Engelmann, S. & Bruner, E.C. (1988). *Reading Mastery I/II Fast Cycle: Teacher's guide*. Chicago, IL: Science Research Associates.

Erickson, G.C., Foster, K.C., Foster, D.F., Torgesen, J.K., & Packer, S. (1992). *DaisyQuest*. Scotts Valley, CA: Great Wave Software.

Ericson, L., & Juliebo, M.F. (1998). *The phonological awareness handbook for kindergarten and primary teachers*. Newark, DE: International Reading Association.

Ferreiro, E. (1986). The interplay between information and assimilation in beginning literacy. In W.H. Teale & E. Sulzby (Eds.), *Emergent literacy*. NJ: Ablex.

Fox, B., & Routh, D.K. (1983). Reading disability, phonemic analysis, and dysphonetic spelling: A follow-up study. *Journal of Clinical Child Psychology, 12*, 28-32.

Flagg, B. (1999). Formative evaluation of "Between the Lions" pilot shows. Unpublished research report 99-099 prepared for WGBH Educational Foundation. Bellport, NY: Multimedia Research.

Frith, U. (1986). A developmental framework for developmental dyslexia. *Annals of Dyslexia, 36*, 69-81.

Galaburda, A. (1985). Developmental dyslexia: A review of biological interactions. *Annals of Dyslexia, 35*.

Garside, A., Hook, P., & Marsh, S. (late 1990s). *Lexia* software, Lincoln, MA: LexiaLearning.

Gates, A.I., & Bond, G.L. (1937). The necessary mental age for beginning reading. *Elementary School Journal, 37*, 495-508.

Gattegno, C. (1968). *Words in Color*. NY: Educational Solutions, Inc.

Gentry, J.R. & Gillet, J.W. (1993). *Teaching kids to spell*. Portsmouth, NH: Heinemann.

Geschwind, N. (1986). Dyslexia, cerebral dominance, autoimmunity and sex hormones. In G.T. Pavlidis, & D.F.Fisher (Eds.), *Dyslexia: Its neuropsychology and treatment*. Chichester, UK: John Wiley & Sons, Ltd.

Gibson, C. (1988). The impact of early developmental history on cerebral asymmetries: Implications for reading ability in deaf children. In D. Molfese & S. Segalowitz, (Eds.), *Brain lateralization in children: Developmental implications*. NY: The Guilford Press.

Goswami, U. (2000). Phonological and lexical processes. In M.L. Kamil, P.B. Mosenthal, P.D. Pearson, & R. Barr (Eds.), *Handbook of reading research*. Mahwah, NJ: Lawrence Erlbaum Associates.

Goswami, U. & Bryant, P.E. (1990). *Phonological skills and learning to read*. Hillsdale, NH: Lawrence Erlbaum Assoc.

Gough, P.B., & Hillinger, M.L. (1980). Learning to read: An unnatural act. *Bulletin of the Orton Society, 30*, 179-96.

Griffith, P.L., & Olson, M.W. (1992). Phonemic awareness helps beginning readers break the code. *The Reading Teacher, 45*, 516-523.

Hall, S.E.M. (1985). OAD MAHR GOS and writing with young children. *Language Arts, 62*, 262-265.

Hall, S.L., & Moats, L.C. (1999). *Straight talk about reading*. Chicago, IL: Contemporary Books.

Heath, S.B. (1986). Separating "things of the imagination" from life: Learning to read and write. In W.H. Teale & E. Sulzby (Eds.), *Emergent literacy*. Norwood, NJ: Ablex Publishing.

Helfgott, J. (1976). Phonemic segmentation and blending skills of kindergarten children: Implications for beginning reading acquisition. *Contemporary Educational Psychology, 1*, 157-169.

Holdaway, D. (1979). *The foundations of literacy.* Sydney, Australia: Ashton Scholastic.

Hynd, G.W., & Semrud-Clikeman, M. (1989). Dyslexia and neurodevelopmental pathology: Relationships to cognition, intelligence, and reading skill acquisition. *Journal of Learning Disabilities, 22.*

Invernizzi, M., Juel, C., & Rosemary, C.A. (1997). A community volunteer tutorial that works. *The Reading Teacher, 50*(4), 304-311.

International Reading Association (1998). *Phonemic awareness and the teaching of reading: A position statement from the Board of Directors.* Newark, DE: International Reading Association.

Juel, C., & Roper-Schneider, D. (1985). The influence of basal readers on first grade reading. *Reading Research Quarterly, 20*, 134-152.

Katz, R.B. (1986) Phonological deficiencies in children with reading disability: Evidence from an object naming test. *Cognition, 22*, 225-157.

Kirk, U. (1989). Neurological aspects of learning difficulty. In F.G. Roswell & G. Natchez, *Reading disability: A human approach to evaluation and treatment of reading and writing difficulties.* NY: Basic Books, 17-40.

Learning First Alliance (1998). Every child reading: An action plan. In *American Educator*, Spring/Summer. Washington, DC: American Federation of Teachers, 52-63.

Lesgold, A.M., & Perfetti, C. (1982). *Interactive processes in reading.* Hillsdale, NJ: Erlbaum.

Lewkowicz, N. K. (1980). Phonemic awareness training: What to teach and how to teach it. *Journal of Educational Psychology, 72*, 686-700.

Liberman, I.Y., & Shankweiler, D. (1979). Speech, the alphabet and learning to read. In L.B. Resnick & P. Weaver (Eds.), *Theory and practice of early reading (Vol. 2).* Hillsdale, NJ: Erlbaum, 109-134.

Lindamood, P., Bell, N., & Lindamood, P. (1992). Issues in phonological awareness assessment. *Annals of Dyslexia, 42.*

Linebarger, D. (2000). Summative evaluation of "Between the Lions." Unpublished report prepared for the WGBH Educational Foundation. Kansas City, KS: University of Kansas.

Lovett, M.W., Borden, S.L., DeLuca, T., Lacerenza, L., Benson, N.J., & Brackstone, D. (1994). Treating the core deficits of developmental dyslexia: Evidence of transfer of learning after phonologically- and strategy-based reading training programs. *Developmental Psychology, 30*, 805-822.

Lundberg, I. (1978). Aspects of linguistic awareness related to reading. In A. Sinclair, R.J. Jarvella, & W.J.M. Levelt, (Eds.), *The child's conception of language.* NY: Springer-Verlag, 83-96.

Lundberg, I. (1987). Phonological awareness facilitates reading and spelling acquisition. In R. Bowler, (Ed.), *Intimacy with language: A forgotten basic in teacher education.* Baltimore, MD: The Orton Dyslexia Society, 56-63.

Lundberg, I., Frost, J., & Petersen, O. P. (1988). Effects of an extensive program for stimulating phonological awareness in preschool children. *Reading Research Quarterly, 23*, 263-284.

102

Lyon, G.R. (1998). Why reading is not a natural process. *Educational Leadership*, 55, no. 6, 14-18.

Maclean, M., Bryant, P., & Bradley, L. (1987) Rhymes, nursery rhymes, and reading in early childhood. *Merrill-Palmer Quarterly, 33*, 255-282.

Manis, F., Savage, P., Morrison, F., Horn, G., Howell, M., Szeszulski, P., & Holt, L. (1987). Paired associate learning in reading-disabled children: Evidence for a rule-learning deficiency. *Journal of Experimental Child Psychology, 43*, 25-43.

Mann, V.A., Tobin, P., & Wilson, R. (1987). Measuring phonological awareness through the invented spellings of kindergarten children. *Merrill-Palmer Quarterly, 33*, 365-391.

Mason, J.M. (1980). When DO children begin to read: An exploration of four-year-old children's letter and word reading competencies. *Reading Research Quarterly, 15*, 203-227.

Mattingly, I.G. (1972). Reading, the linguistic process, and linguistic awareness. In J.F. Kavanagh & I.G. Mattingly (Eds.), *Language by ear and by eye*. Cambridge, MA: MIT Press.

Menyuk, P., & Flood, J. (1981). Linguistic competence, reading, writing problems, and remediation. *Bulletin of the Orton Society, 31*, 13-28.

Modern Curriculum Press (1978). *Six kids*. Phonics Practice Readers. Cleveland, Ohio

Monroe, M. (1932). *Children who cannot read*. Chicago: University of Chicago Press.

Montessori, M. (1912). *The Montessori method (1964 ed.)*. NY: Schocken Books, Inc.

Moats, L.C. (1995). The missing foundation in teacher education. *American Educator*, 19 (2), 9, 43-51.

Morais, J., Cary, L., Alegria, J., & Bertelson, P. (1979). Does awareness of speech as a sequence of phones arise spontaneously? *Cognition, 7*, 323-331.

Morais, J., Cluytens, M., Alegria, J., & Content, A. (1984). Segmentation abilities of dyslexics and normal readers. *Perceptual and Motor Skills, 58*, 221-222.

Morris, D., & Perney, J. (1984). Developmental spelling as a predictor of first-grade reading achievement. *The Elementary School Journal, 84*, 442-457.

Morrison, F.J. (1984). Word decoding and rule-learning in normal and disabled readers. *Remedial and Special Education, 5*, 20-27.

Mullis, I.V.S., & Jenkins, L.B. (1990). *The reading report card, 1971-88: Trends from the nation's report card*. Princeton, NJ: Educational Testing Service and National Assessment of Educational Progress.

NAEP (1985). *The reading report card: Progress toward excellence in our schools*. NJ: NAEP & ETS.

National Reading Panel [NRP]. (2000). *Report of the National Reading Panel: Teaching children to read*. Washington, DC: National Institute of Child Health and Human Development.
[Available at http://www.nichd.nih.gov/publications/nrp.]

National Research Council. (1998). *Preventing reading difficulties in young children*. Washington, DC: National Academy Press.

Olson, R., Wise, B., Conners, F., Rack, J., & Fulker, D. (1989) Specific deficits in component reading and language skills: Genetic and environmental influences. *Journal of Learning Disabilities, 22*, 339-348.

Orton, S.T. (1937). *Reading, writing, and speech problems in children*. NY: Norton & Co., Inc.

Pinnell, G.S., & Fountas, I.C. (1998). *Word Matters*. Portsmouth, NH: Heineman, 191-206.

Rasmussen, D., & Goldberg, L. (1976). *A pig can jig*. Basic Reading Series. Chicago, IL: SRA.

Rath, L.K. (1994). The phonemic awareness of reading teachers: Examining aspects of knowledge. Unpublished doctoral dissertation. Cambridge, MA: Harvard University Graduate School of Education.

Rath, L.K. (2000). Between the Lions: Using television to promote literacy. *Book Links, 9*(4), 41-45.

Read, C. (1971). Preschool children's knowledge of English phonology. *Harvard Educational Review, 41*, 1-34.

Read, C. (1978). Children's awareness of language, with emphasis on sound systems. In A. Sinclair, R.J. Jarvella & W.J.M. Levelt, (Eds.), *The child's conception of language*. NY: Springer-Verlag, 65-82.

Read, C. (1981). Writing is not the inverse of reading for young children. In C.H. Fredericksen & J.F. Dominic (Eds.), *Writing (Vol.2)*. Hillsdale, NJ: Erlbaum.

Read, C., & Ruyter, L. (1985) Reading and spelling in adults of low literacy. *Remedial and Special Education, 6,* 43-52.

Read, C., Yun-Fei, A., Hong-Yin, Nie, Ban-Qing, D. (1986). The ability to manipulate speech sounds depends on knowing alphabetic writing. *Cognition, 26*, 31-44.

Ready Readers (1996). Parsippany, NJ: Modern Curriculum Press.

Rosenberger, P.B. (1992). Dyslexia—is it a disease? *New England Journal of Medicine,* Jan.

Rosner, J. (1974). Auditory analysis training with pre-readers. *The Reading Teacher, 27,* 379-381.

Rosner, J. (1979). *Helping children overcome learning difficulties (2nd ed.)*. NY: Walker.

Rosner, J. (1999). *Test of Audirory Analysis Skills (TAAS) test forms*. Novato, CA: Academic Therapy.

Rosner, J., & Simon, D.P. (1971). The auditory analysis test: An initial report. *Journal of Learning Disabilities, 4*, 384-392.

Roswell, F., & Chall, J.S. (1991). *Diagnostic Assessment of Reading with Trial Teaching Strategies*. Chicago, IL: Riverside Press.

Roswell, F., & Chall, J.S. (1997). *Roswell-Chall Auditory Blending Test*. Cambridge, MA: Educators Publishing Service, Inc.

Rozin, P., & Gleitman, L.R. (1977). The structure and acquisition of the alphabetic principle. In A.S. Reber & D.L. Scarborough (Eds.), *Toward a psychology of reading*. Hillsdale, NJ: Erlbaum.

Rudel, R. (1988). *Assessment of developmental learning disorders: A neuropsychological approach*. NY: Basic Books.

Schickedanz, J. (1990). *Adam's righting revolutions*. Portsmouth, NH: Heinemann.

Seuss, Dr. (1960). *Green eggs and ham*. NY: Random House.

Seuss, Dr. (1965). *Fox in Socks*. NY: Random House.

Share, D.J., Jorm, A.F., Maclean., R., & Mathews, R. (1984). Sources of individual differences in reading achievement. *Journal of Educational Psychology, 76*, 466-477.

Shaw, N. (1986). *Sheep in a jeep*. Boston, MA: Houghton Mifflin.

104

Shaywitz, S.E. (1996). Dyslexia. *Scientific American*, 275, no. 5, November, 99.

Shaywitz, S.E., Escobar, M.D., Shaywitz, B.A., Fletcher, J.M., & Makuch, R.. (1992). Evidence that dyslexia may represent the lower tail of a normal distribution of reading ability. In *The New England Journal of Medicine, 326*, 145-50.

Siegel, L.S., & Ryan, E.B. (1988). Development of grammatical sensitivity, phonological, and short-term memory skills in normally achieving and learning disabled children. *Developmental Psychology, 24*, 28-37.

Slavin, R., Madden, N.A., Kaarweit, N.L., Livermon, B.J., & Dolan, L. (1990). Success for all: First-year outcomes of a comprehensive plan for reforming urban education. *American Education Research Journal, 27*, 255-278.

Snow, C.E. (1983). Language and literacy: Relationships during the preschool years. *Harvard Educational Review, 53*, 165-189.

Snow, C.E, & Ninio, A. (1986). The contracts of literacy: What children learn from learning to read books. In W.H. Teale & E. Sulzby (Eds.), *Emergent literacy*. Norwood, NJ: Ablex Publishing Co.

Snowling, M. (1981). Phonemic deficits in developmental dyslexia. *Psychological Research, 43*, 219-234.

Snowling, M., Goulandris, N., Bowlby, M., & Howell, P. (1986). Segmentation and speech perception in relation to reading skill: A developmental analysis. *Journal of Experimental Child Psychology, 41*, 489-507.

Stanovich, K.E. (1986). Matthew effects in reading: Some consequences of individual differences in the acquisition of literacy. *Reading Research Quarterly, 21*, 360-407.

Stanovich, K.E., Cunningham, A.E., & Cramer, B.B. (1984). Assessing phonological awareness in kindergarten: Issues of task comparability. *Journal of Experimental Child Psychology, 38*, 175-190.

Sulzby, E. (1986). Writing and reading: Signs of oral and written language organization in the young child. In W.H. Teale & E. Sulzby (Eds.), *Emergent literacy*. Norwood, NJ: Ablex Publishing Co.

Tallal, P., Miller, S.L., Bedi, G., Byma, G., Wang, X., Nagarajan, S., Schreiner, C., Jenkins, W., & Merzenich, M. (1986). Language comprehension in language-impaired children improved with acoustically modified speech. *Science, 271*, 81-84.

Tangel, D.M. & Blachman, B.A. (1995). Effect of phoneme awareness instruction on the invented spelling of first grade children: A one year follow-up. *Journal of Reading Behavior, 27*, 153-185.

Taylor, D. (1983). *Family literacy*. Portsmouth, NH: Heinemann.

Teale, W.H. (1986). Home background and young children's literacy development. In W.H.Teale & E.Sulzby (Eds.), *Emergent literacy*. Norwood, NJ: Ablex Publishing Co.

Torgesen, J., & Bryant, B. (1994). *Test of Phonological Awareness (TOPA)*. Austin, TX: Pro-Ed.

Torgesen, J.K., & Davis, C. (1996). Individual difference variables that predict response to training in phonological awareness. *Journal of Experimental Child Psychology, 63*, 1-21.

Torneus, M. (1984). Phonological awareness and reading: A chicken and egg problem? *Journal of Educational Psychology, 76*, 1346-1358.

Treiman, R. (1984). Individual differences among children in reading and spelling styles. *Journal of Experimental Child Psychology, 37*, 463-477.

Tunmer, W.E., Herriman, M.L., & Nesdale, A.R. (1988). Metalinguistic abilities and beginning reading. *Reading Research Quarterly, 23*, 135-158.

Vellutino, F.R. (1978). Toward an understanding of dyslexia: Psychological factors in specific reading disability. In A.L. Benton & D. Pearl (Eds.), *Dyslexia*. NY: Oxford University Press, 63-111.

Vellutino, F.R., & Scanlon, D. (1987). Phonological coding, phonological awareness, and reading ability: Evidence from a longitudinal and experimental study. *Merrill-Palmer Quarterly, 33*, 321-363.

Vernon, M.D. (1957). *Backwardness in reading: A study of its nature and origin*. NY: Cambridge University Press.

Wells, G. (1986). *The meaning makers: Children learning language and using language to learn*. Portsmouth, NH: Heinemann.

Williams, J. P. (1979). The ABDs of reading: A program for the learning disabled. In L.B. Resnick & P. Weaver (Eds.), *Theory and practice of early reading, (Vol. 3)*. Hillsdale, NJ: Erlbaum.

Williams, J.P. (1980). Teaching decoding with an emphasis on phoneme analysis and phoneme blending. *Journal of Educational Psychology, 172*, 1-15.

Wolf, M. (1991). Naming speed and reading: The contribution of the cognitive neurosciences. *Reading Research Quarterly*, 26, 123-141.

Wolf, M., Bowers, P.G., & Biddle, K. (2000). Naming-speed processes, timing, and reading: A conceptual review. *Journal of Learning Disabilities*, 33(4), 388-407.

Wolf, M., Miller, L., & Donnelly, K. (2000). Retrieval, automaticity, vocabulary elaboration, orthography (RAVE-O): A comprehensive, fluency-based reading intervention program. *Journal of Learning Disabilities*, 33(4), 375-386.

Wolf, M., & Obregon, M. (1997). The 'double-deficit' hypothesis: Implications for diagnosis and practice in reading disabilities. *Readings of Language and Literacy*, L. Putnam (Ed.) Cambridge, MA: Brookline Books, 176-210.

Wolf, M., & Segal, D. (1999). Retrieval-rate, accuracy and vocabulary elaboration (RAVE) in reading impaired children: A pilot intervention program. *Dyslexia: An International Journal of Theory and Practice, 5*, 1-27.

Wolff, P. (1989). Presentation at Harvard Graduate School of Education.

Yopp, H. K. (1988). The validity and reliability of phonemic awareness tests. *Reading Research Quarterly, 23*, 159-177.

Yopp, H. K (1992). Developing phonemic awareness in young children. *The Reading Teacher, 45*, 696-703.

Yopp, H.K. (1995). A test for assessing phonemic awareness in young children. *The Reading Teacher*, 49(1), 20-29.

Zifcak, M. (1981). Phonological awareness and reading acquisition. *Contemporary Educational Psychology, 6*, 117-126.

III. LETTERS

Chapter 4. Beginning Reading: Learning Print-to-sound Correspondence

Cheryl Rappaport Liebling, PhD
RMC Research Corporation

It has been more than 15 years since the Commission on Reading issued the report *Becoming a Nation of Readers* (Anderson et al., 1985). That landmark report called for comprehensive early literacy instruction emphasizing explicit instruction and practice in word recognition and spelling strategies along with daily opportunities to read, write, and discuss meaningful, connected text. Recent reviews of early literacy research by the National Reading Panel (2000) and the National Research Council, *Preventing Reading Difficulties in Young Children* (Snow et al., 1998), echo the recommendations of the earlier Commission on Reading. However, today's researchers and practitioners are no longer arguing the need for comprehensive instruction, as was the case in 1985. Rather, they are debating effective ways to mix the ingredients of comprehensive early literacy instructional programs to meet the diverse needs of our nation's learners.

Central to achieving the national early literacy goal of all children reading age-appropriate material fluently with comprehension by the end of grade 3 (U.S. Department of Education, 1997) is an emphasis on decoding print-to-sound during beginning reading instruction. This chapter discusses how to teach beginners to read by emphasizing the code within the context of integrated language arts activities. Learning the code in beginning reading requires direct, systematic, explicit instruction regarding the relationship of print to sound as well as encouragement to practice newly developing reading strategies with connected text. Progress in beginning reading is enhanced by opportunities for learners to listen, and follow along, while fluent readers share children's literature, along with ample occasions to use both written and spoken language.

This chapter begins with a summary of historical trends concerning how beginning reading is taught. This is followed by a description of Stage 1 reading (Chall, 1983) that identifies various aspects of word recognition, along with strategies that help students "break the code." The final section discusses implementation of a Stage 1 beginning reading program by presenting several classroom assessment strategies, a framework for providing instruction within primary-grade classrooms, and several promising intensive intervention programs.

History of Beginning Reading Instruction in the United States[1]

Colonial period through the early 19th century. From colonial times well into the 19th century, the predominant approach to beginning reading was the ABC method. It emphasized the identification of letters by name along with recognition of simple letter-sound relationships. Children learned the names of letters and recited these in sequence in order to memorize words appearing in religious texts. In essence, most children learned to read by spelling aloud written words.

Throughout the colonial period and until the mid-19th century, the primary purpose of reading was to study the *Bible*. A commonly used teaching material was the *New England Primer*, a book that used religious text as the content for instruction. The *Primer* emphasized memorization and recitation as children learned to spell and decode words of one-to-five syllables. Later, children practiced reading words within short verses and religious texts. Many students also used hornbooks, hand-held boards that fit in a child's palm. On each board was written the alphabet, two-letter combinations of a vowel and a consonant, and *The Lord's Prayer*.

---

[1]This discussion is drawn from Adams (1990), Chall (1996), Heilman (1998), and Smith (1986). The reader should consult these texts for more detailed information concerning the history of beginning reading instruction.

Between the Revolutionary and Civil Wars, the reading of patriotic documents became another purpose for reading. Through reading, a sense of pride in the American democratic system of government could be instilled. At this time, Noah Webster developed *The Elementary Spelling Book*. Webster continued to emphasize reading by spelling; his book included spelling rules, lists of words and syllables to memorize and recite, and fables, moralistic stories, and poetry. Stress marks were added to words, within stories and poetry, to encourage correct pronunciation, regardless of regional dialect.

Mid-19th century.   During the mid-19th century, instruction in the **sounds** associated with printed letters gradually came to replace the earlier **alphabet spelling** (Smith, 1986). Using the sound approach, children associated a letter with its most typical sound by means of a key word; for example *B is for ball*. After learning the symbol-sound relationship, children practiced reading one-syllable words containing the phonics generalization.

The *McGuffey Eclectic Readers*, published from 1840 through the turn of the century, provided children with instruction in both the spelling of words and the association of letters with sounds in sequence. The *McGuffey Readers* represented the first attempt to control the complexity of vocabulary and grammar by limiting the number of different words and types of sentence structures within a selection of text. An effort was made to consider the developmental capabilities of students and to provide appropriate reading materials.

During this time, American schools were beginning to place students in separate grades, and the *McGuffey Readers* offered texts for each grade level. Although the *McGuffey Readers* were the most popular instructional texts of the day, they were only one of several series in use. *Bumstead's Reader*, also published at that time, recommended use of a sight method for instruction.

By the mid-1800s, educators were considering alternative teaching approaches for reading instruction. Horace Mann was especially vocal in this debate. He had visited European schools and was inspired by the ideas of Pestalozzi, a Prussian who advocated consideration of the child when designing instruction. As an alternative to the memorization of the alphabet, Pestalozzi proposed that letter sounds be learned, a few at a time, as needed to read a word, rather than in alphabetical order. Mann promoted Pestalozzi's approach, and hence the importance of the relationship of print to meaning. Although it is sometimes thought that Mann wished to abolish phonics instruction, the passage below (in which Mann describes a lesson given in the Pestalozzian manner) suggests quite the opposite. Instead, it indicates that Mann supported the teaching of letter sounds, and their blending into words, but rejected the teaching of letters by name in alphabetical order. Mann writes:

> The teacher first drew a house upon the blackboard....By the side of...it, he wrote the word *house*....With a long pointing rod...he ran over the form of the letters,—the children, with their slates before them and their pencils in their hands, looking at the pointing rod and tracing the forms of the letters in the air....

> The next process was to copy the word *house*, both in script and in print, on their slates. Then followed the formation of the sounds of the letter of which the word was composed, and the spelling of the word. Here the *names* of the letters were not given as with us, but only their powers, or the sounds which those letters have in combination. The letter *h* was first selected and set up in the reading frame, and the children, instead of articulating our alphabetic *h* (aitch), merely gave a hard breathing,—such a sound as the letter really has in the word *house*....

> In every such school, also, there are printed sheets or cards containing the letters, diphthongs, and whole words. The children are taught to sound a diphthong, and then asked in what words that sound occurs (Mann, 1842 in Smith, 1965, pp. 77-78).

Late 19th/early 20th century. Toward the late 19th century, educators decided that the future of the country depended, in part, upon the intellectual abilities of the American people. This realization was coupled with a more enlightened view of childhood as distinctly different from adulthood. The purposes of reading expanded to include acquisition of information, and engagement in a pleasurable activity. As a consequence, many children were introduced to a variety of reading materials including: moralistic verses and stories such as *Mother Goose* and *Aesop's Fables*; adventure stories such as *Robinson Crusoe*; fairy tales such as *Cinderella*; poetry; and, turn-of-the-century contemporary fiction such as *Rebecca of Sunnybrook Farm, The Five Little Peppers, Little Women, and Huckleberry Finn* (Norton, 1999).

As interest in education and literature grew during the early 20th century, so too grew the call to emphasize meaning from the start. The reading textbooks of the late 19th and early 20th centuries such as *Stepping Stones to Literature, The Arnold Primer*, and *The Rational Method in Reading*, emphasized the reading of whole, connected text by whole word identification (Smith, 1986). By the late 1920s, many educators encouraged students to read silently, nearly from the start.

Mid-20th century. By the 1930s, American reading instruction came to rely on basal programs that introduced a set of sight words before sound-symbol relationships were explored. From this time into the 1960s, the "look-say" method received greater emphasis than phonics. Controlled vocabulary and syntactic simplicity characterized the basal stories. Phonics and spelling-sound pattern exercises were offered as supplementary material, while visual configuration and context appeared to be the primary methods for word recognition.

The public reaction of this period nonetheless continued to express desire for the use of phonics as a word recognition strategy during beginning reading. This concern reached its peak in 1955 when many parents in the United States agreed with Rudolph Flesch (1955) that an emphasis on sight word recognition, rather than phonics, was preventing many children from becoming fluent readers and, therefore, from achieving the American dream. Parental interest in Flesch's polemic stirred educators and government leaders alike.

During the 1960s, considerable government resources were allocated to research the relative merits of various beginning reading programs. A number of supplementary phonics programs appeared. Among these were linguistic readers such as *Let's Read* (Bloomfield et al., 1965). These materials were used to teach word families through practice with rhyming word-lists and sentences with rhyming patterns. Another program, *Words in Color* (Gattegno, 1968), used color to help students establish the correspondences between print and sound.

Chall's (1960s) synthesis of the research on beginning reading instruction found that phonics instruction, along with many opportunities to read, was preferable to a sight approach in helping children become independent readers (Chall, 1996). Twenty years after Chall's initial study, her findings were reaffirmed by Adams (1990). Using more sophisticated statistical and research design methods than were available earlier, Adams continued to find that "approaches in which systematic code instruction is included along with meaningful connected reading result in superior reading achievement overall" (Adams, 1990, p. 12).

Late 20th century. Despite the proliferation of supporting research and instructional materials for teaching phonics and word families, by the late 1970s, many educators were still undecided as to the "best" method for instruction. While programs varied in emphasis, the basals of this era tended to include the following: workbooks for the teaching of phonics and spelling-sound patterns; simple stories with controlled vocabulary and syntax; and detailed scripts for the teacher including directions as to how to introduce a story, questions for comprehension discussion, and postreading activities.

While these basals were seen as comprehensive by many educators, others questioned their literary value, the scripting for teachers, the insufficient connection between word recognition exercises and stories, and the limited integration of reading and language arts.

Furthermore, educators began to reexamine their notions of reading. Conceptions of reading now characterized the reading process as constructive since readers create meaning by integrating text information with knowledge gained from prior experience. The Whole Language movement arose in the early 1980s to draw on the use of literature instead of basals in an attempt to focus reading instruction more fully on the meaning of text and the constructive quality of the reading process. This effort reflected a shift in the ongoing debate concerning whether to place more emphasis on decoding or on meaning in beginning reading programs.

It soon became clear, however, that beginning readers need more than exposure to high quality children's literature if they are to become skilled readers. By the late 1990s, a consensus had emerged in the educational community that beginning readers are most likely to achieve the national early literacy goal if they have access to systematic, explicit instruction in phonemic awareness, letter-sound knowledge, and word identification along with daily reading, writing, and discussion of meaningful text (National Reading Panel, 2000; Snow et al., 1998). When the explicit teaching of decoding is combined with frequent opportunities to comprehend text, children advance more quickly toward skilled reading that is characterized by the simultaneous processing of letter, sound, meaning, and contextual information during skilled reading.[2]

Stage 1: Beginning Reading - Learning the Code

During beginning reading, learners need to focus on print, a notion that runs counter to the paramount purpose of reading—understanding the meaning of text (Chall, 1983). Although the central purposes of reading are comprehension and communication, the recognition of words is a necessary step toward comprehension. Since "over 94% of the different words children read occur fewer

---

[2]For further information on conceptualizations of skilled reading, see Chapter 1 of this volume and Adams, M.J. (1990).

than ten times in every million words of text" (Adams, 1990, p. 34), it is crucial that learners become automatic decoders of words as quickly as possible so that their attention in reading can focus upon meaning. Mastery of decoding skills by beginning readers will eventually aid in critical thinking during reading and writing.

Beginning readers generally are learning to decode words that are already in their spoken vocabularies, words for which meaning is immediately associated, once accurate decoding occurs. As Chall (1983) notes, most beginning readers understand 4,000 or more spoken words, yet are learning to read approximately 600 words during Stage 1. Consequently, while being "glued to print" appears to be a less mature approach to reading than reading for comprehension, Chall (1996) makes the convincing argument that attentiveness to the actual words written by the author, rather than the text's overall meaning, is an essential phase in the development of fluent reading.

As discussed in Chapter 3 of this text, the most consistent predictor of beginning reading success is phonemic awareness, a skill that reflects the learner's ability to identify, segment, and blend individual sounds within spoken words. Coupled with the identification of letters by name, phonemic awareness paves the way for the mapping of print to sound during Stage 1 of the reading process.

In addition, children's experiences with language and print prior to learning to read can facilitate early success in reading. Among the characteristics frequently attributed to children who learn to read with ease are: considerable background knowledge gained from wide-ranging experiences, familiarity with written language through listening to books read aloud, drawing and attempting to write for communicative purposes, and pretending to read by telling stories of simple texts (Adams, 1990; Chall, 1996). Furthermore, young children who learn to read easily generally attend to environmental print and communicate ideas and emotions with effective use of vocabulary and grammar.

Chall's Stage 1 describes the transitional alphabetic phase (Juel, 1996) of decoding stage models. Like Ehri's phonetic cue phase (Ehri, 1996), Chall's Stage 1 is characterized as "rudimentary alphabetic" because children are now processing some of the letters when reading words and are beginning to make associations of letters and sounds. Stage 1 is the link between the earlier Stage 0 emergent literacy experiences and the later Stage 2 when automaticity in decoding enables fluent and efficient word recognition and comprehension on the basis of spelling patterns or orthography.

As learners begin to read, they must acquire the range of word recognition strategies that skilled readers call upon when they encounter unfamiliar words. Direct, explicit instruction in these strategies helps beginning readers attend to print and to the relationship of print to sound. At the same time, an effective instructional program also emphasizes the links between spoken and written language.

Such a program includes direct decoding instruction, application of decoding to the reading of connected text, and integration of reading and language arts activities through discussion, writing, and practice in reading simple, engaging stories. In addition, during the school day, beginning readers need to hear more sophisticated texts read aloud by fluent readers in order to become familiar with more complex language patterns, words, and concepts. In combination, these activities constitute a rich instructional program.

INSTRUCTIONAL STRATEGIES

The outcome that signals mastery of Stage 1 reading is the ability to decode and comprehend simple stories independently. Students attain this proficiency by achieving the word recognition goals described below. Such mastery enables readers to shift their attention to comprehension. Most often, these goals are achieved in the primary grades; however, older students and adults who experience difficulties in learning to read need to achieve these goals in order to become fluent readers who concentrate on text meaning.

Goal #1: Use letter-sound correspondences and an understanding of the alphabetic principle when blending sounds to read and write one-syllable words, especially those characterized by the CVC pattern.

Goal #2: Decode by analogy when reading and writing words that are part of rhyming word families. This process enables learners to transfer letter-sound pattern information to words of similar patterns.

Goal #3: Recognize high frequency, irregularly-spelled words by sight as logographic wholes. These words are learned through memorization, participation in language experience, reading aloud, and discussion and writing activities.

Goal #4: Draw on context to confirm word recognition within meaningful sentences.

In combination, mastery of these four goals represents a powerful constellation of strategies for becoming a skilled reader of connected text. The following discussion describes instructional strategies that help learners achieve these goals and illustrates them with sample teaching lessons.

Goal #1 instruction: Use of letter-sound correspondences.

> Phonics is more likely to be useful when children hear the sounds associated with most letters both in isolation and in words, and when they are taught to blend together the sounds of letters to identify words...
>
> (Anderson et al., 1985, p. 118)

Beginning readers need to understand the relationship of letters to sounds, to divide words into subunits, and to blend parts of known words with parts of unfamiliar words before they will succeed in decoding by analogy (Ehri, 1996). Consistent with this perspective, Chall's Stage 1 confirms that it is necessary to emphasize the teaching of letter-sound correspondence and blending.

This initial step involves the teaching of the correspondences of graphemes (printed letters) to phonemes (sounds). Some students already have some familiarity with these correspondences, but others require considerable practice in discriminating the visual shapes of letters, identifying the names of letters, and associating particular sounds with letters. The amount of time spent on instruction should be adjusted to students' levels of understanding. The following broad scope and sequence for teaching letter-sound correspondences is often recommended:

■ Introduce several consonants. These are introduced before vowels since consonants are more frequently found in the initial position in words. However, all consonants need not be taught before introducing some vowels. As suggested in Chapter 3, it is helpful to begin by introducing consonants that are characterized as **continuant sounds** such as **f, m, n, s,** and **w**. These sounds can be pronounced at a slow speed without excessive distortion. Consonants characterized as **stops** such as **p, t, d, b, k,** and **g** can then be introduced.

■ As students begin to learn consonants, they use initial letter-sound correspondences along with context to identify words. They also use some final letter-sound correspondences to identify words. At this point, learners need to become familiar with the terminology *consonant* and *vowel*.

- Next, introduce the short vowels **a, e, i, o, u,** and the vowel digraph **ea** as in **ea**ch. Also teach consonant digraphs **ch, sh, th,** in which two consonants combine to form one sound, and consonant blends, **pl, st, tr,** in which the two consonant sounds can be discerned. (The short vowels and consonant digraphs are introduced before the long vowels in order to reveal the code of CVC words.)

- Then, introduce the consonant digraphs **wh** and **ck,** the consonant blends **br, cr, dr, fr, gr, pr, bl, cl, fl, ld, nd, sc, tw,** silent consonants **kn, wr,** long vowels **a, e, i, o, u, y,** key generalizations such as the **silent e rule,** and vowel diphthongs such as **ow, oi,** and **oy.**

- In addition, introduce the soft sounds for **c** and **g,** the consonant digraph **ph,** consonant blends **sk, sl, sm, sw str, squ, thr,** silent consonants **gn** and **mb,** vowel digraphs **oa, ay,** and **ai, ei** as in **eight** and **receive, ey** as in **honey, oo, ow, ue,** and the vowel diphthong **ou.** Introduce r-controlled vowels: **ar, er, ir, or, ur, ear,** and **our.** Learners also need to tackle final consonant blends such as **ng** and **nt.**

Following is a lesson plan that describes the teaching of a vowel letter-sound correspondence in which a short vowel appears in the medial position of the CVC (consonant-vowel-consonant) pattern. An explicit instructional approach, sometimes termed *synthetic phonics*, is favored so as to avoid confusion during instruction. The example can be followed to teach a range of letter-sound correspondences. A similar lesson plan would be followed to teach an initial consonant. (For an example of a plan that introduces an initial consonant, turn to page 135.)

Sample Lesson Plan for Teaching Vowel Letter-Sound Correspondence with Blending.

Instructional Goal: To teach a decoding strategy that enables students to associate the short *a* with **Aa** as in *tan* and to blend sounds to form one-syllable words of the CVC pattern.

1. Introduce short vowel sounds after students have learned to recognize several consonant letter-sound relationships in the initial and final positions of words. Tell students that they will learn what is called the "short" sound of **a,** and that it corresponds to the letter **Aa.** Short **/a/** can be pronounced in isolation prior to pronouncing it within a CVC word.

2. Begin by presenting, on a piece of oaktag, a short poem that contains words with the short /a/ sound. Read the selection aloud after asking students to listen for words that have the short /a/ sound, as in the word **at** or **hat**. Pronounce the short /a/ in isolation then move to saying the sound within words. While reading the text aloud, pause to underline the **Aa** in the words having the short /a/ sound within one-syllable words of the CVC or VC pattern. In the following text from *One Fish, Two Fish, Red Fish, Blue Fish* (Seuss, 1960), students read about different kinds of fish:

> Some are sad.
> And some are glad.
> And some are very very bad.
> Why are they sad and glad and bad?
> I do not know.
> Go ask your dad.

3. Explicitly demonstrate the blending of a CVC word such as *dad*, **for which the students have already learned the consonant sounds. While blending /d/-/a/-/d/**, point to the word in the text. Next, ask students to practice blending the sounds as you point to each sound in left to right progression. Ask students to write the letters of the word on an index card as they are sounded. Ask students to point to, sound, blend, and read the word on the index card.

4. Now ask students to help you "echo" reread the text. This time, pause to sound and blend those words that contain the short /a/ sound and consonants that have been learned.

5. After the rereading, write on the chalkboard words containing /a/ for students to enter into a wordbank (of index cards) or a reading/writing notebook. Be sure to use words for which students have already learned the consonants. These may include: **sad, fan, pan**, and **man**. As each word is written on the board, make a special effort to point to the letters and blend the sounds from left to right. Students should read each word after the teacher.

Following the reading of the word, write it in a simple sentence on the board. (Use CVC words that also are formed with /a/ to write the sentence.) Students can write the sentence on the back of their index cards while the teacher dictates the sentence slowly. Encourage students to use their letter-sound knowledge to spell words accurately. After a set of words is written on the board and in notebooks or on index cards, ask students to take turns reading their words and sentences. This might be done in pairs.

6. Provide additional practice through matching games, practice exercises, reading of sentences or stories composed of these words, and flashcards. Practice exercises may ask a student to: spell a word containing the short **/a/** such as **_a_** when associated with a picture of a hat; pronounce a word represented by a picture and decide whether the word includes a short **/a/**; identify and color all words in a drawing that contain the short **/a/**; or select the correct word from several choices in order to complete a sentence in a meaningful manner.

Using their set of wordbank cards or their reading/writing notebooks, students can practice reading the words in sentences. Students can also use their wordbank cards to practice reading the words while engaging with peers in games such as BINGO, Fish, or Concentration. Students should be encouraged to refer to their notebooks or index cards during language experience and writing activities.

While teaching a particular letter-sound correspondence, teachers can draw on many simple texts that utilize predictable patterns, rhyming, and particular phonics generalizations. When working on the short vowel sounds, for example, teachers can turn to the following books for compatible text: *Green Eggs and Ham* (Geisel, 1960), *Hop on Pop* (Geisel, 1991), *Wings on Things* (Brown, 1982), or *The Cat in the Hat* (Seuss, 1957). Alphabet books such as *On Market Street* (Lobel, 1981), or *Brian Wildsmith's ABC* (Wildsmith, 1962), offer simple texts that emphasize individual letters, words in which the letters appear, and illustrations to contextualize the words.

Many authors, such as Marjorie Flack, Jack Kent, Molly Bang, Judy Blume, Betsy Byars, Pat Hutchins, and Stan and Jan Berenstain write books that emphasize predictable patterns, rhyme, and phonics generalizations (Norton, 1999; Routman, 1988). Trachtenburg (1990) provides a useful list of stories for beginning readers according to the phonics generalizations that are emphasized in the text. In addition, Modern Curriculum Press and Educators' Publishing Service publish a large variety of stories that emphasize specific phonics generalizations.

Many teachers question whether it is necessary for children to state phonics generalizations that guide pronunciation. Some feel that it is not so important for students to state rules as to apply them through practice in reading and constructing the correspondence. However, it is occasionally beneficial to describe a rule that particularly helps readers and writers decide on the correct pronunciation or spelling of a word. For example, teachers often point out that the vowel within a CVC pattern is generally "short" or that the letters **Cc** and **Gg** generally take "soft" sounds when coming before an *e, i,* or *y*. (See Chapter 6 for other perspectives.)

Summary of goal #1 instruction. Knowing letter-sound correspondences provides learners with a very useful strategy for unraveling unfamiliar words independently in order to read connected text.[3] Exemplary phonics instruction has been characterized as (a) systematic, (b) grounded in a student's phonemic awareness, (c) clear and explicit, (d) integrated into a comprehensive beginning reading and language arts program, (e) focused on reading real words in isolation and in context rather than memorizing rules, and (f) oriented toward helping students become independent in word recognition (Stahl, 1992).

Goal #2 instruction: Decoding by analogy. Once students have developed an understanding of the alphabetic principle, they are ready to learn to decode by analogy (Gaskins et al., 1991; Goswami & Mead, 1992). When readers decode by analogy, they blend the **onset** sound of a word with the larger unit of **rime**, typically composed of a vowel and a final consonant or consonant blend.

For example, in reading the word *hat*, a student learns to blend the onset **/h/** sound with the rime **/at/** to form **hat**. Once students have learned letter-sound correspondences, this may be an easier process and may result in less distortion of sounds than blending individual segments as in **/h/-/a/-/t/**. The following instructional scope and sequence is recommended when teaching students to decode by analogy.

■ First, introduce, one-at-a-time, common word families based on rimes such as **-at, -an, -ap, -it, -ip, -in, -eg, -et, -ot, -og, -ug**. For any one rime, teach students to substitute initial consonants to create familiar words. Also, list unknown words that follow the pattern, and ask students to decode the unknown words by analogy. See also *Decoding and Comprehension Concepts (DCC) Guide* (Appendix B, pages 138-140) by S. Brody for an extended list of components to teach in families and a multisensory sequence of instruction.

---

[3]For more detailed suggestions for the teaching of phonics, see Barr & Johnson (1997), Burns, Roe, & Ross (1999), Heilman (1998), and Leu & Kinzer (1999).

■ Introduce the primary word families throughout Stage 1. Practice blending onset sounds with each rime in reading and writing words. Always follow with opportunities to read these words in sentences to promote decoding in context. Wylie & Durrell (cited in Adams, 1990, p. 85) identify thirty-seven phonograms, or word families, from which at least five hundred primary-grade words can be generated: **-al, -all, -ain, -ake, -ale, -ame, -an, -ank, -ap, -ash, -at, -ate, -aw, -ay, -eat, -ell, -est, -ice, -ick, -ide, -ill, -in, -ine, -ing, -ip, -ir, -ock, -oke, -op, -ore, -uck, -ug, -ump, -unk**.

■ During instruction, introduce students to the major one-syllable patterns: **CVC** (as in *hat*), **CVCe** (as in *cake*), and **CVVC** (as in *boat*).

■ In addition, use poetry and predictable stories to help students decode by analogy. By the conclusion of the beginning reading program, students should decode words that are characterized by the major letter-sound patterns and apply that ability to the reading of simple text.

Sample Lesson Plan for Teaching Decoding by Analogy.

Instructional Goal: To teach a decoding by analogy strategy that enables students to blend the onset sound of a word with the rime in familiar and unfamiliar words within rhyming families.

1. Select a rhyming family such as the **-all** family for instruction. Use the consonant substitution technique to teach students to decode by analogy. Begin instruction by telling the students that they will be reading words in the **-all** family. Write **-all** on the board, pronounce it, and ask the students to read it.

2. Read aloud a poem, or story segment, that emphasizes the word family you will be teaching. Write the text on a large piece of oaktag. Ask students to listen as you read the text aloud, pointing to the words in the **-all** family. Ask students to read along with you as you repeat the text. Read slowly to help students practice blending the onset and rime of each word in the family, as in the following example taken from *Hop on Pop* (Geisel, 1991):

ALL
TALL
We are **all tall.**

ALL
SMALL
We are **all small.**

ALL
BALL
We **all** play **ball.**

BALL
WALL
Up on a **wall.**

ALL
FALL
Fall off the wall.

3. Underneath **-all** on the board, write **tall**. Pronounce **-all** and **tall**, and ask students to repeat after you. Erase the *t* to yield **-all**, and ask students to watch as you substitute *b* for *t* to yield **ball**. Pronounce **ball**, and ask students to repeat after you. Students should then generate new words by substituting the *onset* letter/sound: *c*all, *h*all, *f*all.

As words are generated, make a chart by writing them on the board. You may also want to introduce some unfamiliar rhyming words, such as **gall** and **pall**, to see whether students can decode by analogy even when the words are uncommon. This provides an opportunity to expand your students' vocabulary. Work with students to create short oral sentences that include several of the rhyming words.

4. Ask students to list some target words from the poem and the board exercise in their reading/writing notebooks. Then ask them to copy several sentences from the target poem or story into their notebooks.

5. Now reread the segment, and ask students to underline each word in the **-all** family as the class reads in unison. Students can make word-family index cards and add **-all** family words to their wordbanks. They can also read the charts and sentences from their notebooks to peers and family.

6. As students learn rhyme families, they can spell words of a particular family during dictation of simple sentences. Practice in spelling words that are part of predictable families reinforces the patterns that students are reading. These dictations can be included in word-family notebooks.

7. For those students who require additional support, practice exercises and lists of rhyming words reinforce an understanding of the patterns. In these exercises, students read simple sentences and select rhyming words to complete riddles; circle words that rhyme within stories; connect words to pictures; or select a word that best completes a sentence (Gregorich & Henkel, no date). Using flashcards, a student may be asked to select words from cards that are part of particular word families. The teacher might draw a ladder on the board with **-at** as the bottom rung. Students search the flashcards for words that are part of this family. On each successive rung of the ladder, another word is added: **mat, pat, cat,** etc. (*Golden Step Ahead*, 1989).

Reading by analogy is an important part of an integrated reading and language arts program. Once students become attentive to the rhyming patterns of words in poems and simple stories, they often show an increased interest in reciting and writing poetry as well as participating in choral reading and dramatizations. These activities reinforce the students' knowledge of word families while extending their enjoyment and familiarity with language.

By the conclusion of the beginning reading period, typically by the end of grade 2, most students are very attentive to rhyming patterns; they also recognize words automatically by generating analogous relationships among words in families. This strategy, in combination with a solid understanding of phonics, facilitates the rapid identification of words that is a prerequisite to fluent reading with understanding.

Goal #3 instruction: Rapid recognition of sight words. The primary purpose of sight word recognition is to promote rapid entry to the reading of connected text. Teachers often provide sight word instruction to help students recognize common "glue" words (such as *the, is, are*), as well as content words (such as *beautiful, airplane, pretty*), that appear frequently in beginning reading texts.

Many sight words contain letter-sound correspondences that are not taught until late in the letter-sound instructional sequence. Some of the words contain inconsistent letter-sound correspondences and may always be recognized primarily by visual configurations. Sight words are memorized as logographic wholes through repeated exposures during the reading of stories, short sentences, and flashcards. The following scope of instruction will help beginning readers develop sight word recognition.

■ Teach students to recognize function words, such as **the, their, they, to, do, does, get, have,** and **your**, that carry little meaning, but act as the "glue" that binds content words together in sentences. Many of these words contain consistent letter-sound patterns (such as **it**), but some do not (such as **have**). Whether they are consistent or inconsistent, "glue" words should be overlearned and recognized automatically so that beginning readers can read simple texts.

Common function words include: **a, about, again, all, am, an, and, are, as, at, away, be, but, could, did, do, down, from, for, had, has, have, he, her, here, him, how, I, in, is, it, just, may, me, must, my, near, no, not, oh, of, on, one, she, so, some, soon, that, the, them, then, there, they, this, to, too, two, up, us, want, was, we, were, what, when, where, who, will, with, yes, you,** and **your**.

■ In addition, teach students to recognize common content words that are irregular in the correspondence of letters and sounds. Among these words are: **beautiful, child, father, language, library, mischief, mother, neighbor, special,** and **woman**. In all, some two hundred and twenty-five words that beginning readers frequently encounter can be considered irregular in their letter/sound correspondence (Heilman, 1998). These words need to be taught because they appear so often in texts for beginning readers.

Among common content words are the following: **airplane, apple, baby, back, ball, birthday, black, blue, boy, boat, came, can, come, cookies, cow, cowboy, daddy, dinner, eat, farm, father, girl, good, good-by, happy, house, find, green, known, laugh, little, look, mother, morning, night, party, pie, play, pretty, put, said, saw, show, something, splash, surprise, toy, walk, white,** and **yellow**. Many teachers refer to graded sight-word lists such as the Dale-Chall (1948) list to verify that students have had exposure to words that appear commonly in their reading.

■ Encourage students to read and reread beginning children's literature to promote their skill in sight word recognition.

To learn sight words, students generally write particular words on index cards and generate sentences in which the words appear. For example, *the* is a common sight word. A teacher might take this word from the reading of a simple sentence or text segment, write it on the board, and pronounce it. Students might repeat the pronunciation, trace the letters in the air, close their eyes and spell the word, and enter the word in their word banks or notebooks.

Through practice in reading sight words, either in isolation or within a simple sentence, students are expected to memorize pronunciation and to identify words quickly on the basis of visual configuration. This process can be facilitated if students are encouraged to use phonics for decoding regular letter-sound correspondences such as the *i* in *is*. To identify *is*, students can use their knowledge of phonics to decode the short *i* while the teacher can point out that the *s* represents the sound /z/.

Sometimes teachers select simple text and preteach unfamiliar words as sight words to give students the sense of reading a story long before large numbers of patterns and generalizations can be decoded. When used as a supplement to decoding instruction, and viewed as an initial extension of the stages of emergent reading described by Sulzby (1985), reading primarily by sight with the help of a motivating picture and connection to familiar content may have some benefit among students who can memorize with ease.

For example, in the "Little Book" *Painting* (Cowley, 1990), which is part of the StoryBox series, a student would memorize a set of fourteen words prior to reading the story. These words include: **Toby, painted, the, floor, and, wall, cupboard, table, chair, cat, then, Mom, came,** and, **in**. Many of these words will be decoded through phonics eventually, or by analogy or structural analysis. However, the motivation to read independently can be boosted by success in reading simple texts early, particularly among students who memorize easily.

Additional techniques for sight-word development include: the use of flashcards and word lists to establish a core reading vocabulary; the use of Big Books in which students follow along as the teacher reads aloud and points to individual words; language experience stories; and the use of highly predictable story lines. Many teachers involve students in sight word recognition practice through games such as Concentration, Go Fish, or BINGO.

Summary of goal #3 instruction. While sight words contribute to initial entry to connected text, reliance on sight-word recognition as the primary word-recognition strategy for Stage 1 is an inefficient means for accurate and automatic decoding of text. As studies of fluent readers have shown, unanalyzed sight words are only a small part of all of the words that mature readers recognize automatically. The far greater number of words are identified by means of decoding letter-sound correspondences.

Goal #4 instruction: Using context. With practice, readers learn to couple an understanding of decoding with their background knowledge of vocabulary, syntax, and content to confirm the accuracy of word identification. When combining these strategies, readers generally exhibit a high level of word recognition. Although it is generally inadvisable to encourage readers to guess word identification solely from contextual information, it is important that students use their knowledge of sentence and paragraph context to verify the accuracy of their decoding. In addition, beginners need to rely somewhat on context for word recognition until a full range of decoding generalizations is learned. An instructional scope for teaching students how to use context during decoding is described below.

■ Teach students to use context to provide confirming clues during beginning decoding of letter-sound correspondences. Beginning readers can learn this strategy through exercises in which specific phonics generalizations are highlighted in conjunction with word clues that focus on meaning. For instance, Heilman (1998) offers many examples of exercises in which a learner might be asked to write a word that fits a decoding generalization and a context clue as in the following examples:

> g_t_ Clue: opening in a fence (gate)
> r_s_ Clue: pretty flower (rose)
> pea__ Clue: fruit (peach)
> mo__ Clue: insect (moth).

■ In addition, teach students to use repeating sentence and story patterns to predict word identification and to confirm the appropriateness of an identified word within text. Through the choral reading of "Big Books" with predictable sentence and story patterns and the rereading of familiar stories, beginning readers learn to anticipate repeated words.

■ Encourage advanced beginning readers to self-correct their decoding when their comprehension indicates that they mispronounced a word in context. When a mispronunciation affects meaning, encourage the reader to attempt self-correction. If the error does not affect meaning, let the student continue reading. After the section of reading is concluded, ask the student to pronounce misread words.

Sometimes students are not aware of misreading a word that is important to the understanding of text. In such cases, the students may be reading text that is too difficult and a recommendation to read simpler text may be in order.

SUMMARY OF INSTRUCTIONAL STRATEGIES

A combined strategy of phonics, decoding by analogy, use of sight words, and drawing on context to confirm decoding accuracy helps beginning readers master the outcome of decoding and comprehending simple stories. It is crucial that teachers assure that each student learns the four recognition strategies drawn on by skilled readers. Instruction should provide extra practice for those who need it and the opportunity to move to advanced reading activities for those who have mastered decoding.

Implementation of Stage 1 Reading Programs

When beginning readers are successful in word recognition, they are well on the way to becoming independent readers and writers. Word recognition strategies can be taught in integrated reading and language arts classrooms that provide a variety of oral and written activities. Several factors that contribute to effective implementation of Stage 1 reading programs are taken up below. This section begins by presenting several types of assessments that can facilitate flexible planning. Next, a sample structure for a beginning reading classroom is provided; and finally, a few intensive programs designed to enhance Stage 1 reading are considered.

ASSESSMENT OF STUDENTS' LEARNING

The assessment of students' learning can take many forms: e.g. large-scale state assessments, ongoing classroom assessments conducted by classroom teachers; and formal evaluations of individual students conducted by educational specialists.

Large-scale state assessments. Most states have now established state standards for English language arts and state assessments to measure whether students are achieving proficiency in skills and competencies associated with the standards (Kendall & Marzano, 1997; Schmoker & Marzano, 1999; Tucker & Codding, 1998; Zemelman et al., 1998). The elementary English language arts state assessments, for example, typically measure developing proficiency related to reading, writing, speaking, and listening during the early elementary years (Wixson & Dutro, 1998). These assessments are primarily intended to provide general information on the overall success of the instructional program in helping all students achieve early literacy goals.

Ongoing classroom assessments. To help all children achieve higher standards of proficiency, teachers are now aligning Stage 1 curriculum and instruction to their state's English language arts standards (Marzano & Kendall, 1996). Classroom performance assessments are then developed to measure student achievement of skills and competencies specifically taught within the classroom's instructional program. Often a rubric is established to parallel the competency levels established by the state assessment. When the instructional program is, indeed, aligned with state standards, classroom performance assessment enables teachers to track students' developing proficiency related to the early elementary standards (Glatthorn, 1998; Harris & Carr, 1996; Mitchell et al., 1995).

To gather information from a variety of perspectives, teachers are using student work sample portfolios, daily "kid-watching", and individual conferences. Systematic observation of students at work such as participation in book discussion is an important source of information on student achievement. Culminating performance tasks that serve as exhibitions of learning at the end of standards-based units also provide invaluable information on student achievement: e.g. reading a story to a group of peers or younger children, writing a story in the style of a book recently read; or dramatic retelling of a story that has been read. A regular schedule of individual conferences, such as an eight-week cycle, enables teachers to listen to children reading aloud and gauge a student's developing decoding and comprehension skills in a one-to-one setting. A checklist such as Brody's (2001) *Decoding and Comprehension Concepts (DCC) Guide* offers a useful means of recording and sharing information gathered through informal assessment. (See Appendix B, pages 138-140.)

In addition to ongoing classroom assessments, teachers often use snapshot profiles or informal inventories to monitor student achievement over time, identify students' strengths and needs, and modify instruction accordingly.[4] Print awareness can be assessed simply by classifying the child's ability to read storybooks (e.g. Barr et al., 1995) or by using a more extensive emergent literacy diagnostic survey that includes letter identification, print concepts, and reading isolated words (Clay, 1993; Rhodes, 1992).

To gauge reading abilities, many teachers ask students to read a familiar book of their own choosing, along with a more difficult book selected by the teacher. The teacher conducts an analysis of errors and discusses the story with the child to determine comprehension of the text and the extent that oral reading inaccuracies interfere with understanding (Clay, 1993; Rhodes, 1992). Other

---

[4]For further information on informal assessment, see Roskos & Walker (1994).

teachers use published informal reading inventories to gather similar information (e.g. Bader, 1998; Burns & Roe, 1999; Woods & Moe, 1999).

Formal evaluations. Formal evaluations of individual students conducted by educational specialists provide more detailed information that may help in decisions regarding interventions for students requiring additional support. An assessment instrument such as the *Diagnostic Assessment of Reading with Trial Teaching Strategies* (Roswell & Chall, 1991) draws together the information gathered while teaching with more formal assessment. It provides useful information on strengths and needs along with an opportunity to attempt a variety of instructional interventions while evaluating their effectiveness. For those students who appear to require intensive intervention, formal diagnostic testing is advisable. (See Chapters 11 and 12 of this volume.)

STRUCTURING THE BEGINNING READING CLASSROOM

Teachers in the early grades face a daunting task since their students are quite diverse in their language and literacy knowledge. This diversity in abilities requires substantial flexibility and reflection. Teachers need to provide direct instruction in decoding to students who are learning Stage 1 reading strategies, while providing advanced instruction to students who have mastered Stage 1 reading goals.

Characteristic of the beginning reading classroom is an atmosphere that "invites" learners to engage in spoken and written communication (Routman, 1994). This invitation is grounded in daily, engaging reading and writing experiences. Many teachers allocate at least a daily two-hour block to a reading-language arts program. This block is divided into half-hour segments during which students first participate in a whole group reading, listening, and discussion activity, then move to three other types of activities: guided reading and writing, shared reading and writing, and independent work with words.

Whole group segment. Teachers often begin the reading-language arts block by reading a story to the whole group. Typically, the teacher sits in front of the group of students gathered in the reading corner of the room. While reading aloud, the teacher involves learners in the reading by encouraging them to participate in the story and to respond to the story's content. At the same time, the teacher models effective decoding strategies by using techniques described earlier in this chapter.

For this activity, books are often chosen that use a letter-sound correspondence or word family that is under study. Teachers often use books with repetitive story parts, rhythm, and rhyme as well as songs. As students practice reading stories that contain a high percentage of the patterns that are under study, they can draw analogies between words that they have encountered and unfamiliar words that are consistent with previously learned patterns.

Appropriate stories, poems, and songs for group reading can be written on large sheets of chart paper or may be available as "Big Books." The use of large print facilitates group or "echo" reading in which learners repeat words and phrases as the teacher reads aloud. Beginning readers often need to read aloud since oral reading gives them an opportunity to connect print to speech. They also benefit from practicing word-recognition strategies while reading simple texts containing common words and phonetically regular words.

Guided segment. The heart of the daily instructional program is guided reading and writing—a 30 minute block during which the teacher works with a small group of students (e.g. Fountas & Pinnell, 1996). During guided reading, teachers provide direct instruction in word-recognition strategies using lesson plans such as the examples described earlier (p. 118, 122). Within each guided session, students learn and practice print-to-sound and sound-to-print word recognition and writing strategies.

In addition to direct reading and writing instruction in the four decoding skills and strategies described earlier, students read orally and discuss the reading as soon as they can recognize most of the words in a given selection. For those students who come to school already decoding text fluently, instruction is planned to increase their opportunities to read for meaning along with opportunities to improve their use of letter-sound correspondences in writing.

Some teachers suggest that all aspects of instruction can occur with mixed-ability grouping (Cunningham et al., 1991). However, many others continue to advocate homogeneous groups for the guided reading instruction half-hour block until decoding is mastered to better meet their students' diverse needs.

Teachers are encouraged to utilize flexible regrouping rather than static homogeneous groupings when ability grouping is instituted. Such regrouping lets teachers assess developing skills and regroup according to needs.

Shared segment. During the shared reading and writing segment, pairs of students work collaboratively in reading books and creating stories. At times, teachers find it useful to pair students of different abilities to provide help and encouragement during the shared reading of books. Other times, it is helpful to pair students of similar ability while they practice a skill to mastery, or enjoy shared reading of material they have mastered. Students practice reading aloud to one another, reread stories practiced earlier, and discuss or write about books they have read. They may also collaborate on practice exercises assigned by the teacher.

Beginning readers engage in paired reading and discussion by using books written with familiar language, predictable patterns, rhymes, and repetitive content words. In addition to tackling books on their own, these readers can discuss stories, reread stories, and engage in shared or guided reading with fluent readers.

Among the host of appropriate books and series for young beginning readers are the "I Can Read" Books such as *Little Bear* (Minarik, 1957), *A Bargain for Frances* (Hoban, 1970), *The Smallest Cow in the World* (Paterson, 1991), and *Frog and Toad* (Lobel, 1970). The "Puffin Easy-to-Read" books include titles such as *Tales of Oliver Pig* (Leeuwen, 1979), and the "Ready-to-Read" books include titles such as *Wiley and the Hairy Man* (Bang, 1976).

Independent segment. The final block of the program is devoted to independent work. For 30 minutes each day, students read self-selected books, write or draw in journals about their reading, complete practice exercises, or use computer software that provides additional practice. This is also a time for groups of students to engage in book talks or post-reading sharing activities. For students who can benefit from additional guided direct instruction, the independent block can be used instead to provide additional direct teaching such as the intensive approaches described later in this chapter.

During the independent segment, students sometimes engage in independent writing activities that can have a powerful effect on reading by reinforcing the association of symbols with sounds in word recognition. Beginning readers sometimes make an early entry into independent writing by the use of invented spelling. While teachers may reduce emphasis on spelling and editing skills to motivate students during the "idea generation" phase of writing, instruction should help students produce "final" copy that is grammatically correct and properly spelled. By taking the time to help learners proofread and edit text, teachers encourage beginning readers and writers to become attentive to correct spellings and sentence structure, which reinforces Stage 1 development.

Finally, it is of great importance that beginning readers develop a love of reading and come to see reading as an important activity for free-time and pleasure. Encouraging children to read for pleasure as well as to gather information is an important psychological component of the beginning reading phase of literacy.

INTENSIVE READING-LANGUAGE ARTS INTERVENTIONS

Many educators agree that early and intensive intervention is crucial to preventing later school failure. In addition to sparing children from years of school failure, such programs foster reading development and decrease the need for subsequent special education and remedial services (Slavin, 1996). A variety of instructional interventions have demonstrated success or shown promise in preventing reading failure. Two of these are described below: *Project READ* (Calfee & Wadleigh, 1992; Enfield, 1987), and *Success for All* (Slavin et al., 1996).

Project Read. *Project READ* (Enfield, 1987) is an intensive reading-and-writing approach that uses direct instruction to teach four strands: decoding-spelling, concept-vocabulary development, composition, and story reading. *Project READ* is considered a systematic and multisensory program that can be part of the daily classroom experience for all students. However, some schools use the program only for students who are behind most of their peers in reading ability. The program is generally used in grades one through three, although its materials go through grade nine. Many schools are using the program, and some cite impressive statistics concerning its effectiveness.

The decoding-spelling strand of *Project READ* is based upon the Orton-Gillingham-Stillman approach to the teaching of letter-sound correspondences (Greene & Enfield, 1986)   During Strand 1 of the reading program, students learn to decode one syllable words. As decoding abilities progress, this strand also teaches syllabication, recognition of affixes and roots, and the use of context and the dictionary to aid in word recognition. Strand 2 emphasizes vocabulary and comprehension as well as composition. Strand 3 focuses on writing, as students learn to form letters, spell, and create grammatical sentences.

Students read both linguistically controlled stories and texts with uncontrolled vocabulary. Semantic maps, story graphs, and analysis of story structure are used to help students develop comprehension and create stories. Finally, the program links instruction to assessment through observation of performance and portfolios.

In a typical phonics lesson, the teacher begins by reviewing sounds that were taught in earlier lessons. To emphasize reading, the teacher uses flash letter-cards as the students pronounce corresponding sounds. To emphasize spelling, the

134

teacher pronounces a sound, and students select the matching letter card. New sounds are introduced in a similar manner. In addition, students trace a letter as the sound is pronounced. Kinesthetic approaches include the use of a sand tray, raised letters, and tapping on a table. Students trace letters in the air, on a table, on raised-letter cards that show directionality, or on the board with chalk.

Practice in decoding words occurs as students blend sounds to read short words or syllables. Encoding (spelling) practice reinforces reading as students pronounce each sound while writing its corresponding letter. Oral reading follows as students point, to track each letter, while the sounds are blended. Students read phonetically regular words independently to reinforce correspondences that have been introduced, as in the following examples. The first example provides practice with **Pp-/p/**, **Hh-/h/**, **Jj-/j/**, and the second provides practice with **"Magic E"** and **Ii-/i/**).

Tan

Tan fan,
Tan pan,
Tan ham,
Tan jam.
Tan!
(Greene & Enfield, 1986, p. 11)

A Bike Trip

Mike had his red and white bike.
Mike was on a five mile trip.
Mike sat to rest.
His dog, Spike, was at his side.
"I like to bike," said Mike.
"Next time I will take a nine mile trip!"
(Greene & Enfield, 1986, p. 131)

Students are also encouraged to read any texts that interest them. Termed "stretch reading," this is an opportunity to read uncontrolled vocabulary. Teachers are urged to help with difficult text by pronouncing any words that students are unable to decode independently. Decoding and spelling are linked throughout the program, with emphasis on correct spelling as a means of learning the sequence of sounds in words. In addition, students are expected to use correct capitalization and punctuation. For example, the teacher reads a sentence aloud. Students write the sentences on paper. They correct their own work by underlining errors as the teacher spells aloud and writes the sentence on the board. Correct spellings, capitalization, and punctuation are written above errors.

Success For All. *Success For All* (Slavin et al., 1996) involves a comprehensive restructuring of the educational services provided to children in preschool through grade 5. The goal of *Success for All* is to accelerate the progress of at-risk students. *Success for All* was developed to ensure that students in participating Title I schoolwide programs develop adequate reading ability and receive the instruction needed for academic success. *Success For All* is implemented in many urban schools. It has documented success in drastically reducing retention and special education placements.

Beginning in grade 1, students are flexibly grouped cross-age and cross-grade for 90 minutes per day. This adaptation of the "Joplin Plan" allows a teacher to work with one reading level and to increase the time that a teacher can work with a group of students. Thus, many of the teachers in a school are teaching reading at the same time. In addition, adult tutors are used as teachers to further reduce class size.

The program emphasizes systematic study of print-to-sound correspondences, as students use auditory and visual skills to associate letters and sounds and to blend sounds to form words. As letters are learned, students read "little books" that contain phonetically regular language. Often, the reading of the "mini-books" takes place when pairs of students work together or during the 20 minutes of required reading at home assigned every night. An example of a *Success for All* lesson in the letter-sound correspondence for **Qq-/q/** follows:[5]

A. **Reading review**. A story that has been previously read is reviewed by the entire group or in pairs.

B. **Letter review**. The teacher then reviews letters introduced previously. Students trace the letters in the air, repeating a "cue phrase" that the students have come to associate with the letter.

---

[5]Slavin, R.E., Madden, N.A., Dolan, L.J., and Wasik, B.A. (1996). *Every child, every school: Success for All*. Thousand Oaks, CA: Corwin Press, 29-33; 41-47.

C. **New material**.

    1. *Alphabet song*.

    2. *Tongue twister*. The teacher says, "A lot of words start with the sound **/q/**. Listen to this. `The queen quickly poured the quacking duck some Quaker Oats.'" The teacher pronounces each word that starts with **/q/**, and students repeat each word.

    3. *Introduce /q/ pictures and objects*. A picture or object beginning with **/q/** is pulled from "Alphie's" box. Students name the objects. The objects are shown a second time, and students pronounce the sound they hear at the beginning of each word.

    4. *Make the /q/ sound*. Students make the sound and attend to its "feel." The teacher shows students that **/q/** is actually a blend of **/k/** and **/w/**.

    5. *Introduce the letter Qq*. Write the names of the objects on the board and confirm that the words do indeed begin with **Qq**.

    6. *Write the letter Qq*. Write both upper-case and lower-case forms, discussing the similarities and differences. Students trace **Qq** in the air as they say the cue phrase, "Circle left, up, down, hook right." They write the letter on paper, trace it on a peer's arm, etc. They then add the phrase, "The sound for **Qq** is **/kw/**." The teacher also explains that **Qq** is very shy and seldom goes anywhere without **Uu**: "Never a **q** without a **u**."

    7. *Games*. Several games follow to help students associate the letter and sound.

D. **Working with words.** Practice is provided in reading words that begin with **/qu/**.

E. **Reading practice.** Practice is provided in reading sight words beginning with **/qu/**. Students pronounce the word, use it in a sentence, and clap when they pronounce the target words.

F. **Shared story reading**. The teacher introduces a shared story that includes many examples of **/qu/** words, such as "The Duck in the Pond." The teacher begins by previewing the story with background questions.

    1. *Reading aloud*. The teacher reads the story aloud. A discussion follows regarding the story's meaning.

    2. *Words*. Phonetically regular and sight words are introduced. Students blend the sounds of the phonetically regular words (i.e. *quack*), provide a sentence for the word, and define the word. Sight words are presented on flashcards, pronounced, used in sentences, and spelled until students can identify them.

3. *Guided group reading.* The teacher uses a "teacher script" that offers an elaborated story line and questions and the students read a "student script." The teacher reads the "teacher script" first, followed by the "student script." Then, in unison, the students read their script.

4. *Partner reading.* Pairs of students reread the story to each other. Two comprehension questions follow partner reading. When the group reassembles, each pair responds to the questions. The teacher writes answers to the questions on the board to model the linking of spelling to sound. As students master stories, they are encouraged to read them to other peers or to take the stories home to read with their families.

In Title I programs using *Success for All,* assessment occurs every eight weeks. Students who are falling behind receive one-to-one tutoring from certified teachers. Title I resources are used for tutors—a critical component of the program. The program emphasizes prevention of academic failure by linking preschool and kindergarten instruction, which emphasizes language development and academic readiness, to the elementary program of intensive reading and writing instruction for grades 1 to 5. The program's explicit instruction in reading and writing, illustrated by the shared story lesson above, is enhanced further by low teacher-student ratios, ungraded instruction in reading, and involvement of families in the achievement of literacy.

Conclusion

Stage 1 of the reading process is a time when students are learning word recognition strategies that will help them decode print to understand text. Learning to recognize words requires a direct, systematic approach in which learners focus on the correspondence of letters to sound. Stage 1 learners need to practice decoding strategies with letters, words, and during the reading and writing of simple, meaningful text. Students achieve the paramount outcome of Stage 1 when they can read unfamiliar books composed predominantly of one-syllable words, with adequate comprehension.

Appendix B: Decoding & Comprehension Concepts (DCC) Guide
S. Brody (2001)

The following checklists and teaching guidelines concerning phonological decoding and basic reading comprehension can be used with novice readers of any age. Many teachers find the *DCC Guide* helpful in describing entry skills, planning sequential instruction, and measuring growth over time. The charts provide a convenient visual summary when sharing progress with parents or other professionals. The instructional guidelines offer a means of devising systematic instruction aligned with student needs measured by the charts. The charts can document one student's progress or record concepts introduced and practiced by a whole class. When using the charts for an individual, mark a slash (/) through each concept or example that the student performs proficiently during an informal pretest.

Basic Phonology Concepts	Sample Letter-clusters and Word-families
Continuant Consonants	f, m, n, s, w, r, v, z, l (sound can be extended, e.g. mmmmm)
Stop Consonants	p, t, d, b, k, g (sound cannot be extended)
Short Vowels	a, e, i, o, u
CVC Short Vowel Families (Make three-letter words from the examples by adding onset consonants.)	-at, -ap, -an, -al, -un, -ug, -up, -ut, -et, -en, -ed, -eg, -it, -in, -ip, -im, -ot, -og, -op, -ob (For example, turn -at into cat, hat, mat, rat, Nat, sat, bat, pat.)
Glue Words	is, are, was, were, the, a, an, in, on
R-Controlled Vowels	-ar, -or, -er, -ir, -ur car, far, tar
Double Consonants	ll, ss, zz, ff -ell, -iss, -uzz, -uff hiss, miss fuss, muss toss, loss
Initial Consonant Digraphs (two consonants—one sound)	ch, sh, th, wh, ph chop, shop, whop that, chat shin, chin, thin
Final Consonant Digraphs	sh, ch, th, ck -ash, -ush, -ath, -eck mash, gash, lash, rash
Initial Consonant Blends (two consonants—two sounds)	bl, cl, fl, gl, br, tr, fr, sc, sm, st, tw blob, blot, blab flat, flap, flag twig, brig
Final Consonant Blends	st, ng, ld, mp, nd, nt -est, -ast, -old nest, rest fang, hang
Silent Consonant Blends	kn, wr, gn knot, knob wrap, wren gnat, gnaw
Hard/Soft G	Hard generally precedes a,o,u/soft before e,i,y: gab, got gem, gin
Hard/Soft C	Hard generally precedes a,o,u/soft before e,i,y: cat, cot, cut cell
Long Vowel Sounds	a, e, i, o, u
CVCe Long Vowel-Consonant-Silent e	-ame, -ade, -ake, -ate, -ice, -ute, -ude, -oke fame, name, tame
Vowel Digraph (long-silent vowel pair)	oa, ai, ea, oe, ow, ay, ee boat, coat sail, rail heat, seat
Vowel Digraph (two vowels, 3rd sound)	oo, au, aw, ea, ew soon, moon haul, maul
Diphthongs (two vowels, joined sounds)	oi, ow, ou, oy boil, foil fowl, cowl soy, boy ouch
CV Words (one long vowel ends syllable)	me, go, I, he, we, she

Polysyllabic Phonology and Comprehension Concepts	Sample Letter-clusters, Word-families, and Comprehension Skills
Inflectional Endings	ed, ing, er, s, es, ly, est bat, batted, batting, batter, bats
Contractions	-n't, -'s, -'ll, -'re can't, doesn't, won't he'll, he's, we're
Plural vs Possession	-s, -es, -'s, -s' cat, cats, cat's, cats' (Show with written sentences.)
Compound Words	sailboat, railroad teaspoon, cookbook, somewhere, everything
Prefixes	in-, re-, un-, pre-, sub- inspire, invite, inform, inspect
Suffixes	-less, -ness, -ly, -fully, -ful, -ment, -tion -ance, -ence, ible, -able sadness, kindness, gentleness station, function, junction, action
Syllabic Strategies (Read letter-clusters in long words by six common patterns.)	VC bat/ting, VR bar/ter, V vi/o/(lin), VV sail/boat, VCe (in)/take, CLe (un)/cle
Speed and Accuracy	Read orally with good speaking rate and very few decoding errors. Match voicing to punctuation and content.
Story Patterns	Recognize common story starters (once upon a time), repeating patterns (three bears, five witches magic hats...), structures (beginning, middle, end).
Story Elements	Describe: character(s), setting(s), plot, problem, resolution, theme (message)
Fluency	During oral reading, effortlessly switch attention between meaning and decoding (as needed) while maintaining speed, accuracy, and intonation.

Sample Word-Family Practice Grid and Story
(See steps for use of this grid on following page.)

ab

tab	jab	gab	cab	lab
nab	cab	tab	lab	nab
dab	lab	gab	lab	nab
tab	cab	gab	nab	tab
nab	lab	cab	jab	dab

Nab a cab to the lab.
The tab for the cab is a dab.
Gab in the cab.

Instructional Guidelines: Planning lessons with the *DCC* Charts and Word-Family Grid

Teachers use the *DCC* charts to guide instruction in phonological decoding and comprehension concepts by creating grids and little stories similar to the *ab* example on the previous page, or by using published materials that present the phonological components with lists, grids, and stories. When preparing materials, it is best to make type-written, not hand-written, grids and sentences. Practice with standard print ensures easier transfer to future reading activities.

To select concepts appropriate for instruction, determine which phonological and comprehension concepts students: a) do not know, b) recognize but need to review, c) have mastered. This can be done by making flash cards with examples from the *DCC* charts and asking students to read the flash cards. Sort the cards by how well the concept is known. Follow the order of the *DCC Guide* while offering lessons only on concepts not mastered. When students are already in a polysyllabic reading program, but have occasional difficulty with a few basic phonology concepts, use the chart to note the challenging concepts and supplement the current program with DCC-based lessons. To begin:

1) **Introduce the concept** - state the concept—its letter(s), sound(s), and examples of two or three words in which it appears. For example, to begin a lesson on the letter cluster *–ab*, point to *ab* and say, "Look at *ab*, *ab* says /ab/." Then point to *tab* while saying, "See the *ab* in *tab, t ab, tab."* Then point to *jab* and say the same pattern. Have the student(s) repeat after you.

2) **Provide practice** with reading the concept **in word families** on a five-word by five-word grid. Students use the grid by reading words aloud left-to-right, then top-to-bottom. When a student hesitates with a word, point to the letters in the word, sound the letters one-by-one while pointing, sound the letter-cluster under study (such as *ab)*, then slide-point while reading the whole word. Ask the student to read the difficult word. After the student reads several other words, return to the difficult word for a quick recheck. Explain unknown word-meanings.

3) **Provide practice** with reading the concept **in sentences and stories** of several sentences. Students read sentences orally while paying careful attention to words following the concept pattern. After each sentence or after several sentences, ask students to state the meaning. When students are unsure, ask "Who (or what) was the sentence about," while pointing to the relevant word(s) in the sentence. Then ask, "What did (he, she, it, they) do?" Again, point to the relevant words. Ask the student to tell the meaning. (Explain unknown word-meanings.)

4) **Offer writing practice** with the concept **through dictation** of two or three words that use the concept, followed by two or three sentences using the word. Read dictation slowly, emphasize sounds, help students write the correct letters and link them with their sounds by repeating the sound until it is spelled correctly. Remind student(s) to check letter case and punctuation.

5) **Complete** the teaching session **with shared reading of a slightly challenging story** that uses the concept under study and/or reviews concepts studied earlier. Read together orally with the student reading words that have been studied, while the teacher fills in words not yet learned.

6) Generally, teach one new concept per lesson and **review** a few earlier concepts toward mastery. Some students need multiple lessons on one concept before a new concept is taught.

References

Adams, M.J. (1990). *Beginning to read: Thinking and learning about print.*

Anderson, R.C., Hiebert, E.H., Scott, J.A., & Wilkinson, I.A.G. (1985). *Becoming a nation of readers: The report of the Commission on Reading.* Champaign, IL: Center for the Study of Reading, University of Illinois at Urbana-Champaign.

Bader, L.A. (1998). *Bader Reading and Language Inventory (3rd ed.)* Columbus, OH: Merrill.

Bang, M. (1976). *Wiley and the hairy man.* NY: Macmillan.

Barr, R., & Johnson, B. (1997). *Teaching reading and writing in elementary classrooms (2nd ed.).* White Plains, NY: Longman.

Barr, R., Sadow, M., & Blachowicz, C. (1995). *Reading diagnosis for teachers (3rd ed.).* White Plains, NY: Longman.

Bloomfield, L., Barnhart, C.L., & Barnhart, R. K. (1965). *Let's read.* Cambridge, MA: Educators Publishing Service.

Brody, S. (2001). *The Brody reading manual: An implementation guide for teachers (2nd ed.).* Milford, NH: LARC Publishing. [http://www.LARCPublishing.com/]

Brown, M. (1982). *Wings on things.* NY: Beginner Books.

Burns, P.C. & Roe, B.D. (1999). *Informal reading inventory (5th ed.).* Boston: Houghton Mifflin.

Burns, P.C., Roe, B.D., & Ross, E.P. (1999). *Teaching reading in today's elementary schools (7th ed.).* Boston: Houghton Mifflin.

Calfee, R.C., & Wadleigh, C. (1992, September). How Project READ builds inquiring schools. *Educational Leadership, 50*(1), 28-32.

Chall, J.S. (1983). *Stages of reading development.* NY: McGraw-Hill.

Chall, J.S. (1996). *Learning to read: The great debate (3rd ed.).* Fort Worth, TX: Harcourt Brace.

Clay, M.M. (1993). *An observation survey of early literacy achievement.* Portsmouth, NH: Heinemann.

Cowley, J. (1990). *Painting.* Bothel, WA: The Wight Group.

Cunningham, P.H., Hall, D.P., & Defee, M. (1991). Non-ability-grouped, multilevel instruction: A year in a first-grade classroom. *The Reading Teacher, 44*(8), 566-571.

Dale, E., & Chall, J.S. (1948). A formula for predicting readability and instructions. *Educational Research Bulletin, 27,* 11-20; 37-54.

Ehri, L.C. (1996). Development of the ability to read words. In R. Barr, M.L. Kamil, P. Mosenthal, & P.D. Pearson (eds.), *Handbook of reading research* (Vol. 2, pp. 383-417). Mahway, NJ: Erlbaum.

Enfield, M.L. (1987). A cost effective classroom alternative to 'pull-out' programs. *Intimacy with language: A forgotten basic in teacher education*, 45-46.

Flesch, R. (1955). *Why Johnny can't read.* NY: Harper and Row.

Fountas, I.C., & Pinnell, G.S. (1996). *Guided reading: Good first teaching for all children.* Portsmouth, NH: Heinemann.

Gaskins, R.W., & Others (1991, March). A decoding program for poor readers - And the rest of the class, too! *Language Arts, 68*(3), 213-225.

142

Gattegno, C. (1968). *Words in color.* NY: Educational Solutions, Inc.

Geisel, T.S. (1960). *Green eggs and ham.* NY: Beginner Books.

Geisel, T.S. (1991). *Hop on pop by Dr. Seuss.* [Renewed copyright]. NY: Random House.

Glatthorn, A.A. (1998). *Performance assessment and standards-based curricula: The achievement cycle.* Larchmont, NY: Eye on Education.

Golden Step Ahead. (1989). Racine, WI: Western Publishing.

Goswami, U., & Mead, F. (1992). Onset and rime awareness and analogies in reading. *Reading Research Quarterly, 27*(2), 153-162.

Greene, T., & Enfield, M.L. (1986). *Project READ phonics guide (rev. ed.).* Bloomington, MN: Language Circle Enterprise.

Gregorich, B., & Henkel, A. (no date). *The big phonics book.* Grand Haven, MI: School Zone Publishing.

Harris, D.E., & Carr, J.F. (1996). *How to use standards in the classroom.* Alexandria, VA: Association for Supervision and Curriculum Development.

Heilman, A W. (1998). *Phonics in proper perspective (8th ed.).* Columbus, OH: Merrill.

Hoban, R. (1970). *A bargain for Frances.* NY: Harper & Row.

Juel, C. (1996). Beginning reading. In R. Barr, M.L. Kamil, P. Mosenthal, & P.D. Pearson (eds.), *Handbook of reading research* (Vol. 2, pp. 759-788). Mahway, NJ: Erlbaum.

Kendall, J., & Marzano, R.J. (1997). *Content knowledge: A compendium of standards and benchmarks for K-12 education (2nd ed.).* Alexandria, VA: Association for Supervision and Curriculum Development.

Leeuwen, J. (1979). *Tales of Oliver Frog.* NY: Puffin.

Leu, D.J., & Kinzer, C.K. (1999). *Effective literacy instruction, K-8 (4th ed.).* Columbus, OH: Merrill.

Lobel, A. (1981). *On market street.* NY: Greenwillow.

Lobel, A. (1970). *Frog and Toad are friends.* NY: Harper & Row.

Mann, H. (1842/1844/1965). Teaching young children to read, Vol IV., Method of teaching young children on their first entering school, Vol VI *The Common School Journal.* Boston: William B. Fowle and N. Capen. In Smith, N.B. (1965), *American reading instruction.* Newark DE: International Reading Association.

Martin, B. (1984). *Brown bear, brown bear, what do you see?* NY: Holt, Rinehart, Winston.

Marzano, R.J., & Kendall, J.S. (1996). *A comprehensive guide to designing standards-based districts, schools, and classrooms.* Alexandria, VA: Association for Supervision and Curriculum Development.

Minarik, M. (1957). *Little bear.* NY: Harper Trophy.

Mitchell, R., Willis, M., & Chicago Teachers Union Quest Center (1995). *Learning in overdrive: Designing curriculum, instruction, and assessment from standards.* Golden, CO: North American Press.

National Reading Panel (2000). *Report of the National Reading Panel: Teaching children to read.* Washington, DC: National Institute of Child Health and Human Development [available at http://www.nichd.nih.gov/publications/nrp]

Norton, D.E. (1999). *Through the eyes of a child: An introduction to children's literature (5th ed.).* Columbus, OH: Merrill.

Paterson, K. (1991). *The smallest cow in the world.* NY: Harper Trophy.

Rhodes, L.K. (ed.) (1992). *Literacy assessment: A handbook of instruments.* Portsmouth, NH: Heinemann.

Rhodes, L.K., & Shanklin, N. (1993). *Windows into literacy.* Portsmouth, NH: Heinemann.

Roswell, F., & Chall, J. (1991). *Diagnostic Assessment of Reading with Trial Teaching Strategies.* Chicago: Riverside Publishing Company.

Routman, R. (1988). *Transitions.* Portsmouth, NH: Heinemann.

Routman, R. (1994). *Invitations: Changing as teachers and learners K-12 (Rev. ed.).* Portsmouth, NH: Heinemann.

Schmoker, M., & Marzano, R.J. (1999, March). Realizing the promise of standards-based education. *Educational Leadership, 56*(6), pp. 17-21.

Seuss, Dr. (1957). *The cat in the hat.* NY: Random House.

Seuss, Dr. (1960). *One fish, two fish, red fish, blue fish.* NY: Beginner Books.

Slavin, R.E. (1996). Neverstreaming: Preventing learning disabilities. *Educational Leadership, 53*(6), 4-7.

Slavin, R.E., Madden, N.A., Dolan, L.J., & Wasik, B.A. (1996). *Every child, every school: Success for All.* Thousand Oaks, CA: Corwin Press.

Smith, N.B. (1986). *American reading instruction (3rd ed.).* Newark, DE: International Reading Association.

Snow, C.E., Burns, M.S., & Griffin, P. (Eds.) (1998). *Preventing reading difficulties in young children.* Washington, DC: National Academy Press.

Stahl, S.A. (1992). Saying the "P" word: Nine guidelines for exemplary phonics instruction. *The Reading Teacher, 45*(8), 618-625.

Sulzby, E. (1985). Children's emergent reading of favorite storybooks: A developmental study. *Reading Research Quarterly, 20*, 458-481.

Swartz, S.L., & Klein, A.F. (1997). *Research in Reading Recovery.* Portsmouth, NH: Heinemann.

Trachtenburg, P. (1990). Using children's literature to enhance phonics instruction. *The Reading Teacher, 43*, 648-654.

Tucker, M.S., & Codding, J.B. (1998). *Standards for our schools: How to set them, measure them, and reach them.* San Francisco, CA: Jossey-Bass.

U.S. Department of Education (1997). *The seven priorities of the U.S. Department of Education.* Washington, DC: Author.

Wildsmith, B. (1962). *Brian Wildsmith's ABC.* NY: Watts.

Wixson, K.K., & Dutro, E. (1998). Standards for primary-grade reading: An analysis of state frameworks. *CIERA Report #3-001.* Ann Arbor, MI: University of Michigan, Center for the Improvement of Early Reading Achievement.

Woods, M.L., & Moe, A.J. (1999). *Analytical reading inventory (6th ed.).* Columbus, OH: Merrill.

Zemelman, S., Daniels, H., & Hyde, A. (1998). *Best Practice: New standards for teaching in America's schools (2nd ed.).* Portsmouth, NH: Heinemann.

Chapter 5: Advanced Decoding and Fluency

Linda W. Kemper, PhD
Rivier College

Sara Brody, EdD

Readers enter Stage 2 when they consistently apply phonetic skills to monosyllabic words, use a somewhat considerable sight vocabulary, and sound out simple stories (Chall, 1996). In order to develop **fluency**, Stage 2 readers engage in extensive reading of familiar stories while receiving instruction in advanced decoding skills (National Reading Panel [NRP], 2000). Together, these activities generally lead to automaticity—immediate recognition of simple words, swift recognition of longer, more complex words, and rapid, nearly flawless decoding of connected text. Such automaticity generally enables readers to shift their attention from decoding to meaning in order to enjoy literature and understand expository text.

As with any automatic skill, reading fluency develops through extensive practice. When readers possess effective word-identification strategies, adequate rapid-naming skill, and read regularly, they tend to engage in a cycle of becoming better, more avid readers, through reading. This cycle develops ever stronger vocabulary and background knowledge, increases understanding of syntax and semantics, and enhances understanding of the printed word. Consequently, exposure to print is a crucial factor in predicting long-term development of reading and other verbal skills (Lyon, 2000; Jordan, Snow, & Porche, 2000; Stanovich, 1986). Teachers encourage reading and the desire to interact with books by helping their students acquire the fluency that stimulates reading pleasure and success.

This chapter discusses the development of reading fluency among Stage 2 readers. It begins by exploring two aspects that contribute to decoding automaticity: reading practice, and the learning of advanced decoding skills. Next, comprehension issues are examined, particularly among children with limited exposure to literature. Finally, automatic processes that underlie reading fluency are considered with emphasis on the processes of rapid-serial-naming and attention-switching to produce smooth reading with understanding.

Throughout the chapter, instructional suggestions are offered for readers in elementary classrooms who typically enter Stage 2 in second or third grade. In addition, techniques are recommended for learners of all ages who experience difficulty in making the transition to fluent reading when they lack advanced decoding skills, automatic-processing skills, or sufficient reading practice.

Decoding Automaticity

It was once believed that skilled readers use context clues to facilitate word recognition. However, extensive research reported by Stanovich (1994), indicates that "...word recognition processes of the skilled reader [are] so rapid and automatic that they [do] not need to rely on contextual information" (p. 282). It is now generally accepted that automatic word recognition, achieved through swift and accurate decoding, frees readers' cognitive resources to concentrate on local and global meaning. All attention can focus on comprehension for the purpose of schema construction without the drain of identifying single words. In contrast, less-skilled readers rely heavily on context for word identification; this leads to slow, and sometimes labored, reading (NRP, 2000; Snow, Burns & Griffin, 1998; Stanovich, 1984; Stanovich & West, 1981; 1983; Stanovich, West, & Feeman, 1981).

During mature reading, eye movement is rapid and sequential with the reader's eyes resting on words in linear order. In contrast, the use of context for word identification often requires less-skilled readers to study a complete sentence then return to a challenging word, a process that is reflected in recursive eye movements. Until readers develop automatic decoding skills, their reliance on contextual information to identify words redirects eye movement, slows word recognition rate and, in turn, impedes the process of comprehension (Just & Carpenter, 1981, 1987).

Since readers who lack decoding automaticity need to focus most of their attention on consciously identifying individual words, their attention is drawn away from developing a schema of the story. Whether non-automatic word identification is attempted through use of letter-by-letter decoding, the use of rhyming families, or efforts to guess single words from context clues, the process draws attention away from the more advanced work of constructing an understanding of the text (Bloom, 1986; Perfetti, 1985; Pressley, 2000).

Effective teachers provide instruction in advanced decoding strategies by offering lessons that present specific phonological (letter-cluster/sound decoding) concepts systematically as well as by discussing these concepts as they arise during reading of connected text, for practice and pleasure. Systematic instruction begins with the presentation of a specific decoding concept. Students then practice reading stories and passages that include many examples of the target concept. To supplement systematic instruction, teachers can include lessons that begin with the reading of a story and then pause, when a challenging word appears, to present an advanced decoding concept.

The following discussion examines two important aspects of enhancing automaticity—reading practice and the learning of specific decoding skills. To simplify presentation, separate sections describe the repeated reading of connected text and the teaching of advanced decoding skills. However, effective instruction typically combines both types of strategies within a single reading lesson.

PRACTICE WITH CONNECTED TEXT

Stage 2 readers develop automaticity with newly gained decoding skills through plenty of oral reading practice during broad exposure to connected text. As confidence develops, readers move from word lists and controlled texts to simple literature and expository materials. To help learners feel comfortable with reading, teachers provide a wealth of interesting books that (a) match a variety of reading levels and (b) reinforce advanced decoding skills being explicitly taught. When students practice often with such materials, they generally decode unfamiliar words with ease, and enjoy spending a great deal of time reading.

As learners begin their wide reading to develop automaticity, text with natural language and familiar content encourages them to continue reading (Adams, 1994; Chall, 1996; Snow, Burns, & Griffin, 1998). The familiar language confirms that material was decoded accurately; and, in turn, accurate decoding develops students' confidence. As students engage in reading, books provide models of proper and natural syntax, a wide range of vocabulary, and motivation to continue reading to experience the pleasure of engaging with a variety of interesting topics and genres.

The more time learners spend practicing with familiar material at this level, the more likely they are to move smoothly to Stage 3 where they read to learn about unfamiliar topics. A variety of instructional strategies encourage Stage 2 learners to read often and widely in order to develop decoding automaticity. The suggestions offered below synthesize many techniques appearing in journals, basals, and reading texts and have been reported as useful by classroom teachers during informal observation and discussion (Cooper, 1993; Heilman, 1998; Leslie & Allen, 1999; Leu & Kinzer, 1999; NRP, 2000; Routman, 1994; Savage, 1994; Tunnell & Jacobs,1989).

Select appropriate materials. An environment in which many books are available encourages students to read (Chall, 1996). Appropriate reading materials match learners' interests and are varied in subject and genre. Books that invite reading facilitate independent practice. During early practice with connected text, beginners use short passages that allow them to experience progress as they read slowly to concentrate on each word. Shorter passages at the beginning provide readers with the confirmation that comes with understanding a meaningful piece of text within a brief time span.

Picture books with repetitive patterns (sometimes referred to as "predictable books") are appropriate for younger readers. These books present interesting stories using repetition of ideas and words to reinforce understanding and boost confidence in word recognition skills. Teachers sometimes create short passages that use controlled vocabulary to support fledgling readers. At times, students and teachers create a short story together that can be read many times until it is read fluently (Leu & Kinzer, 1999; Morrow; 1997).

Older students who need to develop automaticity also begin with short readings in which sentence and word length are adjusted to match their reading level. Materials for older students are written in one-page passages that begin as single paragraphs and expand as reading ability and confidence increase. Appropriate content of short passages for older students may include topics such as current events, sports, nature, exploration, or the experiences of characters who draw on inner strength to overcome adversity. Collections of passages at increasing levels of difficulty are available from sources such as Educators

Publishing Service, Jamestown Publishers, LARC Publishing, New Readers' Press, Readers' Digest, Scholastic, and Steck-Vaughn. Or, if sufficient scaffolding is provided by the teacher, students can practice reading paragraphs from newspapers, magazines, or class textbooks (Brody, 2001).

Check and adjust passage difficulty frequently. Diverse needs exist within any classroom. Some students in the early elementary grades have substantial, successful experience with language and books. They eagerly approach books and tackle print enthusiastically. These students progress easily in a solid Stage 2 developmental reading program that provides ample reading materials, adequate time for reading, along with ongoing instruction, encouragement, and appreciation from a teacher who supports their progress.

Other learners, whose exposure to print may be limited, feel less comfortable with books. Since reading does not come as easily for them, they need additional support and encouragement to increase the likelihood that they will practice reading often. In order to develop fluency, these students need to spend more time reading texts that are written with short words and simple sentences before taking on texts that present longer words and complex sentences.

Teachers ensure that students practice for fluency at their highest comfort-level by checking reading progress frequently. Careful monitoring, through informal records of oral reading accuracies and errors along with notes concerning quality of intonation, expression, attention to punctuation, and grasp of content, assures that each reader progresses to the next level as soon as possible (Leu & Kinzer, 1999). When students demonstrate proficiency in materials at one level, the length of stories or passages, as well as word and content difficulty, are adjusted. (For a sample teacher-made reading inventory to assess oral reading informally, see Appendix C, p. 168. And for a guide to record knowledge of specific phonology concepts, see Appendix B, Chapter 4, page 138.)

Guided oral reading. Findings of the National Reading Panel [NRP] (2000, p.7), indicate that:

> ...guided repeated oral reading procedures that included guidance from teachers, peers, or parents had a significant and positive impact on word recognition, fluency, and comprehension across a range of grade levels....These results also apply to all students—good readers as well as those experiencing reading difficulties. (p.7).

These findings have appeared in a variety of classroom studies (Juel & Minden-Cupp, 2000; Leslie & Allen, 1999; Stahl, 1997). Key elements involve modeling of pronunciation, tone, pace by a skilled reader; direct explicit corrective and/or confirming feedback to the novice as words are read; discussion of meaning interjected during the reading; and multiple opportunities for the novice to reread the story or passage orally multiple times to a peer or adult.

Prereading.   An effective approach to introducing guided oral reading involves oral prereading of a story to students by a skilled reader. Stahl (1997) found very positive results with second-graders when using the following procedure. First, the teacher prereads the story aloud to the class. Next, relevant background and vocabulary are presented in a teacher-led discussion that also invites student-generated questions. Then the passage is read orally by students in many venues such as small group, home, and peer pairs.

Oral recitation.   Oral recitation lessons (ORL) offers a group-reading approach to develop fluency (Hoffman, 1985). ORL involves three "routines" or segments used in succession. First, during a direct instruction segment, the teacher introduces a story, reads it aloud as a model, discusses it with students, and helps students summarize it. Next, students read the story chorally, as a group, with teacher assistance as needed. Finally, students take turns reading sections orally to the class. In a study with second graders, students taught with this method demonstrated improved fluency and comprehension (Reutzel & Hollingsworth, 1993).

Paired reading.   Reading with a peer or a more-skilled reader expands opportunities for repeated practice (Leslie, & Allen, 1999; Reutzel & Cooter, 1996; Vacca, Vacca, & Gove, 1999). As described above, when students pair with an adult, the adult reads first to provide a model. Then student and adult take turns reading, discussing, and rereading each part of the story or passage until the learner reads the story fluently. To initiate paired reading activities among peers, a teacher introduces a story by reading it aloud while discussing challenging vocabulary to clarify decoding, word meaning, and story content. After hearing the story and participating in the discussion, peers read stories to each other many times.

During paired reading, the teacher circulates to help with pronunciation and to assess when children are ready for more challenging text. The teacher also encourages students to sound out difficult words rather than passing over them to finish quickly. When students have practiced sufficiently in pairs to read their stories fluently, they read to different adults, volunteers, friends, people at home, or to younger children.

Independent reading time. In contrast to guided oral reading, many classrooms and schools allocate fifteen-to-twenty minutes each day to independent reading through silent reading programs such as Drop Everything And Read (D.E.A.R.) or Sustained Silent Reading (S.S.R.) (Savage, 1994; Vacca, Vacca, & Gove, 1999). Although such programs are popular, the NRP (2000) found no methodologically sound evidence to either support or refute the benefit of this practice for reading fluency at Stage 2.

> In other words, even though encouraging students to read more [silently] is intuitively appealing, there is still not sufficient research evidence obtained from studies of high methodological quality to support the idea that such efforts…result in improved reading skills. (p.8).

Perhaps allocated silent reading time is so intuitively appealing that researchers have not given it careful study. The NRP (2000) report may spur researchers to look at this issue closely in the coming years. If teachers decide to allocate time to silent reading, it is important to remember that while it is a pleasure for skilled readers, it may not be the best use of instruction time for less-advantaged readers who may need more guidance. The following procedure may enhance the use of allocated reading time for less-skilled readers.

Multiple rereadings of recorded stories. With guidance described below, multiple rereadings of recorded stories offers an alternative to silent, independent reading that lets less-skilled readers practice when a partner is not available. Repetition of recorded stories offers a model to make reading practice enjoyable and motivating. Chomsky (1978) formalized the strategy as a means of assisting students who possess basic phonics skills yet need further support to develop reading fluency. Students with less-developed phonology skills could use the procedure for independent practice on material they have already learned.

Chomsky's approach guides readers to "shift their focus from the individual word to connected discourse and to integrate their somewhat fragmented knowledge" (p. 18). She draws on recorded readings, followed by student/teacher interactions, to teach children about the richness of language and the nature of its structure. The approach was researched in a third-grade classroom over four months. During the study, children began to select reading as a preferred activity, to write more often, and to transfer their newfound knowledge to unfamiliar stories with enhanced confidence (Chomsky, 1978).

In Chomsky's approach, readers choose books from a large set preselected by the teacher. The students listen to recordings of their books every day, using headphones, while following along with the printed text. Students replay parts of their tapes often, while rereading sections of their books, many times. As sections of the story are practiced, learners read along with the master tape or record their reading onto another tape. Further, individualized phonics instruction, for any challenging words, is offered in the meaningful context of the increasingly familiar story that highlights its relevance. Children's progress is checked often by adults who listen to the students read as much of their stories as they are ready to share.

Classroom teachers can implement **recorded reading** in the following way. First develop a collection of matching tapes and books by gathering together existing sets and by working with volunteers to make tapes of favorite, short books that are already in the classroom. Next, package the tapes and books in sets to save time when students are searching for materials. Display the sets in a prominent spot in the classroom. Arrange one area of the room with seating, cassette players, and headphones.

Summary of practice with connected text. Whatever the strategy, activities designed to develop fluency include a model of fluent reading, opportunities for plenty of practice, and exposure to interesting materials that motivate students to ever more reading practice (NRP, 2000; Samuels, Schermer, & Reinking, 1992). Generally, teachers and students select books or passages in which the majority of the individual words can be read independently, while fluent reading of the selection, as a whole, remains a challenge. The teacher's reading of the passage is used to model expression, articulation, and fluency. During and after reading, the content is discussed to develop comprehension, work through troublesome words, and clarify word meanings. Students practice reading and rereading in order to develop automaticity with the target passage as well as to transfer automaticity to other materials.

The old adage, "Practice makes perfect," summarizes the focus of instruction designed to improve automaticity. When students read orally often, they become more comfortable with reading and begin to read in many settings. Broader practice with oral reading leads to greater speed and accuracy in word recognition. By engaging in a positive, self-perpetuating cycle, readers develop confidence, read more often, increase their vocabulary, and develop greater understanding (Lyon, 2000; Stanovich, 1986).

ADVANCED DECODING STRATEGIES

As students develop automaticity and confidence in reading simple text, they venture to attempt more advanced material. In their wider reading, students encounter polysyllabic words that cannot be identified with only the basic strategies of letter-sound correspondences, rhyme patterns, sight vocabulary, and context clues. For example, we, as fluent readers, have forgotten the challenges presented to Stage 2 readers who attempt to decode sentences such as, "Pollution is important for us to consider." Without the additional knowledge of syllabication strategies and common suffixes, sentences that rely on the decoding and understanding of polysyllabic words can discourage readers whose decoding skills are limited.

As they progress in Stage 2, readers need additional strategies to consistently figure out longer, less-familiar words. Advanced decoding instruction teaches readers to recognize inflectional endings, compound words, affixes, root words, contractions, and syllabic patterns. These **structural analysis** skills allow readers to analyze a word's construction and sound out its familiar parts. By learning common letter-cluster/sound patterns, readers increase their ability to recognize unfamiliar words (Brody, 1985, 1986a, 2001; NRP, 2000; Roswell & Chall, 1994).

Since Stage 2 readers vary in their knowledge of word elements, effective teaching needs to match instruction with individuals' levels of achievement. Systematic, direct instruction is necessary for teaching unfamiliar decoding elements. Direct, guided practice increases familiarity with elements that are known but not recognized with confidence. In addition, oral reading encourages progress from familiarity to automaticity. The discussion that follows describes advanced decoding elements and suggests a variety of strategies for their instruction.

Inflectional endings. Students encounter common inflectional endings during Stage 1 and Stage 2 reading. Readers who do not recognize them readily need direct instruction and practice in noticing *-s, -ed, -ing, -ly, -er,* and *-est* (Brody, 2001; Moats, 2000). These inflectional endings often are introduced by writing a known word (such as *bat*) on the board and asking students to say the word. The inflectional ending *-s* is added and the teacher states that the word now means "more than one." Students read the new word. After this process is repeated with many words and the same inflection, a target word with multiple inflections is used to teach changes in endings.

Some students have difficulty not only in differentiating among inflectional endings but also in noticing **whether** an ending is present. These students often read only the first syllable or first few letters of a word and then guess the rest from context. Learning to read all parts of a word, rather than guessing the ending, can develop when students practice with word lists or flash cards in which the base word remains constant and only the inflectional **endings** change. After reading words on lists, students practice noticing endings of words in context by reading sentences composed of target words along with their various inflectional endings. In addition, students may practice by responding to oral or written sentences by filling in blanks with the target words, with or without inflectional endings. For example:

(dog, dogs)   Five _____ ran through my yard.
               My _____, Shep, ate his dinner.

Compound words. While mastering basic inflections, students also begin to encounter compound words. Teachers foster students' awareness of compound words by asking students to notice small words within larger words. For example, they point out that a *firefighter* is a *fighter* who puts out a *fire*.

Many compound words are introduced in the primary grades, or during Stage 2 reading for older students; some of these include: *into, outside, inside, within, mailman, fisherman, landlady, upon, something, baseball, sailboat, roadway, moonlight, airplane, waterfall, notebook, herself,* and *anyone* (Heilman, 1998).

Many beginning readers are unaware of compound words and need instruction that goes beyond encouragement to look for compound words or to divide longer words into their component parts. Teachers can introduce the concept of compound words by beginning with familiar words. First the compound word is presented (either in text, on the chalkboard, or on a card) and students are asked to find the two small words in the larger word. As students identify them, the teacher circles the two words and explains that the two words were "put together" to form one **compound word**. Additional compound words are presented and students are asked to identify the small words within the word. Again, the smaller words are circled to note them clearly. Compound words can also be presented on separate cards with each smaller word written in a different color to aid students in discriminating and attending to the separate words.

Students can practice building and segmenting compound words by playing a matching game in which they select two small word-cards to form one compound word. For example, a game card for *baseball* is made by writing the word on an index card in large print and cutting the card in half between *base* and *ball*. *Baseball* is written on the back of each half-card to allow for self-checking. Separate pieces of several compound words are placed on a table and students search for two halves that form a compound word. They look on the back of each half to check their accuracy and engage in additional practice in reading the parts and reading the whole word. Cards also can be cut in varied shapes to let the puzzle configurations assist younger readers in self-checking.

Affixes and base words. Stage 2 readers often need direct instruction to notice **affixes**, the prefixes and suffixes added to base words to alter their meanings. When teaching affixes, it is important to discuss meaning as well as decoding of the words. Common **prefixes** include: *after-, dis-, extra-, counter-, inter-, mid-, mini-, mis-, non-, post-, pre-, re-, sub-, super-,* and *un-*. Common **suffixes** include: *-able, -ance, -tion, -less, -ness, -ful, -ment,* and *-able* (Bebko, Alexander, & Doucet, 1998; Brody, 1984; Heilman, 1998).

Prefixes and suffixes are introduced separately. The teacher begins by presenting a base word such as *pay* and reviewing its meaning. Next a prefix, such as *re-* is added, and students are asked to pronounce the new word. The change in meaning is discussed to convey that each affix carries meaning and that *repay* means to pay again. In order to help students understand the meaning of the prefix, other examples are provided using the same prefix, but different base words. Suffixes are introduced in the same way.

Students need to use their knowledge of affixes when reading connected text. When readers hesitate at a word with an affix, teachers can remind them, "This is a word with a suffix (prefix)," and then direct the student to, "Find the base word." This procedure guides students to help themselves by using affixes as part of the decoding process while reading for pleasure.

To provide additional awareness and practice in identifying common affixes, teachers and students can create prefix and suffix charts and display them in the classroom. Such charts include common affixes, their meanings, and examples of words constructed from the affixes as shown in Figure 5.a, below.

Many words constructed with prefixes and suffixes are part of most Stage 2 readers' speaking and listening vocabularies. As readers learn to recognize common affixes during advanced decoding instruction and practice, they more easily identify additional words from their listening vocabularies when they appear in print. Practice in identifying words by reading their affixes leads to greater automaticity during reading of more advanced material.

PREFIXES		
Prefix	**Meaning**	**Examples**
re-	to do again	repay, redo, remake, retell
un-	not	unfair, unlike, unbelievable
pre-	to do before	prepay, prejudge

SUFFIXES		
Suffix	**Meaning**	**Examples**
-less	without	hopeless, careless, homeless
-ness	quality or state of	happiness, playfulness
-ful	full of	hopeful, cheerful, gleeful

Figure 5.a. Prefix and suffix charts.

Complex base words and affixes. It is convenient and effective to introduce affixes and **base words** simultaneously. Although students often recognize simple combinations, many readers need direct instruction to master the more complex constructions. Lessons in the analysis of words such as *disagreeable, reconstruction, imperfection, displacement,* and *uncomfortable* help prepare students to decode the challenging words in advanced textbooks with accuracy.

Analysis of complex polysyllabic words can be taught with the following steps. First, several such words are listed on the board, on cards, or on charts. The teacher selects the first word (for example, *disagreeable*) and asks a student to identify and read its base by dropping the prefix and suffix. The teacher assists by circling the prefix and suffix, as needed, so that the student can identify *agree* as the base. Next, the teacher asks the student to read the prefix (*dis*), and the suffix (*able*). Finally, the student is asked to "put the word together" by reading each part in order. The process is continued with other words on the list. Then students read a small text selection that incorporates several of the words under study.

When a brief introduction is insufficient, it is helpful to introduce many words of similar construction in order to help students identify specific affixes automatically (Brody, 2001). For example, students may study a list of words ending in *tion*, then a list of words ending in *ous*, and next a list of words ending in *able*. Again, reading of the words on lists is followed by reading a small text selection that incorporates the base or affix pattern. Opportunities to construct complex words from base words and affixes are also helpful (Biemiller, 2000; Heilman, 1998; Steere, Peck, & Kahn, 1971), as in the following exercise:

> *Select from the prefixes and suffixes below to construct a word that replaces the underlined word(s).*
>
> **Prefixes:** *dis, un, re, pre*
> **Suffixes:** *ful, ment, ness, less, able*
>
> 1. My friend and I <u>do not agree</u> on which movie to see.
>   (_____agree)
>
> 2. I had to <u>pay</u> the bill <u>again</u>.
>   (_____pay).
>
> 3. The ache in my tooth is <u>giving me pain</u>.
>   (pain_____)

Contractions. Some students need many exposures in order to recognize contractions, while other learners generalize easily from a few examples. When presenting contractions, explain that they are words formed from two words, by omitting one or more letters, and inserting an apostrophe. Point out that contractions have the same meaning as the two original words. Model contractions by writing several sets of words on the board, erasing the appropriate letters, and filling in an apostrophe. At the same time, ask students to follow the model on their own papers.

Some students need the additional support of learning common contractions one set at a time. The chart in Figure 5.b, below, can be posted in an elementary classroom or copied into the writing notebook of an older student as a ready reference.

Not n't		will 'll	is 's	are 're
does not doesn't	Cannot can't	you will you'll	he is he's	we are we're
did not didn't	would not wouldn't	she will she'll	she is she's	you are you're
is not isn't	could not couldn't	he will he'll	it is it's	they are they're
has not hasn't	should not shouldn't	they will they'll		

Figure 5.b. Chart of common contractions.

Syllabic patterns.   Another approach to analysis of polysyllabic words teaches students to read longer words in small, manageable parts by dividing the words into syllable-sized chunks and identifying the sounds of these smaller units. Students read each segment, then blend the segments to read a whole word. Readers use word lists or word cards to practice identifying common syllabic patterns.   Teachers encourage students to divide words in small segments that approximate syllabic patterns, rather than striving for precise dictionary divisions. This enables students to use the strategy with ease and independence. In addition to word-list practice, students use the strategy when polysyllabic words appear in passages, news articles, and texts. Further practice occurs during writing activities (Brody, 1984).

Programs that teach identification of words through segmentation-by-syllables generally teach six common syllabic types. The markings and names for the syllables vary, but the patterns remain the same across programs since they reflect the syllabic structure of English words. For example, Brody (2001) uses the pattern names that appear in Figure 5.c.

158

Common Syllable Patterns (Brody, 1984, 2001)

VC -   a single vowel (short) followed by a consonant,
         as in *cat* or *is*.

VR -   a single vowel followed by the consonant *r*,
         as in *car* or *her*.

V -   a single vowel (long) ending a syllable,
         as in *me* or *go*.

VV -   two adjacent vowels giving one vowel sound,
         as in *boat* or *seen*.

VCe -   a single vowel (long) followed by a consonant and
         silent *e*, as in *like* or *fame*.

CLe -   a consonant followed by the letter *l* and silent *e*,
         as in *uncle* or *apple*.

Figure 5.c. Chart of common syllable patterns.

Summary of advanced decoding skills. Stage 2 learners practice decoding strategies and read widely in connected text in order to develop automaticity. Identification of polysyllabic words is enhanced by knowledge of word-analysis strategies such as recognition of inflections, compound words, affixes and base words, contractions, and syllabic patterns. As students learn word analysis techniques, they read literature or expository text written at a level that reinforces their decoding skills and lets them increase their automaticity. Effective teachers adjust the amount of instruction in word-analysis skills to match the needs of individual students. Good instruction provides time for plenty of practice and application during oral reading of interesting literature and expository text.

Comprehension

In addition to accurate and speedy decoding, reading fluency depends on rapid recognition of common literary and expository forms at the sentence, paragraph, and story level (NRP, 2000; Spiegel & Whaley, 1980; Stanovich, 1986). Students without learning disabilities who have been read to often, by others, are more likely to recognize simple literary conventions such as repeated refrains, rhyming words, and dialogue patterns. When these students read, knowledge of literary conventions enables them to check that they have decoded accurately and that they have interpreted the text content meaningfully. Such confirmation is reassuring and encourages further reading.

Research indicates that there is a direct relationship between readers' listening comprehension and their reading comprehension (deLone, 1990; Stanovich, 1993). Teachers can assess students' listening comprehension level informally by asking questions related to a story read to them or by asking students to retell a story (Bembridge, 1994; Brown & Cambourne, 1987; Glazer, 1992). DeFina (1992) offers a helpful checklist for assessing comprehension through retelling. A hearing check, initially by the school nurse, is also important when listening or reading comprehension are in question.

Unless a learning-disability is present, students who come to Stage 2 with a solid background in vocabulary meanings and literary language often develop automatic decoding and begin to comprehend written stories with ease when provided with advanced decoding instruction and plenty of reading practice. Their understanding of stories, developed during earlier listening experiences, prepares them to comprehend any materials that they can decode (Chall, 1996). These students have developed an understanding of story syntax and discourse through their past involvement in listening to and discussing stories (Irwin, 1986; Pressley, 2000).

These students possess **syntactic** knowledge—awareness of how the **order** in which words are placed within a sentence communicates meaning (Goldman & Rakestraw, 2000; Leu & Kinzer, 1999). Although students may not understand the terms *noun* and *verb*, they can select a word of correct, syntactic form to complete sentences. A solid base of syntactic knowledge enables readers to anticipate and confirm when words have been read correctly within a sentence.

Students with substantial syntactic knowledge also make use of **discourse knowledge**, an understanding of various types of writing (newspapers, fairy tales, fiction, nonfiction, mysteries, etc.). Discourse knowledge helps readers form a framework within which to understand the text they are reading. For example, when a story begins with, "Once upon a time..." readers with knowledge of literary discourse recognize that a fairy tale is beginning. These readers anticipate a fairy tale, frame their schemata of the story as a fairy tale, and expect elements of a fairy tale to emerge.

When students listen to stories often while being guided to recognize the elements of character, plot, setting, problem, and resolution, they build discourse understanding. These better-prepared readers also become familiar with cause and effect in stories (if Goldilocks eats the porridge, they expect that the bears will be upset). Such readers understand story sequence (*first*, Goldilocks sits in the chairs, *next*, she eats the porridge, *then*, she sleeps in the beds). When students are familiar with common story elements, their understanding of common structures confirms that readings have been decoded and comprehended with accuracy.

Increasing familiarity with literary language. Students who have had little exposure to print need to learn the basic conventions of literary language in addition to learning to decode print. They need to hear stories read aloud and participate in guided discussions of stories. In order to help students increase their understanding of literary conventions, teachers read to their students often and encourage them to reread stories from books that can be decoded with relative ease (Leslie & Allen, 1999).

During reading, teachers interject relevant questions regarding literal and inferential comprehension. Literal questions, which seek specific information written in the text, tend to be easier for students to answer. When literal answers elude readers, teachers encourage them to reread a pertinent section of text and, if necessary, point to the exact words in which the answer is located. Students then reread the sentence that contains the answer. Finally, they state the answer in their own words.

Inferential questions, which ask for information not specifically stated in the text, are also asked during or after reading. These questions are more difficult for students with limited knowledge of literary conventions since answers often depend on an understanding of what is implied or anticipated by the convention. For example, if asked what Goldilocks will do next after lying on Mama Bear's bed, a reader who knows the repetition convention suspects that she will head for Baby Bear's bed, while a student who is unfamiliar with the convention is unsure. In order to expand readers' understanding of story pattern, the teacher and students look back in the story to note how Goldilocks has gone from one chair to another, then one porridge to another, and then to the beds.

During reading, teachers ask questions concerning main characters, and discuss the story's setting. They also prepare students for the story line by asking them to watch for a problem that will arise in the story. When students read about the problem, the teacher stops the reading to ask students to describe it. If they did not recognize it, the teacher helps them return to that section of text in order to reread the relevant material and engage in discussion for clarification. After the story is finished, the teacher encourages students to discuss how the problem was solved and to summarize the story briefly.

In summary, instruction in literary conventions is provided to enhance comprehension among students who lack knowledge of common story structures.

In turn, comprehension of simple stories facilitates enjoyment of reading, confirms decoding accuracy, and encourages students to read common stories more often as a means of developing decoding automaticity.

Automatic Processes

A variety of automatic, unconscious, mental processes contribute to reading fluency. In the majority of readers, these processes appear, as students mature, without direct instruction. However, some students exhibit learning disabilities that impair one or more of the automatic processes underlying fluent reading. For these students, the use of not-so-automatic processes must be developed through extensive instruction and practice, rather than unfolding incidentally with maturation and experience.

In the past, special educators had hoped that use of automatic processes could be taught in one area and then transferred to other areas—this proved to be ineffective. For example, students could not learn to shift their attention from one word to the next by practicing shifting their weight from one foot to another, nor by shifting markers from one bin to another. When teachers want their students with processing deficits to know how to process words to read, they need to teach their students to do this with words. And reading words needs to be practiced extensively both in isolation—to learn recognition of phonological word features systematically, and in stories and passages—to learn how to rapidly make use of those features to process connected text (Torgesen et al., 2001).

Reading disabilities may require instruction in one or more processes related to decoding or comprehension. Two of the processes crucial to fluent reading—rapid-naming and attention-switching—are described below along with several instructional suggestions. In addition, intensive instruction and/or instructional guidance for specific students should be obtained from a skilled language and/or disabilities specialist when automatic processes are implicated.

RAPID-AUTOMATIZED-SERIAL-NAMING (RAN)[1]
Definition. Although researchers and educators have been aware for some time that phonological skills are a strong predictor and contributor to decoding skill, the unique role of rapid-automatized-serial-naming became clearly evident more slowly. Wolf, Bowers, & Biddle (2000) built on earlier work in this area to provide a clear assessment of the role of rapid-naming in reading fluency. They

---

[1] Rapid-automatized-serial-naming is sometimes referred to as RAN, rapid-naming, rapid-automatized-naming, or rapid-serial-naming.

describe rapid-naming as the ability to "name rapidly the most familiar visual symbols and stimuli in the language: letters, numbers, colors, and simple objects." (p. 387). Rapid-naming skill is assessed by asking students to look at lists or grids of numerals, single letters, color swatches, or small pictures of common objects (such as the draft examples below), and rapidly name each item on the grid.

Sample Grid of Objects

Sample Grid of Numerals

2	6	5	12	7
3	5	7	4	8
1	9	11	6	10

Figure 5.d. Sample grids of common visual symbols.

Because these assessments require students to say the names of familiar visual symbols instead of reading words, the ability to rapidly call up and say the name of one-symbol-after-another is measured separately, without interference from the ability to match letters and letter-clusters with their phonological sounds—the phonological skills aspect of reading. Wolf, Bowers, & Biddle (2000) describe various studies showing that poor readers can exhibit rapid-naming difficulties yet not show difficulties with articulation, accuracy in naming familiar visual symbols, or matching letter-clusters with their sounds *when timing is not a factor.* Thus, rapid-naming processes seem to be particularly involved with identifying and saying names of symbols *quickly* and *serially* and seems to be a process separate from phonological skills.

Rapid-serial-naming difficulties appear across languages and are not more apparent in languages with more complex spelling patterns, such as English. In non-disabled readers, rapid-naming appears to be fully developed by first or second grade—and thus is typically available to process word information to achieve fluent reading during Stage 2.

Lovett, Steinbach, & Frijters (2000) describe students with three types of underlying reading disabilities: those with phonological processing deficits, those with rapid-naming impairments, and those with "double-deficit"—impairments in both phonological processing and rapid-naming. Not surprisingly, students with a double-deficit need the most intensive instruction and practice to master reading fluency.

Instruction. Effective instruction for students with rapid-naming deficits is grounded in providing plenty of models, examples, and scaffolded-practice concerning specific reading tasks (reading lists of words or phrases, sentences, and longer passages). These tasks are practiced while utilizing specific word information (meanings and phonological letter-sound/clusters) that is taught in a direct and systematic manner.

For students with a double deficit, intensive and extensive instruction time needs to be spent on both teaching the word information and practicing the use of that information during reading. For students with only a rapid-naming deficit but intact phonological knowledge, less time is needed to teach the word information, but extensive practice in using that information during reading tasks is still needed. Since students with rapid-naming deficits often have weaker vocabulary knowledge as well, it is important to check knowledge of word meanings in material under practice, and teach meanings directly when necessary.

Programs and materials available to assist in teaching rapid-naming include multiple components. They provide lists of words and phrases, sentences, paragraphs, and passages. Students use this material to repeatedly practice words and letter-cluster/sound patterns that they are studying. Students orally read these materials repeatedly to increase both reading speed and the length of the material that can be read with speed and accuracy. In addition, spelling, dictation, and/or writing activities are included to engage the kinesthetic modality and enhance learning. Materials generally include a word-meaning component as well to ensure that students clearly attach correct meaning to the words they are learning to rapidly name (Brody, 2001; Fischer, 1995; Wolf, Miller, & Donnelly, 2000).

For example, Brody (2001) and Enwright (2001) recommend improving rapid-naming while teaching a letter-cluster/sound pattern in the following way. First introduce a letter-cluster/sound pattern such as "*tion* says /shun/" by showing the letter-cluster and telling its sound. Next ask a student to look at a list of words that include that letter-cluster. Students are asked to look at the first word, divide it into letter-clusters (making the *tion* one cluster). Thus *action* would be divided into *ac tion*. The student then reads *ac*, then *tion*, then reads *ac tion,* and finally combines the two letter-clusters to read *action.* Next, the teacher checks whether the student knows the meaning of the word *action.* If not, the meaning is given by the teacher along with examples of the use of the word in sentences. Student-generated sentences are then elicited to ensure the word's meaning is understood. These steps are repeated for the remaining list of 10–20 words, each containing the letter-cluster *tion.*

After reading each word, part-by-part, and with parts combined, the student reads the whole list. The list is read multiple times until the student reads the words with a high level of accuracy and with natural speed and intonation. Some programs give specific reading speeds for particular lists or passages. Others recommend that the teacher judge adequate speed and accuracy based on a natural rate, with good intonation, and nearly 100% accuracy (Brody, 2001). The repeated practice, intended to improve speed and accuracy, should not be so demanding as to induce anxiety. If a word, previously read several times correctly, is misread in otherwise fluent delivery, correct it and move on.

When a specific phonological letter/cluster-sound pattern is taught, prior patterns are reviewed as well to help students integrate and coordinate their knowledge. This can be done by making a list of several words following a prior pattern along with several words following the pattern currently under study. For example, students could be asked to read *action, function, suddenly, gladly, nearly* to practice *tion* and *ly.* These same five or six words can be listed in many different sequences to ensure that the student attends to the endings, and differentiates between them, to rapidly-name the words correctly (Fischer, 1995).

Next, the student reads sentences and paragraphs that include words spelled with the pattern under study. For example, when students are practicing *tion*, they read a passage written about Pollution (Brody, 1986b). Reading of passages offers another opportunity to practice rapid-naming of words that follow prior patterns along with words following the pattern under study. While practicing with passages, students apply decoding strategies to read and reread until sentences and paragraphs flow fluently. During the oral reading and rereading, comprehension of sentences and paragraphs is checked by asking students to state the meaning, with coaching provided as needed. Time spent on both decoding and comprehension activities during passage reading creates opportunities for the student to practice utilizing and coordinating all the cognitive processes that need to work together for fluent reading.

During oral reading and rereading, it is crucial that the teacher scaffold the student's decoding accuracy with unobtrusive prompts such as a confirming "yes," or a quiet "uh" to repeat misread words correctly. The attention to accurate reading improves the speed and accuracy of rapid-naming by increasing the number of accurate exposures and links that the student practices between the letter-cluster/sounds, words, phrases, sentences and their meanings. In addition, this commitment to accuracy decreases the number of confusing exposures and inaccurate links formed by the student and embedded through practice.

In addition to oral reading of words, phrases, sentences, and paragraphs using the letter-cluster/sound pattern under study, students are also asked to write the pattern during dictation of several words and short sentence using words that were studied. In time, and with further systematic instruction, students develop the skill to write their own sentences and paragraphs with these words.

Sometimes, students have difficulty recalling and applying basic phonology concepts studied previously. When this occurs, it is crucial to go back and review the less-than-fluent concept by using a routine such as the one described in the *Decoding & Comprehension Concepts (DCC) Guide* (Brody, 2001). (See Appendix B, pages 138-140, or use another systematically structured approach.) With repeated, accurate practice, students with single-deficits learn the letter-cluster pattern under study *and* how to rapidly name words composed with that letter-cluster while reading connected text. The repeated practice enhances students' ability to decode words while gathering, maintaining, and integrating the meaning presented by the printed symbol or cluster of symbols. While students with double-deficits may not reach rapid-naming fluency, extensive practice slowly improves their decoding and understanding of text (Torgesen et al., 2001).

ATTENTION

When a reader begins Stage 2, "the combined attention demands of decoding and comprehension are greater than the reader's attention resources [can handle]," (Samuels, et al., 1992, p. 130). Until advanced decoding skills and rapid-naming are automatic, and literary conventions are well understood, readers may experience difficulty in shifting attention between decoding and meaning. As these abilities develop, readers generally enter a more sophisticated level of reading. No longer do they attend only to decoding or only to content. Instead, they integrate these elements to read fluently and with understanding (Lyon, 2000; Pressley, 2000; Walczyk, 2000).

When decoding and rapid-naming are automatic, most readers unconsciously shift their attention to comprehension. In turn, clear comprehension confirms the accuracy of students' automatic decoding and encourages readers to remain attentive to meaning as they move smoothly through text. When mismatches arise between decoding and comprehension, misunderstandings unconsciously signal readers to double-check their decoding for accuracy. When appropriate repairs are made, readers' understanding of text, solidly based in common literary conventions, supports a seamless return of attention to comprehension.

Some readers learn to shift between decoding and meaning with relative ease; others need specific instruction to develop the ability. Readers with learning disabilities sometimes experience particular difficulty in switching attention between decoding and comprehension (Denckla, 1983). Several types of instruction are offered in an effort to enhance these students' attention-switching capacities. As discussed earlier in detail, reading practice is provided, and advanced decoding skills are taught to mastery level, and rapid-naming of words is practiced, in order to develop facile decoding and free attention for comprehension. For those who need it, practice with learning and recalling word meanings is provided to increase the speed and thus the fluency with which students move from decoding to meaning.

Teachers can also directly cue attention switches during oral and silent reading as needed. When directly cuing attention-switching, teachers begin a lesson by asking a question that sets a purpose for reading in order to cue attention to meaning. When an unknown word is encountered, the teacher prompts students to "decode it" as a cue for students to shift attention to pronouncing the word correctly. Once a word is identified, a request for students to summarize the earlier reading, or a brief summary provided by the teacher, cues readers to return their attention to meaning. When the story plot, up to the point of interruption, is reestablished, the teacher asks another question to cue attention to the portion about to be read. The process involves: 1) asking questions to focus attention on meaning; 2) providing cues to switch to decoding when errors arise; 3) providing reminders of the plot of the text already read to scaffold and cue a shift back to meaning; and, 4) asking a question to focus on the next section of text to resume reading. Much practice is needed before students with attention difficulties can focus as deeply as they must on decoding or meaning while also providing these cues for themselves. As students become more adept at cuing themselves to shift attention and select relevant strategies as needed, teacher-cues are faded.

At times, providing plenty of practice in decoding of word-lists and connected text develops automaticity that indicates students are rapidly naming and knowing the meanings of the words they read, along with shifting attention effortlessly between decoding and meaning. However, some students need much more intensive instruction and extensive practice to develop the processes of rapid-naming and attention-switching. In either case, teachers need to provide plenty of reading practice, and, when the "automatic processes" that support fluent reading do not occur coincidentally, seek assistance from the speech and language pathologist and/or learning disabilities specialist to obtain the intensive instruction needed to develop these abilities.

Conclusion

Fluent readers move through text smoothly while closely understanding the author's meaning and attending to decoding aspects of reading, as needed. Mastery of decoding patterns, vocabulary word meanings, and common literary conventions, along with development of skillful use of automatic reading processes enhance readers' ability to read fluently and with understanding. Readers develop fluency by reading connected text, practicing advanced word-analysis strategies, and reading, listening to, and discussing stories and expository passages that follow familiar text structures.

When students exhibit disabilities in one or more of the automatic reading processes, they can learn to process information (such as decoding concepts or vocabulary meanings) through step-by-step instruction and practice. When learners read text that is at an appropriate level and receive sufficient instruction and scaffolds, they experience confirmation and success that, in turn, stimulate an ongoing cycle of reading to learn, and of enhancing their reading ability by reading.

168

Appendix C: Informal oral reading inventory prepared by Barbara Goebel, LD Specialist, Thorntons Ferry School, Merrimack, NH.

Informal Oral Reading Inventory

Student's Name_____ **Reviewed by**_____
Date_____ **Book or passage selection**_____

Accuracy (Note ability with phonetically regular words, glue words, unfamiliar words.)

_____

Errors

_____

Quality of Intonation

_____

Expression/Fluency

_____

Attention to Punctuation

_____

Grasp of Content

_____

Passage Level (Note sentence complexity, word length, and word meaning difficulty.)

_____

General Comments:

References

Adams, M.J. (1994). *Beginning to read: Thinking and learning about print.* Cambridge: MIT Press.

Bebko, A., Alexander, J., & Doucet, R. (1998). *Language! Roots.* Longmont, CO: Sopris West.

Bembridge, T. (1994). A multilayered assessment package. In S.W. Valencia, E.H. Hiebert, & P.P. Afflerbach (Eds.) *Authentic reading assessment.* Newark DE: International Reading Association.

Biemiller, A. (2000). Vocabulary: The missing link between phonics and comprehension. *Perspectives*, 26(4), 26-30.

Bloom, B.S. (1986). Automaticity: "The hands and feet of genius." *Educational Leadership, 43*, 70-77.

Brody, S. (1984). *Patterning: Reading becomes easy.* Milford, NH: LARC Publishing.

Brody, S. (1985). Patterning: Reading becomes possible, In *Resource Papers, NH Task Force on Secondary Special Education.* Concord, NH: NH Department of Education.

Brody, S. (1986a). The Brody reading method: A successful approach to reading and written-language skills for at risk students. Paper presented at the Annual Meeting of the Association for Children and Adults with Learning Disabilities (23rd, NY, NY, March 12-15). ERIC ED275 103.

Brody, S. (1986b). *Patterning: Companion Passages.* Milford, NH: LARC Publishing.

Brody, S. (2001). *The Brody reading manual: An implementation guide for teachers (2nd ed.).* Milford, NH: LARC Publishing. [http://www.LARCPublishing.com/]

Brown, H., & Cambourne, B. (1987). *Read and retell.* Portsmouth, NH: Heinemann.

Chall, J.S. (1996). *Stages of reading development (2nd ed.).* Orlando, FL: Harcourt Brace.

Chomsky, C. (1978). When you still can't read in third grade: After decoding what? In S.J. Samuels (Ed.), *What research has to say about reading instruction (1st ed.).* Newark, DE: International Reading Association.

Cooper, J.D. (1993). *Literacy: Helping children construct meaning.* Boston: Houghton-Mifflin.

DeFina, A.A. (1992). *Portfolio assessment: Getting started.* NY: Scholastic.

deLone, H.T. (1990). *Reading skills and metacognition of fourth grade students.* Unpublished Doctoral Dissertation, Harvard Graduate School of Education.

Denckla, M.B. (1983). Learning for language and language for learning. In U. Kirk (Ed.), *Neuropsychology of language, reading and spelling*, 33-43. NY: Academic Press.

Enwright, K. (2001) Personal communication concerning effective implementation of rapid-naming instruction using the Brody Reading Method in elementary classrooms.

Fischer, P.E. (1995). *Speed drills for decoding automaticity.* Farmington, ME: Oxton House.

Glazer, S.M. (1992). *Reading comprehension.* NY: Scholastic.

Goldman, S. & Rakestraw, J. (2000). Structural aspects of constructing meaning from text. In M.L. Kamil, P.B. Mosenthal, P.D. Pearson, & R. Barr (Eds.), *Handbook of reading research.* Mahwah, NJ: Lawrence Erlbaum Associates.

Heilman, A W. (1998). *Phonics in proper perspective (8th ed.).* Columbus, OH: Merrill.

Hoffman, J.V. (1985). *The oral recitation lesson: A teacher's guide.* Austin, TX: Academic Resource Consultants.

Irwin, J.W. (1986). *Teaching reading comprehension processes*. Englewood Cliffs, NJ: Prentice Hall.

Jordan, G.E., Snow, C.E., & Porche, M.V. (2000). Project EASE: The effect of a family literacy project on kindergarten students' early literacy skills. *Reading Research Quarterly*, 35(4), 524-546.

Juel, C. & Minden-Cupp, C. (2000). One down and 80,000 to go: Word recognition instruction in the primary grades. *The Reading Teacher*, 53(4), 332-335.

Just, M.A., & Carpenter, P.A. (1981). Cognitive processes in reading: Models based on readers' eye fixations. In A.M. Lesgold & C.A. Perfetti (Eds.), *Interactive processes in reading*. Hillsdale, NJ: Lawrence Erlbaum. 177-213.

Just, M.A., & Carpenter, P.A. (1987). *The psychology of reading and language comprehension*. Needham Heights, MA: Allyn & Bacon.

Leslie, L. & Allen, L. (1999). Factors that predict success in an early literacy intervention project. *Reading Research Quarterly*, 34(4), 404-424.

Leu, D.J., & Kinzer, C.K. (1999). *Effective literacy instruction, K-8 (4th ed.)*. Columbus, OH: Merrill.

Lovett, M.W., Steinbach, K.A., & Frijters, J.C. (2000). Remediating the core deficits of developmental reading disability: A double-deficit perspective. *Journal of Learning Disabilities*, 33(4), 334-358.

Lyon, G.R. (2000). Learning to read: A call from research to action. *NEBIDA Newsletter,* Spring/Summer 15-18.

Moats, L.C. (2000). *Whole language lives on: The illusion of "balanced" reading instruction*. Washington, DC: Thomas Fordham Fooundation. [Available at http://www.edexcellence.net/.]

Morrow, L.M. (1997). *Literacy development in the early years: Helping children reading and write (3rd ed.)*. Boston, Allyn & Bacon.

National Reading Panel [NRP]. (2000). *Report of the National Reading Panel: Teaching children to read*. Washington, DC: National Institute of Child Health and Human Development. [Available at http://www.nichd.nih.gov/publications/nrp.]

Perfetti, C.A. (1985). *Reading ability*. NY: Oxford University Press.

Pressley, M. (2000). What should comprehension instruction be the instruction of? In M.L. Kamil, P.B. Mosenthal, P.D. Pearson, & R. Barr (Eds.), *Handbook of reading research*. Mahwah, NJ: Lawrence Erlbaum Associates.

Reutzel, D.R., & Cooter, R.B. (1996). *Teaching children to read: From basals to books (2nd ed.*. NY: Merrill.

Reutzel, D.R., & Hollingsworth, P.M. (1993). Effects of fluency training on second graders' reading comprehension. *Journal of Educational Research, 86*(6), 325-331.

Roswell, F.G., & Chall, J.S. (1994). *Creating successful readers: A practical guide to testing and teaching at all levels*. Chicago: Riverside Publishing Co.

Routman, R. (1994). *Invitations: Changing as teachers and learners K-12 (Rev. ed.)*. Portsmouth, NH: Heinemann.

Samuels, S.J., Schermer, N., & Reinking, D. (1992). Reading fluency: Techniques for making decoding automatic. In S.J. Samuels & A.E. Farstrup (Eds.), *What research has to say about reading instruction (2nd ed.)*. Newark, DE: International Reading Association.

Savage, J.F. (1994). *Teaching reading using literature*. Madison, WI: Brown & Benchmark.

Snow, C.E., Burns, M.S., & Griffin, P. (Eds.) (1998). *Preventing reading difficulties in young children*. Washington, DC: National Academy Press.

Spiegel, D.L., & Whaley, J.F. (1980). Elevating comprehension skills by sensitizing students to structural aspects of narratives. Paper presented at the Annual Meeting of the National Reading Conference (30th, San Diego, CA, December 3-6). ED199 634.

Stahl, S.A., Heubach, K., & Cramond, B. (1997). *Fluency-oriented Reading Instruction. Reading Research Report #79.* Athens, GA: National Reading Research Center.

Stanovich, K.E. (1984). The interactive-compensatory model of reading: A confluence of developmental, experimental, and educational psychology. *Remedial and Special Education, 15,* 11-19.

Stanovich, K.E. (1986). Matthew effects in reading: Some consequences of individual differences in the acquisition of literacy. *Reading Research Quarterly, 21*(4), 360-407.

Stanovich, K.E. (1993). The construct validity of discrepancy definitions of reading disability. In G.R. Lyon, D.B. Gray, J.F. Kavanagh, & N.A. Krasnegor (Eds.), *Better understanding of learning disabilities.* Baltimore, MD: Brookes Publishing Co.

Stanovich, K.E. (1994). Romance and reality. *The Reading Teacher, 47*(4), 280-291.

Stanovich, K.E., & West, R.F. (1981). The effect of sentence context on ongoing word recognition: Tests of a two-process theory. *Journal of Experimental Psychology: Human Perception and Performance, 7,* 658-672.

Stanovich, K.E., & West, R.F. (1983). On priming by a sentence context. *Journal of Experimental Psychology: General, 112,* 1-36.

Stanovich, K.E., West, R.F., & Feeman, D.J. (1981). A longitudinal study of sentence context effects in second-grade children: Tests of an interactive-compensatory model. *Journal of Experimental Child Psychology, 32,* 185-199.

Steere, A., Peck, C.Z., & Kahn, L. (1971). *Solving language difficulties.* Cambridge, MA: Educators Publishing Service.

Torgesen, J.K., Alexander, A.W., Wagner, R.K., Rashotte, C.A., Voeller, K.S., & Conway, T. (2001). Intensive remedial instruction for children with severe reading disabilities: Immediate and long-term outcomes from two instructional approaches. *Journal of Learning Disabilities,* 34(1), 33-58.

Tunnell, M.O., & Jacobs, J.S. (1989). Using "real" books: Research findings on literature based reading instruction. *The Reading Teacher, 42,* 470-477.

Vacca, J.L., Vacca, R.T., & Gove, M.K. (1999). *Reading and learning to read (4th ed.).* NY: Harper Collins.

Walczyk, J.J. (2000). The interplay between automatic and control processes in reading. *Reading Research Quarterly,* 35(4), 554-566.

Wolf, M., Bowers, P.G., & Biddle, K. (2000). Naming-speed processes, timing, and reading: A conceptual review. *Journal of Learning Disabilities, 33*(4), 388-407.

Wolf, M., Miller, L., & Donnelly, K. (2000). Retrieval, automaticity, vocabulary elaboration, orthography (RAVE-O): A comprehensive, fluency-based reading intervention program. *Journal of Learning Disabilities, 33*(4), 375-386.

Chapter 6. Spelling: A Window on Linguistic Development[1]

Louisa Cook Moats, EdD
National Institute of Child Health and Human Development,
Washington, DC
University of Texas, Houston, Health Sciences Center

In 1967, Johnson and Myklebust characterized spelling as a complex entity, requiring more simultaneous perceptual discrimination, memory, sequentialization, and analysis and synthesis of linguistic information than any other academic skill. During the past three decades, research has confirmed their viewpoint and deepened our understanding of why this apparently simple form of language output presents so much difficulty for so many.

Far from being "mechanical," spelling has been shown to be a multifaceted linguistic skill that integrates and depends upon several layers of language

---

[1]Louisa C. Moats is project director of the Washington DC site of the National Institute of Child Health and Human Development (NICHD) Early Interventions Project, and clinical associate professor of pediatrics, University of Texas, Houston, Health Sciences Center. Her work is supported in part by grant HD30995, "Early Interventions for Children with Reading Problems," funded by the NICHD.

knowledge: *phonological*, or awareness of speech sounds in words; *morphological*, or awareness of the meaningful parts that make up words; *semantic*, or knowledge of word meanings and word relationships; and *orthographic*, or knowledge of the letter sequences and patterns that are used to spell words (Ehri, 1989; Fischer, Shankweiler, & Liberman, 1985; Henderson, 1990; Read, 1986).

Good spellers do not depend upon better visual-orthographic memory alone. In comparison to poor spellers, they are more sensitive to language structure, more able to think about language and manipulate language, and more able to learn linguistic complexities. Spelling is a visible record of language processing, a window through which to view development of orthographic knowledge, phonological development, and understanding of word structure. Through careful analysis of spelling errors, we can learn which speech sounds, spelling correspondences, syllable patterns, and morphemes are challenging for students, and illumine these structures for those who need to gain familiarity with the details of words (Moats, 1995; Sawyer, Wade, & Kim, 1999). In fact, spelling instruction presents an opportunity to teach students how their own language works, an aspect of curriculum in great need of revival (Stotsky, 1999).

Reading and spelling are two sides of the same coin—the linguistic processing of print (Ehri, 1997). The study of one enhances the study of the other. Most commonly, individuals who are instructed systematically in word structure not only learn to spell but become better readers and expand their vocabularies. Even so, some people read well but spell quite poorly. Spelling is inherently more difficult than reading because all the letters in a word must be remembered to write it, whereas partial visual memory will support word recognition for reading.

Learning to spell presents a significant problem for more than those few individuals who are referred for special education services with learning disabilities. The average adult in our society attains the equivalent of only an eighth grade spelling level (Wide Range Achievement Test Manual, Wilkinson, 1993). Spelling disabilities are ubiquitous among individuals with learning disabilities and usually coexist with disorders of oral language, reading, written expression, and attention. Many successful adolescents and adults with a history of early reading disability continue to be less-than-exemplary spellers even though they may eventually learn to read (Bruck, 1987; Finucci, Gottfredson, & Childs, 1985; Moats, 1996).

This chapter will consider the complex process of spelling. First, the nature of regularity in the English spelling system is reviewed. Next, the stage-like progression in which spelling is generally learned is explored. Then, principles for helping able and less-able spellers are proposed. Finally, a recommended order of instruction is examined along with specific strategies for reducing spelling problems.

The English Spelling System is Pattern-Based and Predictable

English orthography is often maligned as unpredictable. On the contrary, although there are complexities and irregularities, English orthography is a structured and predictable system in which spellings for phonemes, syllables, and morphemes are rule-governed or explainable according to a word's historical origins, meaning, and sound structure (Hanna, Hanna, Hodges, and Rudorf, 1966; Venezky, 1970).

Hanna, Hanna, Hodges, and Rudorf's (1966) computer-based analysis of English orthography tested the predictability of sound-symbol correspondences in English, and documented that one-half the words in English could be spelled accurately and another 37% could be spelled with one error using phoneme-grapheme correspondence rules alone. Hanna et al.'s estimate of predictability took into account the fact that many graphemes or spellings for phonemes involve more than one letter (*igh*; *ay*; *oi*; *ck; tch; dge*, for example). A variety of additional factors, described below, influence the nature of predictable patterns of English spelling.

Phonemic context. Many spellings for sounds are influenced by the phonemes that come before or after them, or by their phonemic context. For example, the sound /f/ is spelled *ff* at the ends of words following a short vowel (*fluff, off*), *ph* after an /s/ (*sphere, sphynx*), or *gh* at the ends of a small set of Anglo-Saxon words (*tough, laugh, rough, cough, enough, trough, slough*).

Stress patterns. In addition, spellings are determined in part by stress patterns. For example, the speech sound /j/ is spelled *dge* at the ends of syllables with stressed short vowels (*dodge, fudge, wedge, badger, ridge*) but is spelled *ge* after long vowels or unaccented vowels (*college, village, stooge, wage*). Because syllable stress can be difficult for writers with learning disabilities to identify, it is not surprising that they may fail to internalize the spelling patterns that are governed by the stress feature of vowels.

Orthographic rules. English spelling is also determined by purely orthographic rules that specify what letter sequences are allowed and what letters can be used to spell speech sounds in certain contexts (Venezky, 1970). For example, no word in English ends in the letter *v*; words ending in /v/ use a marker letter *e* to prevent *v* from ending a word (*love, mauve, shove, above*). Because of orthographic constraints, many of the letter sequences that make up words are redundant or repetitious, and we learn the probabilities of these constraints unconsciously through exposure to print. Readers know, for example, that the names *Nkruma*, *Rajiv*, and *Khrushchev* are not English spellings, although they may not be able to explain exactly why without more language study.

Lexical relationships. English spelling is also determined by the meaningful parts that words comprise (Henry, 1993; Moats & Smith, 1992; Templeton, 1992). In fact, meaning often takes precedence over sound in spelling because lexical roots, base words, and affixes are usually spelled consistently in spite of pronunciation changes, as in *preside - president; define - definition.* Consonant shifts in pronunciation occur in *social - society; precocious - precocity; medic - medical - medicine*, and vowel shifts occur in words such as *divine - divinity; obscene - obscenity; compete - competition*. One of the reasons that English orthography is not a simple phonetic transcription system is that lexical relationships are preserved in our spelling to communicate meaning even when the words change in pronunciation from one derived form to another.

Other spelling consistencies preserve lexical relationships in the presence of silent letters: *sign - signal - signature; muscle - muscular; hymn - hymnal*. Still others involve phonological and orthographic assimilation rules so that prefixes are compatible with the root: *in-* is assimilated in *irregular, illegitimate,* and *immortal* by changing the *n* to match the first consonant of the base word. Similarly, *ad-* is changed in *affix, approach, arrest, attend.*

Anglo-Saxon exceptions. Many common words of Anglo-Saxon origin are exception words, or words that do not follow common spelling patterns, such as *said, they, does, was, one, do*, and *to*. About 350 of the 500 most often used words in English have odd or unusual spellings, according to Horn (1969), who was a strong advocate of memorization techniques in spelling instruction. The most commonly misspelled words in children with spelling disabilities tend to be those oddities, words such as *done, because, again, buy, some, their, were, would, where, of* and *who* (Moats, 1996).

Phonological rules. The relationship between speech and spelling is complex, indirect, and multifaceted. Even words that seem to use straightforward, predictable spellings can present problems to novices. For example, short or lax vowels that precede the voiced consonant /g/ are changed slightly in pronunciation, by phonological rule, so that the vowel in *big* is closer to long *e* than the vowel in *bit*; the vowel in *egg* is closer to long *a* than the vowel in *bed*; the vowel in *bag* is pronounced as a diphthong with two parts, unlike the vowel in *back*. The /t/ phoneme in words like li*tt*le and a*tt*itude is reduced to tongue flap /D/ in such spoken words and is affricated in the /tr/ blend in *train*.

These distinctions might seem petty or irrelevant to those of us who can spell already, but the child learning to spell must learn to ignore such phonetic detail and treat the phoneme as an abstraction that can vary in pronunciation. Spelling is not a literal phonetic transcription of speech such as a linguist would accomplish with a phonetic alphabet. Therefore, children can only progress so far with "invented" spelling, or guessing at a phonetic transcription.

The Course of Spelling Development

Spelling develops in a broadly predictable sequence between kindergarten and about sixth grade, even among children who have had different instructional experiences. Much work during the past twenty years has been directed toward defining this stage-like progression (Ehri, 1997; Henderson, 1990; Read, 1986; Templeton & Bear, 1992; Treiman, 1993), and although there is some disagreement among researchers, a common framework has been constructed (see Table 6.1, following page).

Early and late phonetic stages. After a prephonetic or logographic stage, in which letter-like forms are made without regard to alphabetic speech representation, children begin economically and rulefully to produce syllabic representations of the salient consonants and vowels in words, often using letter name strategies. With practice and instruction, children later learn to represent all of the prominent phonemes of the word, including the vowel nucleus.

In both early and late phonetic spelling, children often use their knowledge of alphabet letter names creatively. They will derive short vowel spellings from the letter name articulated in similar position (/E/ derived from *a*; /I/ derived from *e*; /U/ derived from *o*, for example, BAD/bed; FES/fish; OP/up). Long vowels are often represented with one letter: FET/feet, NIT/night, or SA/say. Diphthongs and back vowels are often spelled in a way that expresses phonetic detail: PIYL (pile), BOE (boy) and BOWT (boat). Phonetic features are represented, such as the affrication on the initial blends *tr* and *dr* (CHRAN/train; JRS/dress), and the reduction of /t/ to tongue flap [D] (LEDR/letter). One letter will often represent syllabic segments [l], [r], [m], and [n]: (LIDL/little; METN/mitten; NHR/nature).

Table 6.1. Stages of Spelling Development.

Stages of Spelling Development

1. **Preliterate Stage**
    a) idiosyncratic symbols used
    b) letters and numerals combined
    c) no use of a phoneme-grapheme correspondence system
    d) may or may not go left to right
    e) only the child can read the message back

2. **Semiphonetic or Prephonetic Stage (Early Letter Name)**
    a) growing awareness of left to right
    b) incomplete or abbreviated spellings
    c) use of single letters for whole syllables
    d) use of letter names for sounds
    e) salient consonants represented
             Examples: RUDF? IWILGEVUAKNOPENR   HAPEBRTDA
             (Are you deaf? I will give you a can opener.)   (Happy Birthday)

3. **Later Phonetic Stage**
    a) systematic representation of all sounds
    b) surface phonetic features represented
    c) systematic and principled, based on awareness of what mouth is doing
    d) not aware of correct spellings for sounds
    Examples: a) tense (long) vowels:
           DA (day) KAM (came) FEL (feel) MI (my) LIK (like) TABIL (table)
    b) lax (short) vowels: derived from letter name close in articulation:
           a for /E/ BAD (bed) SAD (said),   e for /I/ WEL (will),   i for /U/ KIT (cut)
    c) preconsonantal nasals omitted:
           JUP (jump) AD (and) BAK (bank) ED (end)
    d) syllabic consonants *m, n, l, r*:
           LITL (little) BIGR (bigger) SOGR (sugar) OPN (open)
    e) inflected endings spelled phonetically (ed, s):
           WAKT (walked) ARIVD (arrived) HALPT (helped) RASTD (rested) DAWGZ (dogs)
    f) vowel spellings show phonetic detail:
           SOWN (soon) GOWT (goat) BOE (boy) POWLEOW (polio)
    g) affrication of *tr* and *dr*:
           CHRA (tray) CHRIBLS (troubles) JRADI (dreidel) JRΛGN (dragon)
    h) intervocalic flaps shown as D:
           LADR (letter) WODR (water) BEDR (better)
    i) letter names Y for /w/ and H for /ch/:
           YOH (watch) YL (will) HRH (church)

4. **Transitional or Syllable Juncture Stage and Beyond**
    a) awareness of syllable patterns
    b) nasals are represented
    c) no more syllabic *l, r, m, n*
    d) use of silent letters such as *e*
    e) visual awareness of letter groups
    f) awareness of vowel teams
    g) automatic spelling of sight words
    h) rules over-generalized
           Examples: EIGHTE (eighty) YOUNITED (united) TAOD (toad) HUOSE (house)

Children who succeed with inventive, phonetic spelling have achieved an essential milestone toward mastery of decoding in reading. As discussed in Chapter 3, the ability to spell phonetically is a powerful predictor of early reading success, and a powerful measure of early reading progress, because phonological awareness, alphabet knowledge, and realization of the alphabetic principle are necessary for both early spelling and early decoding (Adams, Foorman, Lundberg, & Beeler, 1997; Tangel & Blachman, 1995). Phonological awareness and phonological processing permit and facilitate the connection between phonemes and graphemes in memory and are the foundation for acquisition of specific word knowledge.

Transition to standard spelling. To make the transition to correct spelling, children must absorb many concepts and facts about English orthography, and accumulate a store of knowledge in the orthographic memory system. After phonetic spelling is achieved, children must learn the actual graphemes that spell syllable parts and the ways in which syllables are joined. Bear, Templeton, Invernizzi, & Johnston (1996) have labeled these stages "within word pattern" and "syllable juncture" according to the primary orthographic content to be learned at each level.

For example, children must realize that many vowels are spelled with letter combinations, some letters can be doubled, spellings change when endings are added, and much phonetic detail is not represented in spelling. Further, children must learn the constancy of many morpheme spellings and consider sound, pattern, meaning, and even syntax to spell correctly. The teacher's interpretation of spelling errors must be informed by awareness of these developmental principles. Otherwise, errors that, in fact, are developmentally common and stage-appropriate will be viewed as pathological (Invernizzi & Worthy, 1989; Moats, 1983).

Development when spelling disabilities are present. Children with reading and spelling disabilities, who usually have related difficulties with language processing, follow the normal course of spelling development more slowly (Invernizzi & Worthy, 1989) and with ultimate limits on their achievement (Moats, 1996). Most dyslexic students with average verbal intelligence achieve gross phonetic accuracy in their misspellings after sufficient instruction (Bailet, 1990; Bruck, 1988; Moats, 1983; Pennington et al., 1986).

However, there are certain phoneme-grapheme correspondences, aspects of word structure, and specific lexical spellings that appear to be insurmountably difficult for many poor spellers to learn, and students with phonological processing deficits often remain stuck below a fifth grade level of spelling accuracy even though they may learn to read close to grade level in adolescence (Moats, 1996). The growing disparity between reading and spelling in the remediated dyslexic appears to be a consequence of the much greater precision in word memory that is required for spelling than is needed for word recognition (Bruck, 1988; Ehri, 1989).

Linguistic challenges for the person with spelling disability. In the past, researchers and test makers have focused on whether children were better or worse at spelling "predictable" or "unpredictable" words in order to characterize a disability. This approach has very limited value, however. More recently, it has been shown that error patterns in the misspellings of both good and poor spellers may be influenced by at least four factors.

First, individual phoneme characteristics, such as the presence or absence of voicing or aspiration in a consonant, or the place of articulation of a vowel, may influence the accuracy with which it is spelled (Hoffman & Norris, 1989). Second, the phonological characteristics of spoken syllables, such as their stress and whether they contain a liquid (/l/, /r/) or a nasal (/n/, /m/, /ng/) after a vowel are related to spelling difficulty (Moats, 1996; Read & Ruyter, 1985; Sawyer et al., 1999; Treiman, 1993).

Third, morphophonemic aspects of word structure, such as the presence of an inflected ending (-ed, -s, -er, -ing) or the distance between a root and a derivation, determine the likelihood of correct spelling (Bailet, 1990; Carlisle, 1987; Fischer, Shankweiler, & Liberman, 1985).

Finally, orthographic structure itself is related to difficulty, such as the presence of doubled letters. Words whose spellings represent complex relationships between morphology, phonology, and orthography are in general the hardest to recall. Poor spellers usually are stymied by certain linguistic constructions as well as specific, irregular words. Their ultimate level of success with spelling depends in large part on the intactness of their phonological processing capabilities.

Principles of Spelling Instruction

Up through the 1970s, spelling instruction research focused on questions that face every classroom teacher: Should word lists be grouped according to word frequency or word pattern? Should English be taught as a predictable, logical system of orthography? What kind and what amount of practice would result in the most efficient and generalizable learning? What role should tests play in word study? How can teachers ensure that word study generalizes to writing? Although traditional studies of classroom spelling instruction generally did not define or group their subjects according to their developmental spelling level or their cognitive characteristics, some findings regarding classroom-based spelling instruction were replicated consistently from the 1920s to the 1970s (Fitzsimmons & Loomer, 1977; Hillerich, 1985; Horn, 1969):

1. The test-study-test method is desirable, especially if students correct their pretests immediately and use the information to focus their study.

2. Ten to fifteen minutes per day is sufficient for most students to master a week's spelling lesson of twenty words.

3. Words should be grouped by both frequency and spelling pattern.

4. Practice should entail writing the unknown words several times daily in meaningful exercises; spelling improves most when children are asked to write often.

5. Active word analysis, involving both speech and print, rather than passive "looking the words over" or spelling words orally, gets the best results.

If even this much were practiced from one grade to another, within an organized, consistent plan for skill development, spelling might not be the cause for concern that it has become in many schools. Unfortunately, philosophies of instruction have dominated classroom practice for the past 15 years that have minimized the importance of direct, organized teaching of language structure at any level, including spelling. Systematic, direct, and sequential spelling practice has been casualty of whole language theories that have advised teachers to teach spelling only in the context of written expression (e.g., Powell & Hornsby, 1993).

Teachers are to avoid teaching planned, structured spelling lessons because a focus on spelling would divert students' attention from written composition. In lieu of skills development, teachers are encouraged to emphasize written expression, and then to ask students to make lists of spelling words they might not know how to spell. Proofreading and self-correction are claimed to be sufficient methods for spelling study.

Such advice is not grounded in research and is especially harmful to students who are dyslexic. As Berninger (1998, 1999) and her group have documented, students who have learned to form letters and spell words are better writers than students who have not automatized the basic skills of transcription. Learning to spell facilitates learning to write because students expend less cognitive energy wondering how to spell words and devote more attention to what they want to say.   Beyond the middle of first grade, students benefit from a comprehensive approach to written expression that includes the formal study of spelling (Bear et al., 1996; Berninger, 1998).

INSTRUCTION FOR GOOD SPELLERS

Some children learn to spell rather effortlessly; nevertheless, they do benefit from organized instruction. Such children easily remember orthographic patterns as they encounter them in print. They also do well on tests of phonological processing, as the ability to discriminate and analyze speech sounds is a prerequisite for spelling competence as well as decoding proficiency (Sawyer et al., 1999; Tangel & Blachman, 1995). Children with good spelling memories can learn by almost any method, as long as some type of systematic practice is present, and the spelling instruction is at an appropriate level of spelling development.

A qualitative inventory of spelling development is an efficient and effective way to group children for spelling instruction. Henderson's (1990) text, *Teaching Spelling*, contained a validated inventory that has since been revised and adapted by others (Bear at al., 1996; Ganske, 1993, 2000). The inventory consisted of word lists that used progressively more complex and advanced correspondences, and that reflected the order in which orthographic knowledge is typically acquired. An inventory of spelling development (see Appendix D, page 203) can be used to determine what elements of orthography a student knows, or needs to learn.

Basal programs, designed for use by grade level with large classes of students, vary considerably from one another and need to be used with caution. Many contain information that is not linguistically accurate.   Some provide wasteful "busywork" practice, and often provide no valid rationale for including words on lists. Sometimes they oversimplify, or explain poorly, the complexities of sound-symbol correspondence. Because they are designed for the average child at a given grade level, the programs may not match the instructional level and unique needs of less-able learners. Too many words and too many concepts are presented at once; too many confusing stimuli are offered in one lesson; and insufficient review and practice of previously learned material may be present for the poor speller. Further, basal texts often fail to give the linguistic or historical reasons why English words are spelled the way they are—information that can help spelling make sense.

Basal texts can be useful if the level of difficulty is matched to the students' developmental spelling level, using an informal assessment (see Appendix D, page 203) and if the teacher follows the research-supported steps listed on page 180. Newer programs that are well designed include Houghton Mifflin's *Spelling and Vocabulary* and Scholastic's *Scholastic Spelling*.

INSTRUCTION FOR POOR SPELLERS

What can be done for the person who spells poorly? Too often, the poor speller in the elementary grades is deemed not ready for instruction; the poor speller in the intermediate grades is deemed unresponsive to instruction; and the poor speller in high school or beyond is viewed as a hopeless case. When such attitudes prevail, it is not surprising that poor spellers often remain untaught. Although research on general classroom instruction of spelling is plentiful, research on spelling instruction for the student with well-defined spelling disability is much more limited.

Spelling improvement can occur in poor spellers if it is carried out systematically over a long period of time. Very poor spellers seldom progress in spelling as fast as they can improve in reading. Although the ultimate gains may be modest, they provide a basis for simple written communication. An effective instructional program for poor spellers will be integrated with other language instruction and will include the following components:

- direct teaching with teacher-student interaction
- controlled presentation of less information
- modeling and immediate feedback
- simultaneous, multisensory methodology
- systematic, sequential, and cumulative teaching of sounds, syllables, and morphemes

Teacher-directed, systematic practice with controlled amounts of new information. The term "systematic" spelling instruction means that patterns of correspondence and English orthography are emphasized in the lesson design. Instruction proceeds step-by-step, providing sufficient practice with concepts and patterns already taught in previous lessons. Thus, systematic teaching is also cumulative and redundant. The teacher assumes that students will forget, even as they study, and that some students need a great deal of practice before associations and concepts are internalized. Instruction is carried out with the aid of careful record-keeping to determine when words, patterns, and concepts are learned.

Why is it necessary to be systematic? First, our orthography is a system of correspondences that are predictable by rule and pattern; second, children are more likely to learn the system if they receive organized, sequential practice. Many children will not remember the spelling of words simply from reading them or from writing them occasionally. Spelling requires explicit and precise recall of orthographic sequences and many examples of a pattern should be presented at once. In addition, many of the most commonly used words in English are of Anglo-Saxon origin and have retained low frequency or odd spellings that also must be memorized.

Regardless of the content, people with dyslexia or spelling disabilities generally learn better when the amount to be learned is controlled, the amount of practice is monitored, and reinforcement theory is applied deliberately by the teacher (Lyon & Moats, 1988). To build up word images in memory and to ensure that words are so well learned that they can be recalled without delay or extra attention, a great deal of practice of a few elements at a time is required. A good rule of thumb is 80% old information, 20% new information in a lesson plan designed for a person who spells poorly. Fernald (1943) showed that some children required up to 40 opportunities to write a word correctly before they remembered it.

Limit number of words. The number of words presented at one time also needs to be limited for poor spellers. Rieth et al. (1974) found that poor spellers recalled more words by the end of the week if they learned five or six a day and were tested on those daily. Good spellers, however, learned well with all twenty words given on Monday. Bryant, Drabin, and Gettinger (1981) found that students with severe spelling disabilities did best with only three new words a day. This data is most applicable to situations when students are trying to *memorize specific words*.

When students are being taught a concept, rule, or generalization about sound-symbol correspondence, such as the "f, l, s doubling rule," only one concept or pattern should be taught at a time. However, ample practice with 30 or more examples in one lesson is often necessary for the redundant pattern to be internalized. Children learn patterns through repeated exposure to many examples. Poor spellers need more experience with print and more focus and repetition during that experience than good spellers.

Modeling and immediate feedback. With poor spellers, effective teaching also entails direct teaching and much interaction between student and teacher. Activities such as quiet completion of worksheets and looking at words on flash cards until they can be written from memory do not result in useful learning. Students should be asked to write words and sentences to dictation and then receive immediate corrective feedback from the teacher, who might use an overhead projector to proofread sentences with the class. One strategy that has been validated with students with learning disabilities is error imitation and modeling (Nulman & Gerber, 1984). The teacher reproduces the child's error and then corrects it, explaining the difference between the incorrect and correct words, before asking the student to write the word correctly.

Multisensory instruction. The term *multisensory* refers to the simultaneous engagement of hearing, seeing, saying, and feeling during spelling practice. The initials VAKT - visual, auditory, kinesthetic, tactile - refer to multisensory instruction. Children might be asked to say a word while writing it with fingers on a rough surface, or might be asked to say a word slowly, segment its sounds, say the letters that correspond to sounds, and write them, for example. Although it is not entirely clear from research why multisensory techniques are most efficacious with dyslexic children, experienced remedial teachers have recommended them for decades (e.g., Birsh, 1999; Fernald, 1943; Gillingham & Stillman, 1960; King, 1984). Multisensory practice has been shown experimentally to produce better results than unisensory techniques with novice or dyslexic children (Thomson, 1991).

One likely reason for the efficacy of the multisensory approach is that it encourages the child to externalize and focus upon the phonemic elements of the word by saying it slowly and deliberately, noticing how each phoneme is represented. This activity facilitates the "comparator function" viewed as central to spelling by Lindamood, Bell, and Lindamood (1992)—the active differentiation of similar word forms and conscious matching of sound to symbol. Moreover, more attention is deployed when several sensory modalities are engaged simultaneously, probably resulting in increased brain activation levels and increased chances for information storage.

Systematic, sequential, cumulative instruction. Children who are poor spellers are insensitive to the structure of spoken and written language. They need much more practice than good spellers to remember sound-symbol associations. They do not spontaneously perceive the semantic, phonological, or orthographic relationships among words that are part of a derivational network. When the correspondences, syllable patterns, and other redundancies of language are presented one at a time in logical sequence, the elements are differentiated, brought into focus, and related to each other. All elements are not equally difficult. Repetition of the hardest concepts and associations can be provided as needed.

Components of Spelling Instruction

Whether there is an ideal sequence for teaching spelling is open to debate. However, there seems to be substantial commonality in the basic scope and sequence of most spelling programs. The sequence seems to represent a natural order of word learning that corresponds to phonological, word recognition, and vocabulary development. Such a sequence allows for orderly introduction of redundant elements and systematic exploration of their relationships.

The components of spelling instruction will be described following the outline in Figure 6.a (below) and the scope and sequence of Table 6.2 on the following page. The scope and sequence is not intended to be used in a lock-step manner. Teaching should be recursive and flexible, in response to students' needs. New concepts can be introduced while others are being mastered and automatized through varied practice.

Sequence of Spelling Instruction

Explicit Practice with Phonological Analysis
Basic Sound-symbol Correspondences
One-syllable Patterns
Inflections
Conditional Word and Syllable Patterns
Homophones
Syllable Patterns and Syllable Junctures
Latin and Greek Morpheme Patterns
Ending Rules

Figure 6.a. Sequence of spelling instruction.

Table 6.2. Spelling Scope and Sequence Chart. (Developed by L.C. Moats in collaboration with G. Giveans and teachers from Dresden School District, Hanover, New Hampshire.)

Grade Level	1	2	3	4	5	6	7	8
Beginning Consonants	b c d f g h j k l m n p r s t v w y z		qu	c: cent g: gent				
Ending Consonants	b d g m n p t	x ff ll ss zz			ck-k ge-dge			
Beginning Blends		bl cl fl gl pl sl br cr dr fr gr pr tr sc sk sl sm sn sp st sw	scr spr spl str squ	shr thr		sch		
Ending Blends		mp nd ft lt nt lf st nk ng						
Digraphs		ch sh th	wh-	ph	ch-tch	ch: ache chorus		
Silent Letters			ck lk	wr kn	gn			
Vowels	short a e i o u	long a-e e-e i-e o-e u-e	y as long i: sky	y as long e: happy		ie ei schwa (ə)	y as short i: system eigh augh ough	
Vowel Digraphs		ai ee oa ea	au aw oo: boot ew	oo: foot				
Diphthongs			ou ow oi oy					
r- control			ar er ir or ur	air ear				
Prefixes				un- re-	pre- en- dis- mis- ex- in-	con- per- com- a -	bi- mal- circum- inter- intra- super- trans-	Derivational doubling: immature irregular
Grammatical Endings		No base change -s -ed -ing	Double final consonant Drop final e -ed -ing	Change y to i -ed -ing -er -est			Double final consonant of accepted syllable: regretted	
Suffixes				-ly -ful -ness -less	-tion -sion -teen	-ment -en	Adjective suffixes: -ous -able -ible -ic -al	Noun suffixes: -tion -sion -al -ment -ian -ance -ence -tious -cial -ture
Syllables: open and closed		Concept of syllable	Divide compound words sail/boat	Divide words with prefixes and suffixes: re/turn sad/ly	Divide cvc words: mo/ment Divide vccv words: trum/pet	Suffix -le takes preceding consonant: ta/ble	Vowel digraphs and diphthongs remain undivided in syllables: com/pound	
Contractions			I'm he's she's it's	'll: he'll n't: aren't	'd: we'd 're: you're 've: they've			
Sample Words	lap run flop yet big	sniff stamp chops made load	quitting striding why snoop smart	rice shrilly unhook hurried phone	gnat prediction token napkin judge	school receive neither noble compartment	submitting humorous destructive horizontal agreeable	accord funeral version librarian spacial

EXPLICIT PRACTICE WITH PHONOLOGICAL ANALYSIS

Because accurate spelling begins with an internal representation of a word's phonemic structure, phonological awareness activities should be incorporated into spelling lessons for children who cannot represent words phonetically. Awareness can be developed through a variety of games and activities that are brief, fun, and interspersed with activities throughout the day (Adams, Foorman, Lundberg, & Beeler, 1997; Blachman, Tangel, Ball, & Black, 1999); also see Chapter 3 of this volume.

Introductory phoneme awareness activities.

a) Create silly words, such as names for puppets, animals, and characters, using rhyme and alliteration (Bino the Rhino).

b) Point out that known names begin with certain sounds.

c) Contrast words that differ only in one sound (goal - gold).

d) Have children purchase store items or play guessing games by saying a "little bit" of a word or getting ready to say a word and producing the first sound only.

e) Select a target sound for the day, and reward the student when the sound is spontaneously identified.

More explicit forms of word analysis.

a) Identify initial phonemes in words through analysis of rhymes. Using blocks or other counters, show children how a rhyme is formed by changing the initial phoneme. Say, "Your name is Jason. Now, if I take off the /j/ and add an /m/, I can make a rhyme—Mason! Now you try it."

b) Identify an initial phoneme in words while moving a block or counter to show completion of the word. Use continuant phonemes (/f/, /s/, /m/, /n/, /l/, /r/, /th/, /v/, /z/) rather than stops (/t/, /k/, /p/) since it is easier to blend a continuant than a stop.

c) Identify the phonemes in a consonant-vowel combination by changing the initial consonant (Sue, moo, new, shoe). Move a block for each sound and blend the sounds together. Then change the vowel and show with the counters what happened (Sue, see, say, so).

d) Add a final consonant to consonant-vowel combinations and represent each phoneme with a block (su + p = sup).

e) Use Ball and Blachman's (1991) "Say It and Move It" procedure, modeled after Elkonin (1973): The child is presented with a line drawing of an object she can name. Below the picture is a rectangle divided into sections that correspond to the number of phonemes in a word. The teacher models, then the child puts a counter in a section while saying the word slowly. Then the child says the blended word fast.

After playing this game with many different words, the child can be given chips of different colors to represent the consonants and the vowels. Later, letter tiles can be substituted for chips and beginning spelling can occur. (Ambiguous vowels, diphthongs, r-controlled vowels, and consonant blends should be avoided at this stage.) Beginning awareness of inflections such as plural /s/ can be developed at this stage.

f) Play sound deletion games after Rosner's (1973) auditory analysis activities:
1. syllable deletion from a compound (say "treetop" without "tree")
2. syllable deletion (say "cucumber" without the "cu")
3. initial consonant deletion ("part" without the /p/)
4. final consonant deletion ("seat" without the /t/)
5. initial phoneme in a blend ("stake" without the /s/)
6. final phoneme in a blend ("past" without the /t/)
7. second consonant in an initial blend ("stake" without the /t/)

g) Coding with colored blocks: The child uses colored blocks to represent sounds and shows changes where they occur in spoken syllables by changing the color of a block, adding a block, or taking a block away. If sounds are the same, the same color should represent them; if sounds are different, different colors should be used. An order for level of difficulty is as follows:
1. add a sound (if this says /i/, show me /i+p/)
2. delete a sound (if this says /kap/, show me /ap/)
3. change a consonant (if this says /slap/ show me /snap/)
4. change a vowel: (if this says /slap/, show me /slop/)
5. change the order of sounds (pats to past)
6. duplicate a sound already in the word (art to tart)

Once skill is developed with colored blocks, then letter tiles can be gradually substituted for them.

Additional phonological awareness activities for older students:

a) With one-syllable words, have the student say each word slowly, separating the phonemes, and marking each sound on a finger. Model this as often as necessary.

b) Given an array of counters that correspond to the phonemes in longer words such as *silver*, ask the student which one corresponds to /l/ or some other sound.

c) If the student has difficulty representing a vowel, be sure the reader has identified the vowel in the syllable correctly by saying it in isolation and giving a cue word beginning with the vowel.

d) Deliberately contrast prefixes and words that have subtle differences in pronunciation, such as *pre*, *per*, and *pro; migrate* and *migraine*, by dictating these slowly and having the student spell them with letter tiles.

e) Words in a student's writing vocabulary can be categorized by sound. For example, awareness of similar blend sounds such as *fr* and *fl* can be enhanced by grouping words such as *flagrant* and *fragrant* with others beginning with the same clusters.

TEACHING BASIC SOUND-SYMBOL CORRESPONDENCES

The most basic multisensory drill advocated by Gillingham and Stillman (1960) and other programs based on similar principles (Birsh, 1999; Clark & Uhry, 1995) includes viewing a letter form on a card, saying the letter name, saying a key word, and then saying the target phoneme in isolation ("*i*, itchy, /I/"). The letter form is traced on a rough surface as the student recites.

To spell, the order of drill is changed to saying the sound, the key word, and the letter that makes it, and then writing the letter. The Orton-Gillingham approach strives automatic learning of these associations, and even after longer words are being spelled successfully, the student is asked to repeat the drill at the beginning of each lesson. As associations are learned, words are spelled using the Gillingham Simultaneous-Oral-Spelling (S.O.S.) technique (Gillingham & Stillman, 1960) to establish reliance on a phonetic encoding strategy:

1) The teacher pronounces the word.

2) The child hears the word and repeats the word. (He is hearing his own voice and feeling the articulation.)

3) The child says the word sound by sound. After identifying each phoneme, the child says the name of the letter that represents the sound, and writes the letter as it is being named.

4) The child reads orally the word that was written.

Many older children are not sure of all the alphabet letter names or forms even though they have been in school for several years. Some of the most confusing letters are *u*, *y*, and *w*, because their names, sounds, and forms relate in misleading ways to one another.

Choice of an unambiguous key word containing each phoneme is critically important in the basic sound-symbol drill. Desirable key words to associate with the short vowel phonemes would avoid nasalized vowels, r-controlled vowels, or vowels that are distorted by the following consonant. Suggested key words are as follows:

Vowel	Key Word	Words to Avoid
/ă/	at, apple	ant, bag, air
/ĕ/	Ed, Eddy	egg, elephant
/ĭ/	it, icky	igloo, Indian, ink
/ŏ/	ox, octopus	on, off
/ŭ/	up, us	umbrella, uncle

If students are severely learning disabled and affected by severe deficits in phonological processing, they must be taught speech sound awareness before and during sound-symbol instruction. Methods such as Lindamood's *LIPS Program* (Lindamood & Lindamood, 1984) that emphasize place, manner, and contrasts of phoneme production can be effective where others fail (Alexander et al., 1991; Torgesen, Wagner, & Rashotte, 1997). Vowel discrimination and memory for vowel correspondences can be enhanced when the articulatory placement of vowels is associated with their most reliable spellings (see Figure 6.b, following page).

A practice of the Lindamood and Gillingham approaches that should be incorporated into any remedial spelling program is the explicit and correct definition of linguistic concepts. Vowels are a set of speech sounds; digraphs are different from blends; schwa is the unaccented vowel, and so forth. Even young

Vowel Spellings by Mouth Position

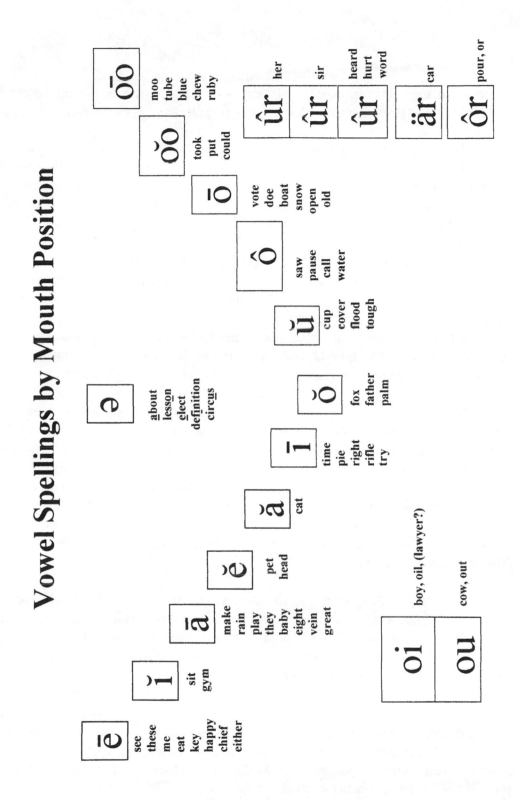

Figure 6.b. Vowel correspondences by vowel placement. © Louisa Moats.

children can learn this terminology. It serves to clarify, not confuse, but of course the teacher must be well informed about language to teach these concepts.

Persistent letter confusions and letter reversals can usually be corrected with a multisensory drill and daily practice reading and writing words with the confusing letters. Immediate corrective feedback must be available at first until the student internalizes a self-checking strategy. Reference to a mnemonic image, such as a bed for *b* and *d*, is often very helpful.

TEACHING REGULAR ONE-SYLLABLE PATTERNS
The basic units of spelling should be presented and learned in an order progressing from high frequency, high regularity units to complex, more unusual units that operate within several constraints. Forbes (1968), for example, organized her word lists into those that could be "sounded out," those that could be "sounded out and thought out," and those that required memorization or thorough knowledge of complex rules and probabilities.

The first level of practice occurs with predictable short-vowel word families or recurring syllable patterns. When first introduced to a new spelling pattern, the student should actively reorganize, compare, contrast, and sort words by their initial consonant(s), vowel, or rime unit (ending phonogram). Lists of words sharing rime features should be kept for later reference (e.g., *mass, grass, compass*) and for adding new words as they are encountered. Comparison, sorting, and classification are much more effective than rule recitation for learning about patterns, although ample practice writing words will be necessary to reinforce their automatic recall.

Vowel spellings, again, are the most varied and require the most practice. At first, the single letter and vowel-consonant-e patterns should be taught, then the vowel digraphs and diphthongs, one at a time. Vowels followed by /l/, /r/, and nasals /m/ and /n/ will be the most challenging for students because the presence and identity of the consonant as separate from the vowel is difficult for dyslexic students to realize. These constructions are phonologically ambiguous or obscure. In addition, the spellings in *hurt*, *bird*, *learn*, *were*, *her*, and *favor* all map to the same indistinct vowel plus /r/, and the word *fire* sounds as if it has two syllables, as in *higher*. Many poor spellers never quite master these complexities, so repeated practice with different patterns should be ongoing even when more advanced polysyllabic words are being studied.

Corrective feedback should take into account the reason for a child's confusion about spelling. Very often, the phonological ambiguity of the words themselves will be the cause of a misspelling. For example, if the child spells BAG for *beg*, the student could be taught that the vowel in *beg* is in fact pronounced like a "long a," but that this distortion in speaking is ignored in writing, and the word is to be grouped with the family that includes *leg*, *keg*, *Meg*, and *egg*.

EARLY INTRODUCTION OF INFLECTIONS

As soon as students are reading and writing verb forms, they are ready to be introduced to the past tense *-ed* morpheme. As soon as they are reading and writing noun forms, they are ready to learn the plural /s/ spelling. Learning that these morphemes are spelled consistently in spite of variations in pronunciation is the first step to realizing that spelling represents meaning, often in preference to sound. Explicit teaching of the past tense necessitates identification of the /d/, /t/, or /ed/ that ends words such as *begged, walked*, and *wanted*, before words are written to dictation. Spellings of inflections should be reviewed and practiced often for many years. It is insufficient to present one lesson on each and expect the learning to be internalized.

CONDITIONAL WORD AND SYLLABLE PATTERNS

Many patterns and generalizations are predictable but conditional. They include the spellings of *tall*, *annoy*, *glue*, *glove*, and *most*. In these cases, the student can either be asked to understand a pattern from examples (inductive learning) or to apply a given rule or principle to examples (deductive learning). The inductive approach is a powerful tool with bright students who enjoy solving puzzles. It is illustrated by the following exercise to teach the *ch*, *tch* generalization:

Given this list of words,

inch	catch	bunch	kitchen
starch	pouch	fetch	butcher
pitch	march	ranch	pinch
hatchet	pooch	botch	stitch,

students state when *tch* is used to spell /ch/ at the ends of words or syllables. Students may realize there are a few exceptions, including *rich, much, such, which, attach, sandwich,* and *bachelor*, and these should be presented as atypical. The "word sort" activity (Bear et al., 1996) is helpful for discovering patterns and can be carried out with words on cards.

If the inductive approach is confusing or ineffective with students because they are unable to see the patterns in the examples, then a deductive approach must be taken. A deductive approach calls for the teacher to state the rule and ask the student(s) to apply it to examples. With the word list above, the teacher might state, "A one-syllable word ending in /č/ is spelled with *tch* after an accented short vowel. In all other cases, /č/ is spelled *ch*." Then words could be grouped, read, and spelled to dictation.

HOMOPHONES

Their, there, and *they're; you're* and *your; its* and *it's* are among the most often misspelled words in the language. Other spellings of words that sound the same but differ in meaning and spelling, such as *course* and *coarse*, *knight* and *night*, *prophet* and *profit*, are commonly confused by children who cannot rely on letter memory. The best one can hope for in cases of very poor spellers is to clarify confusions among words they use most often, because practice of these words **in context** is what eventually develops the correct word habit.

Teachers often claim it takes an entire year of repeated practice to straighten out the *there/their/they're* confusion in older children. Matching games in which spelling and meaning are paired are helpful, at least in sensitizing the writer to what must be looked up, along with dictated phrases given regularly. Spell checkers on computers do not catch such errors and they can be embarrassing (like the letter from the ski coach who asked parents to learn the *coarse* before *gait*-keeping).

A comprehensive list of homophones can be found in *The New Reading Teacher's Book of Lists* (Fry, Fountoukidis, & Polk, 1985). Recall is facilitated when the words are placed in meaningful contexts repeatedly, including phrases, sentences, cloze exercises, analogies, jokes, cartoons, and puns. Homophones should be taught a few at a time, however; only the most able learners can work with the long lists that often appear in workbooks.

SYLLABLE PATTERNS AND SYLLABLE JUNCTURE

The syllable should be defined as a pronounceable unit that always contains a vowel sound and vowel letter (exceptions *rhythm*; *-ism*). Children with spelling difficulties benefit from learning the six syllable types (see Table 6.3, following page). One reason for teaching syllables is that redundant patterns in longer words can be much more quickly discerned; another is that the rules for adding endings to words and the way in which syllables are combined into longer words depend on the type of syllable(s) in the word; and finally, spellings become more predictable when the type of syllable is taken into account. For example, the most common spelling of "long a" in an open syllable within a polysyllabic word (*radio, vacation, stable*) is simply the letter *a*, and not the other seven alternatives.

Table 6.3. Syllable Types.

Syllable Type	Characteristics
Closed *rabbit* *basket* *picnicking*	These syllables contain a single short vowel followed by a consonant. In a polysyllabic word, a short vowel is usually protected from an adjacent vowel by two consonants. Thus, if a short vowel is heard in the first syllable, there are most likely two consonants between it and the next vowel.
Open *moment* *radar* *decide*	An open syllable ends with a long vowel spelled with a single letter. The long vowel in an open syllable is usually separated from the next syllable with only one consonant letter or no consonant.
R-Controlled *bird* *berth* *server*	When a vowel is followed by /r/, the vowel loses its identity as a long or short vowel, and is coarticulated with the /r/. A similar phenomenon occurs when /l/ follows a vowel. Students must learn that syllabic /r/ and r-controlled vowels are spelled with a vowel letter plus the letter *r*.
Vowel Team *sailboat* *seafood* *seesaw*	Many long vowels are spelled with two vowel letters including *ai, ay, ee, ea, ie, oa*. Diphthongs are also spelled with two vowel letters such as *oi, oy, ou*. In addition, the letter *w* can act as a vowel in a team, as in *ow, aw*. These teams, which are difficult for many poor spellers, can appear at the middle or end of words or before certain consonants (e.g. *aw* before *n* and *l*).
Vowel-e *write* *pace* *bake*	In the vowel-consonant-silent *e* pattern, the first vowel is long, there is one intervening consonant, and the *e* is silent. The silent *e* can be removed when adding a suffix that begins with a vowel to take the place of the silent *e* to keep the first vowel long: *writing, pacer*.
Consonant-le *juggle* *rifle* *table*	When the syllabic /l/ sound occurs at the ends of spoken words, it is often preceded by a consonant and spelled *le*. This forms a C-*le* syllable. Sometimes the first syllable needs to end with a consonant. For example, *little* has a first syllable closed by the first *t*, while the word *bugle* has an open first syllable. The sound of the vowel in the first syllable determines whether two consonants are needed.

If one knows about syllable types and syllable division, one can remember more easily that *supper* has two *p*'s and *super* has one. In *supper*, the first vowel is short, the first syllable is closed by a *p*, and another *p* separates the first vowel from the second. Most commonly, a short vowel (closed) syllable is separated from the vowel of a following syllable by two intervening consonants. A double *n* is necessary in words like *beginning* because the second syllable is closed and the double letters protect the "short I" vowel sound when the *ing* is added. There are many excellent programs for teaching syllable structure, including the *Brody Reading Method, 2ⁿᵈ Edition* (Brody, 2001), Jane Greene's *Language!* (Greene, 1995), *Patterns for Reading and Spelling* (Henry & Redding, 1996), *Megawords* (Johnson & Bayrd, 1983), and the *Wilson Language Program* (Wilson, 1996).

LATIN AND GREEK MORPHEME PATTERNS

Latin patterns. Latin-based words are usually taught after basic Anglo-Saxon vocabulary has been learned (Henry, 1993). In some ways, Latin-based words are easier to spell than Anglo-Saxon words. They do not use the problematic digraphs so common in Anglo-Saxon spellings, and because many spellings are meaning-based prefixes, roots, and suffixes, they tend to be constant even though many are reduced to /ə/ when they are unaccented. If students learn to recognize those meaningful units, many spellings will seem more logical. For example, *recommend* does not have two *c*'s, because the prefix *re* is added to the root *commend*.

There is ample evidence from cognitive psychology that words sharing derivational relationships should be taught together (Moats & Smith, 1992; Templeton, 1992). Many roots of Latin origin have consonants whose phonetic form changes in derived words such as the *t, c*, and *s* that appear in *partial, magician, confusion*. In addition, reduced vowels can be ambiguous in various derived forms (*confidence, sedative, competition*). In many words with ambiguous vowels or chameleon consonants, the correct spelling of a base word or derivation can be recovered more easily if it is learned in partnership with a word sharing the same root and more transparent.

On any list of "hard to spell" words, there are some that can be taught so that root-derivative relationships are made clear: *differ, different; favor, favorite; child, children; autumn, autumnal; sign, signal, resign, resignation; vacate, vacation; athlete, athletic; theater, theatrical; magic, magician.*

Many other words that turn up on "hard to spell" lists are rule-based or comprise affix-root constructions that make the spelling make sense. There is no reason why *beneficial, advice, attend*, or *misspell* should be learned in isolation as sight words, when all have prefixes. The method for teaching such words should call attention to the word's structure at the levels of sound, syllable, and meaningful parts.

Greek patterns. Words of Greek origin compose a large segment of our scientific vocabulary, and are best studied in the context of science and math. The spellings of *y* for /I/ (*gym, sphynx, krypton*), *ph* for /f/ (*photo, sphere, graph*) and *ch* for /k/ (*chorus, chameleon, ache*) signify a Greek derivative. Greek words combine morphemes but assign them equal status, like English compounds (*stratosphere, phonograph, thermometer*). The spellings tend to be very consistent and phonically transparent, and thus easier than words from other languages. Programs that teach Greek roots are the *Roots* supplement to *Language!* (Bebko, Alexander, & Doucet, 1997) and *Patterns for Reading and Spelling* (Henry & Redding, 1996).

The word *mnemonic* might seem obscure and difficult to spell until one considers its Greek origin and the related forms that have entered English. Mnemosyne was the Greek goddess of memory. The words *amnesia* (without memory) and *amnesty* (literally, forgetting a transgression) are cousins of *mnemonic*. Such knowledge helps clarify for most people that the other phonetically confusing Greek root, *pneumo* (*pneumatic*, *pneumonia*) is an altogether different form having to do with air. Memory and air, are, we hope, dissociated.

ABOUT ENDING RULES

The three major rules requiring an orthographic change when endings are added to words seem daunting for students to learn and frustrating for teachers to teach (see Table 6.4, following page).

The only hope for teaching these rules is to present them at intervals over several years, along with repeated reinforcement when corrective feedback about spelling is given. Consistent practice is needed rather than one or two lessons in sixth grade. Furthermore, these rules should be introduced after students have the conceptual underpinnings: a firm grasp of single-syllable spellings; the concepts of consonant, vowel, and syllable; and the ability to read multiple examples.

Most people begin to internalize the patterns for spelling word endings through repeated exposure to them in print. A good speller can produce a rule-based construction without necessarily stating the rule accurately, although knowledge of the rules helps clarify what is right when specific word memory fails. Individuals with mild spelling difficulties profit from practice with rules because their attention can be focused on the entire letter sequence in words such as *beginning* and *easier* when the spelling makes sense.

The internalization of orthographic change rules is very difficult for many poor spellers. Very often, students with spelling disabilities will fail to recognize when a rule needs to be applied, even if they know the rule (Carlisle, 1987; Liberman, Rubin, Duques, & Carlisle, 1985). Spelling research suggests that poor spellers will often recall specific word spellings without evidence that they have internalized or automated the rule that governs them.

Table 6.4. Orthographic Change Rules for Adding Endings.

Rule	Characteristics
Doubling Rule *running* *wettest*	When a one-syllable word with one vowel ends in one consonant, double the final consonant before adding a suffix beginning with a vowel.
Advanced Doubling *conferring* *occurred* *opening*	When a word has more than one syllable, double the final consonant when adding an ending beginning with a vowel *if* the final syllable is accented and has one vowel followed by one consonant.
Silent-e *confining* *wasteful*	When a root word ends in a silent *e*, drop the *e* when adding a suffix beginning with a vowel. Keep the *e* before a suffix beginning with a consonant.
y *studied* *studying* *monkeyed*	When a root word ends in a *y*-preceded-by-a-consonant, change the *y* to *i* before a suffix, except *ing*. When adding *ing*, or when the root word ends in *y*-preceded-by-a-vowel, make no change, just add the suffix.

Instructional Strategies Across the Sequence

MEMORIZING WORDS AS WHOLES

Multisensory techniques can be applied to the memorization of individual words. Even Horn (1969), who was generally hostile to linguistic or rule-based spelling instruction, notes that word study was more effective when several sensory images were stimulated simultaneously. His word study method follows:

1) look at the word
2) pronounce the word
3) say the letter names
4) recall how the word looks with the eyes closed
5) look back at the word and check
6) write the word
7) check and repeat if necessary

Horn's method, however, avoided explicit analysis of speech sounds and their representations. In contrast, the Fitzgerald method (Fitzgerald, 1951), places more emphasis on linking meaning with spelling, and remains an effective multisensory technique for memorizing words with somewhat unpredictable or complex spelling patterns. This method uses the following steps:

1) *Meaning and pronunciation.* Have the child look at the word, pronounce it, and use it in a sentence.

2) *Imagery.* Ask the child to see the word and say the word. Have the child say the word by syllable, spell the word orally, and trace over the word with a finger or write it in the air.

3) *Recall.* Ask the child to look at the word and then close her eyes to see the word in her mind's eye. Have her spell the word orally with her eyes closed. Ask her to open her eyes and see if the spelling was correct.

4) *Write the word.* The child writes the word from memory, and then checks against the original.

5) *Mastery.* The child covers the word and writes it. If she is correct, she should cover it and write it two more times.

The Fernald (1943) technique is similar to the above, but the whole word is traced repeatedly with the index and middle fingers on a rough tactile surface until the child can write it from memory. The learned word is then placed in the context of a meaningful sentence. There is no concern for grouping words by phonic pattern in Fernald's approach.

Such techniques foster the recall of whole word images for words that a student must commit to memory. They should accompany explicit instruction in the patterns and logic of the spelling system which, if learned, will facilitate the whole word learning process. There is some evidence (Vaughn, Schumm, & Gordon, 1993) that a variety of motoric conditions can be used for multisensory practice of spelling words—writing, tracing, or typing on a computer—and each of these is equally beneficial.

PROMOTING THE USE OF ACTIVE RECALL STRATEGIES
Although many programs offer suggestions for mnemonic devices that will aid spelling recall, the most effective mnemonics are those that students make up themselves. Because more active mental processing is necessary to create an idea than to listen to one, the self-generated strategy is the one most likely to be used. Gerber (1984) and others also have shown that children's word recall could be enhanced if they were taught to identify which words they were unsure of and to write plausible alternatives.

PLANNED GENERALIZATION OF SKILL

Most children who spell poorly can learn some words in lists with sufficient practice, but they regress to old habits during spontaneous writing. Instruction is not worthwhile unless it generalizes. Regular dictation exercises, personal spelling dictionaries with words listed alphabetically, and proofreading practice can strengthen the bridge between spelling skill development and its automatic use. Furthermore, overlearning basic sound-symbol associations and syllable patterns, and rehearsing words using multisensory drills prior to writing them in text, facilitates generalization.

Brody (2001), for example, suggests that informal classroom use of syllabication and multiple word writing improves spelling. Her steps include:
1. Student says word in syllables.
2. Student writes word in syllables while subvocalizing pronunciation of each syllable (syllables are separated with empty spaces, not lines).
3. Student writes word as whole.
4. Words are written 5 times each in syllables, repeatedly over 3 - 5 days.

INTEGRATED LESSON PLANNING

A systematic teacher plans the major elements of a lesson according to a predefined sequence of skills, and keeps an informal record of a student's responses to instruction. Although the plan can always be adjusted, it serves as a guide by which good teaching principles are implemented. Such a plan includes a choice of appropriate examples, sufficient review and practice, and application of skills to writing. With detailed record keeping, the next lesson can be tailor-made.

Systematic spelling instruction usually occurs in coordination with reading and vocabulary instruction. A structured lesson plan within a multisensory, linguistic approach might be similar to this:
1. phonogram drill
    a) sound-symbol
    b) symbol-sound
2. writing to dictation and immediate correction of errors by reference to logic or known words; review of previously learned material
3. sight word practice using multisensory writing-saying technique
4. introduction of new concept using inductive method or deductive method, as appropriate; exploration of phonological, orthographic, and etymological facts about the concept
5. writing nonsense and real words to dictation
6. sentence writing activity using new words

INDIVIDUAL DIFFERENCES AND FLEXIBLE TEACHING

Various strategies work for different types of words and different types of children. All of the specific suggestions offered here may be useful at some point, with some students. For example, some learners need quick integration of basic patterns into advanced vocabulary (*patch, dispatch, dispatcher; cent, century, percent, centennial*), but other learners might be overwhelmed by exposure to the harder words or words not in their speaking vocabulary. It is essential to have available a comprehensive word list that includes examples of each sound-symbol correspondence, syllable type, spelling pattern, rule, or generalization (e.g., Bear et al., 1996; Forbes, 1968; Ganske, 1993, 2000) and to use it with discretion.

As others have concluded after reviewing the historical literature on teaching spelling, there is no one right way to represent word structure for children or to help them remember this information. Techniques for making word structure memorable should vary according to the words under study. These strategies should match the properties of the target word presented as well as the learner's capabilities.

ADDITIONAL STRATEGIES TO AID MEMORIZATION

Several additional strategies for spelling instruction can be helpful when employed selectively and sensibly:

1. *Invoke a "spelling pronunciation."* This works well for words with silent letters, and foreign or irregular spellings that do not match pronunciation, such as *Wednesday*, *was*, and *antique*.

2. *Group words with like, but unusual, spelling-meaning patterns.*

two	one	there	their
twenty	once	here	heir
twelve	only	where	

3. *Employ mnemonic devices (association links):* He **mean**t to be **mean**. There's **a rat** in sep**arat**e. Knights would **die val**iantly in me**dieval** times. **Loose** as a **goose**. It's hard to **lose** your **nose**. **Sally** fin**ally** came home.

4. *Highlight visual-orthographic features of words.* People with poor orthographic memory may store and retrieve word images more readily if novelty or contrast is used to highlight letter sequences. Techniques that may be useful include: color coding (to contrast vowels and consonants); underlining; using different fonts on a word processor; or writing letters in different sizes. The effectiveness of such manipulations is not well researched at present, however.

SPECIAL CONSIDERATIONS FOR TEACHING ADOLESCENTS

Adolescents and adults often view themselves as hopeless cases if they have spelling disabilities, especially if prior instruction has been haphazard or linguistically uninformed. Many of them, however, can make significant improvement if their disabilities are worked with systematically, sequentially, and logically over a sustained period of time. When instruction is aimed at their developmental level of word knowledge (see Appendix D, following page), adolescents can develop confidence that language makes sense and that many spelling problems can be solved with knowledge of language structure.

Adolescents often know many individual words but do not understand spelling principles or word relationships. They have a much larger oral vocabulary to draw upon, so that rimes and other syllable units can be applied immediately to many examples. Their vocabulary can be used to build understanding of redundant language patterns. Goals for accuracy must be modest and realistic. Instruction should be aimed at improving the person's chances to communicate clearly and recognize the need to check spelling even when using technological aides to proofreading.

Conclusion

The teacher of spelling who knows language intimately can clarify the patterns of English for the learner. When a teacher understands the course of spelling development and the meaning of various error patterns, the level of instruction can be matched to the instructional level of each student. Individual variation in spelling is extremely wide in any classroom. A successful teacher will survey the developmental levels of the students and provide meaningful practice at those levels. Methods of instruction and practice will depend upon the nature of the vocabulary to be learned, the developmental levels of the students, and the types of any learning difficulties present. Effective spelling instruction will improve spelling, strengthen the learner's knowledge of word structure and vocabulary, and increase students' ability to use words fluently when writing.

Appendix D: Directions for Administering
the Primary & Elementary Spelling Inventories

These two tests are designed to assess the word knowledge elementary students have to bring to the tasks of reading and spelling. Students are not to study these words. That would invalidate the purpose of this inventory which is to find out what they truly know. You can administer this same list of words three times: in Sept, Jan and May; to measure children's progress.

These words are ordered in terms of their relative difficulty for children in grades K to 5. For this reason you need only call out the words which sample features your children are likely to master during the year. However, do call out enough words to give you a sense of the range of ability in your class. For kindergarten you may only call out the first five to eight words on the primary list for most children. For the first grade call out at least 15. For 2nd and 3rd use the entire primary list. Use the entire elementary spelling inventory for grades 4 and 5 and for any 3rd graders who are able to spell more than 20 of the words on the primary list. You should also call out additional words for any children who are spelling most of the words correctly at the K or 1st grade level.

Testing. Call the words as you would for any test. Use them in a sentence to be sure your children know the exact word. Assure your students that this is not for a grade but to help you plan better for their needs. Seat the children to minimize copying or test the children in small groups (recommended for K and early 1st grade).

Scoring the test. Copy a scoring sheet for each child and simply check off the features for each word which are spelled according to the descriptors at the top. Add an additional point in the "correct" column if the entire word is correct. Note that some words are scored for some features and not others and the number of possible points varies by words.

Assigning points and analyzing the results. Total the number of points under each feature and across each word. Staple the child's spelling test to the individual form. The total point score will give you a number which can be compared over time but the most useful information will be the feature analysis. Look down each feature column to determine the needs of individual students. Transfer these numbers to a class composite sheet to get a sense of your group as a whole and to form groups for instruction. Highlight children who are making two or more errors on a particular feature. For example, a child who gets 6 of 7 short vowels correct on the primary list can be considered in pretty good shape although some review work might be in order. A child who gets only 2 or 3 of the 7 short vowels needs a lot of work on that feature. Since the total possible number will vary depending on how many words you call out the criteria for mastery will vary. I generally think like this. If X is the number of possible correct responses then X or X-1 indicates good control of the feature while X-2, or more, indicates the need for instruction. If the child did not get any points for a feature it is beyond their instructional range and earlier features need to be addressed first.

Appendix D continued: **Primary Spelling Inventory** – Individual Score Sheet (adapted from Francine Johnston, 7/98)

Name of Child _____ Teacher _____ Grade ____ Date ____ Total Pts ____

	Initial Consonant	Final Consonant	Di-graph	Blend	Short Vowel	Long Vowel VC e	Vowel Team/diphthong	R-control Vowel	Inflec-tions	Correct	Word Totals
1. fan	f	n			a						
2. pet	p	t			e						
3. dig	d	g			i						
4. mob	m	b			o						
5. rope	r	p				o-e					
6. wait	w	t					ai				
7. chunk			ch	nk	u						
8. sled				sl	e						
9. stick		-ck		st	i						
10. shine			sh			i-e					
11. dream				dr			ea				
12. blade				bl		a-e					
13. coach			-ch				oa				
14. fright				fr			igh				
15. snowing				sn			ow		-ing		
16. talked							-a		-ed		
17. camping				-mp					-ing		
18. thorn			th					or			
19. shouted			sh				ou				
20. spoil				sp			oi				
21. growl				gr			ow				
22. chirp			ch					ir			
23. clapped				cl					-pped		
24. tries				tr					-es		
25. hiking									-king		

Appendix D continued: **Elementary Spelling Inventory** – Individual Score Sheet (adapted from Francine Johnston, 7/98)

Name of Child _____ Teacher _____ Grade _____ Date _____ Total Pts _____

	Short vowel	Blend/ digraph	Long vowel	Other vowel	Complex consonant	inflection	Syllable juncture	Unaccented syllable	suffix	Correct	Word Totals
1. speck	e	sp			ck						
2. switch	i	sw			tch						
3. throat			oa		thr						
4. nurse				ur							
5. scrape			a-e		scr						
6. charge		ch		ar	ge	ai					
7. phone		ph	o-e								
8. smudge	u	sm			dge						
9. point		nt		oi							
10. squirt		squ		ir							
11. drawing		dr		aw		-ing					
12. trapped		tr				-pped					
13. waving						-ving					
14. powerful				ow				-er	-ful		
15. battle							tt	-tle			
16. fever							v	-er			
17. lesson							ss	-on			
18. pennies						-ies	nn				
19. fraction									-tion		
20. sailor							l		-or		
21. distance							st		-ance		
22. confusion									-sion		
23. discovery								dis-	-ery		
24. resident								si	-dent		
25. visible									-ible		
Feature Totals											Total Pts:

206

References

Adams, M.J., Foorman, B.F., Lundberg, I., & Beeler, T. (1997). *Phonemic Awareness in Young Children: A Classroom Curriculum.* Baltimore: Paul Brookes.

Alexander, A., Andersen, H., Heilman, P., Voeller, K., & Torgesen, J. (1991). Phonological awareness training and remediation of analytic decoding deficits in a group of severe dyslexics. *Annals of Dyslexia, 41,* 193-206.

Bailet, L.L. (1990). Spelling rule usage among students with learning disabilities and normally achieving students. *Journal of Learning Disabilities, 23,* 121-128.

Ball, E., & Blachman, B. (1991). Does phoneme awareness training in kindergarten make a difference in early word recognition and developmental spelling? *Reading Research Quarterly, 26,* 49-66.

Bear, D.R., Templeton, S., Invernizzi, M., & Johnston, F. (1996). *Words their way: Word study for phonics, vocabulary, and spelling instruction.* Englewood Cliffs, NJ: Merrill.

Bebko, A., Alexander, J., & Doucet, R. (1998). *Language! Roots.* Longmont, CO: Sopris West.

Berninger, V. (1998). Assessment, prevention, and intervention for specific reading and writing disabilities in young children. In B. Wong (ed.), *Learning About Learning Disabilities (2nd ed.)* (pp. 529-555). New York: Academic Press.

Berninger, V. (1999). The "write stuff" for preventing and treating writing disabilities. *Perspectives, 25*(2), 20-22.

Birsh, J. (ed.) (1999). *Multisensory teaching of basic language skill.* Baltimore: Paul Brookes.

Blachman, B., Tangel, D., Ball, E., & Black, R. (1999). Combining phonological awareness and word recognition instruction. *Perspectives, 25*(2), 7-10.

Brody, S. (2001). *The Brody reading manual: An implementation guide for teachers (2nd ed.).* Milford, NH: LARC Publishing.

Bruck, M. (1987). The adult outcomes of children with learning disabilities. *Annals of Dyslexia, 37,* 252-263.

Bruck, M. (1988). The word recognition and spelling of dyslexic children. *Reading Research Quarterly, 23,* 51-69.

Bryant, N.D., Drabin, I.R., & Gettinger, M. (1981). Effects of varying unit size on spelling achievement in learning disabled children. *Journal of Learning Disabilities, 14,* 200-203.

Carlisle, J.F. (1987). The use of morphological knowledge in spelling derived forms by learning-disabled and normal students. *Annals of Dyslexia, 37,* 90-108.

Clark, D.B., & Uhry, J. (1995). *Dyslexia: Theory and Practice of Remediation (2nd ed.).* Baltimore: York Press.

Ehri, L.C. (1989). The development of spelling knowledge and its role in reading acquisition and reading disability. *Journal of Learning Disabilities, 224,* 349-364.

Ehri, L.C. (1997). Learning to read and learning to spell are one and the same, almost. In C.A. Perfett, L. Rieben, & M. Fayol (eds.), *Learning to Spell: Research, Theory, and Practice across Languages.* Mahwah, NJ: Lawrence Erlbaum.

Elkonin, D.B. (1973). USSR. In J. Downing (Ed.), *Comparative reading.* NY: Macmillan.

Felton, R.H., & Wood, F.B. (1989). Cognitive deficits in reading disability and attention deficit disorder. *Journal of Learning Disabilities, 1,* 3-13.

Fernald, G. (1943). *Remedial techniques in basic school subjects.* New York: McGraw Hill.

Fink, R. (1998). Literacy development in successful men and women with dyslexia. *Annals of Dyslexia, 48,* 311-346.

Finucci, J., Gottfredson, L.S., & Childs, B. (1985). A follow-up study of dyslexic boys. *Annals of Dyslexia, 35*, 117-136.

Fischer, F.W., Shankweiler, D., & Liberman, I.Y. (1985). Spelling proficiency and sensitivity to word structure. *Journal of Memory and Language, 24*, 423-441.

Fitzgerald, J.A. (1951). *A basic life spelling vocabulary*. Bruce.

Fitzsimmons, R.J., & Loomer, B.M. (1977). *Excerpts from spelling, learning and instruction - research and practice*. Iowa State Department of Public Instruction and the University of Iowa, Iowa City.

Forbes, C.T. (1968). *Graded and classified spelling lists for teachers grades 2-8*. Cambridge, MA: Educators Publishing Service.

Frauenheim, J.G., & Heckerl, J.R. (1983). A longitudinal study of psychological and achievement test performance in severe dyslexic adults. *Journal of Learning Disabilities, 16*, 339-347.

Fry, E., Fountoukidis, D.L., & Polk, J.K. (1985). *The new reading teacher's book of lists*. Englewood Cliffs, NJ: Prentice Hall.

Ganske, K. (2000). *Word Journeys*. NY: Guilford.

Gerber, M. (1984). Techniques to teach generalizable spelling skills. *Academic Therapy, 20*, 49-58.

Gillingham, A., & Stillman, B. (1960). *Remedial training for children with specific disability in reading, spelling, and penmanship*. Cambridge, MA: Educators Publishing Service.

Greene, J. (1995). *Language!* Longmont, CO: Sopris West.

Hanna, P.R., Hanna, J.S., Hodges, R.E., & Rudorf, E.H. (1966). *Phoneme-grapheme correspondences as cues to spelling improvement*. Washington, DC: U.S. Government Printing Office, U.S. Office of Education.

Henderson, E. (1990). *Teaching spelling (2nd ed.)*. Boston: Houghton Mifflin.

Henry, M. (1993). Morphological structure: Latin and Greek roots and affixes as upper grade code strategies. *Reading and Writing: An Interdisciplinary Journal, 5*, 227-241.

Henry, M., & Redding, N. (1996). *Patterns for reading and spelling*. Austin, TX: Pro-Ed.

Hillerich, R.L. (1978). *A writing vocabulary of elementary children*. Springfield, IL: Charles C. Thomas.

Hillerich, R.L. (1985). *Teaching children to write, K-8: A complete guide to developing writing skills*. Englewood Cliffs, NJ: Prentice Hall.

Hoffman, P.R., & Norris, J.A. (1989). On the nature of phonological development: Evidence from normal children's spelling errors. *Journal of Speech and Hearing Research, 32*, 787-794.

Horn, E. (1969). Spelling. In C.W. Harris (Ed.), *Encyclopedia of Educational Research* (pp. 1282-1299). New York: Macmillan.

Invernizzi, M., & Worthy, M.J. (1989). An orthographic-specific comparison of the spelling errors of learning disabled and normal children across four grade levels of spelling achievement. *Reading Psychology: An International Quarterly, 10*, 173-188.

Johnson, D., & Myklebust, H.R. (1967). *Learning disabilities: Educational principles and practices*. New York: Grune & Stratton.

Johnson, K., & Bayrd, P. (1983). *Megawords*. Cambridge, MA: Educators Publishing Service.

208

King, D. (1984). *Teaching written expression to adolescents*. Cambridge, MA: Educators Publishing Service.

Liberman, I.Y., Rubin, H., Duques, S., & Carlisle, J. (1985). Linguistic abilities and spelling proficiency in kindergartners and adult poor spellers. In D.B. Gray & J.F. Kavanaugh (Eds.), *Biobehavioral measures of dyslexia* (pp. 163-176). Parkton, MD: York Press.

Lindamood, P.C., Bell, N., & Lindamood, P. (1992). Issues in phonological awareness assessment. *Annals of Dyslexia, 42*, 242-259.

Lindamood, C., & Lindamood, P. (1984). *The A.D.D. Program: Auditory discrimination in depth (2nd ed.)*. Allen, TX: DLM, Inc.

Lyon, G. R., & Moats, L.C. (1988). Critical issues in the instruction of the learning disabled. *Journal of Consulting and Clinical Psychology, 56*, 830-835.

Mann, V.A., Tobin, P., & Wilson, R. (l987). Measuring phonological awareness through the invented spellings of kindergarten children. *Merrill Palmer Quarterly, 33*, 365-391.

Moats, L.C. (1983). A comparison of the spelling errors of older dyslexics and second-grade normal children. *Annals of Dyslexia, 33*, 121-139.

Moats, L.C. (1995). *Spelling: Development, disability, and instruction*. Baltimore: York Press.

Moats, L.C. (1996). Phonological spelling errors in the writing of dyslexic adolescents. *Reading and Writing: An Interdisciplinary Journal, 8*, 105-119.

Moats, L.C., & Smith, C. (l992). Derivational morphology: Why it should be included in assessment and instruction. *Language, Speech and Hearing in the Schools, 23*, 312-319.

Nulman, J.H., & Gerber, M.M. (1984). Improving spelling performance by imitating a child's errors. *Journal of Learning Disabilities, 17*, 328-333.

Orton, S. (1937). *Reading, writing, and speech problems in children*. New York: W.W. Norton and Co.

Pennington, B.F., McCabe, L.L., Smith, S.D., Lefly, D.L., Bookman, M.O, Kimberling, W.J., & Lubs, H.A. (1986). Spelling errors in adults with a form of familial dyslexia. *Child Development, 57*, 1001-1013.

Powell, D., & Hornsby, D. (1993). *Learning phonics and spelling in a whole language classroom*. New York: Scholastic Professional Books.

Read, C. (1986). *Children's creative spelling*. London: Routledge and Kegan Paul.

Read, C., & Ruyter, L. (1985). Reading and spelling skills in adults of low literacy. *Remedial and Special Education, 6*, 43-52.

Reith, H., Axelrod, S., Anderson, R., Hathaway, F., Wood, K., & Fitzgerald, C. (1974). Influence of distributed practice and daily testing on weekly spelling tests. *Journal of Educational Research, 68*, 73-77.

Rosner, J. (1973). *The perceptual skills curriculum*. New York: Walker Educational Book Co.

Sawyer, D., Wade, S., & Kim, J. (1999). Spelling errors as a window on dyslexia. *Annals of Dyslexia, 49*, 137-159.

Stoner, J. (1985). *Syllable plus*. Cambridge, MA: Educators Publishing Service.

Stotsky, S. (1999). *Losing our language: How multicultural classroom instruction is undermining our children's ability to read, write, and reason*. New York: The Free Press.

Tangel, D.M., & Blachman, B.A. (1992). Effect of phoneme awareness instruction on kindergarten children's invented spelling. *Journal of Reading Behavior, 24*, 233-261.

Templeton, S. (1992). Theory, nature, and pedagogy of higher-order orthographic development in older students. In S. Templeton and D. R. Bear (Eds.), *Development of orthographic knowledge and the foundations of literacy: A memorial Festschrift for Edmund H. Henderson.* (pp. 253-277). Hillsdale, NJ: Erlbaum.

Templeton, S., & Bear, D. (Eds.) (1992). *Development of orthographic knowledge and the foundations of literacy: A memorial Festschrift for Edmund H. Henderson.* Hillsdale, NH: Lawrence Erlbaum.

Thomson, M. (1991). The teaching of spelling using techniques of simultaneous oral spelling and visual inspection. In M. Snowling and M. Thomson (Eds.), *Dyslexia: Integrating theory and practice.* (pp. 244-250). London: Whurr Publishers.

Torgesen, J., Wagner, R., & Rashotte, C. (1997) The prevention and remediation of severe reading disabilities: Keeping the end in mind. *Scientific Studies of Reading*, *1*, 217-234.

Treiman, R. (1993). Beginning to spell: *A study of first grade children.* New York: Oxford.

Vaughn, S.V., Schumm, J.S., & Gordon, J. (1993). Which motoric condition is most effective for teaching spelling to students with and without learning disabilities? *Journal of Learning Disabilities, 26*, 191-198.

Venezky, R. (1970). *The structure of English orthography.* The Hague: Mouton.

Wilson, B.A. (1988). Instructor Manual. Millbury, MA: Wilson Language Training.

IV. THOUGHT

Chapter 7. Comprehension: Gathering Information and Constructing Understanding

Sara Brody, EdD

When students read fluently—with speed, accuracy, and comprehension they begin Chall's Stage 3—"reading to learn." During Stage 3, students learn how to process unfamiliar information and develop understanding while reading. With guidance, they begin to use reading as a highly versatile problem-solving tool. They rapidly discover that reading enables them to gather ideas and useful details from sources as diverse as the information superhighway and their own shopping lists. Further, some students turn to reading for the pleasure of fantastic adventure, enthralling romance, or a close-up encounter with the thoughts of a respected role model.

As they progress through Stage 3, students use reading itself, along with relevant instruction, as a means to enrich their vocabulary, broaden their background, and increase their agility in developing clear understanding of unfamiliar concepts. As they build their background resources and continue in their cognitive maturation, successful students later use reading as a process that lets them synthesize and share deep understanding concerning complex systems of thoughts, concepts, and structures.

Teachers enhance comprehension development among Stage 3 readers through instruction that facilitates reading to learn and deeply understand specialized information. As students mature toward Stages 4 and 5, teachers can provide scaffolds that help advanced readers become adept at gathering information from multiple sources in order to construct new understanding while reading challenging text.

Research suggests that during Stage 3, effective instruction needs to draw on the skills emphasized in classic instructional techniques while providing enhancement with more recent experimental approaches (National Reading Panel [NRP], 2000). In particular, until the 1980s, reading comprehension activities generally focused on teaching students the skills needed to determine the main idea and details of a selection, along with how to compare and contrast concepts, identify cause and effect, and draw inferences and conclusions. Such activities foster Stage 3 reading—using text to learn new concepts, information, thoughts, feelings, relationships, etc. These activities remain central to constructing a clear understanding of text.

In addition, during the last few decades, researchers and educators began exploring means of facilitating Stage 4 and 5 reading—gathering information from multiple perspectives to actively construct new knowledge—by teaching a variety of metacognitive strategies. As a whole, studies of these strategies yielded rather mixed findings among 4th and 5th graders who were at the stage of learning to gather specialized content from text (Brody, 1989; Haller, Child, & Walberg, 1988; NRP, 2000; Pressley, 2000). The mixed findings mirror the experiences reported to me informally by reading specialists and teachers who have found inconsistent results in their own classrooms. Teachers often indicate that strategy effectiveness is related to students' needs, abilities, and background, with skilled readers generally performing well on comprehension tasks no matter which strategy is employed.

It is tempting to conclude that teachers must rely solely on experimentation in order to find activities that can be used during classroom instruction to meet the individual needs of both advanced and less-skilled learners. However, it seems that instructional planning can be enriched by a guiding framework if it delineates the effective elements of Stage 3 instruction, profiles additional elements that facilitate higher level comprehension, and specifies when and how these elements may be integrated effectively.

In order to seek such guidelines, I sifted through the mixed findings in the literature concerning Stage 3 reading comprehension instruction. First, I reviewed and synthesized dozens of research studies, from the 1980s to '90s, concerned with classroom reading comprehension instruction of 4th and 5th graders—readers beginning the process of gathering specialized information from print (Brody, 1989; 1991; 1993). Then, I examined these practices and findings along with the findings from similar studies conducted with older students (Flood & Lapp, 1990; Graves, Cooke, & LaBerge, 1983; Hayes, 1989; Palincsar & Brown, 1984; Slater, Graves, & Piche, 1985). In addition, these studies were compared with findings reported by the National Reading Panel (2000).

The review indicated that, across the age range, certain *underlying elements* were **present** along with any method under study when it exhibited a comprehension advantage over a comparison procedure. Further, when any method found effective in one instance showed no advantage in another study, the core *underlying elements* did **not** appear to be **present** in the latter studies.

This chapter draws on these studies to consider the nature of effective reading instruction, particularly at Stage 3. First, underlying **core elements** related to comprehension among Stage 3 readers are identified. Next, these elements are examined by considering factors that contribute to their effectiveness, along with instructional approaches in which they are incorporated during classroom reading instruction. This is followed by a review of strategies that are commonly recommended to facilitate higher levels of reading comprehension. Finally, the chapter describes a process that integrates core elements of Stage 3 instruction with strategies that facilitate preparation for Stage 4 and 5 reading.

Core Elements and Comprehension Instruction

The core instructional elements that continually reappear when Stage 3 reading comprehension methods appear effective seem almost too common-sense to study or consider. And yet, it is the presence or absence of these elements that seems consistently related to strategy effectiveness. The core elements are summarized below:

1) assure that students are able to read the words in which the material is written (introduce specialized polysyllabic words before assigning reading to **enhance decoding fluency**, or use text written at readers' decoding competency level);

2) provide multiple exposures to the meanings of unfamiliar words, or assure that readers possess the necessary

background from which to **develop knowledge of word meanings** while reading (teach word meanings before and during reading along with teaching the background concepts needed to infer word meanings from context);

3) **pose questions** that develop an organizing focus and purpose for reading and continuing to read (use questions, before and during reading, that prime readers to process what they read);

4) assure that readers possess crucial background knowledge that is needed in order to grasp the concepts in the material under study (**explain background** needed to form inferences);

5) provide many exposures to unfamiliar ideas in the reading, and offer many opportunities to organize, summarize, and express these concepts (arrange **plenty of practice and application** of unfamiliar concepts).

Validation. The effectiveness of the core elements in facilitating reading comprehension is corroborated in several ways. As discussed above, these elements commonly appear as an integral part of instruction when any reading comprehension approach is found effective. In addition, research concerning the habits of skilled readers indicates that "strategic" readers *use these same elements* in their own self-directed reading processes (Flood & Lapp, 1990; Lyon, 2000). In addition, these elements are stressed in the findings of the National Reading Panel (2000).

Flood & Lapp (1990) and Pressley (2000) report that skilled readers slow down, when needed, to **decode unfamiliar words**; use various strategies to **determine the meanings** of unknown words; **ask questions** of themselves to focus on relevant concepts in the reading; search through their prior knowledge to **seek background** that will let them form appropriate inferences; and engage in **repeated rehearsal, summarization, and review** of a text under study as a means of developing meaningful and complete schemata.

The match is quite close between the behaviors of skilled readers and the instructional elements that assist less-skilled readers. This match suggests that when instruction incorporates these core elements, it serves as a scaffold that enhances less-skilled readers' comprehension until they develop the rich background and ability needed to use "strategic" habits independently.

It appears that various instructional strategies are likely to enhance the comprehension of Stage 3 readers *provided* that the methods include the effective elements noted above. This section presents core elements in detail in order to clarify how and why these "active ingredients" help readers comprehend text. Several elements are discussed in separate chapters of their own and are mentioned only briefly in this section. (See Chapter 8 concerning background concepts; Chapter 9 concerning vocabulary concepts; and Chapter 10 related to multiple exposures and expression through writing.)

Element One: Develop Decoding Fluency Before and During Reading

As discussed in Chapter 5, decoding fluency sets a reader's mind free to focus on comprehension of the information and concepts relayed by text (Bloom, 1986; Lyon, 2000; Samuels, Schermer, & Reinking, 1992; Stanovich, 1994). After much debate, it is generally accepted that word decoding ability is a prerequisite to understanding content text (Biemiller, 2000; NRP, 2000).

In addition, through the nature of their research designs, most researchers acknowledge that decoding fluency is a prerequisite to the use of a variety of reading comprehension strategies whether applied to literature or content texts. For example, researchers design their comprehension studies to avoid limited decoding competency by selecting only students whose decoding skills are at grade level, or students otherwise judged to be competent decoders (Anstey & Freebody, 1987; Palincsar & Brown, 1984). Other times, studies use reading materials that are written well below the grade level of the students in the study as a means of assuring that all subjects can decode the study materials with fluency (Hansen & Pearson, 1983; Spiegel & Whaley, 1980).

Many studies provide evidence to substantiate the positive influence of decoding fluency on reading comprehension in the upper elementary grades (e.g., Durkin, 1984; Pressley, 2000; Sadoski & Page, 1984). They compare decoding error rates with reading comprehension scores and find a significant correlation. Occasionally, researchers speculate that a strategy under study is not as effective as expected because the metacognitive requirements of the strategy are overwhelming when accompanied by the demands of less-than-fluent decoding among less-skilled readers (Gordon & Pearson, 1983).

One study, comparing silent and oral reading, found that upper-elementary grade readers with limited decoding competency understood text no better whether reading silently or orally. During silent reading, these students completed the assigned reading task more quickly, by skipping over unfamiliar words, but this did not enhance their understanding of what was read (Juel & Holmes, 1980).

The procedures used by researchers to rule out decoding limitations during research activities are not available routinely to classroom teachers. Consequently, several alternatives are suggested below.

Develop decoding fluency with unfamiliar content words. Many readers beyond the primary years generally decode fluently but stumble on long words that convey unfamiliar content in tradebooks or textbooks. Teachers can ease the burden of decoding long words by introducing them before assigning independent reading. The introduction can follow these steps:

Teacher:
- write the word on the board
- say the word
- break the word into syllables and say syllables while pointing to them
- tell word meaning if unknown

Students:
- repeat the above activities following the teacher's model.

The approach can be combined with a variety of prereading strategies such as text-structure frames, focus questions, or reading previews (described later in this chapter). Whatever strategy is in use, referring to the activity as a vocabulary procedure reduces embarrassment that may accompany explicit recognition of limited decoding competency. This prereading practice showed promise during informal research in elementary, middle, and high school classes (Brody, 1986, 2001).

Teachers who recognize the burden of less-than-fluent decoding skills respond willingly to students' requests for assistance in reading unknown words. This scaffold lets learners get on with the project of reading the passage. Since readers need to build efficient visual-phonological-lexical links through extensive, **accurate** repetition (Goswami, 2000; Perfetti, 1985), teachers need to provide correct pronunciation, when asked, rather than encouraging students to "get by" with many inaccurate guesses (Adams, 1994). Providing pronunciation will **not** deprive students of an opportunity to identify a word through context since students tend to ask for help only when they feel that the strategies they possess have failed.

Compensate with alternatives to reading. The great diversity in students' reading abilities presents a particular challenge during instruction in the content areas. When decoding limitations lie deeper than a lack of fluency with a few specialized content words, students risk falling far behind in background knowledge development (Lyon, 2000; Stanovich, 1986, 1994). In order to convey important content concepts, teachers can provide alternative exposures through oral language presentations accompanied by visual materials such as pictures, graphs, videos, and experiences. Class lectures, discussions, and group projects allow opportunities for multiple non-print exposures to the central concepts of a lesson. In order to assure that the **language** for expressing these concepts is learned as well, teachers need to accompany visual and experiential instruction with **oral descriptions** and **discussion** (Brody, 1993).

At the same time, it is important to offer many reading opportunities for students who *can* decode, since proficient reading may provide a broader range of information than may be available from listening to a single source. These opportunities capitalize on the apparent advantage of reading as a means of developing vast stores of background knowledge (Chall, 1996; Stanovich & Cunningham, 1993).

Ensure that oral activities remain on topic and sequential. Students with limited decoding competency need to experience rich, oral exposure by engaging in fruitful discussions concerning the topic under study. These students lose the opportunity to learn when class discussions wander aimlessly or in multiple directions that scramble topics and issues with irrelevant trivia (Mangano, 1983).

Discussions that enhance comprehension focus on central points as well as clearly illustrate the connections between secondary issues and main concepts (Manzo & Manzo, 1990; Pressley, 2000). In this way, class discussion can serve as an effective vehicle for sharing concepts with students who lack decoding ability. Discussion also needs to be focused in order to effectively confirm and clarify the important aspects of what was read by efficient decoders. (See Chapter 10 concerning the use of writing to facilitate discussion, application, and deep conceptual understanding.)

Element Two: Knowledge of Word Meanings

Readers need to possess sufficient knowledge of the meanings of the words in a passage in order to "get the meaning from context" when unfamiliar words are encountered (Biemiller, 2000; McKeown, 1985). Readers who lack this competency sometimes can be identified by their ability to read with deep comprehension in subject areas that are familiar to them, but with little or no understanding concerning unfamiliar subjects. It is as if someone had deleted nearly every content word and left the reader to glean meaning only from the short "glue" words in the paragraphs.

This comprehension problem can plague readers whose learning disabilities have limited their vocabulary development, or it may afflict readers who have not been read to by others, or who have not read widely to themselves (Biemiller, 2000; Chall, Jacobs, & Baldwin, 1991; Cunningham & Stanovich, 1997). Reading and oral language comprehension strategies need to provide multiple exposures to unfamiliar words by defining, explaining, clarifying, or demonstrating the meanings of words that appear in text (McKeown, 1985, 1993; Moats, 2000; NRP, 2000).

Some students seem more "motivated" to read material on a familiar favorite topic than to read about an unfamiliar concept. By consistently providing adequate vocabulary exposure when *introducing* a unit, teachers can enhance motivation and encourage readers to explore unfamiliar concepts. Engagement in broad reading, in turn, extends readers' knowledge of word meanings and background concepts (Chall, 1987; Chomsky, 1972; Snow, Burns, & Griffin, 1998; Stanovich, 1986; Stanovich & Cunningham, 1993). (See Chapter 9 concerning vocabulary development.)

Element Three: Use Questions to Organize Focus Before and During Reading

Readers need to identify and sequence what is important in text and sort it from what is extraneous. Some students can understand expository or narrative text that is well organized and thus "considerate of the reader," but experience difficulty when text is scattered and thus "inconsiderate" (Armbruster, 1984, 1991; Goldman & Rakestraw, 2000). For example, some readers become confused when reading a story that employs flashbacks or shifts in author's voice. Similarly, readers may be confused when the running text of a social studies book is broken by insertions of fictionalized historical accounts or reproductions of authentic artifacts such as newspaper articles.

Strategies that assist readers in locating important information and recognizing subordinate material seem to **pose questions**, in some format, to be answered by gathering information from text (NRP, 2000). Some strategies pose questions directly (Wixson, 1983); other strategies couch questions within a problem to solve or in a framework to complete during reading (Slater et al, 1985). Yet others direct students to develop their own questions (Helfeldt & Henk, 1990; Palincsar, 1986; Palincsar & Brown, 1984). Relevant questions help students focus on important content under study while irrelevant questions lead readers to remember tangential concepts (Wixson, 1983).

The effectiveness of questions as a means of focusing readers' attention on central information is reflected in research on human motivation and our need to make sense of the world. Humans have a driving need to resolve cognitive dissonance (Csikszentmihalyi, 1990; Festinger, 1957). Teachers can create cognitive dissonance by posing questions that demand focused reading to achieve resolution.

Textbook questions. A great volume of material is crammed into typical classroom textbooks. Publishers try to accommodate audiences that vary widely across the nation (Chall & Squire, 1991). Consequently, they often include so much information in any one chapter that it is very difficult for an inexperienced reader to sort out the extraneous detail. Since the publishers could not decide what was pertinent and what could be left out, it is not unreasonable that an inexperienced reader, with limited background concerning the subject, would also have difficulty with that task. It is important, then, for teachers to determine what material should be read and what ignored. These decisions can be communicated, to some extent, through questions that accompany the reading (Lyon, 2000; Santa, 1986).

When asked questions before reading, learners typically remember question-related information and forget information that was not related to a question (Pressley, 2000; Wixson, 1983). Thus questions give readers a way to recognize what is important and what is less important. In addition, as questions are answered, they offer students concrete evidence that progress has been made in understanding what was to be learned.

Sometimes teachers are dismayed that students have a tendency to read assigned questions *before* reading the related text. However, students who are learning how to learn-from-text have not yet mastered the art of differentiating important and unimportant, or central and supporting, concepts. They preview questions to assist themselves with this differentiation (and to finish the assignment quickly). Teachers can capitalize on their students' tactic by providing questions that draw together the relevant information. Such questions help students construct meaningful schemata while reading to find answers to specific questions. If important or sufficient information is not highlighted by questions printed in the text, teachers can develop and assign alternative or additional questions of their own.

During reading of content texts or literature, much of the cognitive process of arranging lexical units to form a schema seems to be an unconscious questioning of whether information is making sense in a particular arrangement and whether the information is important enough to include in the schema (Goldman & Rakestraw, 2000; Perfetti & Curtis, 1986). In a sense, readers form a text schema to answer the question, "What is this all about?" As readers make their way through text, answering questions may confirm that relevant schemata are being formed.

Cue questions. When developing questions, teachers can use several strategies that lead to particularly effective study. Carefully worded questions subtly preteach or reteach relevant background. Such questions are phrased to include relevant background that clarifies the focus expected in the answer. For example, rather than asking the very broad question, "Why is sexism a problem?" teachers prepare students to seek the issue of relevance by asking, "Given that women generally earn less than men when working at the same job with equal or better efficiency, and given that the nation's poor are predominantly women and children, why is sexism a problem and what steps might decrease its influence?"

As a general rule, questions should follow the sequence of the text. This practice helps students develop cohesive schemata composed of relevant points. When literature or expository texts are assigned, less-skilled readers may attempt the material, if they are given the scaffold of questions that include (in parentheses) the page number and paragraph heading in which an answer is located. Less-skilled readers also may be aided by varied spacing, between questions, that indicates the size of the answer that is anticipated. For example, one line of space would appear under a question asking for the date of an event, while a quarter or third of a page would appear under a question that requires an answer listing several points.

Questions to facilitate pleasure reading. The effectiveness of posing questions to guide reading is well established (NRP, 2000; Wixson, 1983). Questions encourage independent pleasure reading when they appear in book-report or reading-record formats to be completed for bonus credit.

Reading-record formats include questions such as: What is the story title? Where is the setting? Describe the main characters. What five major events occurred (plot)? What is the author's message about life (theme)? How can you apply the author's lesson to your life or the life of a friend (application and transfer)? Or, with expository text: What are three interesting concepts presented? Describe several aspects of each concept. How do these concepts affect society?

Questions that stimulate problem-solving. Problem-solving offers an alternate form of posing questions. Perkins (1986) and Perkins & Salomon (1988) propose that problem-solving facilitates the learning of information as "active" (accessible and applicable) knowledge rather than as an "inert" collection of facts that cannot be recalled or applied to appropriate situations.

Csikszentmihalyi (1990) suggests that the greatest challenge in creative work is defining the problem to be solved. He proposes that once the problem is found—the question framed—a paradigm is formed and material can take shape as a meaningful and cohesive set of concepts. In essence, problem-solving is completed when one gathers and arranges information into a meaningful and cohesive sequence (schema).

Problem Types. Several types of problems can engage readers with text.

Type One. Type One problems focus on a problem of completing an assignment. Some students enjoy solving the problem of completing work, checking it off, and handing it in on time.

While this aspect of problem-solving develops important organizational skills, it can lead to erroneous understanding since it **does not** assure meaningful engagement with reading material. (A student could check off a Type One problem after **in**accurately completing an assignment.) While assignment-completing behaviors are crucial, they do not assure that unfamiliar concepts are learned.

Type Two. Another, more effective, type of problem assures direct engagement with the content of a specific passage under study. Perkins (1986, p.101-106) suggests a variety of ways to frame text-specific problems. A few of his approaches, described below, adapt easily to assignments related to literature or content area texts:

> **develop a definition**—identify a class of cases important in a situation, or a statement of the

conditions under which something occurs. (What is a setting? What are bacteria?)

explain—account for what is known to be fact. (Why did the character act sheepishly? How does mitosis occur?)

classify—make order out of a chaos of information by developing a structure or a set of rules for sorting the material. (What factors differentiate two genres of fiction? Why are some living things classified as plants and others as animals?)

Solutions to these Type Two problems emerge through reading and clarifying information found in text.

Type Three. A third type of problem is related to the community or environment (Dahlberg, 1990). Readers use texts and literature as references while solving real-life problems. (Students may read from a text to find information on pollution while they develop an answer to solve a community recycling problem. Or they may read relevant poetry in order to locate quotations for a recycling flyer.)

Question-Text-Organize-Practice-Share (Q-TOPS). This strategy illustrates a means of implementing Type Two problem-solving. During my informal research with middle and high school students, the approach seemed to provide motivation, focus, and understanding of concepts under study. A teacher using **Q-TOPS** follows these steps:

- **Q**uestion. When preparing for class, select several topics from a study-unit and develop questions that pose a problem that requires construction of a definition, explanation, or classification. (See examples on previous page.)

- **T**ext. Begin class by dividing students into small groups; assign one problem to each group. Distribute reading materials that will enable a group to answer questions that solve the problem. For example, when studying protists, groups may be assigned to define protists, to explain how bacteria are helpful and harmful, or to classify forms of life. Reading materials that span mixed abilities could come from the grade-level science text, junior library books, introductory or advanced science magazines, and even a simple summary written by the teacher.

Allocate 10 to 20 minutes for students to search for data relevant to their group problem. Suggest that each student jot at least five brief notes concerning related information. Circulate during reading to assist less-skilled readers in finding information.

- **Organize.** When most students have written five informative notes, ask each group to pool its findings into a group list and organize the material into a coherent answer.

- **Practice.** When group lists seem to be in order, ask students within the group to break into pairs or triplets to rehearse the information with each other.

- **Share.** Ask each group to share its solution with the class. Students record these solutions in their notebooks while the teacher writes them on the board. During this process, engage the class in discussion to clarify and refine the solutions.

Teachers can stimulate Stage 4 reading and multiple-viewpoint thinking by providing a variety of source materials and by eliciting applications to other contexts during a discussion that enhances and elaborates on the concept.

Pose questions to fill in frameworks while reading. A variety of strategies for developing and filling in frameworks have been proposed. These strategies were devised with the intent of sensitizing students to text structure and its value as a framework upon which to form a schema (Armbruster, Anderson, & Ostertag, 1989; Call, 2000; Jones, Pierce, & Hunter, 1989).

For example, students might be asked to fill in a framework or flow chart related to a piece of literature or expository text that follows the structure of cause-reactions-effect, or a temporal sequence such as first-next-finally. Research concerning framework strategies yielded mixed results. Typically, skilled readers remember relevant information requested by the frame, while less-skilled readers tend to remember a mix of relevant and irrelevant information (Alvermann & Boothby, 1986; Armbruster, Anderson, & Ostertag, 1987; Gordon & Pearson, 1983).

Less-skilled readers' inability to sort and focus on relevant information could arise from not understanding the language of the structures, such as cause-effect, enumeration, etc. Or, it could reflect that readers lack sufficient background to recognize which concepts are relevant. In their confusion, less-skilled readers might view frame completion as a Type One Problem and focus on simply filling the frame.

This difficulty can be circumvented with study guides, such as those recommended by Slater et al. (1985), Santa (1986), or Armbruster (1991), that guide students in sorting the important from the unimportant. These study guides offer specific questions that elicit answers to fill in the framework. When completing frames while guided by carefully phrased questions, students learn how to use textbooks, trade books, and other resources to gather needed information.

As readers become familiar with this process, some of the questions and structures that form a study guide can be withdrawn slowly, at a rate that allows students to continue to experience success. Some students are ready sooner than others to have parts of the frame withdrawn. Eventually, many students construct their own frames, and develop questions to fill the frames (Santa, 1986), while others continue to need a full study guide indefinitely.

Conclusions concerning questioning techniques. Questions appear in effective comprehension strategies for Stage 3 readers whether presented as cues to guide the use of frameworks that reflect text structure, as problems in need of solutions, or as probes to gather, sequence, summarize, and synthesize relevant information. Effective questions lead students to focus on relevant and important concepts in text. Appropriate questions assist readers in organizing information into a meaningful understanding.

Element Four: *Provide* **crucial background from which to form inferences.**

Readers need to possess **sufficient, accurate, background knowledge** in order to form inferences and understand unfamiliar text. When there are too many gaps in readers' background knowledge, they are unable to form cohesive schemata that accurately represent the concepts expressed in narrative or expository text. Without broad and deep background, readers lack building blocks from which to develop new understanding (August, Flavell, & Clift, 1984; Goldman & Rakeshaw, 2000; Lipson, 1984; Wilson & Anderson, 1986).

Activities that provide or review accurate and relevant background can assist readers in better comprehending the major points and subtle nuances of unfamiliar material (Brody, 1991; Dole, Valencia, Greer, & Wardrop, 1991; Graves et al., 1983; Stahl, 1997). (A discussion of effective strategies and teachers' crucial roles in building readers' background knowledge appears in Chapter 8.)

Element Five: Offer *Multiple Opportunities* to Absorb, Process, Rehearse, and Express Unfamiliar Material Under Study

Readers need to **process and express unfamiliar concepts** in order to expand their fluent use of knowledge in an area of study. Lack of automaticity with language that expresses a concept is indicated when readers successfully choose among several possible answers proposed to them, but have difficulty wording an answer independently (Bloom, 1986; Curtis & Glaser, 1983).

Skilled readers rehearse and repeat unfamiliar information for themselves (Flood & Lapp, 1990; Pressley, 2000). In preparation for Stage 4 and 5 reading, students seem to need multiple exposures to unfamiliar concepts. These exposures may help them access neural representations of reviewed concepts with confidence and fluency. Extensive practice seems to lead to automatic retrieval, selection, and sequencing of concepts. As agility develops in retrieving a broad array of lexical units, readers seem to begin experiencing the fluency of thought that will let them eventually progress to Stage 4 and 5 reading, perhaps during high school or college.

Depth and breadth. Provide enriched depth and breadth by layering multiple meanings, nuances of meaning, and varied applications of a concept (McKeown et al., 1985; NRP, 2000). Schema theory suggests that this richness of understanding fosters multifaceted neural connections. Multiple exposures range from simple repetition to varied activities centered on one concept.

At times, students need repetitive practice to master complex concepts (Bloom, 1986; Just & Carpenter, 1987). After a concept is understood from one perspective, exposures in multiple contexts, with varied activities, increase its accessibility for use in other contexts during further reading, thinking, and problem-solving (Perkins & Salomon, 1988).

Multiple exposures develop the precise meaning and nature of a concept. Such clarity assists in its appropriate retrieval and use. For example, if students learn that *explicit* means clear, they may try to describe a blue sky on a clear day as *explicit*. Guided and varied exposures offer opportunities to repair misconceptions.

Activities. Teachers and students can express concepts through explanations, oral reports, or class discussions. Writing, reading-and-retelling what was read, or summarizing subtopics during reading also offer opportunities for students to absorb and express unfamiliar concepts (Flood & Lapp, 1990; Hayes, 1989; Manzo & Manzo, 1990; NRP, 2000). Book reports, vocabulary study, and outlining-while-reading are other assignments that encourage multiple exposures and expression (Brody, 1987). (See Chapter 10 for suggestions concerning multiple exposures and written expression.)

It is important to differentiate whether a strategy provides **students**, or their **teacher**, with multiple exposures and opportunities to express a concept. A **teacher** engages with a concept when using strategies that require the teacher to repeat or demonstrate the same concept. **Students** engage with a concept when using strategies that require a teacher to model the concept followed by a variety of activities in which **students** say, read, write, observe, or demonstrate the concept.

This does not imply that teachers remain silent while students flounder. Instead, teachers provide initial models along with supports such as alternative explanations and confirmations of comprehension accuracy. However, each time that a teacher needs to provide an alternative explanation, students need multiple opportunities to express the concept as well.

Students can practice stating unfamiliar concepts by explaining them to other classmates during group activities. Classmates' questions generate careful reconsideration and restatement of the content (Palincsar, 1986; Palincsar & Brown, 1984). Students and teachers can prepare to present unfamiliar concepts by reading a text, a secondary source, a fictionalized account, or technical support material, as well as through seeing a video, hearing a lecture, or conducting an experiment.

Strategies Proposed to Elicit Higher Level Comprehension

Teachers who know a variety of strategies possess a convenient means of keeping themselves alert and fresh as well as a means of continuing to use the element of surprise that can engage students in the ongoing challenge of learning. In order to assure that students continue to expand their reading comprehension while engaging in novel activities, teachers need to check that their strategies amply incorporate one or more of the five core elements of comprehension instruction as discussed in this chapter.

Students need to allocate some of their attentional resources to understanding an unfamiliar strategy, and this draws concentration away from text comprehension. Consequently, teachers should use caution when switching among strategies. Some teachers like to develop a small range of strategies that they use consistently in order to offer variety as well as familiarity with several methods.

Following are descriptions of various activities designed to teach higher level reading comprehension. The discussion highlights those features of the activities that implement some of the basic elements of effective comprehension instruction. In addition, the description suggests adjustments that may enhance the effectiveness of strategies that did not appear to be particularly effective during classroom studies.

Text-structure frames. As discussed earlier, classroom research remains mixed on the effectiveness of text frames in aiding reading comprehension. In instances when framing strategies seem to facilitate reading comprehension, the framing procedure is explicitly taught and modeled (Pressley, 2000) and is accompanied by detailed note-taking activities (Slater et al., 1985), specific questions and elaboration that help students focus on text (Santa, 1986), or summarization activities (NRP, 2000). Armbruster (1991) suggests the following process for developing frames to help students understand science text:

1. While preparing a lesson plan, outline the important ideas of the topic and the points contributing to those ideas. Develop a flow chart or grid that includes boxes to record this information as well as **questions** or headings to elicit the information.

2. During the lesson, ask students to fill in the frames by answering the questions **while reading the related text**.

3. Use the frames as a basis for class discussion during or after reading as well as for writing projects.

4. Encourage students to refer to the frames as questions and answers while studying for tests.

Frames can be used with science and social studies texts to list characteristics, compare types, record a time line, present cause-reactions-effect, etc. (Armbruster,

1991). Readers can use frames with literature to record the problem, climax, and resolution of a story or to note the author, setting, plot, and theme (Brody, 1987).

Study guides. Teachers use study guides to: ask questions that focus on important concepts; provide a glossary of vocabulary definitions; offer multiple exposures to material under study; and elicit a variety of written responses concerning the content (Just & Carpenter, 1987). Study guides can facilitate higher level comprehension and stimulate self-directed active learning, particularly when direct modeling by the teacher is faded out slowly as the process is mastered (Santa, 1986).

Study guides that encourage two-column note-taking are particularly helpful (Palmatier, 1973; Santa, Havens, & Harrison, 1989). In Column One, readers list main ideas, important vocabulary, and specialized concepts. In Column Two, important details, elaborations, and definitions are listed directly across from their related concepts in Column One. Later, readers can use the material in Column One to elicit the details in Column Two in order to study for a test (Santa, 1986).

Study guides have been used over time to ask questions that elicit literal, inferential, and applied responses. When constructing study guides, teachers can vary both the comprehension level of response desired and the format in which students respond to the questions. Study guides can include activities such as taking notes, defining vocabulary terms, and drawing a diagram of an object or process under study (Tierney, Readence, Dishner, 1985).

Semantic mapping. Semantic maps offer an alternative format for outlining information from text. Rather than organizing information by stating the main idea and listing supporting details beneath, a semantic map or web places the main concept in a box or circle at the center of a page, with supporting or related details springing out as spokes from the main concept. Semantic maps offer variation in how material is presented. Vocabulary acquisition studies indicate that semantic maps are as effective as other means of teaching a concept and its definition provided that they offer **multiple exposures** to the word, its *correct* meaning, and its use in **multiple contexts** (McKeown et al., 1985).

Questioning techniques. Approaches such as Reciprocal Questioning (Palincsar & Brown, 1984) or ReQuest (Flood & Lapp, 1990; Manzo, 1969) teach students to ask their own questions while reading. (See Chapter 10 of this volume as well.) To initiate these activities, teachers model how to pose relevant questions that draw on important concepts and their elaborations. This is followed by students asking questions. Questions are asked while the text is read in small segments, sentence-by-sentence or paragraph-by-paragraph, silently or aloud.

When working in a one-on-one setting, the teacher and student take turns asking questions, with the teacher modeling and shaping the quality of questions. Within a group, students as well as the teacher respond to questions and comment on how to improve the effectiveness of questions. Eliciting questions from students seems to stimulate active involvement in reading. Forming teams to ask questions may also heighten motivation (Helfeldt & Henk, 1990; Vacca & Vacca, 1993).

Lesson formats. Classic approaches such as the Directed Reading Activity (Betts, 1946) provide an instructional process that introduces, studies, reviews, and applies concepts encountered in literature or content texts. When using the Directed Reading Activity (DRA), the teacher introduces a reading by sharing relevant background information and unfamiliar vocabulary meanings and pronunciation, along with posing guiding questions. Students read a section of text silently then take part in clarifying their comprehension through questions and discussion. Next, students reread the text orally for further understanding. Finally, students apply what they have learned during follow-up activities.

Guided Reading Procedure (GRP) (Manzo, 1975; Ruddell, 1993) is introduced similarly to DRA. However, after initial silent reading, students close their books and state all that they can recall, while the teacher writes their responses on the board. This is followed by students checking the passage to add or correct any concepts that were missed or recorded inaccurately. Next, the teacher guides students to organize the material that they have gathered from the text, and facilitates discussion that lets them link what they are learning with other concepts that are familiar. Finally, students are tested on the reading.

Over the years, elements of DRA and GRP have appeared commonly in basal and content area reading texts. These strategies include many of the core elements of effective comprehension instruction presented earlier in this chapter. Since they include these elements in their design, it is understandable that newer strategies do *not* consistently outperform basal activities such as DRA or GRP.

Synthesizing Core Elements and Advanced Comprehension Strategies to Optimize Understanding

Theories of cognitive development suggest that when learners perform relatively simple activities at one stage nearly independently, they are ready to practice the activities within a set of more complex demands that constitute a higher stage *if* they are supported with **sufficient** scaffolding (Case, 1980; Fischer, 1980).

Several studies discussed earlier suggest that such scaffolding may be helpful in the transition from Stage 3 to Stage 4 and 5 reading. Palincsar & Brown (1984) found that 7th and 8th grade students could learn to ask focus questions of themselves when teachers first provided a model and plenty of scaffolding. Santa (1986) found that high school students, who were Stage 3 readers, could learn to construct their own study guides when teachers provided models and questions that were slowly withdrawn when the supports were no longer needed. In addition, Slater et al. (1985) report that text-structure organizers, when used in conjunction with note-taking, were beneficial to ninth-grade students' comprehension of expository text.

These studies suggest that teachers can expose readers to activities associated with advanced critical thinking and construction of new knowledge while teaching Stage 3 competencies. It seems that such exposure may be helpful *if* teachers carefully include core elements to scaffold more advanced reading. In addition, when working with younger readers, teachers need to monitor when advanced strategies place too great a stress on beginners' attention and simplify activities until core elements are handled successfully (Gordon & Pearson, 1983).

In short, as we continue to search for ways to improve readers' comprehension, we need to include, and use plentifully, the core elements that seem to facilitate Stage 3 comprehension. At the same time, we can draw on newer strategies to provide elaboration, active questioning, application to real problems, and frameworks that arrange concepts into meaningful schemata. In heterogeneous classrooms, such instruction can enable Stage 3 readers to engage with core elements of comprehension instruction while at the same time enabling more advanced readers to engage with higher level strategies.

Building Effective Elements into Teacher-Designed Strategies

Teachers can use a checklist (Table 7.1, below) to review any practices under consideration for adoption from a journal or by requirement of a school district. Alternatively, teachers can develop strategies of their own by assuring that their plans include many of the elements appearing on the checklist. Strategies that focus on the core elements recorded on the checklist are likely to assist students in developing reading comprehension ability. When strategies lack these elements, teachers can use the checklist as a guide to develop adaptations that can enhance instruction.

Table 7.1. Checklist of Core Comprehension Elements.

Strategy Name:		
Core Elements	**Yes/No**	**Plans that Add Element**
1. Teaches accurate decoding of unfamiliar words.		
2. Provides **unfamiliar** word meanings before and during reading.		
3. Poses **relevant** questions concerning the text under study.		
4. Teaches **accurate** and **crucial** text-related background concepts.		
5. Offers **multiple** opportunities to **study, summarize,** and **express** unfamiliar concepts.		

Below is an example of a comprehension strategy that was developed to incorporate some of the checklist elements.

Spell-Vocabulary-Schema (SVS). Stage 3 readers sometimes have difficulty forming appropriate schemata. They may be hampered by limited decoding fluency, insufficient vocabulary knowledge, or difficulty processing textual material in their own words. SVS was developed and informally researched in order to help students engage with challenging concepts while reading unfamiliar text selections (Brody, 1986; 2001). This strategy previews the decoding and meaning of difficult content words from the assigned text, then provides opportunities for readers to articulate their understanding as they read. By answering text-related questions that lead them to state their learnings as they read, students share their schema-building process, during construction, and receive scaffolding as needed.

Spelling: List potentially difficult words on the board before a selection is read. Introduce each word by clearly pronouncing it while pointing to its syllables. Blend the sounds of the syllables to say the whole word and ask the class to segment, blend, and say the word. Post these words in a highly visible spot for the remainder of the unit, and encourage students to refer to them for accurate spelling during related writing assignments.

Vocabulary: Follow the pronouncing of a word by presenting its meaning. Offer several sentences that illustrate the meaning of the word. Ask students to generate additional sentences. Students write the words, and their use in meaningful sentences, in notebooks.

Schema: Students read from a content text or a short story while pausing after a paragraph, or short section, to enumerate important details by answering questions such as, "What is one thing you learned?" or "What is one important thing that happened?" After discussing details, readers also articulate a brief schema—a summary that relates the details to the main idea by answering questions such as, "So what is the main point?" or, "How does this tie in with what happened earlier?" As needed, teachers provide scaffolding that assists in locating and forming relevant responses. The frequency of pauses should be planned to assure that readers construct accurate schemata by thinking over what has been read, looking back and clarifying any confusions, and describing central concepts in their own words.

SVS draws on many core elements. In addition, teachers can scaffold Stage 4 reading from multiple viewpoints by using SVS when students read and discuss several related passages written from varied points of view. The strategy shows promise for elementary, middle, and high school classrooms among students who are beginning Stage 3 reading (Brody, 1986; 1987).

Conclusion

As students read widely in literature and content texts to gather information and develop understanding during Stage 3, teachers can support them with a variety of strategies that incorporate "active ingredients" of effective instruction. Such instruction assists with the decoding and meaning aspects of unfamiliar words, uses questions to provide a guiding focus, offers crucial background concepts required to form inferences and understand the reading, and creates multiple opportunities to absorb, process, and express the material under study.

In addition, teachers can encourage middle grade and high school students as they begin the transition to higher level comprehension and application by arranging for scaffolded use of strategies such as: solving problems and applying the findings to several contexts; completing text-structure frames by answering accompanying questions; organizing information with semantic maps; or engaging students in self-questioning during reading.

When used consistently during the reading of content texts and engaging literature, core comprehension elements can assist students in becoming confident Stage 3 readers who possess broad and deep background that prepares them for Stage 4 and 5 critical thinking, wide reading, and synthesis. With teachers' scaffolding, Stage 3 readers can begin to apply concepts to multiple contexts while participating in shared efforts to construct new knowledge.

236

References

Adams, M.J. (1994). *Beginning to read: Thinking and learning about print*. Cambridge, MA: MIT Press.

Alvermann, D.E. & Boothby, P.R. (1986). Children's transfer of graphic organizer instruction. *Reading Psychology* 7(2), 87-100.

Anstey, M.M. & Freebody, P. (1987). The effects of various pre-reading activities on children's literal and inferential comprehension. *Reading Psychology*, 8(3), 189-209.

Armbruster, B.B. (1984). The problem of "inconsiderate text." In G.G. Duffy, L.R. Roehler, & J. Mason (Eds.), *Comprehension instruction*. New York: Longman.

Armbruster, B.B. (1991). Framing: A technique for improving learning from science texts. In C.M. Santa & D.W. Alvermann (Eds.), *Science learning: Process and applications*. Newark DE: IRA.

Armbruster, B.B., Anderson, T.H. & Ostertag, J. (1987). Does text structure/summarization instruction facilitate learning from expository text? *Reading Research Quarterly*, 22(3).

Armbruster, B.B., Anderson, T.H. & Ostertag, J. (1989). Teaching text structure to improve reading and writing. *The Reading Teacher, 43*(2), 130-137.

August, D.L., Flavell, J.H. & Clift, R. (1984). Comparison of comprehension monitoring of skilled and less skilled readers. *Reading Research Quarterly*, Fall, 20(1), 39-48.

Betts, E.A. (1946). *Foundations of reading instruction*. New York: American Book Co.

Biemiller, A. (2000). Vocabulary: The missing link between phonics and comprehension. *Perspectives*, 26(4), 26-30.

Bloom, B.S. (1986). "The hands and feet of genius" Automaticity. *Educational Leadership*. February.

Brody, S. (1986). The Brody Reading Method: A successful approach to reading and written-language skills for at risk students. Paper presented at the Annual Meeting of the Association for Children and Adults with Learning Disabilities (23rd, NY, NY, March 12 - 15). ERIC ED275 103.

Brody, S. (1987). *Study Skills: Teaching and learning strategies for mainstream and specialized settings*. Milford, NH: LARC Publishing.

Brody, S. (1989). Elements of effective reading instruction in grades 4 and 5: Lessons from recent research. Unpublished Qualifying Paper, Harvard Graduate School of Education.

Brody, S. (1991). *Clarifying the role of prereading instruction in 4th graders' comprehension of social studies text*. Unpublished Doctoral Dissertation, Harvard Graduate School of Education.

Brody, S. (1993). Developing background knowledge: A context enrichment strategy that may provide more consistent results than activation of prior knowledge. *Proceedings: UKRA '94 Annual Conference*, United Kingdom Reading Association, Exeter, England.

Brody, S. (2001). *The Brody reading manual: An implementation guide for teachers (2nd ed.)*. Milford, NH: LARC Publishing.

Call, P.E. (2000). Reflective questioning: A strategy to review notes. *Journal of Adolescent and Adult Literacy*, 43(5), 487-488.

Case, R. (1980). The underlying mechanism of intellectual development. In *Cognition, development, and instruction*. Academic Press.

Chall, J.S. (1987). Two vocabularies for reading: Recognition and meaning. In M.G. McKeown & M.E. Curtis (Eds.), *The nature of vocabulary acquisition*. Hillsdale, NJ: Lawrence Erlbaum.

Chall, J.S. (1996). *Stages of reading development (2nd ed.)*. Orlando, FL: Harcourt Brace

Chall, J.S., Jacobs, V.A., & Baldwin, L.E. (1991). *Why poor children fall behind in reading: What schools can do about it*. Cambridge, MA: Harvard University Press.

Chall, J.S. & Squire, J.R. (1991). The publishing industry and textbooks. In R. Barr, M.L. Kamil, P. Mosenthal, & P.D. Pearson (Eds.), *Handbook of reading research, volume II*. NY: Longman.

Chomsky, C. (1972). Stages in language development and reading exposure. *Harvard Educational Review*, 42(1).

Csikszentmihalyi, M. (1990). *Flow: The psychology of optimal experience*. NY: Harper.

Cunningham, A.E. & Stanovich, K.E. (1997). Early reading acquisition and its relation to reading experience and ability 10 years later. *Developmental Psychology*, 33, 934-945.

Curtis, M.E. & Glaser, R. (1983). Reading theory and the assessment of reading achievement. *Journal of Educational Measurement*, 20(2).

Dahlberg, L.A. (1990). Teaching for the information age. *Journal of Reading* 34(1).

Dole, J.A., Valencia, S.W., Greer, E.A., & Wardrop, J.L. (1991). Effects of two types of prereading instruction on the comprehension of narrative and expository text, *Reading Research Quarterly*, 26(2), 142-159.

Durkin, D. (1984). The decoding ability of elementary school students. Reading Education Report No. 49. Bolt, Beranek and Newman, Inc., Cambridge, MA. Illinois University, Urbana. Center for the Study of Reading. (ERIC Document Reproduction Service No. ED 244 228)

Festinger, L. (1957). *A theory of cognitive dissonance*. White Plains, NY: Row, Peterson and Company.

Fischer, K.W. (1980). A theory of cognitive development: The control and construction of hierarchies of skills. *Psychological Review*, 87(6), 115-169.

Flood, J. & Lapp, D. (1990). Reading comprehension instruction for at-risk students: Research-based practices that can make a difference. *Journal of Reading, 33*(7), 490-496.

Goldman, S. & Rakestraw, J. (2000). Structural aspects of constructing meaning from text. In M.L. Kamil, P.B. Mosenthal, P.D. Pearson, & R. Barr (Eds.), *Handbook of reading research*. Mahwah, NJ: Lawrence Erlbaum Associates.

Gordon, C.J. & Pearson, P.D. (1983). The effects of instruction in metacomprehension and inferencing on children's comprehension abilities. Technical Report No. 277. Bolt, Beranek and Newman, Inc., Cambridge, MA. Illinois University, Urbana. Center for the Study of Reading. (ERIC Document Reproduction Service No. ED 232 132)

Goswami, U. (2000). Phonological and lexical processes. . In M.L. Kamil, P.B. Mosenthal, P.D. Pearson, & R. Barr (Eds.), *Handbook of reading research*. Mahwah, NJ: Lawrence Erlbaum Associates.

Graves, M.F., Cooke, C.L., & LaBerge, M.J. (1983). Effects of previewing difficult short stories on low ability junior high school students' comprehension, recall, and attitudes. *Reading Research Quarterly*, 20(2).

Haller, E.P., Child, D.A., & Walberg, H.J. (1988). Can comprehension be taught? A quantitative synthesis of "metacognitive" studies. *Educational Researcher, 17*(9), 5-8.

Hansen, J. & Pearson, P.D. (1983). An instructional study: Improving the inferential comprehension of good and poor fourth-grade readers. *Journal of Educational Psychology*, 75(6), 821-29.

Hayes, D.A. (1989). Helping students GRASP the knack of writing summaries. *Journal of Reading, 33*(2), 96-101.

238

Helfeldt, J.P. & Henk, W.A. (1990). Reciprocal question-answer relationships: An instructional technique for at-risk readers. *Journal of Reading, 33*(7), 509-515.

Jones, B.F., Pierce, J., & Hunter, B. (1989). Teaching students to construct graphic representations. *Educational Leadership*, December 88/January 89.

Juel, C. & Holmes (1980). Comparison of processing strategies in oral and silent reading by good and poor readers. Paper presented at the Annual Meeting of the American Educational Research Association (Boston, MA, April 7-11). ERIC Document Reproduction Service No. ED 192 289)

Just, M.A. & Carpenter, P.A. (1987). *The psychology of reading and language comprehension*. Boston: Allyn & Bacon.

Lipson, M.Y. (1984). Some unexpected issues in prior knowledge and comprehension. *Reading Teacher, 37*(8), 760-764.

Lyon, G.R. (2000). Learning to read: A call from research to action. *NEBIDA Newsletter,* Spring/Summer 15-18.

Mangano, N.G. (1983). The effects of teacher explanation and questioning patterns on fourth grade students during basal reading instruction. Paper presented at the Annual Meeting of the National Reading Conference (33rd Austin, TX, Nov. 29-Dec. 3). (ERIC Document Reproduction Service No. ED240 502)

Manzo, A.V. (1969). The request procedure. *Journal of Reading*, 11, 123-126.

Manzo, A.V. (1975). Guided reading procedure. *Journal of Reading*, 18, 287-291.

Manzo, A.V. & Manzo, U.C. (1990). Note cue: A comprehension and participation training strategy. *Journal of Reading.* May.

McKeown, M.G. (1985). The acquisition of word meaning from context by children of high and low ability. *Reading Research Quarterly*, 20(4), 482-496.

McKeown, M.G. (1993). Creating effective definitions for young word learners. *Reading Research Quarterly*, 28(1), 16-30.

McKeown, M.G., Beck, I.L., Omanson, R.C., & Pople, M.T. (1985). Some effects of the nature and frequency of vocabulary instruction on the knowledge and use of words. *Reading Research Quarterly*, 20(5), 522-35, Fall.

Moats, L.C. (2000). *Speech to print: Language essentials for teachers*. Baltimore, MD: Paul H. Brookes Publishing Co..

National Reading Panel [NRP]. (2000). *Report of the National Reading Panel: Teaching children to read.* Washington, DC: National Institute of Child Health and Human Development.
[Available at http://www.nichd.nih.gov/publications/nrp.]

Palincsar, A.S. (1986). The role of dialogue in providing scaffolded instruction. *Educational Psychologist*, 21(1-2), 73-98.

Palincsar, A.S. & Brown, A.L. (1984). Reciprocal teaching of comprehension-fostering and comprehension-monitoring activities. *Cognition and Instruction.* 1(2), 117-175.

Palmatier, R.A. (1973). A notetaking system for learning. *Journal of Reading*, October.

Perfetti, C.A. (1985). *Reading ability*. New York: Oxford University Press.

Perfetti, C.A. & Curtis, M.E. (1986). Reading. In R.F. Dillon & R.J. Sternberg (Eds.) *Cognition and instruction.* Academic Press.

Perkins, D.N. (1986). *Knowledge as design*. Hillsdale, NJ: Lawrence Erlbaum.

Perkins, D.N. & Salomon, G. (1988). Teaching for transfer. *Educational Leadership, 46*(1), 22-33.

Pressley, M. (2000). What should comprehension instruction be the instruction of? In M.L. Kamil, P.B. Mosenthal, P.D. Pearson, & R. Barr (Eds.), *Handbook of reading research*. Mahwah, NJ: Lawrence Erlbaum Associates.

Ruddell, M.R. (1993). *Teaching content reading and writing*. Boston: Allyn and Bacon.

Sadoski, M. & Page, W.D. (1984). Miscue combination scores and reading comprehension: Analysis and comparison. *Reading World*, 24(1), 43-53.

Samuels, S.J., Schermer, D.R., & Reinking (1992). Reading fluency: Techniques for making decoding automatic. In S.J. Samuels & A.E. Farstrup (Eds.), *What research has to say about reading instruction (2nd ed.)*. Newark DE: International Reading Association.

Santa, C. (1986). Content reading in secondary schools. In J. Orasanu (Ed.). *Reading comprehension: From research to practice*. Hillsdale, NJ: Lawrence Erlbaum.

Santa, C. Havens, L. & Harrison, S. (1989). Teaching secondary science through reading, writing, studying, and problem solving. In D. Lapp, J. Flood, N. Farnam, (Eds.), *Content area reading and learning: Instructional strategies*. Englewood Cliffs, NJ: Prentice Hall.

Slater, W.H., Graves, M.F. & Piche, G.L. (1985). Effects of structural organizers on ninth-grade students' comprehension and recall of four patterns of expository text. *Reading Research Quarterly* 20(2).

Snow, C.E., Burns, M.S., & Griffin, P. (Eds.) (1998). *Preventing reading difficulties in young children*. Washington, DC: National Academy Press.

Spiegel, D.L. & Whaley, J.F. (1980). Elevating comprehension skills by sensitizing students to structural aspects of narratives. Paper presented at the Annual Meeting of the National Reading Conference (30th, San Diego, CA, December 3-6). (ERIC Document Reproduction Service No. ED199 634)

Stanovich, K.E. (1986). Matthew effects in reading: Some consequences of individual differences in the acquisition of literacy. *Reading Research Quarterly*, 21(4), 360-406.

Stanovich, K.E. (1994). Romance and reality. *Reading Teacher,* 47(4).

Stanovich, K.E. & Cunningham, A.E. (1993). Where does knowledge come from? Specific associations between print exposure and information acquisition. *Journal of Educational Psychology* 85(2), 211-229.

Stahl, S.A., Heubach, K., & Cramond, B. (1997). *Fluency-oriented Reading Instruction. Reading Research Report #79*. Athens, GA: National Reading Research Center.

Tierney, R.J., Readence, J.E. & Dishner, E.K (1985). *Reading strategies and practices: A compendium (2nd ed.)*. Boston: Allyn & Bacon.

Vacca, R.T. & Vacca, J.A.L. (1993). *Content area reading (4th ed.)*. NY: Harper Collins.

Wilson, P.T. & Anderson, R.C. (1986). What they don't know will hurt them: The role of prior knowledge in comprehension. In J. Orasanu (Ed.), *Reading comprehension: From research to practice*. Hillsdale, NJ: Lawrence Erlbaum.

Wixson, K.K. (1983). Questions about a text: What you ask about is what children learn. *The Reading Teacher* 37, 287-294.

Chapter 8. Previews: Learning Pertinent Background and Text Concepts

Sara Brody, EdD

Readers understand text more completely and with greater ease when they possess broad and deep background knowledge. Such knowledge develops during a lifetime of exposure to a vast array of learning experiences. When these experiences are understood and stored with the use of language, they become available for later processing or recall during language-dependent activities such as reading, writing, and speaking. In addition to developing language-based background by interpreting and storing experiences linguistically, learners who can understand unfamiliar text enhance their background knowledge by reading.

Rich background knowledge enables learners to supply missing details to infer a text's meaning when an author's explanation is incomplete. At times, the problem of insufficient background may be avoided by selecting a text that matches the background possessed by a reader. However, this practice limits the extent that learners develop broader background. When texts rely on the unfamiliar, crucial background knowledge needs to be developed through instruction. Less adept readers can increase their background knowledge by reading, when they receive the support needed to learn new concepts with accuracy (Lyon, 2000).

Readers in the upper elementary grades and beyond generally possess the intellectual ability to comprehend specialized concepts (Chall, 1996; Gazzaniga, 1992; Inhelder & Piaget, 1958). However, when science and social studies lessons present unfamiliar and specialized topics, many Stage 3 readers need assistance in order to understand their texts. The issue is not one of waiting for readers to mature sufficiently to become able to learn new material, but rather one of providing instructional activities that assure sufficient background knowledge to promote the learning of unfamiliar information (Biemiller, 2000; National Reading Panel [NRP], 2000).

This chapter examines the nature of background knowledge and its instruction during Stage 3 reading development. First, the role of background in readers' understanding of text is considered. Next, evidence from classroom research related to background knowledge is explored. Finally, teaching strategies that appear to enhance the availability and use of appropriate background knowledge during reading are presented.

The Role of Background in Text Comprehension

A note on terminology. In this chapter, **background knowledge** refers to concepts, experiences, information, and text structures that are relevant to a text under study. These concepts are accurate and *may or may not be known by the reader*. However, knowledge of them would be useful to a reader who is trying to fully comprehend a text. In contrast, the reading literature generally uses the term **prior knowledge** to refer to accurate or inaccurate text-related knowledge that a reader *actually possesses*. This knowledge is stored in a reader's memory in a form that is accessible through written or spoken language. Thus, background knowledge is the broader term, encompassing relevant accurate knowledge known or not known by the reader; and prior knowledge is a reader-specific term, since the experiences, exposures, and memory of the reader define its parameters.

Interaction of text and prior knowledge. Theorists postulate that a reader's prior knowledge plays an important role in the comprehension of text. Reading theory suggests that comprehension occurs when a reader constructs a schema (an understanding of the text) by combining the information presented in a text with knowledge the reader already possesses. Schema theory suggests that it is this interaction of what is in print and what is in the reader's mind that produces what is finally understood or misunderstood (Adams, 1994; Goldman & Rakestraw, 2000; Kintsch, 1998; Perfetti & Curtis, 1986).

Readers' comprehension of text is influenced by the related prior knowledge that they bring to their reading as well as by how clearly a writer states relevant and crucial concepts. In addition, comprehension is influenced by the **mis**conceptions and preconceived **mis**understandings that readers possess before beginning to read a passage. When readers' prior knowledge conflicts with material written in a text, readers tend to misread the text to make it fit their previously formed schemata, whether they are accurate or not (Goldman & Rakestraw, 2000; Lipson, 1984; Pressley, 2000; Wilson & Anderson, 1986).

National assessments of educational progress suggest that reading comprehension is related positively to the amount of time students spend reading (Campbell, Hombo, & Mazzeo, 2000). Further, it appears that, among college students, spending time reading enhances general background knowledge (Stanovich & Cunningham, 1993). During Stage 3 reading and beyond, learners who engage in extensive reading generally increase their store of background knowledge—concepts, vocabulary, experiences, and text patterns (Chall, 1996; Pressley, 2000; Stanovich, 1994). As their background knowledge broadens and deepens, these readers appear to develop lexical resources that allow them to select for relevance and appropriateness, quickly and effectively, when engaging with varied materials that express multiple points of view concerning an area of interest.

Related Research

A variety of studies concerning background knowledge were conducted during the 1980s and 1990s. Some explored whether comprehension would be enhanced by "activating" prior knowledge—encouraging readers to recall whatever they knew related to a topic before reading (Anstey & Freebody, 1987; Hansen & Pearson, 1983). Others explored the effects of teaching relevant and related background during prereading activities (Brody, 1991; Dole, Valencia, Greer, & Wardrop, 1991; Graves & Cooke, 1980; Graves, Cooke, & Laberge, 1983; Graves, Prenn, & Cooke, 1985; Stahl, 1997).

"Activation" studies. Several classroom studies drew on theoretical models of reading comprehension as justification for developing instruction that would "activate" a reader's prior knowledge. Researchers postulated that the possession of activated prior knowledge, along with the strategy of making conscious use of prior knowledge, would lead a reader to form a schema of a text more easily. Although results with such approaches were mixed, activation of prior knowledge often continues to be recommended as a means of making the reader's background more available to contribute to reading comprehension.

For example, if a text on farming in Switzerland were assigned, a teacher might probe to activate students' prior knowledge by asking students what they think people do to produce milk and milk products. A related approach teaches the strategy of consciously using one's knowledge to make sense of text when a difficult section is encountered during reading. For example, if a passage concerning Swiss grazing practices were confusing, students would be prompted to think about what they know about farming in general. They would be encouraged to use their knowledge as a context within which to interpret the confusing text.

Problems related to the strategy of activating prior knowledge. The knowledge that readers possess before they begin to read is very powerful. People tend to remember and rely on what they already know when new information that they see, hear, or read contradicts what they know. Even when readers' prior knowledge is inaccurate, it often overrides the accurate information read in a text, especially among weak readers (Pressley, 2000; Wilson & Anderson, 1986). Lipson (1984) describes several studies in which elementary students with no prior knowledge concerning a topic understood a related passage better than students with related but inaccurate prior knowledge. This is congruent with neurological research that suggests "the human capacity to hang on to our beliefs in the presence of confounding data is astounding" (Gazzaniga, 1992, p. 136).

For example, based on their inaccurate prior knowledge, readers may continue to think that whales are fish, not mammals, even after reading a text that explains that they are warm blooded, need to surface for air every 10 to 30 minutes, and nurse their young. Even though the text presents explanatory information, the reader's prior knowledge may still override what is in print. Consequently, it seems that the strategy of activating prior knowledge inadvertently may lead to a *misunderstanding* of text by refreshing readers' misconceptions before reading, by raising inaccurate predictions before reading, or by sharing students' misconceptions with others before reading.

During prereading activities that encourage readers to recall their prior knowledge, teachers often ask students to discuss their thoughts and experiences related to a topic to be studied. The usefulness of information learned during these activities depends upon the accuracy and relevance of the prior knowledge that classmates share during prereading activation. For example, prereading instruction concerning a passage about whales may begin by asking students to tell their ideas about whales. If students indicate that whales are fish because they swim, this may reinforce misinformation or provide misinformation to students who knew nothing about whales.

Even when readers work independently, if their knowledge concerning a topic under study is limited, recalling that knowledge may not offer a sufficiently rich context to support the reading of unfamiliar text. In such instances, an activation approach does not account for readers who need to learn unfamiliar concepts for which they *lack* any relevant prior knowledge. Computers provide a helpful analogy. We can do many applications and innovative projects using the software already in our computers. However, for some projects, we may need to expand our versatility by installing completely new programs. If we were to insist that all our work and applications derive only from one, beginning program, we would limit our potential to develop breadth of knowledge. Similarly, strategies designed to activate the knowledge that readers already possess, before coming to a text, may not compensate sufficiently for the limited, or inaccurate, prior knowledge that many young readers possess as they begin to read unfamiliar and specialized text.

Classroom studies of prior knowledge activation strategies. The issue of instruction in activation of prior knowledge has been particularly confusing since early, mixed results were considered encouraging. In order to clarify why the findings were mixed, several studies comparing activation strategies with other methods of instruction, conducted with 10 to 12 year olds, are reviewed below.

One study (Hansen & Pearson, 1983) finds mixed results, sometimes favoring an activation strategy, other times favoring a brief introduction of the topic and several pertinent points, but finding little difference between approaches overall. It appears that when the prior knowledge activation was more effective, the strategy also generally conveyed some of the pertinent and central concepts of the text under study while the comparison approach gave only cursory introduction to the topic. In this study, the activation approach previewed relevant text concepts during an activity in which the teacher used specific information taken from the text, while modeling how to use text information, and prior knowledge, to form inferences.

A later study (Anstey & Freebody, 1987) found somewhat similar results. In this study, several approaches designed to activate prior knowledge were compared. One activation approach provided exposure, through a picture, to the central concept of a text before reading. In this approach, students wrote their ideas concerning the content of a passage while viewing a picture that depicted the main concept of the story. In two comparison activation approaches, no direct exposure to the central text concept was provided. Instead, students wrote free associations either from the story title or from questions related to the topic to be read. In this study, only the strategy of exposing the main story concept (with a picture) was related to an advantage over reading the passage without any prereading instruction. These findings suggest that students may have benefitted from exposure to pertinent concepts or information before the reading of unfamiliar text rather than from activation of prior knowledge.

Directly teaching relevant background knowledge. Several studies examine the role of background knowledge by directly providing readers with accurate background before reading, through instruction in crucial related concepts. The findings from these studies consistently suggest that directly providing upper-elementary and secondary-school students with accurate and relevant background before reading literature or social studies passages seems to be related to enhanced reading comprehension of the passage under study (Brody, 1991; Dole et al., 1991; Graves & Cooke, 1980; Graves, et al., 1983; 1985).

Two of these studies (Brody, 1991; Dole et al., 1991) explore further the questions raised by classroom activation studies. They examine whether it is the activation of prior knowledge or, instead, the teaching of pertinent and important background concepts that is related to enhanced comprehension of a text among upper-elementary school students. These studies compare methods that teach central background concepts and information related to upcoming text with approaches that ask students to recall knowledge that they already possess. These strategies are also compared with the reading of a passage after no prereading instruction at all.

The results of these studies (Brody, 1991; Dole et al., 1991) indicate an advantage associated with the teaching of background information related to the text under study when compared with either activation or with no prereading instruction at all. These findings lend further evidence suggesting that reading comprehension of an assigned text is enhanced when the teacher directly conveys relevant background knowledge and important concepts before reading. Further, they suggest that drawing out prior knowledge does not seem to be associated with enhanced comprehension of a passage.

Teaching Strategies

The following discussion describes several strategies researched in the classroom studies noted above.

Present crucial concepts before reading. Teachers can present crucial concepts related to the text that students are about to read by following several steps that require very little change from directions given in teachers' manuals, yet that are related to a marked increase in students' understanding of text (Brody, 1991). First, during planning, the teacher selects several concepts crucial to understanding of the text and develops clear 3- to 5-sentence explanations of each. When a complex concept needs longer explanation, the teacher breaks the concept into smaller elements in order to present each smaller element in a 3- to 5-sentence explanation. Developing these brief presentations ensures that students will be attentive during presentation rather than getting lost in a lecture and drifting from the content. When preparing the lesson, teachers may draw on class texts, parallel texts, encyclopedias, trade books, visual media, or other resources to enhance their own background.

To begin the lesson, the teacher tells, reads, or demonstrates one concept by using the 3-5 sentence explanation. Next, the teacher asks questions that lead students to explain and apply what they have learned from the teacher's presentation. When a student's response to a question is accurate, the teacher confirms the response and sometimes repeats it in similar words to reinforce the concept for all the class.

Alternatively, when a student's response is inaccurate, the teacher says, "Actually, ..." and then explains the information again using other wording and perhaps a diagram or picture as well. In this case, the teacher would ask additional questions that draw out further explanation or application from students in order to assure that the clarification was understood.

Concepts are introduced in small steps, one-at-a-time. The process of first presenting a concept, then asking questions that require explanation and application, and finally confirming or reiterating the concept, is repeated several times. The number of concepts presented will vary with the background of the class. The teacher needs to present sufficient background concepts to provide a rich context from which to read the text. Introduction of 2 to 4 concepts crucial to understanding a section of text may take no more than 5 to 10 minutes, since the teacher keeps the class focused on pertinent material through brief instruction, questions that elicit explanation and application, and statements that confirm or clarify responses.

For example, students could be presented with an explanation of the concept "irrigation" by the teacher. Then they could be asked to tell how it is used to solve a problem, or how irrigation works, in order that they might actively apply the concept in their own words. If a student's answer indicates a misunderstanding of irrigation, the teacher would acknowledge the student's response by saying, "Actually, irrigation is used in this way..." The teacher then asks the same student the question again, in order to provide an opportunity for the student to experience success and in order to be sure that the teacher's revised explanation was understood.

Such a strategy can be used along with the materials and manuals that teachers already have in their classrooms. The only adjustment necessary is to **begin** by providing students with information concerning a concept and to **follow** with questions that encourage students to discuss the concept. This is in contrast to beginning as well as ending the prereading lesson by encouraging students to discuss a concept without first receiving accurate information to use in developing thoughts and responses. The approach can be used for whole class, small group, or individual instruction. The crucial elements appear to be: 1) accurate presentation of relevant concepts by the teacher; 2) an opportunity for students to express their understanding of each concept, as soon as it is presented, through the answering of questions that require an explanation or application of the concept; and, 3) immediate confirmation or else clarification by the teacher when the student's response suggests a misunderstanding of the concept (Brody, 1991).

Previews. Graves et al. (1980; 1983; 1985) suggest that teachers frame prereading instruction as a preview similar to that for a movie. Students are given an overview of a story that introduces its main characters and setting. In addition, the preview offers background that leads to, but does not reveal, the story climax. In this procedure, students are given an opportunity to discuss the preview information, and have their misunderstandings clarified, before reading. Graves et al. indicate that learners found these previews helpful in understanding where to focus attention during reading and that their understanding of the text was fuller when given such previews. Informal questioning of students in the study suggests that previews contribute to understanding without detracting from motivation, suspense, or interest.

Preteaching vocabulary. Teaching meanings of unfamiliar words prior to reading is an effective way to directly convey relevant background (Biemiller,

2000; Brody, 1987). Biemiller recommends daily instruction in core vocabulary that appears across many reading selections accompanied by direct instruction in meanings of words specific to a particular passage prior to reading. Prior to assigning a reading, the teacher selects words that are crucial to comprehension of the passage and presents the words and their meanings. It is important for the teacher to state the relevant meaning clearly and to demonstrate use of the word in several meaningful sentences. This is followed by helping students form meaningful sentences that correctly use the word.

Preteaching Background for Active Learning

Direct teacher contribution of background knowledge is sometimes viewed as a more traditional approach to instruction when compared with expecting students to activate their prior knowledge to figure out meaning independently. However, preteaching of accurate background differs from lecture instruction in several ways. First, the teacher's presentation of crucial concepts is given in short, 3-5 sentence segments rather than long lectures that exceed many students' attention spans. Next, it is accompanied by opportunities for students to actively apply the concepts.

In addition, rather than passively listening, learners actively engage in a dialog initiated by the teacher and guided by questions that tap the crucial background concepts. This dialog provides multiple opportunities for learners to process, articulate, and examine relevant, accurate background and vocabulary before reading. When properly implemented, presentation of background knowledge engages students in meaningful processing of accurate concepts rather than in spinning inappropriate and inapplicable schemata (Brody, 1993).

This practice is compatible as well with educational reform efforts that strive to implement school-based experiences that reflect community-based applications. For example, in the workplace, if an employee is to learn a new process, the manager would teach the unfamiliar practice before asking an employee to use it with customers or in a costly production routine. Similarly, medical students are not encouraged to make their first surgical incisions by drawing inferences from their related prior knowledge. Instead, they are shown precisely where and how to cut. Much later, when the concept of how and where to make a particular incision is embedded in their prior knowledge of medical practice, they can innovate in unusual circumstances.

Direct instruction and creativity. Many educators fear that children's creativity will be stifled unless they are left to develop understanding completely on their own from their prior knowledge, without the interference of adults' formalized background knowledge. However, research suggests that creative expression seems to unfold in a stage-like progression similar to the development of reading and language (Gardner, 1982).

Howard Gardner's studies (1982) suggest that young, artistic children take great delight in creating from what they know, with little concern for adult conventions during the early years. This is somewhat parallel to the pretend reading and language development play of Stage 0. As artistic children mature, they develop an intense desire to learn the conventions of perspective and other techniques that will allow them to make their drawings appear "real." They are pleased to be shown how to make objects in the picture plane come forward or recede and how to turn a line to make a familiar figure. Although their drawings at this stage do not seem as "creative" as earlier productions, this stage appears to lead to enhanced creative expression. As young artists practice their drawing, they use conventional techniques as convenient tools that let them go on, in the high school years and beyond, to create their personal style and expression with a sense of control and power rather than happenstance.

Promoting creativity, active learning, and self-confidence. Active integration and application of concepts are integral elements of strategies that directly develop background knowledge. In these strategies, the concepts presented by the teacher are immediately applied by students. Such application occurs through discussions that are stimulated by asking readers to answer questions by explaining or describing the concepts under study. These opportunities for thoughtful explanation and application of relevant background to text-related contexts contrast greatly with the practice of rote repetition without understanding.

For example, students could be presented with a description of the concept "pollination" by the teacher. Then they could be asked to explain the concept in their own words by describing how farmers plant their crops to increase pollination. The offering of information by the teacher does not replace active involvement in learning; instead it offers students rich and accurate background knowledge to use while developing and articulating their thoughts. Further, students may be able to use the information, while reading, to understand the text more clearly. Rather than coming to the process of constructing meaning with inaccurate background, students enter the process with a context of pertinent and enriched background. As suggested by the results of the studies reviewed above, this seems to assist students in constructing accurate schemata that let them comprehend unfamiliar texts more fully.

Whatever the strategy in use, the crucial elements to include when developing background involve directly presenting students with accurate concepts while providing opportunities for students to apply those accurate concepts to relevant situations or examples. When misconceptions emerge during discussion, the teacher corrects or clarifies them to assure that they do not persist during reading of the text.

Compatibility with schema theory. Schema theory suggests that readers comprehend text by integrating what they read with what they know in order to construct text schemata. Studies suggest that literal and inferential comprehension are associated positively with prereading instruction in which teachers accurately present text related concepts in order to develop enriched background knowledge (Brody, 1991; Dole et al., 1991; Graves et al., 1983; 1985). This research suggests that effective instruction develops accurate and relevant background knowledge, and thereby facilitates the forming of a meaningful text schema. This conforms with research indicating that readers who possess accurate and relevant knowledge concerning a new text understand it better than those who possess inaccurate or tangential knowledge (Barnitz & Morgan, 1983; Biemiller, 2000; Goldman & Rakestraw, 2000; Lipson, 1984; NRP, 2000; Wilson & Anderson, 1986).

Self-esteem. We need to examine the popularly-held notion that students' self-esteem decreases when teachers correct **in**accurate views. In fact, Carnine (2000) reports that self-esteem does **not** seem to be harmed by providing correct information along with additional opportunities for students to practice correctly. He indicates that students seem to develop self-esteem and confidence when they competently grasp subject matter through direct instruction. Perhaps readers sense when they lack the background knowledge needed to understand a concept and realize that their understanding of unfamiliar information is unclear and vague. Avoiding the correcting of inaccurate responses may leave students feeling insecure and unsure.

We need to respond to inaccurate statements sensitively while providing accurate background that lets readers clarify misconceptions. This occurs with methods such as saying "actually" and providing the correct information then asking a question that lets the same student respond accurately. Such approaches generate feelings of success while neither alienating learners through a gesture of rejection nor binding learners to continued confusion through condescending, though well-intentioned, acceptance of inaccurate responses.

Summary.   Relevant background knowledge appears crucial to understanding of unfamiliar and specialized text. Comprehension appears to be enhanced when prereading instruction provides learners with accurate information and concepts, along with opportunities to discuss and clarify understanding of such concepts. Such instruction seems to fill in gaps in prior knowledge and to provide opportunities for students to express their newly developing understanding in their own words. Such instruction is provided through previews of relevant concepts followed by the posing of questions that encourage students to reformulate, articulate, and apply the previewed concepts and background. With such preparation, students seem to experience enhanced comprehension when reading unfamiliar and specialized text. This success may lead them to view reading as an opportunity for constructive interaction with new concepts and ideas rather than as an exercise in frustration and confusion.

References

Adams, M.J. (1994). *Beginning to read: Thinking and learning about print.* Cambridge: MIT Press.

Anstey, M.M. & Freebody, P. (1987). The effects of various pre-reading activities on children's literal and inferential comprehension. *Reading Psychology, 8*(3), 189-209.

Barnitz, J.C. & Morgan, A.L. (1983). Aspects of schemata and syntax in fifth grade children's inferential reading comprehension of causal relations. *Reading Psychology, 4*(3), 337-48.

Biemiller, A. (2000). Vocabulary: The missing link between phonics and comprehension. *Perspectives*, 26(4), 26-30.

Brody, S. (1987). *Study skills: Teaching and learning strategies for mainstream and specialized classrooms.* Milford, NH: LARC Publishing.

Brody, S. (1991). *Clarifying the role of prereading instruction in 4th graders' comprehension of social studies text.* Unpublished Doctoral Dissertation, Harvard Graduate School of Education, Cambridge, MA.

Brody, S. (1993). Developing background knowledge: A context enrichment strategy that may provide more consistent results than activation of prior knowledge. In D. Wray (Ed.), *Proceedings: 1994 United Kingdom Reading Association Annual Conference*, Exeter, England: UKRA.

Campbell, J.R., Hombo, C.M., & Mazzeo, J. (2000). *Trends in academic progress: Three decades of student performance.* Washington, DC: U.S. Department of Education.

Carnine, D. (2000). *Why education experts resist effective practices.* Washington, DC: Thomas Fordham Foundation. [available at http://www.edexcellence.net].

Chall, J.S. (1996). *Stages of reading development (2nd ed.).* Orlando, FL: Harcourt Brace

Dole, J.A., Valencia, S.W., Greer, E.A., & Wardrop, J.L. (1991). Effects of two types of prereading instruction on the comprehension of narrative and expository text. *Reading Research Quarterly, 26*(2), 142-159.

Gardner, H. (1982). *Art, mind, and brain: A cognitive approach to creativity.* New York: Basic Books.

Gazzaniga, M.S. (1992). *Nature's mind: The biological roots of thinking, emotions, sexuality, language, and intelligence.* New York: Basic Books.

Goldman, S. & Rakestraw, J. (2000). Structural aspects of constructing meaning from text. In M.L. Kamil, P.B. Mosenthal, P.D. Pearson, & R. Barr (Eds.), *Handbook of reading research.* Mahwah, NJ: Lawrence Erlbaum Associates.

Graves, M.F., & Cooke, C.L., (1980). Effects of previewing difficult short stories for high school students. *Research on Reading in Secondary Schools, 6*, 38-54.

Graves, M.F., Cooke, C.L., & Laberge, M.J. (1983). Effects of previewing difficult short stories on low ability junior high school students' comprehension, recall, and attitudes. *Reading Research Quarterly, 18*(3) 262-276.

Graves, M.F., Prenn, M.C., & Cooke, C.L. (1985). The coming attraction: Previewing short stories. *Journal of Reading, 28*(7), 594-598.

Hansen, J. & Pearson, P.D. (1983). An instructional study: Improving the inferential comprehension of good and poor fourth-grade readers. *Journal of Educational Psychology, 75*(6), 821-29.

Inhelder, B., & Piaget, J. (1958). *The growth of logical thinking from childhood to adolescence.* NY: Basic Books.

Kintsch, W. (1998). *Comprehension: A paradigm for cognition.* New York: Cambridge University Press.

Lipson, M.Y. (1984). Some unexpected issues in prior knowledge and comprehension. *Reading Teacher, 37*(8), 760-764.

Lyon, G.R. (2000). Learning to read: A call from research to action. *NEBIDA Newsletter,* Spring/Summer 15-18.

National Reading Panel [NRP]. (2000). *Report of the National Reading Panel: Teaching children to read.* Washington, DC: National Institute of Child Health and Human Development. [Available at http://www.nichd.nih.gov/publications/nrp.]

Perfetti, C.A. & Curtis, M.E. (1986). Reading. In R.F. Dillon & R.J. Sternberg (Eds.), *Cognition and instruction.* NY: Academic Press.

Pressley, M. (2000). What should comprehension instruction be the instruction of? In M.L. Kamil, P.B. Mosenthal, P.D. Pearson, & R. Barr (Eds.), *Handbook of reading research.* Mahwah, NJ: Lawrence Erlbaum Associates.

Stahl, S.A., Heubach, K., & Cramond, B. (1997). *Fluency-oriented Reading Instruction. Reading Research Report #79.* Athens, GA: National Reading Research Center.

Stanovich, K.E. (1994). Romance and reality. *The Reading Teacher, 47*(4), 280-291.

Stanovich, K.E., & Cunningham, A.E. (1993). Where does knowledge come from? Specific associations between print exposure and information acquisition. *Journal of Educational Psychology, 85*(2).

Wilson, P.T. & Anderson, R.C. (1986). What they don't know will hurt them: The role of prior knowledge in comprehension. In J. Orasanu (Ed.), *Reading comprehension: From research to practice.* Hillsdale, NJ: Lawrence Erlbaum.

Chapter 9. Vocabulary: Teaching Words and Their Meanings

Paula H. Sable, EdD
Measured Progress

Reading is greatly enhanced when learners possess substantial vocabulary knowledge. Extensive knowledge of word meanings offers a solid underpinning as readers peruse text to understand an author's message. Such background assists readers in forming inferences more accurately and efficiently and also contributes to a sense of confidence that the author's meaning is understood (Biemiller, 2000; National Reading Panel, 2000).

A range of knowledge is used to build an extensive vocabulary—surface and deep meanings, connotations and contextual meanings all contribute to understanding a word's potential communicative intent. This chapter examines the nature of rich reading vocabulary and its development. First, the types of vocabulary knowledge that readers use are described. Next, issues related to direct and indirect instruction are considered. And, finally, strategies used to increase word knowledge are presented.

Types of Vocabulary Knowledge

A reader's lexicon, or mental dictionary, is composed of what the person knows about words and their meanings. The term **vocabulary** refers to one's lexical understanding; this is the case whether words represent tangible items, abstract ideas, or concepts. Lexical knowledge includes both meaning—purely semantic aspects of words—and the syntactic or technical elements of words, such as word endings that signify tense or possession. Together, semantic and syntactic knowledge constitute a reader's lexicon. This body of information can be drawn on to understand and engage in linguistic thought. What readers know *about* words, as well as the words readers know, influences the clarity with which learners understand a range of spoken and written language.

The act of reading draws heavily on an understanding of word meanings. Proficient readers connect printed words to their meanings with ease. In addition, they negotiate meanings of unfamiliar words by drawing on text content and knowledge of syntax, semantics, and synonyms. In order to consider thoroughly the contribution of vocabulary knowledge to reading, it is helpful to explore the kinds of "vocabularies" readers possess and the extent to which they understand these words.

Depth and breadth. By the time learners develop reading fluency, one of the primary functions of instruction is the extension of their substantial lexicon in order to enhance the development of both depth and breadth of vocabulary knowledge. Readers encounter a variety of words (breadth); they also learn that some words have meanings that vary by context (depth).

These multiple meaning words are especially important when learners study in different disciplines. For example, readers may know that the term *cabinet* describes a particular type of furniture. When readers learn about forms of government, the term *cabinet* indicates a body of people with a specific governmental function. The learning of such multiple-meaning terms becomes an important focus for the development of vocabulary depth, especially when reading within the academic content areas.

Denotation and connotation. Vocabulary development reflects an additional dimension as well. Not only are unfamiliar words and/or meanings encountered, but denotative and connotative aspects of meaning are explored. Although individual words may have very specific denotations, or definitions, they may also convey very different connotations, or suggested meanings, when used in unusual situations.

With instruction, practice, and wide reading, students learn to clarify a word's connotative meanings in relation to the words surrounding it. Such clarification occurs very quickly when fluent readers, with strong vocabularies, engage with well structured text. However, the process requires careful instruction for readers who lack a range of background that can aid in negotiating an author's intended meaning. The following example illustrates how a reader may draw on both semantic and syntactic knowledge to learn a connotative meaning:

> Samantha knows that *unique* means one of a kind. She can identify a unique object when asked to select it from several others.

> Samantha also knows that *circumstances* is used to identify situations. If presented with two situations, Samantha can select the unique one.

> However, Samantha must draw on syntactic, as well as semantic, knowledge when she encounters the following sentence: *When the unique circumstances occurred repeatedly, policy changed.*

> In order to fully comprehend this sentence, Samantha draws on her syntactic knowledge of the suffix *ly* in order to be aware that what has been unique is now occurring, not one time, but often. She makes use of semantic knowledge as well. By knowing that policy is promulgated to reflect common circumstances, Samantha more fully comprehends the sentence.

In addition, connotation alone can affect word meaning. Compare the implications of these two sentences.

> *The students described their teacher as very patient.*

> *The students described their teacher as very meek.*

In these two syntactically similar sentences, the words *patient* and *meek*, though quite close in meaning, represent very different personalities. Such connotations can only be understood when the reader possesses considerable semantic knowledge.

Oral and literary language. A writer's or speaker's choice of words varies to match the context in which the words are used. For example, when sharing information concerning vocabulary in an educational column of a local newspaper, one's choice of wording and phrasing would differ from that used when writing a paper to present at a research convention. To accommodate these differences in level of formality, we need to develop a broad vocabulary that enhances communicative flexibility.

Learners who have experienced very little exposure to books or conversations in which literary language is used tend to rely primarily on informal expressions.   In contrast, avid readers and those regularly exposed to conversations that draw on literary conventions tend to possess broader vocabularies. This breadth reflects both exposure to literary language and exposure to informal, oral language through daily experience and wide reading in which both formal and informal vocabulary is encountered. Learners who begin Stage 3 reading with both formal and informal language exposure tend to increase their reading ability with greater ease (Chall, 1987; Stanovich, 1986).

Receptive and productive vocabulary. When listening to another person talking, or when reading, students rely on their stored knowledge of words in order to comprehend the content. These words make up their receptive vocabulary. When readers' receptive vocabulary is weak, they search to bridge their knowledge gaps in one of several ways. They may try to discern a meaning in relation to the context of a topic or sentence, or seek help from another source, such as a dictionary or another person.

Often, readers with limited vocabulary lack sufficient receptive word knowledge to fill in, from context, and understand with accuracy (McKeown, 1985).   In addition, their weak receptive vocabulary makes it difficult to comprehend dictionary meaning (McKeown, 1993) and may leave them too self-conscious to ask for help. If these students are to learn from reading, teachers need to preview vocabulary related to assigned text. This preview, coupled with subsequent, active engagement with the word, while reading it in multiple contexts, helps to insert the words into the memory bank of receptive vocabulary.

Productive, or expressive, vocabulary refers to those words used during speech or writing.   Students transfer a word from receptive to expressive vocabulary when they know its meaning well and feel comfortable or competent using it actively (Graves, 1987). Words that are part of receptive vocabulary do not necessarily become part of productive vocabulary, or may require a considerable number of encounters before transfer. Consequently, receptive vocabulary is usually more expansive than productive vocabulary. One of the tasks of good vocabulary instruction is to enhance students' productive vocabulary in order to facilitate independence in active, linguistic processing of unfamiliar concepts.

Completeness. Completeness of word knowledge can be described in terms of various developmental schemes. The one presented here was introduced by Edgar Dale (1965) and its usefulness further expanded by Mary E. Curtis (1987). It delineates four states of word knowledge that reflect a word's increasing accessibility in receptive and/or productive vocabulary.

Unknown Words. Dale describes the earliest level of word knowledge as no knowledge—words to which one cannot attach meaning. Dale describes a student's response at this stage as, "I never saw it before." Learners may not even be sure that a word in this stage is a real word, as has been demonstrated when they have been asked to identify "real" words from a list of real and nonsense words (Curtis, 1987).

Vague Knowledge. At this level of word knowledge, a student may respond, "I've heard of it, but I don't know what it means." A student at this stage is aware of a term but has not yet associated clear meaning with it. Such a word cannot be part of the student's productive vocabulary since no meaning is available to initiate its use. Further, the word is of little value in the reader's receptive vocabulary since it can only elicit quizzical looks or awareness that it would be wise to consult a dictionary or other reference source.

Partial Knowledge. Dale indicates that a reader with partial knowledge would have a general association of a word within a specific context. Thus, a response would be, "It has something to do with...." Words in receptive vocabulary are often initially those for which partial understanding is held. Usually, such words require additional encounters, within several contexts, before a reader feels confident that the meaning is perceived accurately. Still further exposure is needed before learners attempt to use these words in speaking or writing. Thus, these words are tentatively embedded in receptive vocabulary, and unlikely to be part of productive vocabulary.

Deep Knowledge. Curtis describes this level of vocabulary as that at which a reader can define a word without tying it to a specific context (1987, p. 43). In order to do this, the reader must possess sufficient understanding to relate the word to synonyms, use it in differing contexts, and explain its meaning in some detail. Since such knowledge is necessary to allow use in productive vocabulary, it is worth teaching toward this level.

Partial knowledge of words is often sufficient to recognize meaning when context is explicit. Curtis (1987) found such knowledge adequate to produce correct responses on multiple choice vocabulary tests. But partial knowledge is troublesome when it leads students to misunderstand what they read. Further, problems arise when partial understanding leads teachers to assume that students have developed a greater depth than is actually the case (Sable, 1992).

When selecting words for instruction, teachers sometimes pass over words for which students possess partial knowledge. The importance of instruction in such words becomes evident during productive use or when content is less explicit. Many teachers who have asked students to look up word meanings in the dictionary, then use these words in sentences, have encountered examples of partial understanding. Miller and Gildea (1987) illustrate with this example:

> A fifth grader, having read in the dictionary that *meticulous* means being very careful about details, wrote the following sentence: *I was meticulous about falling off the cliff* (p. 98).

Deep knowledge of word meanings is particularly important when readers add technical and specialized words to their productive vocabulary during Stage 3 reading and beyond. Such words carry a great deal of the content load. Fluent use of the words allows readers to think about material under study and to use language to actively apply content to a variety of contexts and circumstances. This processing aids in remembering the material and in understanding its relevance (Perkins & Salomon, 1988). In addition, such use enables readers to communicate the content to others during discussion or in writing.

Teachers need to recognize the importance of developing deep understanding of words as a goal of vocabulary instruction. Since their students generally perform well on multiple choice or matching quizzes with only partial knowledge of word meanings (Curtis, 1987), teachers may not recognize the limitations imposed by knowledge developed only to the level of exposure. Insufficient knowledge of word meanings may persist when teachers provide only brief exposure to vocabulary, in expectation that mastery of meanings will come later, through other means (Sable, 1992).

Direct and Indirect Vocabulary Instruction

Vocabulary is acquired through direct instruction and incidental exposure. Both types of learning contribute to the development of a rich and varied vocabulary (Chall, 1987). Since both instruction and exposure enhance word knowledge, teachers need to assist students in developing vocabulary through each of these means.

Prior to schooling, very young children develop an understanding of words through instruction by parents who point to objects while saying their names, and through repeated labeling of actions and ideas during daily routines. This occurs primarily during speaking, being spoken to, and listening to others. Language development and vocabulary acquisition are further enhanced by exposure to print, as occurs when adults read aloud. (See Chapter 2, of this volume, concerning language development.)

Children continue to expand their vocabulary through these avenues when they enter school. At this point, opportunities expand with exposure to unfamiliar activities and routines. In addition, as children develop reading proficiency, they enhance their capability to learn word meanings from printed context. The rate of such learning is quite varied since some children select and read books and other materials avidly, while others read little or not at all.

Independent reading can provide a positive opportunity for expansive development of vocabulary among children who are avid readers (Nagy, Herman, & Anderson 1985). The more these children read, the more they encounter new words. Extensive vocabulary expansion can occur as a result of this exposure. Consequently, many educators suggest that an important contribution to vocabulary instruction lies in turning children loose with books and encouraging them to read, read, read (Green, 1984; Nagy & Herman, 1987).

However, simply exposing children to books does not develop vocabulary sufficiently in the upper elementary grades and beyond (Beck & McKeown, 1983; Chall, 1987; Graves, 1987). Learners at these levels need to comprehend unfamiliar information in a variety of subject areas but do not gain sufficient exposure to all areas of knowledge through independent reading alone.

Numerous studies attest to the need for an instructional approach that includes direct, systematic instruction as well as encouragement to read frequently and broadly (Mezynski, 1983; Nagy, 1988; Stahl & Fairbanks, 1986). The need for direct instruction becomes especially evident when considering the learning characteristics of the readers described below:

Infrequent Readers.   Many students lack the habit of frequent and independent reading (Mullis, Campbell, & Farstrup, 1993). These readers are exposed to words through context less frequently than their peers who read often.   Consequently, they require direct instruction in order to develop depth and breadth of vocabulary. In turn, this word knowledge can support greater understanding during reading and perhaps promote greater reading frequency among some students.

Readers from Limited-literacy Backgrounds. Much research has examined the relationship between reading development and family/situational backgrounds (Chall, Jacobs, & Baldwin, 1990; Chall & Snow, 1982; Feitelson, Kita, & Goldstein, 1986).   This research demonstrates that children who have little reading material available in their homes are less likely to read frequently. When children come to school with limited exposure to print and literary language, direct instruction in words and their meanings particularly enhances recognition of a broad variety of words and their meanings in literary discourse and expository text.

Readers from Varied Cultural Perspectives. The teacher's role, and the way learning is perceived and achieved, differs among cultures. Since students' expectations often influence how they learn (Heath, 1983), children who look to the teacher to initiate instruction will benefit from direct instruction (Delpit, 1986; 1988).

Readers who Lack Extensive Vocabulary. As readers enter the upper elementary grades, they need to draw on broad and deep vocabulary to help them determine word meanings accurately from context (McKeown, 1985). Lack of such knowledge affects skilled readers, as well as those less skilled, when they try to understand text that was written with many specialized words. Direct instruction provides meanings of crucial content words as a foundation from which to develop accurate word meanings from context (Graves, 1984).

Less-Skilled Readers. Research comparing the practices of skilled and less-skilled readers (Golinkoff, 1975-76; Sullivan, 1978; Harmon, 1999) indicates that less-skilled readers rely on fewer strategies for negotiating meaning. In order to learn unfamiliar words through the exposure of independent reading, students need to recognize whether they understand a word or concept. Research on metacognition indicates that some readers, particularly those who are younger or less skilled, lack this awareness; consequently, they do not know when to seek an unknown definition (Paris & Lindauer, 1982). These learners need direct instruction to develop sufficient vocabulary knowledge to recognize whether they know words.

Risk-avoiding Readers. Reading often requires learners to take risks. Skilled readers usually take risks. When one strategy fails, they try another (Sullivan, 1978). In contrast, less-secure readers tend to be more rigid and to give up easily when a first attempt at meaning fails (Bransford, Vye, & Stein, 1984). These students need direct instruction in word meanings to build their vocabulary as a means of bolstering their confidence during independent reading. Direct instruction that includes consistent reinforcement of a variety of word-learning strategies in turn increases readers' attempts to try multiple strategies.

Independent Readers. Even skilled readers in the elementary grades experience difficulty in learning the meanings of specialized content words solely from context or context-with-dictionary-support. They need some direct instruction for assistance, since most dictionary meanings are too broad to define specific concepts clearly (McKeown, 1993).

Readers come to Stage 3 with a variety of learning characteristics that contribute to their need for focused vocabulary instruction. Such instruction teaches words directly through multiple exposures to words, their meanings, and synonyms; it also provides many opportunities for independent reading (Chall 1987; Mezynski, 1983; Stahl & Fairbanks, 1986).

Vocabulary Instruction

Classroom research suggests that effective vocabulary instruction integrates four components: a clear statement of, and focus on, the definition of unfamiliar words; multiple opportunities to use words under study in spoken and written contexts; the association of words under study with related words and concepts; and use of activities that require reasoning about word meanings and their relationships with other words (Beck, McKeown, & Omanson 1987; Beck, Perfetti, & McKeown, 1982; Mezynski, 1983; Sable, 1988; Stahl & Fairbanks, 1986). The following discussion offers guidelines concerning how to select words for direct instruction and then suggests a variety of instructional strategies that incorporate the four components described above.

SELECTING WORDS FOR DIRECT INSTRUCTION

Teachers need to select words for instruction carefully since time allows only a limited number of words to be taught directly. Some research suggests that lessons involving 10 - 12 words seem appropriate for most students in the intermediate grades (Beck et al., 1982; McKeown, Beck, Omanson, & Pople, 1985; Wixson, 1986; Wysocki & Jenkins, 1987). Vocabulary lessons in commercial materials sometimes exceed these numbers; however, these materials often include many words that students already know (Sable, 1988). Recent analyses of current commercial materials suggest that fewer words are being recommended for study today (Sable, 1998) and that, often, these words do not contribute to rich vocabulary development (Stotsky, 1999). Thus, it is even more important that teachers judiciously select words for study. Maria (1990) and Graves, Slater, & White (1989) offer helpful criteria for selecting words to study. These are described below:

Relevant Words. Words for study should be taken from material that students will actually read, such as textbooks and trade or story books used in the classroom. These establish a functional basis for inclusion.

Unfamiliar Words Not Easily Inferred from Context. Words that students are not likely to know, or to figure out from context, should be selected. Teachers can focus instruction on these words by choosing carefully among lists of words recommended in commercial programs (Sable, 1988) or by previewing reading materials and selecting those words for which students are likely to require instructional elaboration.

Maria (1990) advises that words whose meanings may be easily inferred from context should not be selected for instruction. For such words, a brief query during the actual reading of the text with repeated use during post-reading discussion may ensure comprehension and word learning.

When text includes more words requiring instruction than can fit a lesson, Maria (1990) and Graves (1987) suggest the following additional criteria to narrow word selection:

Words Essential to Comprehension. Since only a limited number of words can be taught, content words most essential to understanding should be selected. Klein (1988) refers to these as "enabling" words.

Words that Foster Strategic Skill Development. In addition to essential words, it is also useful to select words that provide opportunities to

264

develop word-learning strategies. For example, sometimes several words in the text have the same affix or root word. Part of the lesson can focus on the common element in these words to provide a strategy for identifying other similar words.

Words of General Utility. Essential words that appear often in other contexts may also be taught. When a text contains several unusual words, some may be defined briefly **during actual reading** to reserve vocabulary lesson time for those higher frequency words that can influence reading comprehension more broadly. For example, in a science lesson on bacteria, appropriate vocabulary words may include *chloroplast, flagella,* and *cilia,* while brief instruction during reading would suffice for a passing reference to *trypanosoma.*

Words that Pique Interest. Maria also suggests selecting words of particular interest. She cites educators (e.g., Richek, 1988) who demonstrate that focus on words of interest to students can increase word knowledge and interest in the study of words.

These criteria offer guidelines to consider when choosing words for direct instruction. By culling words selectively, teachers maximize the extent that vocabulary lessons increase students' knowledge of word meanings along with their skill in determining meaning independently.

When selecting words to teach, it is helpful to consider the type of knowledge that students need to develop concerning each target word. Graves, Slater, & White (1989) describe six specific word-learning skills that may be needed to enhance receptive or productive vocabulary. Their classification system is delineated below:

Type One: Recognition of Known Words. The most basic word learning task is learning to decode words whose meanings are already known. By learning to "crack the code," learners can recognize, in print, words that they already possess in their listening vocabulary. (See Chapters 3, 4, and 5 of this volume for a detailed description of instruction.)

Type Two: Polysemous Words. The second word type described by Graves et al. is recognition that a word's meaning may differ when the context is changed. Instruction of polysemous, or multiple-meaning words, occurs especially in relation to various content areas. Devine (1986) indicates that there are two kinds of polysemous words. One includes common words for which a variety of meanings are already known, such as *stop, store, ice*. The other includes words whose meanings vary in different disciplines such as *charged* used in war, finance, and electronics.

Type Three: Unfamiliar Words for Familiar Concepts. Readers need to learn unfamiliar words that represent well known concepts. For example, students may not know the word *daguerreotype*, but readily recognize the concept that it represents, an old-time photograph. Unfamiliar synonyms can be linked with a concept that is already understood by providing a simple explanation of the meaning, coupled with examples that associate the word with the reader's existing schema.

Type Four: Unfamiliar Words for Unfamiliar Concepts. Perhaps the most difficult vocabulary task is learning unfamiliar words for unknown concepts. Such words appear frequently in content area reading. Terms such as *entropy, isolationism* or *imaginary number* often require conceptual development before they can be fully understood. Johnson and Pearson (1984), suggest that students learn unfamiliar concepts through multiple experiences with central and related information in similar and varied contexts.

Type Five: Depth and Precision of Word Meaning. Another vocabulary development task described by Graves et al. is "clarifying and enriching the meanings of known words" (1989, p. 216). Such instruction helps students increase depth of understanding and use greater precision in word usage as in clarifying the difference between *assertive* and *aggressive*.

Type Six: Moving Words to Productive Vocabulary. The final, ongoing, task described by Graves et al. involves the expansion of productive vocabulary. Since most individuals comprehend more words than they speak or write, expanding productive vocabulary tends to require additional instruction. A variety of strategies foster habits of vocabulary awareness, interest in words, and the use of new words.

The classifications provided by Graves et al. underscore the importance of the vocabulary word selection process and the need to vary teaching rate to accommodate the kinds of words under study. A fifteen-minute lesson may introduce six or more synonyms for familiar concepts; however, at least that time may be needed to introduce one unfamiliar word and its related unfamiliar concept.

INSTRUCTIONAL STRATEGIES

A crucial element of effective vocabulary instruction is the provision of multiple and varied exposures to the word and its meaning. This exposure includes explanation and demonstration by the teacher as well as opportunities for students to use the word many times in many contexts to assure clear understanding and transfer to productive vocabulary. The following strategies can be effective in vocabulary instruction:

Concrete examples. The critical factor in teaching polysemous words is knowing the appropriate match between meaning and context. When the meaning is already known, instruction simply needs to teach explicitly the match between the word and its unfamiliar context. This can be done by providing students with the unfamiliar usage and several concrete examples, prior to encounter in print. For example, the teacher might turn on a flashlight with a dead battery, then replace it with a *charged* battery before students read about electricity. The demonstration could be followed by asking students to describe other gadgets that require charged batteries.

Linking unfamiliar synonyms with familiar meanings. Graves et al. (1989), Sable (1988), Curtis (1986), Johnson & Pearson (1984), and Beck & McKeown (1983) discuss a variety of ways to link synonyms with existing schemata. When used in combination, such strategies effectively provide multiple exposures to words and their meanings. These activities include:

- Provide the definition of a word orally.
- Offer a definition and use the word orally in a context laden sentence.
- Ask students to look up the word in a dictionary or glossary.
- Offer multiple examples by using a word in several contexts, followed by asking students to deduce word meaning.
- Engage students in adapted card games such as Concentration.
- Develop semantic maps of the word and its synonyms.

Presentation and discussion of words in multiple contexts. Discussion of the definitions and use of a word in multiple contexts can enhance memory of the word and understanding of its meaning (Curtis & Longo, 1999; Stahl & Vancil, 1986). Group discussion of sentences and meaning offer opportunities for associations among words as well as opportunities for students to use the words themselves in unfamiliar ways. Throughout the discussion, it is crucial that the teacher directly confirms accurate usage and correct inaccuracies to assure that students embed the term appropriately in their lexicon. Whatever the strategies used, as with all types of vocabulary words, they will be learned and remembered best if students are given many exposures to the word and its meaning (Beck et al., 1983).

Word maps. Word mapping, developed by Schwartz (1988), assists students in learning unfamiliar concepts and their related words. This activity, which may be completed with a text frame (see Chapter 7), provides a strategy that teaches a concept by noting its class, distinguishing characteristics that separate it from other members of its class, and several examples of the concept in use. Schwartz recommends that the following questions be used during instruction:

- What is it? (categorize by class)
- What is it like? (compare with similar concepts or describe attributes)
- What are some examples? (demonstrate understanding)

For example, when defining the term *republic*, students would answer questions to fill in a word map with responses such as:

- What is it? *form of government*
- What is it like? *citizens vote for representatives, head is elected*
- What are some examples? *U.S.A., Canada*

Clarifying meaning by example and non-example. Research suggests that work with semantically related words clarifies and deepens word knowledge (Beck & McKeown, 1983; Johnson & Pearson, 1984; Marzano & Marzano, 1988). Graves et al. (1989) and Frayer, Frederick, & Klausmeier (1969) offer a strategy that clarifies word meaning by comparing familiar and unfamiliar terms.

To use this approach, teachers first introduce a target word, its meaning, and its attributes. Next, they compare the target word to similar, but different, words while noting similarities and distinctions. Then, they provide examples of appropriate uses of the target word. This is followed by demonstrating non-examples (related contexts in which a different word needs to be used for accuracy) along with examples (related contexts for which the target word is appropriate). Teachers offer additional examples and non-examples while leading students through a discussion to clarify the concept. Finally, teachers ask students to present their own examples and non-examples. When students do this successfully, they understand the concept.

Semantic maps. Semantic maps, sometimes called word webs, are diagrams that show how words are related to one another (Johnson & Pearson, 1984, p. 12). Semantic maps are developed by noting associations among words. When discussion is guided carefully, it can verify, correct, and expand students'

268

understanding of word meanings (Heimlich & Pittelman, 1986). This process seems especially appropriate for refining depth and precision of word meanings. (See Figure 9.a.)

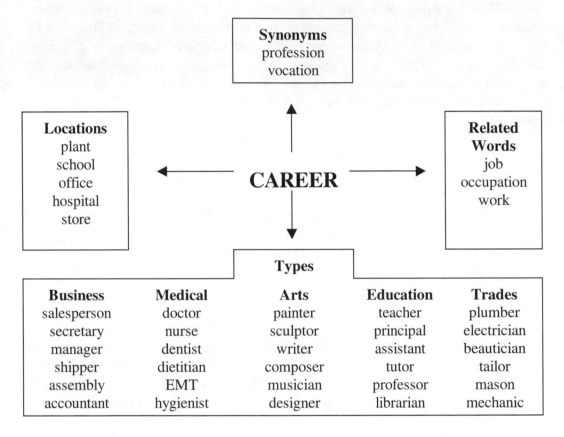

Figure 9.a. Semantic map.

It is helpful to follow a mapping lesson with activities that require students to use words from the map in speaking, reading, and writing. Questions that encourage students to think, respond, and provide reasons for their responses seem particularly effective in the development of depth of word knowledge (Beck et al., 1987). In particular, the additional exposure to target words during such activities reinforces meaning (Beck & McKeown, 1983; Beck et al., 1982; Curtis & Longo, 1999).

Semantic feature analysis. Another method of refining word meaning involves a comparison-contrast activity conducted while developing an attribute grid. In this activity, a particular category is selected and target words within the category are listed. These, and a row of attributes, form a matrix. Students identify the attributes of each target word by placing a check or plus/minus in appropriate spaces on the matrix. (See Figure 9.b, below.)

Word	Characteristics				
	Lasting	Pleasant	Food Related	Mild	Strong
aroma	+	+	+/-	+	-
fragrance	+	+	-	+	-
odor	+	-	+/-	?	+
stench	+	-	-	-	+
scent	-	+	?	+	-
whiff	-	+/-	+/-	+	-

Figure 9.b. Semantic feature analysis grid.

Marzano & Marzano (1988) suggest using such matrices in several ways: to develop generalizations concerning related words; to note how few words possess the same attributes; to describe similarities and differences among words; and to develop definitions. As with semantic maps, feature analysis matrices lend themselves to activities that raise questions, analyze meaning, and develop connotative understanding. They may also be used to note terms that are formal and those that are reserved for informal contexts.

Analogies. The completion or construction of analogous relationships is a form of word play that promotes depth of understanding. However, in order for students to engage in this activity, they need to understand the kinds of relationships displayed in analogic equations. Johnson & Pearson (1984) suggest several relationships that are demonstrated by analogy. A few examples of these include:

Characteristics: Stone is to hard as fur is to soft.
Part/Whole: Page is to book as spoke is to wheel.
Location: Clerk is to store as teller is to bank.
Action/Object: Skate is to ice as fry is to griddle.

Analogies are used to depict relationships, and students clarify their vocabulary understanding by explaining the analogy. Students actively process the words and their meanings through discussion or writing. Once students master the relationships of analogy, teachers can help them develop their own analogies using related words under study.

Vocabulary notebooks. Vocabulary notebooks are especially helpful in expanding productive vocabulary. Marzano & Marzano (1988) suggest that students develop these notebooks arranged by category and concept. For example, under the category "personality traits," the student would list the concept "peevish." Within this format, students list the target word, words that are similar, and a definition (see figure 9.c, below). Since the three-ring notebook is arranged with at least one page per category, students can add words by category without concern for alphabetical order. Activities involving the notebook provide opportunities to note differences among similar words and encourage students to use the words accurately.

Category:	words that convey emotion	
Concepts:	anger, joy, sadness, apathy	
WORD	RELATED WORDS	DEFINITION
ire	anger, wrath, fury	deep anger
dejection	sadness, misery, melancholy	depression
ecstatic	overjoyed, delighted, blissful	full of happiness

Figure 9.c. Vocabulary notebook page arranged by category and concept.

Klein (1988) recommends the use of vocabulary notebooks when teaching theme-related words, particularly in content-area learning. He suggests that students use notebooks to record times and places where unfamiliar words are heard or used both in school and other settings. He cautions that the notebooks must be coupled with brief, daily discussion if entries are to be mastered. In a similar program, Word Wizard (Beck & McKeown, 1983), students earn points by sharing, in class, target words seen, heard, or used outside of class.

Etymology. Interest in expanding productive vocabulary can be sparked through lessons that explore the origin of words and their meanings. Etymology, the history of words, can intrigue students when properly presented. A focus on etymology is particularly appropriate for learners at or beyond Stage 3 reading development since these readers possess a rudimentary facility with dictionaries and basic research skills. Klein (1988) suggests that lessons can focus on word evolution by noting semantic changes, word formation, and dialect.

Students are often interested in how new words are formed. Even at very young ages, children experiment with new names for objects and play at developing their own words. (See Chapter 2 for detail.) Discussion of word formation enhances this curiosity and offers specific knowledge as well. The following examples describe a variety of ways in which words are formed:

Acronyms are developed by shortening longer titles or phrases to the initial letter of each word in the descriptor as in *SCUBA* (self-contained underwater breathing apparatus; or, *EMT* (emergency medical technician).

Abbreviations evolve from longer words through deletion as in *gym* (gymnasium).

Blends develop from two or more existing words as in *smog* (smoke and fog).

Coined words express a concept in a new field as in *interface* (coined to describe connectors that let various computer accessories work together).

Role shifts occur when words used as one part of speech are used in another, as in *service* (a noun used as a verb to explain that *the car was serviced*).

Whatever teaching strategy is selected, teachers can facilitate the learning of unfamiliar words by assuring that instruction defines words clearly and offers students multiple opportunities to use the words appropriately in a variety of contexts. Such instruction aids in the learning of unfamiliar words and in moving words from receptive to productive vocabulary (Beck et al., 1982; 1987).

Conclusion

Comprehension of literature and expository text is enhanced by broad and deep vocabulary knowledge that leads a reader to fully understand word meanings. Mastery of word meaning requires frequent exposure to words in a variety of contexts. Word knowledge is enhanced by a program of consistent instruction that includes systematic review of word meanings along with encouragement to use these words during oral communication (Sable, 1988).

In addition, maintaining a learning atmosphere where students are comfortable exploring the use of words is a crucial instructional goal. Effective programs teach sets of semantically-related words; offer daily practice that involves semantic association, connotation, and production of definitions; and create opportunities for students to use the words often when writing or speaking.

References

Beck, I.L., & McKeown, M.G. (1983). Learning words well: A program to enhance vocabulary and comprehension. *Reading Teacher, 36,* 622-625.

Beck, I.L., McKeown, M.G., & Omanson, R.C. (1987). The effects and uses of diverse vocabulary instructional techniques. In M.G. McKeown & M.E. Curtis (Eds.), *The nature of vocabulary acquisition.* Hillsdale, NJ: Erlbaum.

Beck, I.L., Perfetti, C.A., & McKeown, M.G. (1982). Effects of long-term vocabulary instruction on lexical access and reading comprehension. *Journal of Educational Psychology, 74,* 506-521.

Biemiller, A. (2000). Vocabulary: The missing link between phonics and comprehension. *Perspectives*, 26(4), 26-30.

Bransford, J.D., Vye, N.J. & Stein, B.S. (1984). A comparison of successful and less successful learners: Can we enhance comprehension and mastery skills? In J. Flood (Ed.), *Promoting reading comprehension.* Newark, DE: International Reading Association.

Chall, J.S. (1987). Two vocabularies for reading: Recognition and meaning. In M.G. McKeown & M.E. Curtis (Eds.), *The nature of vocabulary acquisition.* Hillsdale, NJ: Erlbaum.

Chall, J.S., Jacobs, V.J., & Baldwin, L.E. (1990). *The reading crisis: Why poor children fall behind.* Cambridge, MA: Harvard University Press.

Chall, J.S., & Snow, C. (1982). *Families and literacy.* NIE Report.

Curtis, M.E. (1986). The best kind of vocabulary instruction. *Massachusetts Primer, 15,* 5-9.

Curtis, M.E. (1987). Vocabulary testing and vocabulary instruction. In M.G. McKeown & M.E. Curtis (Eds.), *The nature of vocabulary acquisition.* Hillsdale, NJ: Erlbaum.

Curtis, M.E., & Longo, A.M. (1999). *When adolescents can't read: Methods and materials that work.* Cambridge, MA: Brookline Books.

Dale, E. (1965). Vocabulary measurement: Techniques and major findings. *Elementary English, 42,* 895-901; 948.

Delpit, L.D. (1986). Skills and other dilemmas of a progressive black educator. *Harvard Educational Review, 56,* 379-385.

Delpit, L.D. (1988). The silenced dialogue: Power and pedagogy in educating other people's children. *Harvard Education Review, 58,* 280-298.

Devine, T. G. (1986). *Teaching reading comprehension: From theory to practice.* Needham, MA: Allyn & Bacon.

Feitelson, D., Kita, B., & Goldstein, Z. (1986). Effects of listening to series stories on first graders' comprehension and use of language. *Research in the Teaching of English, 20,* 339-356.

Frayer, D.A., Frederick, W.C., & Klausmeier, H.J. (1969). *A schema for testing the level of concept mastery.* (Working Paper Number 16.) Madison, WI: Wisconsin Research and Development Center for Cognitive Learning.

Golinkoff, R.M. (1975-76). A comparison of reading comprehension processes in good and poor comprehenders. *Reading Research Quarterly, 11,* 623-659.

Graves, M. (1984). Selecting vocabulary to teach in the intermediate and secondary grades. In J. Flood (Ed.), *Promoting reading comprehension.* Newark, DE: International Reading Association.

Graves, M. (1987). The role of instruction in fostering vocabulary development. In M.G. McKeown & M.E. Curtis (Eds.), *The nature of vocabulary acquisition.* Hillsdale, NJ: Erlbaum.

274

Graves, M., Slater, W., & White, T. (1989). Teaching content area vocabulary. In D. Lapp, J. Flood, and N. Farnam (Eds.), *Content area reading and learning: Instructional strategies.* Englewood Cliffs, NJ: Prentice-Hall.

Green, G. (1984). On the appropriateness of adaptations in primary level basal readers: Reactions to remarks by Bertram Bruce. In R. Anderson, J. Osborn, & R. Tierney (Eds.), *Learning to read in American schools.* Hillsdale, NJ: Erlbaum.

Harmon, J.M. (1999). Initial encounters with unfamiliar words in independent reading. *Research in the Teaching of English, 33,* 304-338.

Heath, S.B. (1983). *Ways with words: Language, life, and work in communities and classrooms.* Cambridge: Cambridge University Press.

Heimlich, J.E., & Pittelman, S.D. (1986). *Semantic mapping: Classroom applications.* Newark, DE: International Reading Association.

Johnson, D.D., & Pearson, P.D. (1984). *Teaching reading vocabulary, (2nd ed.).* New York: Holt, Rinehart, & Winston.

Klein, M.L. (1988). *Teaching reading comprehension and vocabulary: A guide for teachers.* Englewood Cliffs, NJ: Prentice-Hall.

Maria, K. (1990). *Reading comprehension instruction: Issues and strategies.* Parkton, MD: York Press.

Marzano, R.J., & Marzano, J.S. (1988). *A cluster approach to elementary vocabulary instruction.* Newark, DE: International Reading Association.

McKeown, M.G. (1985). *The acquisition of word meaning from context by children of high and low ability.* (Outstanding Dissertation Monograph, 1985). Newark, DE: International Reading Association.

McKeown, M.G. (1993). Creating effective definitions for young word learners. *Reading Research Quarterly, 28,* 16-31.

McKeown, M.G., Beck, I.L., Omanson, R.C., & Pople, M.T. (1985). Some effects of the nature and frequency of vocabulary instruction on the knowledge and use of words. *Reading Research Quarterly, 20,* 522-535.

Mezynski, K. (1983). Issues concerning the acquisition of knowledge: Effects of vocabulary training on reading comprehension. *Review of Educational Research, 53,* 253-279.

Miller, G.A., & Gildea, P.M. (1987). How children learn words. *Scientific American, September,* 94-99.

Mullis, I.V., Campbell, J.R., & Farstrup, A.E. (1993). *Reading report card for the nation and the states.* Washington, DC: United States Printing Office.

Nagy, W.E. (1988). *Teaching vocabulary to improve reading comprehension.* Newark, DE: International Reading Association.

Nagy, W.E., & Herman, P.A. (1987). Breadth and depth of vocabulary knowledge: Implications for acquisition and instruction. In M.G. McKeown & M.E. Curtis (Eds.), *The nature of vocabulary acquisition.* Hillsdale, NJ: Erlbaum.

Nagy, W.E., Herman, P. A., & Anderson, R.C. (1985). *Learning word meanings from context: How broadly generalizable?* (Technical Report Number 347.) Urbana-Champaign: University of Illinois, Center for the Study of Reading.

National Reading Panel [NRP]. (2000). *Report of the National Reading Panel: Teaching children to read.* Washington, DC: National Institute of Child Health and Human Development. [Available at http://www.nichd.nih.gov/publications/nrp.]

Paris, S.G., & Lindauer, B.K. (1982). The development of cognitive skills during childhood. In B. Wolman, (Ed.), *Handbook of developmental psychology.* Englewood Cliffs, NJ: Prentice-Hall.

Perkins, D.N., & Salomon G. (1988). Teaching for transfer. *Educational Leadership, 46*(1), 22-33.

Richeck, M.A. (1988). Relating vocabulary learning to world knowledge. *Journal of Reading, 32,* 262-267.

Sable, P.H. (1988). *Vocabulary instruction in basal readers: Does it reflect research?* Unpublished qualifying paper, Harvard Graduate School of Education.

Sable, P.H. (1992). *Vocabulary instruction in fourth and fifth grades: What teachers say they do.* Unpublished doctoral dissertation, Harvard Graduate School of Education.

Sable, P.H. (1998). *Evaluation of two reading series: Houghton-Mifflin Invitations to Literacy and Harcourt Brace Signatures.* [Analysis prepared for the Haverhill (MA) School District].

Schwartz, R. M. (1988). Learning to learn vocabulary in content area textbooks. *Journal of Reading, 38,* 108-118.

Stahl, S.M., & Fairbanks, M.M. (1986). The effects of vocabulary instruction: A model-based meta-analysis. *Review of Educational Research, 56,* 72-110.

Stahl, S.M., & Vancil, S.J. (1986). Discussion is what makes semantic maps work in vocabulary instruction. *Reading Teacher, 40,* 62-67.

Stanovich, K.E. (1986). Matthew effects in reading: Some consequences of individual differences in the acquisition of literacy. *Reading Research Quarterly, 21*(4), 360-406.

Stotsky, S. (1999). *Losing our language: How multicultural classroom instruction is undermining our children's ability to read, write, and reason.* N.Y.: Free Press.

Sullivan, J. (1978). Comparing strategies of good and poor comprehenders. *Journal of Reading, 21,* 710-715.

Wixson, K.K. (1986). Vocabulary instruction and children's comprehension of basal stories. *Reading Research Quarterly, 21,* 316-329.

Wysocki, K., & Jenkins, J.R. (1987). Deriving word meanings through morphological generalization. *Reading Research Quarterly, 22,* 66-81.

Chapter 10. Writing: The Royal Road to Reading Comprehension

Sandra Stotsky, EdD
Massachusetts Department of Education

In 1982, I published an article describing a number of writing activities that might enhance students' reading comprehension. The activities I discussed were dictation, paraphrasing, summary writing, sentence combining, outlining, copying, and the reproduction exercise. Although they were all potentially useful for developing a variety of reading (and listening) skills, some had never been the direct focus of research. However, there was support from related studies, if not direct research, for using all of them. In addition, many of these activities had been used for years if not centuries, in this country and elsewhere, as a regular feature of language instruction.

As I suggested at the time, these strategies generally provide a vehicle for encouraging students to engage actively with a text whether that text is presented orally or in writing. And as writing researchers and teachers have long observed, writing is an active learning process that focuses attention and demands thinking if sensible written expression is to emerge. It seemed reasonable to conclude that when students are asked to manipulate new information and ideas in some form of purposeful and meaningful writing, they must engage in active thinking and hence are likely to improve their comprehension of these new ideas and information.

Two years later, Anderson and Armbruster (1984) reviewed the research on a number of cognitive strategies—activities that were once referred to as the study skills. The studies that they critiqued focused on underlining, mapping, outlining, notetaking, networking, summary writing, self-generated questioning, and responding to attention-focusing questions interspersed throughout an instructional text. The review was not able to comment on academic journal writing because research on it had only just begun. Although there was still little research on summary writing and self-generated questioning, Anderson and Armbruster were able to conclude from the limited results they reviewed that any strategy could be useful if its use was appropriate to the task demanded of the student. However, they noted that some strategies, such as mapping or outlining, seemed to have more potential than others for promoting the processing of new information at deep conceptual levels.

And they believed, on the basis of the research that had been done, that students could benefit from using these strategies if they were taught their use, if they were helped to improve their use of these strategies, and if, in addition, they were taught metacognitive skills, that is, taught to make judgments about when a strategy might or might not be used most fruitfully or when understanding was or was not adequate. As the research suggested, students needed to be taught *how* to use and improve their use of study strategies that required them to recall, restate, reorganize, integrate, elaborate upon, or identify relationships among ideas. Without such instruction, students generally were not able to benefit from using them. If a student could not use a strategy to process informational material at a deep level, then the strategy was no more effective than just reading the text and reviewing it, or repetitive reading. And if a student could not use a mind-intensive strategy appropriately and efficiently on his or her own, then, as Anderson and Armbruster suggested, the student might not be willing to expend effort to use it at all.

More recently, the National Reading Panel (NRP, 2000) conducted a meta-analysis of over two-hundred methodologically sound studies concerning strategic reading comprehension instruction. Their findings indicate that question-generation, summarization, and readers' monitoring of their understanding during reading all contribute to improved comprehension for non-disabled readers.

Combining these strategies was found to enhance their effectiveness. However, questions remain concerning which strategies are most effective for specific age groups, genres, and levels of text difficulty.

It seems clear from my article, from Anderson and Armbruster's review, and from the NRP findings that students should be taught how to use cognitive strategies effectively, especially if they entail writing. Moreover, although much depends on the student's age, ability, and metacognitive skills, strategies that require both thinking and writing would seem to have educational value in the literature class as well as in the content area class.

In this chapter, I focus on four writing techniques that can be used productively in these settings: self-generated questioning, academic journal writing, summary writing, and dictation. I have chosen the first three because of their potential for developing higher level reading skills and because the NRP (2000) findings seem to support their usefulness fairly consistently. I have chosen dictation because it is an exercise that can affect the learning of a number of lower level reading skills and it thus provides a useful balance to the other three strategies, even though students cannot engage in a dictation exercise independently of a teacher (or capable student) who must read the material that is being dictated. While dictation is not a study technique and is a very circumscribed writing activity in comparison to the other three, I believe it has much untapped potential for enhancing the learning of lower level skills in an integrated way and should be used more frequently than it is by both reading and writing teachers. Interested readers can refer to my 1982 article for details on copying, paraphrasing, sentence-combining, and the exercise in reproduction or recall. For an update on the results of research on the effects of sentence-combining practice on reading comprehension, readers may refer to the succinct synthesis of the research literature in Wilkinson & Patty (1993).

Self-Generated Questioning

Self-generated questioning may be the single most important intellectual process in which students engage for developing understanding of idea-centered prose. Indeed, it seems to be an effective study technique in almost every study in which it is examined. According to Brown et al. (1983) and Palincsar & Brown (1984), asking and answering their own high-level questions as part of their learning seem to facilitate students' comprehension by inducing such cognitive activities as focusing attention, organizing the new material, and integrating the new information with existing knowledge. Further, as King (1992) suggests in a comparison of self-questioning, summarizing, and notetaking-review as strategies for learning from lectures, self-questioning provides learners with a way to test themselves; that is, it helps them to check how well they are comprehending what they are studying. And this is one kind of metacognitive skill many students need to develop. Indeed, King's own study found that self-questioning seemed to be even more effective than summarizing for long-term retention of the material.

As I have suggested in an earlier article on student-generated questioning (Stotsky, 1986) the ability to ask appropriate and substantive questions about ideas may be the essential component in critical thinking. For students who have been accustomed only to answering questions—and answering them in the way in which they think their teachers want them to be answered—learning how to ask questions may be a difficult learning experience. But it is a necessary one in view of the fact that asking questions does not seem to be a "natural" activity for students in school. According to reviews of research on question-asking behavior in the elementary school, children rarely ask questions in school (Dodl, 1965; Floyd, 1960), and when the quality of the few questions they ask is examined, they are usually judged to be extremely low-order ones that produce yes/no or single word answers concerning literal features of the material they are studying (Gallagher, 1965; Guszak, 1966).

One possible reason for the failure of teachers to encourage question-asking by their students is the seeming obsession in educational research with the questions the teacher asks. A great deal of effort has also focused on teaching students at all levels of education how to answer not only their teachers' questions and the questions that appear in their textbooks but also the questions that appear on standardized tests. However, there appears to be little research on how to teach students to ask intelligent, perceptive questions. This gap in the research is particularly surprising in view of the fact that most, if not all, textbooks on the teaching of reading recommend a technique for studying in the content areas called SQ3R—Survey, Question, Read, Recite, and Review. It is apparently assumed that students know how to ask questions, as I can find no helpful discussions in these texts on how to help students learn to ask the kinds of questions that will initiate genuine in-depth involvement with a particular subject. At best, these texts suggest that students invert the boldface section headings in their informational material into questions. While this is useful to do, this suggestion tends to make the students' questions completely textbased. Students' questions should also go beyond the text at hand.

How questions are formulated. What happens when children or adults try to formulate a question? First, in order to formulate any relevant question at all about a given topic, they focus on the subject under discussion, think about what it is or could be, and consider what questions could be directed to it. Then, as I have discovered in talking to teachers in workshop sessions over the years, questioners do several things, although not necessarily in the same order. They may try to classify the new subject with known subjects judged to be similar in nature so that questions that are appropriate for the known subject can be used for the new topic. I have called that "a transfer of knowledge-based categories." For example, the kinds of knowledge that most of us in this country are apt to have about the beliefs and practices of Judaism or Christianity are easily turned into questions for learning about a relatively unknown religion such as Buddhism or Islam. I have regularly seen participants at question-storming sessions ask if there are holy books, holy places, or places of worship for the new religion they are hypothetically about to study because they know that these exist for Christianity and Judaism.

Questioners may also search through their minds for what is known about the new subject, connecting ideas in some way. This kind of thinking—to recall to mind what is already known about a subject—can serve two purposes. First, it helps the questioner begin with the more obvious questions; these ease initiation into the activity of questioning. It also helps learners discover questions at the edge of their knowledge of the subject, particularly after the more obvious questions have been formulated and less obvious ones are being sought. These kinds of questions are extremely important for they can often turn the learner's attention to completely new areas to explore. In this way, asking questions not only requires thinking, it develops thinking.

Enhancing question formulation. Students at all educational levels seem to need some guidance in learning how to generate their own questions about a topic they have been asked to read or that they have chosen to explore. Students need to learn both how to ask questions and how to ask "good" questions. The first hurdle is getting students to ask questions at all. They can probably learn best how to generate questions by participating in question-generating sessions with their peers in preparation for reading about a particular topic in a content-area textbook. These question-storming sessions might well be considered one kind of collaborative learning. The opportunity to hear the kind of questions their peers raise is beneficial to all students and encourages even reluctant students to ask questions. And by accepting almost any question offered so long as it is at all relevant, the teacher provides a non-threatening environment for students to learn how to ask good questions.

For example, suppose students are to read an essay about national holidays. The teacher can start them off by asking students to come up with questions that they would expect to see answered or would like to see answered in this essay. Phrasing the directions in this way stimulates both prediction (what do they expect to see answered) and self-interest (what would they like to see answered). As they call out their questions, the teacher should be writing them on the chalkboard. Students might come up with such questions as:

> What is a national holiday?
> What are our national holidays?
> How do we celebrate a national holiday?
> Do we go to school on any national holiday?
> How does a national holiday get to be one?
> Who decides?
> Why do we have national holidays?
> Are they like other countries' national holidays?
> Have we recently added or taken away any national holidays?
> Has the way in which holidays are celebrated changed over time?

What is happening is that students are learning what specific questions are possible to raise about a particular subject. Moreover, every question that is put on the chalkboard may stimulate several others. This kind of cross-fertilization causes students to become aware of the many potentially critical attributes of the subject under discussion. It also helps students to learn different ways of forming questions.

The second hurdle is helping students appreciate the worth of self-generated questioning. Once a large number of questions have been generated, students can be asked to read the essay. They are apt to discover that their interest in the text material was piqued by the questions, and that material that addressed the questions became salient as they read through the chapter. They may also come to realize the value of non-textbased questions, as they will undoubtedly discover that many of their questions have not been answered by the chapter. Students could be asked to discuss how reasonable it was to expect information to answer these questions and what could account for the lack of information addressing them. The absence of information that one hopes to find in a particular source is often as informative as the information itself.

The third hurdle is helping students improve the quality or usefulness of their questions. Students can be helped to judge the quality of their questions in several ways. First, the teacher can show how questions can be divided into two general classes, open and closed. Closed questions are those that can be answered simply by yes or no or with one or two words or simple phrases, such as "When are the holidays?" Open questions are those that elicit a great deal of material, such as "Why do we have national holidays?" Even though closed questions lead to much more limited information, both kinds of questions are useful, and students should learn that they need to generate and explore both open and closed questions. Second, the teacher can ask students to judge for themselves which questions would seem to elicit more interesting or useful material, and which do not. It is important for the teacher to let students use their own judgment, and to encourage them to evaluate and prioritize any sets of questions they might generate on their own.

Although the goal of all this is to help students learn how to generate and write down their own questions as a regular study strategy before they undertake reading on their own, a number of sessions of group question-storming is invaluable for helping students discover the range of questions that can be generated about any topic. It also helps students learn how to set their own purposes for reading informational material, even if the material has been assigned by the teacher because it is part of the curriculum.

Contexts for question formulation. Once students have begun to learn how to ask their own questions about a variety of topics, there are many pedagogical contexts for the activity. The doing of the research paper is a chief one. Evaluation of self-generated questions is most useful when students are about to undertake a research paper. Before plunging into reference books and other sources of information, students should be guided to generate and evaluate a series of questions that could get them into their material most productively. Students who are not guided initially by their own questions as they begin to investigate a topic either take voluminous notes on everything they find on their topic or copy large sections of the texts they find because they have no specific focus for their reading. Researchers usually pursue questions of their own in their reading of the literature on a subject rather than read through everything they can find on a topic in order to discover a question. Student researchers need to be taught a similar way of proceeding so that their focus is narrowed to something manageable.

The literature class provides a very different but equally appropriate context for self-generated questioning. Jane Schaffer, a high school English teacher (1989), describes the way in which she uses student-generated questions to guide discussion after a literary text has been read. She asks students to generate three interpretive questions each in advance of class discussion, and she then selects the best ones to use for initiating discussion. Having all students write down their own questions before class discussion is also useful for ensuring that all students engage in some critical thinking about the text they have just read. Class discussions are so often dominated by a small number of students that such an activity makes sure that all students have to do some thinking of their own.

In another article on questioning by a high school English teacher, Valerie Hobbs (1988) describes how she developed and used "question" journals. Students had to formulate a number of "good" questions in a response journal as they proceeded on their own through an assigned informational or literary text. Afterwards, they had to work out a more formal piece of writing in response to the one they judged was the best. Over the course of the year, her students developed a number of criteria for a "good" question. A "good" question was one that:

> we all wanted the answer to,
> wasn't boring,
> would help us understand the whole chapter/book,
> made us want to answer it,
> couldn't be found at the end of the chapter,
> made us think,
> couldn't be answered easily or forever,
> helped us learn/understand something about life that we didn't know before,
> made us ask more questions, and
> encouraged lots of answers.

As wonderful as this all sounds, Hobbs notes that at the end of the year some students reported that "thinking is just 'too hard'" and that they "prefer to write to assigned topics...rather than write their way into their own." For many students, "it is 'just too confusing' and, besides, there are too many questions that will never be answered" (p. 12). Such comments tell us about the current needs of our students and the critical importance of Hobbs' pedagogy.

Academic Journal Writing

The "question" journal that Hobbs evolved for use with her students is an excellent illustration of the way in which two useful study strategies have been intertwined. Just a few decades ago, it would have been difficult to find teachers who even tried to use journals for academic learning; at that time the journal was considered chiefly a repository of the writer's intimate thoughts on personal concerns, like a diary. But this situation was dramatically changed by teachers' responses to the views expressed by the authors of a study on the development of writing abilities from 11-18 carried out in England in the early 1970s and first published in 1975. After analyzing the kinds of writing assignments that British teachers gave their secondary students, James Britton and his associates concluded that most teachers tended to overemphasize, if not focus exclusively on, formal writing.

They did not give their students the opportunity to use more informal writing—"expressive" writing, as they termed it—for exploring and developing their ideas before shaping them in "transactional" writing—writing to convey knowledge or information to an external audience. Because these ideas seemed to make a lot of sense to teachers, the use of informal journal writing—or writing-to-learn activities, as they later came to be called—mushroomed throughout all areas of the curriculum, far beyond the composition class: in the literature class, this informal writing became known as the response journal; in other academic subjects, it was called the reading log, the learning log, or the academic journal. Students were not prevented from writing about their own experiences or making connections between their personal lives and what they were learning about. But the primary purpose of these journals was to encourage students to see writing as a way to elaborate and reflect on their own thinking about the ideas they were attempting to understand in their school subjects. They were to do so without concern for genre conventions, the requirements of the written code, and textual coherence, all of which are expected in formal writing to others—whether the teacher or another reader.

In-class journal writes. Teachers have found many ways in which to work in brief episodes of informal writing during ongoing classroom work. They may introduce a discussion class with a five-minute journal-write, using the journal to bridge the gap between the previous day's discussion and the focus of the current discussion. Or teachers may ask students to respond briefly to a quotation from a reading assignment as a way to get them to focus their attention on the subject and to compose their thoughts. Teachers may also end a class with a brief journal-write. Students may be asked to pull together information or ideas that they have learned during the class or write down questions that remain unanswered. As a way to refocus students during a rambling class discussion, teachers may interrupt the discussion and ask students to write about what the class is trying to explain and have them restate some of the main points of the argument. Simply as a change in pace during a lecture, teachers may ask students to write down briefly what is being discussed and any confusions or questions they may have.

Journal assignments for homework. In contrast to these examples of in-class journal writing, teachers may assign it as homework. Students may be asked to record their thoughts and questions as they read an assigned chapter in a literature class or a content area class, or to maintain a record of and response to a current issue that they may be following in the media. Some teachers provide students with starter questions or sentence beginnings to get them going. Part of the purpose in doing so is to make sure that students approach their writing from a variety of perspectives. For example, one list of sentence-beginnings I have seen used successfully by a science teacher to assist her students in writing journal entries on a regular basis includes:

> I realized...
> I noticed...
> I think...
> I was reminded of...
> I'm surprised that..,
> I'd like to know...
> I'm not sure...
> Although it seems...
> I don't understand....

As an illustration, after reading and discussing rheumatoid arthritis in a health and disease class at the community college level, a student used several sentence beginnings to write the following as a homework assignment:

> I was surprised to find out that rest is recommended to someone with rheumatoid arthritis. I thought exercise would help so that the joints would not become stiff. I realized that there is no cure for rheumatoid arthritis but perhaps if early detection through a blood test treatment with anti--inflammatory drugs can begin.
>
> I was reminded that simply by being my age and gender, I am prone to yet another disorder in which I have no control. Also that every time I give

blood I might get a little card in the mail telling me that my blood is no good because they ran a test on it which revealed some factor that no one else wants.

I was surprised that x-rays showed rheumatoid arthritis. Too bad the joints have to be eroded away in order for it to be clear, other than the obvious soft tissue swelling. I'd like to know if stress has been directly linked to rheumatoid arthritis. Because I'm not sure if rheumatoid arthritis is the body's turning on itself in response to continual stimulants, as suggested by a few people.

For another journal entry, this time in a radiography class at the community college level, a student answered the teacher's question: What did you learn about producing radiographs from today's lab?

Some new things that I learned was for one how to operate the x-ray machine. I also learned about setting the dials on the controller. I also learned how to develop an x-ray, but it is not that new to me because I work in a dental office and make x-rays all the time and I also develop them and somewhat understand how they work because I am in charge of cleaning the machines. I think it helped me to understand what I am doing. I also learned about the dosimeter which measures the amount of radiation the object is receiving.

The basic question posed by these writing assignments—what new things did you learn?—can be asked of students in any class at any level after any piece of informational reading. As can be seen, what these students have done through their informal journal entries is to recall and summarize the main points of their recent learning experiences.

Application in science class. Learning logs can be used productively in the science class and even by young children. In the elementary grades, students can be asked to keep a science journal in which they must simply write a page-long entry once or twice a week. The entry can be their own free writing based on a science observation or what they have read in a science book, or it can be a page of interesting facts they have copied verbatim. Just the activity of thinking about and writing down the information they find of interest to themselves is useful for vocabulary development and comprehension.

Learning logs can also be used in the science class to help students pull together what they have learned and to stimulate their curiosity for further information or observation. The teacher can ask the students simply to write down (1) what they learned, (2) what they didn't understand, and (3) what questions they want the answers to after they have completed a lesson or an observation. Or the teacher can ask students to fill out regularly on a response form the "answers" to the three following sentence beginnings after each science lesson:

> Today in science I learned...
> I don't understand...
> I'd like to know more about...

One first grader, after a lesson on the sun and the moon, wrote down in answer to the first stem "that the sun lite reflects off the moon. And I learned that the earth turns like a spinning ball." Another child wrote "about the world. At the Surprise Center we are using the globe. We shine the flashlight on the earth and it goes to the moon." In response to the third stem the first child wrote "I would like to know more about the sun and the moon," while the second child wrote "the world and how the moon reflects onto the ground." As can be seen from these responses, further benefit of journal writing in the science class is that it provides students with the opportunity to use the vocabulary they are learning in meaningful writing, whether they write just phrases or complete sentences.

As these examples suggest, journal entries can be totally uncontrolled and unstructured by the teacher, as in an assignment to respond to a particular reading selection in whatever way the student wishes. Or they can be completely teacher-directed and teacher-structured, as in an assignment to summarize a particular reading selection or class discussion. These differences in use reflect the teacher's judgment as to what will benefit the students most, a judgment that is based largely on the needs of a particular discipline, the teacher's goals for a particular lesson, and the student's ability level. Some journals have become the opportunity for a written dialogue between the student and the teacher, with the teacher responding to a few of the student's entries with comments or questions. The size of the class and the time that the teacher is willing to give these assignments are critical factors in the decision to turn journal entries into a dialogue between teacher and student.

Cautions concerning journal use. Teachers need to know that despite the voluminous literature that now exists on writing across the curriculum and on writing to learn, there is little empirical literature to support the values claimed for academic journal writing. Anson & Beach (1990) did a study of their own at the college level after reviewing the research literature, and reported that the kinds of thinking encouraged by journal writing had little to do with the students' learning as measured on the objective tests given in the course. They also found that how much students wrote in their journals had little or no bearing on the kinds of entries they wrote. Although they acknowledged that the ways in which thinking and learning were measured in their study might not have been the best measures, nevertheless they noted that teachers need to monitor their use carefully and remain alert to what seem to be productive and unproductive ways in which students might use them.

A number of other cautions are in order for teachers who wish to use informal journal writing as a regular study strategy. First, beware of overuse. Any new idea is prone to overkill, and journal writing has become one of them. Students who are asked to keep journals in almost every subject are apt to develop an intense dislike of writing in any of them. Journal writing needs to be coordinated across the curriculum if it is a regular assignment. Second, avoid romanticizing them. Journals are not the magic strategy that will naturally lead to a high level of learning for all students. Much depends on the effort students are willing to put in. Even if there were a great deal of research evidence supporting the use of journal writing, no one technique can entail the exercise of all the intellectual processes that students must use for in-depth comprehension of any topic. Third, as with all strategies, many students need to look at a range of models that suggest the sorts of entries a teacher thinks might be appropriate. Fourth, as with all writing assignments, journals should be read through occasionally by the teacher and graded. Although journal writing should remain unevaluated writing from a compositional perspective, fluency and cogency should be rewarded as part of the students' final grade.

Summary Writing

Summary writing is an exercise in reading comprehension par excellence; it is also, according to Hood (1967), an exercise in vocabulary building, in sentence construction, and in clear, concise expression. Although students are frequently asked to summarize material they have read or heard, it is not clear how frequently or how well they are given instruction in summarizing. Summarizing entails a specific set of skills in its own right and should not be assigned (or expected in journal entries) with the assumption that students can compress ideas and information into at least one-third of their original bulk easily and without instruction. Summary writing needs to be taught and can be taught to students in the upper elementary grades as well as to secondary or postsecondary students. When a specified number of words is required, summary writing is called precis writing.

The basic tasks confronting the student in summary or precis writing are the selection of important facts, the rejection of unimportant ones, the brief restatement of key ideas by means of generalization, and determination of the controlling idea. Many researchers and educators have offered their ideas on how to teach summary writing (e.g., Brown & Day, 1983). However, I will draw heavily here on Karen D'Angelo's article (1983) on teaching summary writing to fourth grade students because it is the best I have seen for young students and can easily be adapted for older students.

According to D'Angelo, students must remember three things to help them write an accurate summary: they must identify topic sentences, rephrase material in their own words, and keep the order of the text, at least in the beginning. To help them with these tasks, she recommends lessons in each of the following: selecting topic sentences, identifying paragraph shapes, using synonyms, and rephrasing. D'Angelo points out that identifying the main ideas of paragraphs is often difficult, but students must be able to locate them before beginning to write a summary.

To help students learn how to identify the main ideas in each paragraph of the materials they are learning to summarize, D'Angelo suggests that students first should be taught that there are four possible locations for a topic sentence in a paragraph (at the beginning, at the end, at both the beginning and the end, and within the paragraph) and that sometimes the topic sentence is not stated. Then they should be given practice selecting topic sentences and rejecting sentences that contain unimportant ideas in all these paragraph types. For help in finding the topic sentence, they should look for the most general and inclusive sentence in the paragraph. Students should also discuss their reasons for selecting a certain topic sentence. To help students use their own words to paraphrase important ideas in a text, students should be asked to supply synonyms for key words, if possible, using a dictionary or thesaurus if necessary.

D'Angelo recommends giving students many opportunities to practice these steps as a group so that they can discuss their choices and develop oral skill in rephrasing. As with the initial teaching of self-generated questioning, D'Angelo believes that students should learn to write group summaries as part of a group lesson before trying to write summaries on their own.

D'Angelo does not discuss how students can determine the controlling idea of the whole article when, as can happen, it is not simply the topic sentence of the opening paragraph. Colleen Rae (1986), a college teacher, recommends that students try to determine the author's main idea only after they have read through each paragraph and written the topic sentence or a one-sentence summary of each one. Then, she suggests, students should go through these topic sentences to try to come up with a word or short phrase that suggests what the author's focus is for the whole work. Most likely the controlling idea contains the key words in the article, whose importance can be determined by their frequency throughout the article but especially in its opening and closing paragraphs.

Dictation

Dictation has generally been used in this country only for teaching and testing in foreign language classes. However, it has long been used in many other countries as a regular part of their native language teaching. By dictation, I do not mean the dictation of isolated spelling words or sentences using those words. I mean the dictation of well-written, interesting, and complete passages from literature or non-literary informational prose for students to transcribe. At a surface level, it is a way to teach spelling, punctuation, capitalization, grammar, and handwriting in a meaningful context. At a deeper level, it is a highly structured way to give students practice in listening to, writing, and then reading worthwhile vocabulary and ideas or information in complete sentences in connected discourse. Thus, it is an exercise that contextualizes important skill work and integrates listening, writing, and reading.

In addition to providing contextualized practice for handwriting and spelling, regular dictation practice can enlarge a student's vocabulary. It clearly provides structured but active practice in listening to and writing words in context. Further, as research by Gipe (1978-1979) and Wolfe (1975) suggests, reading and studying new words in context seems to be the most effective method for developing vocabulary. It may also be a way of helping students incorporate part of their reading vocabulary into their writing vocabulary.

Finally, dictation gives students regular practice in proofreading, a skill and a habit that is rarely fully developed even by high school age. Structured proofreading practice may help them to proofread their own free writing more effectively.

Preparation for dictation. Well-written passages for dictation can easily be found in the unadapted literary and non-literary informational selections that are in the student's regular curriculum. It is important that the reading level of a passage be close to the students' reading level so that its ideas and vocabulary are within their reach. Unless the whole class can benefit from the same dictation passages, dictation groups might be similar to reading groups.

As I have discussed in an earlier article (Stotsky, 1983), the length of the passage depends upon the grade level and capability of the students. It is better, generally speaking, to begin with short passages of about three to four sentences in order to work out a smooth procedure for regular use. It is also best not to use passages with dialogue, as the language of dialogue is not usually enriching; third-person narrated passages or informational passages are much more satisfactory. Before a passage is given, it should be marked off in syntactic groups appropriate for the students' span of attention. Before the first dictation is given, the teacher should explain clearly what procedures he or she will use. If students are asked to skip every other line on their papers, it will be easier for them to insert omitted words and correct misspellings when these are discovered.

Dictation procedures. In traditional dictation, the passage is read aloud three times. The first reading acquaints students with the meaning of the selection, but students should not write. Difficult proper nouns and long words with unfamiliar spellings may be written on the chalkboard so that they do not serve as obstacles to fluent writing. Then the entire passage should be read slowly according to the syntactic phrases that have been marked off, with a pause after each one while the students write. There should be no repetitions. This is critical for developing their span of attention. Of course, the pace of reading and the length of the phrases should be adjusted for different ability groups, but students should be warned in advance that no repetition is allowed during the second reading. (If necessary, students with serious learning disabilities may need to have the second reading presented one-word-at-a-time at first in order to achieve success.) Punctuation may or may not be given orally depending on the learning focus of the dictation. In the earliest grades, telling the students "end of sentence" when the end of a sentence has been reached may be helpful and should automatically clue them into capitalizing the next word. For the third reading, the passage should be read at normal speed while students check for omitted or superfluous words.

292

To make the dictation a learning experience, not a testing session, students must make their own corrections by proofreading from the original passage. The passage can be either on the chalkboard (covered up during the dictation) or in their textbooks. Students will have a powerful incentive to improve their handwriting and to proofread carefully if they are graded only on the number of errors they do not find themselves. In this way, only unwillingness to proofread carefully is penalized, and no student is penalized for lack of spelling ability. Needless to say, when students have to read their own writing regularly to find their own errors, the care they take to make the dictation legible increases automatically. A dictation corrected by the student can also be given several days later as a test. Students can also be given the option of studying a passage as homework the night before a dictation lesson or a dictation test. Although teachers may collect the corrected dictations to give them a grade based on the number of errors the student did not find, they may also have students exchange papers and let them determine how many errors their peer failed to correct. Doing this reduces the amount of student work the teacher must grade herself, making the dictation exercise a more welcome addition to classroom practice.

After the dictation lesson has been completed, the dictation passage can be used as the basis for a vocabulary or grammar lesson or even as free writing. There are many ways to use a good piece of writing, and each passage will suggest a different focus.

Outcomes of using dictation. Although we have as yet no research on the benefits of frequent dictation practice, dictation exercises may be useful at all grade levels and for all kinds of students. It may be particularly beneficial for bilingual, learning disabled, and other special-needs students. As Pappas (1977) notes, dictation is a simple technique for developing the power of concentrated listening, for increasing the span of attention for phrases and sentences, and for developing facility in recording words exactly. It is obvious that students must pay attention in order to reproduce the dictated passage, and an immediate writing activity reinforces what the student has comprehended orally.

Moreover, dictation of syntactic phrases in increasingly larger units may be an effective way to develop students' span of attention for reading and writing in longer and longer phrases; as Amble's (1967) research found, training in phrase reading improved elementary school students' reading comprehension. And, finally, training in recording accurately the exact words of a passage may be important for limited English-speaking students who need to become more familiar with the variety of inflectional and derivational endings in English words in order to develop a better understanding of their semantic and syntactic uses. Frequent practice in writing exactly the vocabulary of informational prose in an interesting context may be far more effective for these students than simply reading it in context—or filling in blanks in multiple-choice exercises. In addition, regular practice in writing complete well-written sentences may help them develop a stable sense of English sentence structure and the sense of a complete sentence.

Concluding Remarks

One thing we should try to avoid as much as possible is teaching study strategies or writing exercises in isolation from each other. As Valerie Hobbs' "question" journal demonstrated, useful pedagogical techniques often reflect integration of several strategies. But that is not the only kind of integration that is useful. Teachers can also coordinate different thinking and writing activities across a series of lessons concerning one reading selection to allow for accumulated learning.

To show how one thoughtful teacher coordinated several activities for a series of lessons with some sixth and seventh grade students in a Chapter One program, I present the outline of her lessons and the summary that one of the students produced. The teacher first read the short opening paragraph of a six-paragraph selection about the Loch Ness Monster to her students. She then asked her students to raise as many questions as they could about what they thought the rest of the selection might tell them or what they wanted to know about. Next she read the story aloud, discussed it, and answered questions about it. She asked them to write down the main idea for the whole story and then write down the main idea for each paragraph and form a summary. She next dictated the opening paragraph and had students proofread for errors. Finally, she discussed with them the use of the comma in the first sentence to separate a word from an explanation of the word and had students punctuate similar types of sentences. The following is the summary produced by one of her students, with spelling and punctuation corrected.

> People believe that the Loch Ness monster exists, but other people don't believe it. Loch Ness is a lake in Scotland where they say there is a monster that exists in the lake. They call it Nessie. People say they have seen the Lock Ness monster at night. Other people say that they are imagining things. Robert Rines, a scientist, went to Loch Ness. He came from Boston. He set up a trap that the monster would come close to the cameras so they can take

294

pictures of it. After a few weeks the monsters came towards them and they took pictures of it. It seems to be a picture of two monsters not just one. There might be two monsters not just one. But some people still don't believe the pictures are enough. Some scientists are trying to take more pictures. People believe that the monster came in by an inlet and there was an avalanche that cut off the ocean from the lake.

I believe this teacher's lesson outline represents a fine effort to create a meaningful sequence of learning activities. I also think the student's summary reflects an excellent response.

As most teachers know from experience, we must try to avoid assumptive teaching. We cannot assume students know how to use study strategies—or how to use them well. It may be self-defeating to ask students to summarize material or to generate their own questions or outlines without teaching them how to do so and without giving them opportunities to learn how to improve their use of these strategies. We cannot teach reading comprehension explicitly in the sense that we teach students exactly how to construe something. But we can give them instruction and practice in using study techniques that require them to make connections between prior experience or knowledge and new information. Such instruction will show them how to construct their own understanding of something as well as give them practice in how to go about constructing an understanding of new information and ideas when they read on their own.

There is another, perhaps more important reason for us to give this kind of instruction regularly. Students need to learn that quality comprehension (or composition) requires hard work—and steady work. Neither reading well, nor writing well, comes easily and quickly to most people. To read (or write) effectively requires much mental effort as well as regular reading and writing. There are no magic pedagogical bullets that, if fired, turn students into good readers and writers. We do a grave disservice to our students if we let them think that there are shortcuts or substitutes for regular and thoughtful reading and writing. The rewards for active thinking are there, but they are intangible and internal. The intellectual and emotional satisfaction that results from having used one's mind well is the reward for the effort. The supreme challenge for teachers today is how to convince more students that the satisfaction they will gain from using their minds well is worth the effort.

References

Amble, B. (1967). Reading by phrases. *California Journal of Educational Research, 18,* 116-24.

Anderson, T., & Armbruster, B. (1984). In P. D. Pearson (Ed.), *Handbook of reading research.* NY: Longman, Inc. 657-679.

Anson, C., & Beach, R. (1990). *Research on writing to learn: The interesting case of academic journals.* Unpublished paper presented at the Conference on College Composition and Communication, Chicago, Illinois.

Brown, A.L., & Day, J. D. (1983). Macrorules for summarizing texts: The development of expertise. *Journal of Verbal Learning and Verbal Behavior, 22,* 1-14.

Brown, A.L., Bransford, J.D., Ferrara, R.A., & Campione, J.C. (1983). Learning, remembering and understanding. In J.H. Flavell and E.M. Markman, (Eds.), *Handbook of Child Psychology. Vol. III: Cognitive Development* (77-166). NY: Wiley.

Britton, J., Burges, T., Martin, N., McLeaod, A., & Rosen, H. (1975). *The development of writing abilities* (11-18). Great Britain: Macmillan Education Ltd.

D'Angelo, K. (1983). Precis writing: promoting vocabulary development and comprehension. *Journal of Reading,* March, 534-539.

Dodl, N. (1965). *Pupil questioning behavior in the context of classroom interaction.* Unpublished doctoral dissertation, Stanford University.

Floyd, W.D. (1960). *An analysis of the oral questioning activity in selected Colorado primary classrooms.* Unpublished doctoral dissertation, Colorado State College.

Gallagher, J. (1965). Expressive thought by gifted children in the classroom. *Elementary English, 42,* 559-569.

Gipe, J. (1978-1979). Investigating techniques for teaching word meaning. *Reading Research Quarterly, 14,* 624-644.

Guszak, F. (1966). *A study of teacher solicitation and student response interaction about reading content in selected second, fourth and sixth grades.* Unpublished doctoral dissertation, University of Wisconsin, 1966.

Hobbs, Valerie. (1988). Collective survival: Using question journals in the classroom. *The Quarterly of the National Writing Project and the Center for the Study of Writing, 10,* 9-12.

Hood, R. (1967). *Precis writing practice.* Cambridge, MA: Educators Publishing Service.

King, A. (1992). Comparison of self-questioning, summarizing, and notetaking-review as strategies for learning from lectures. *American Educational Research Journal, 29,* 303-323.

National Reading Panel [NRP]. (2000). *Report of the National Reading Panel: Teaching children to read.* Washington, DC: National Institute of Child Health and Human Development.
[Available at http://www.nichd.nih.gov/publications/nrp.]

Palincsar, A., & Brown, A.L. (1984). Reciprocal teaching of comprehension fostering and monitoring activities. *Cognition and Instruction, 1,* 117-175.

Pappas, G. (1977). You mean you still give dictation? *Language Arts, 54,* 401-402.

Rae, C. (1986). Before the outline--the writing wheel. *College Teaching, 34,* 99-102.

Schaffer, J. (1989). Improving discussion questions: Is anyone out there listening? *English Journal,* April, 40-42.

Stotsky, S. (1982) The role of writing in developmental reading. *Journal of Reading, 25*(4), 330-341.

Stotsky, S. (1983). Dictation: Building listening, reading, and writing skills together. (1983). *The Leaflet*, Spring, *82*, 6-12.

Stotsky, S. (1986). Asking questions about ideas: A critical component in critical thinking. *The Leaflet.* Fall, *85*, 39-47.

Wilkinson, P., & Patty, D. (1993). The effects of sentence combining on the reading comprehension of fourth grade students. *Research in the Teaching of English, 27*, 104-125.

Wolfe, R. (1975). *An examination of the effects of teaching and reading vocabulary upon writing vocabulary in student composition.* Unpublished doctoral dissertation, University of Maryland. ED 114 818.

V. ASSESSMENT

Chapter 11. Reading Assessments and Interpretations

John O. Willis, EdD
Rivier College
Regional Services & Education Center

A well planned assessment of reading skills provides useful information to help determine an instructional program for a student in reading. Valid and relevant assessment results can help with decisions of what to teach and how to teach the content effectively. Reading tests measure components of reading by using a broad variety of formats. When reading tests are selected, administered, and interpreted carefully, with an understanding of their specific characteristics, they can provide results that enhance planning.

Some authorities recommend that reading assessments include the testing of skills other than reading. Acuity of vision and hearing certainly contribute to reading. Social and emotional issues can sometimes play parts in the drama of a student's reading abilities. Certain authors (e.g., Hynd & Cohen, 1983) recommend extensive testing of underlying neurological processes. And some suggest that assessments need to trace reading difficulties back to weaknesses in oral language or fundamental auditory skills.

Nonetheless, a reading assessment is generally most productive when it focuses on the determination of what components of reading abilities are in need of instruction (Chall & Curtis, 1990). Consequently, the process of identifying areas in need of reading instruction is the focus of this chapter.

CHAPTER ORGANIZATION

The assessment of reading is an extremely broad topic. This chapter concentrates primarily on issues concerned with how to provide a comprehensive assessment of a student's reading skills. The assumption underlying most of the discussion below is that the evaluator will work individually with the student for an hour or more and spend that time assessing the student's reading skills.

A note concerning specific reading tests. Specific tests are discussed in this chapter as examples that illustrate various points, but several caveats are in order. First, the mention of a test does not indicate endorsement of that test, in some cases quite the opposite. The absence of a test does not necessarily indicate disapproval. New tests and revisions of old ones are being published every day. Some of the citations of specific tests may be outdated before the chapter is printed. In most cases, revisions of tests are improvements, but this is not always true and earlier or later editions of tests may vary in features from the edition(s) discussed here.

The reader will also note that I seldom, if ever, recommend using only one test or all aspects of one test. Furthermore, the needs of many students dictate assessment of underlying skills as well as actual reading skills, so their evaluations must go beyond the scope of "reading" tests. In addition, sometimes the more skills that a single test battery attempts to cover, the less depth it gives to any skill. A point of diminishing returns can be reached where each subtest becomes so brief that reliability becomes low.

A note on terminology. Although this chapter is generally written in standard English, some technical terminology and jargon (such as "reliability" in the paragraph above) are used. Because different readers will be familiar with different terms, most of the definitions will be found in the Glossary rather than within the text. Throughout, I refer to the person assessing reading as the "examiner" and the person whose reading is being assessed as the "student."

Assessment of reading is not possible without an understanding of the processes of reading, and it is not likely to be of much value without an understanding of approaches to instruction that might be recommended. This chapter assumes an understanding of reading competencies and instructional approaches presented earlier in this book.

Chapter format.   The chapter is presented in the following format (see Figure 11.a. below). It begins by placing reading assessment in the context of other assessments, such as intellectual testing.   Here, "IQ" tests and what they do and do not contribute to reading assessments are discussed.   Next, a section titled "Planning the Assessment" carries the examiner through the initial steps of planning.

These introductory sections are followed by discussion of various reading components: Passage Comprehension, Reading Vocabulary, Oral Vocabulary, Oral Reading of Passages, Oral Reading Decoding, and Auditory Skills and Phonemic Awareness.   Each of these subsections examines some specific tests and attempts to highlight their strengths and weaknesses for various purposes.   The hope is that the sometimes-detailed discussion will provide enough background to allow the examiner to understand, evaluate, and select tests and subtests with greater understanding, and to interpret test results effectively.

The chapter closes with guidelines for conducting an assessment.   These include suggestions for introducing and concluding an evaluation, along with "Some Rules for Testing Reading," a prescriptive list of procedures for planning and implementing an assessment.

READING ASSESSMENTS AND OTHER ASSESSMENTS

PLANNING THE ASSESSMENT

TESTING READING AND ITS SUBSKILLS
Passage Comprehension
Vocabulary Tested Through Reading
Vocabulary Tested Orally
Fluency and Accuracy in Oral Reading of Passages
Oral Decoding of Words
Auditory Skills and Phonemic Awareness

INTERACTIONS WITH THE STUDENT

SOME RULES FOR TESTING READING

CONCLUSIONS

Figure 11.a. Format of Chapter 11.

Reading Assessments and Other Assessments

Often, a student with reading difficulties is referred to a reading specialist who is asked to perform a reading assessment and report on the student's reading skills and needs. In many other instances, the reading assessment is part of a broader evaluation, such as a psychological, psychoeducational, neuropsychological, neurological, speech and language, or vocational evaluation. Regardless of its context, the reading assessment should be thorough and valid. Otherwise, it may generate incorrect information and plans. Brief "screenings" can lead to poor decisions about students' programs.

IQ AND READING

There can be considerable value to a thorough, comprehensive intellectual assessment that includes a thoughtful interpretation of intelligence testing. However, the relationship between tested IQ scores and reading is much weaker than is supposed. In fact, it is so weak that examiners interested primarily in testing reading might do best to ignore the student's IQ score (e.g. Siegel, 1989).

For example, Hammill and McNutt (1981) collected all of the studies they could find, over a period of 30 years in 25 major journals, that compared Wechsler IQ scores and reading test scores. The median correlation between Full Scale Wechsler IQs and total scores on various reading tests was only 0.44. This means that only 19% ($0.44 \times 0.44 = 0.19$) of the variance in total reading scores was attributable to Full Scale Wechsler IQ scores. The remaining 81% of the variance in total reading scores was attributable to other, unknown factors, such as, perhaps, number of books in the home, parental education, or auditory discrimination ability.

Even more surprising was Hammill and NcNutt's examination of correlations between individual Wechsler subtests and total reading scores. The subtest with the highest correlation with reading was not, for example, Vocabulary, general Information, or verbal Comprehension. It was Arithmetic. Arithmetic is the Wechsler subtest that, at least for children, is most like an achievement test and least like an IQ test. Achievement tests correlate better with each other than they do with IQ tests.

Classroom evidence further indicates that students with low IQ scores can learn to read.   Fuller (1983) invented the Ball-Stick-Bird method of reading instruction and reported relatively little difficulty teaching not only reading decoding, but reading comprehension skills through a sixth grade level, to students with IQ scores lower than 60.   Ursula Willis (1971) and many other teachers have taught elementary reading skills to students classified as moderately intellectually challenged ("moderately mentally retarded").

In short, the correlation between reading and IQ test scores is very modest; much of that small correlation comes from the achievement-test aspect of the IQ tests; and direct efforts to teach reading skills to intellectually challenged students are often successful.   Furthermore, modern IQ test scores cannot be converted directly into mental ages.[1]   Consequently, there remains no justification for computing potential reading levels from IQ test scores.   Nor should IQ test scores be used to terminate reading instruction.   The goal of reading assessment is to determine how—NOT whether—the student can be taught to read better.

THE ACID PROFILE

At least as far back as Altus (1953), researchers have attempted to find patterns of Wechsler (1949; 1974; 1991) subtest scores that are associated with reading difficulty.   The most famous and most enduring is Altus's (1953) ACID profile: low scores on **A**rithmetic, **C**oding, **I**nformation, and **D**igit Span.   The mental Arithmetic test and oral questions of general Information are, of course, at

---

[1]Over time various formulae have been developed with the intent to predict reading ability levels from IQ test "mental ages."   However, modern IQ test scores are not based on mental ages.   Until 1949 (Wechsler, 1949), children's IQ test scores were ratios between a "mental age" score and the child's actual age.   They were literally intelligence "quotients." The abbreviation, IQ, has endured long beyond the concept.   Since 1949, the now essentially universal trend has been toward "deviation IQs" based on the relationship of the child's score to the average and the variability of scores of other children the same age.   "Mental ages," if they are used at all, are computed from the child's raw scores on the test or subtests, independently of the IQ scores.   One simply cannot compute a "mental age" directly from the IQ score on a modern test.

304

least as much achievement tests as intelligence tests, so low scores for weak readers on those tests are hardly surprising. Both tests also require considerable receptive language ability, some expressive language, auditory discrimination, and auditory memory, among other abilities.

Digit Span asks the student to repeat increasingly long series of digits dictated by the examiner and to repeat additional series in correct, reversed order. Weaknesses in rote, short-term, auditory, sequential concentration and memory, in auditory discrimination, or in hearing acuity might be expected to impair beginning reading progress.

The Coding subtest, for children of ages eight and over, asks the child to mark rows of randomly sequenced, printed digits with certain symbols according to a digit-symbol code at the top of the page. The score is the number marked correctly in two minutes. The Coding subtest requires, among other abilities, sequential organization, facile learning of written symbols, left-to-right organization, sustained concentration for two minutes, and willingness to work hard on an apparently pointless task simply because a teacher said to do it.

The ACID profile makes sense and is supported by research findings. However, there is less there than meets the eye. When students are referred for testing **because** of reading difficulty, the ACID profile sometimes does and sometimes does **not** reveal low scores. Either way, the students still exhibit reading difficulty.[2]

---

[2]There are many handbooks and pamphlets that offer varying opinions concerning the Wechsler IQ test subtests and what each subtest is proposed to measure In the 1960s and 1970s, students with learning disabilities were given exercises with balance beams, tether balls, and dittoed mazes in the hope of "remediating" deficiencies in "basic processes" to provide a foundation for academic progress. Myriad instruments were designed to "pretest" and "posttest" these "basic processes," and the Wechsler scales were also used for this, a purpose never anticipated by the author. In my experience, much of the material in many of these handbooks is not useful and could be misleading.

SUMMARY

The best way to assess reading is by testing, observing, and listening to the student's reading. If the examiner suspects, from the reading assessment, that weaknesses in basic processes underlie the student's reading difficulty, those processes can be assessed further by methods designed for those purposes. Such methods include, for example, tests of phonological awareness and rapid automatized naming. Intelligence testing is an essential part of a comprehensive assessment of a student's total intellectual functioning. In conjunction with a reading assessment, it can provide the valuable context of a more complete understanding of a student's cognitive functioning. It is not, even with well-designed instruments that yield profiles of scores, such as the various Wechsler scales, a very efficient or thorough means of directly assessing reading abilities and needs. A simple, uninterpreted IQ score by itself offers no contribution to a reading assessment.

Planning the Assessment

INITIAL STEPS

A good reading assessment is a planned process directed toward a goal. It attempts to answer specific questions. This process is much more than a routine application of a standard battery of tests.

Given this philosophy, the reading assessment must begin by collecting questions and concerns from teachers and, at least for minor students, from parents. The student's own questions are also essential, but must await the first meeting between the student and examiner. The examiner needs to know the specific reasons someone thinks there is a reading problem, such as difficulty understanding questions on science tests, apparent boredom with grade-level reading material that seems to be too easy, or failure to master the beginning, first-grade instruction in letter sounds.

Some observations may be in conflict; for example, there may be disagreements among various parents and teachers about how well or poorly the student reads. One party may be deeply concerned and another not at all. The student's reading behavior may actually vary among different settings. Various observers may have different standards or may be using different reference groups, such as classmates or older siblings. All of this information is important and should be catalogued by the examiner. Questionnaires, interviews, or telephone calls may be needed to clarify and refine questions, concerns, and observations.

The concerns and observations are summarized in writing before the assessment begins, and the refined questions are written so that they can be quoted and answered in the report. It is wise, almost essential, to write each portion of the report as soon as the information is available. The report will be written better than if it is postponed to some future time when long-forgotten events and sketchy notes may prove inadequate.

The examiner also reviews previous testing, including group tests, and previous report cards and progress reports. Limited knowledge of phonetic rules has a very different meaning for a student who has been exposed to only "whole language" than for one who has been receiving intensive training in phonics. A table of report card marks and a chronological report of comments can convey the information clearly.

ORDER OF ASSESSMENT

The examiner plans the initial stages of the assessment to test those skills that certainly need to be evaluated. The first stage of the evaluation may suggest other areas that need to be explored as well. A good strategy is to begin with higher-order skills and work down until a floor of solid competence in more basic skills is reached. This approach usually requires less time and effort than beginning with the most basic, underlying skills and working up toward higher-order ones. In addition, the top-down approach lowers the likelihood focusing on apparent weaknesses in basic skills that are no longer relevant at the student's present reading level or for which the student is successfully compensating.

Testing Reading and its Subskills

This section examines assessment practices and instruments by starting with broad comprehension skills, next moving to reading vocabulary, then to oral vocabulary, followed by oral decoding and finally phonemic awareness. This order reflects the hierarchy of broad to basic skills that a planned assessment might follow. When planning an assessment, this order should be applied with some thoughtful flexibility. For example, if a student is known to have very limited broad comprehension, extensive oral vocabulary, but difficulty with decoding, the assessment might take one measure of reading comprehension as a benchmark then focus more on identifying subskills of decoding in need of instruction rather than on broad comprehension.

In contrast, if a student is known to decode fluently, but to exhibit reading comprehension weaknesses, the assessment might examine comprehension and knowledge of word meanings from multiple vantage points and pick up a benchmark of decoding efficiency while testing comprehension of passages read orally. The reader may find it helpful to refer to Table 11.1 (following page) as an organizing framework while reading the following descriptions of various tests and subtests.

PASSAGE COMPREHENSION

Reading comprehension is a complex process that involves the interaction of many abilities. These include, but are not limited to, language, decoding, thinking, remembering, checking, and synthesizing. Efforts to measure this activity have produced many tests of reading comprehension arrayed in a vast number of formats.

There is a danger that these very different tests will be considered interchangeable measures of a monolithic skill of "reading comprehension." Yet no single test of reading comprehension is able to test all of the major components of reading comprehension, and each test of reading comprehension is unavoidably limited by compromises among various constraints and mutually exclusive objectives. The examiner's goal, therefore, cannot be to select THE correct reading comprehension test, or even THE correct reading comprehension test for a particular student. Instead, the examiner must select one, or probably more than one, reading comprehension test and use it or them with a lively awareness of the limitations of each test.

The following discussion of several popular reading comprehension tests is intended to give the examiner a few examples of the many available instruments, some insight into major strengths and weaknesses of those instruments and, especially, to provide a model of the type of analysis that the examiner should apply when selecting and interpreting any reading comprehension test. The tests used for examples below are grouped by format.

Table 11.1. Subtests of A Few Reading Tests. (Test inclusion, exclusion, or order of appearance does not reflect test quality or usefulness. Use blank rows to add others.)

Test	Passage Comprehension	Reading Vocabulary	Oral Vocabulary	Oral Passages	Oral Word Decoding	Phonemic Awareness	Spelling
Diagnostic Assessment of Reading with Trial Teaching Strategies	S		L	O	O		W
Woodcock Reading Mastery Tests-R/NU	S	O			O		
Kaufman Test of Educational Achievement Comprehensive Form/NU	S				O		W
Peabody Individual Achievement Test-R/NU	S,M				O		M
Wechsler Individual Achievement Test	S				O		W
Gates-MacGinitie Reading Tests, 4th ed.	S,M	S,M					
Gray Oral Reading Test-3	O,M			O			
Diagnostic Reading Scales-81	O,S			O	O	L	
Wide Range Achievement Test-3					O		W
Slosson Oral Reading Test-R					O		
Goldman-Fristoe-Woodcock Auditory Skills Test Battery					O	L	W
Woodcock-Johnson III	S	O	L		O	L	W
Gray Silent Reading Test	S						

Key: **S = silent reading   O = oral reading   M = multiple choice   W = written response   L = listen and respond orally**

Read and answer. The traditional measure of reading comprehension is a test in which the student reads a passage and answers questions about the passage. Even this single procedure offers several variations—some examples follow.

Most items on the Kaufman Test of Educational Achievement, Comprehensive Form (K-TEA/NU) (Kaufman & Kaufman, 1998) ask the student to read a brief passage and orally respond to one or two written questions at the end of the passage. The format is straightforward and appealing in its simplicity. Sometimes the student has more difficulty with the wording of the questions than with the passage itself, which is not a problem in the scoring, because this difficulty is part of the standardization and norming of the test. However, particular difficulty with the questions would be a valuable observation worth pursuing with additional assessment, since following written directions is an important skill for school work (Brody, 1987). The student's answers to the test questions, spontaneous comments, and replies to an examiner's inquiries can sometimes suggest whether there is more difficulty with the level of the vocabulary or with the complexity of the language of the passages.

The K-TEA/NU diagnostic analysis classifies each question as factual or inferential comprehension with norms to indicate whether the student showed a strength or weakness in each area compared to other students in the same grade with the same ceiling item. This analysis must be used with great caution since the student could miss a question due to difficulty decoding a long word, rather than from lack of recall or reasoning skill. In such a case, specific categories of comprehension never come into play. In addition, the use of only one or two questions per passage may be a limitation.

The Wechsler Individual Achievement Test (WIAT) (Wechsler, 1992) Reading Comprehension test is similar to the K-TEA/NU, but the student announces completion of the reading and the examiner asks comprehension questions orally. Scoring is strict, and the examiner must not deviate from the scoring, as this was how the test was normed. The WIAT Reading Comprehension can be compared to the WIAT Listening Comprehension.

Both the WIAT and the K-TEA/NU mostly use relatively short passages of one to a few sentences. If a referral question involves study skills, the ability to sustain attention during long reading assignments, or comprehension of lengthy material in content-area reading (see Chapter 7), a test of brief passages will not be sufficient. Comprehension of brief passages may provide valuable information, but a longer test, such as the Gates-MacGinitie Reading Tests (4th ed.) (MacGinitie & MacGinitie, 2000), will also be required. The Gray Silent Reading Test (Wiederholt & Blalock, 2000) is intermediate in length.

Some tests, such as the Diagnostic Reading Scales-Revised (DRS-81) (Spache, 1981) and the Gray Oral Reading Test—Third Edition (GORT-3) (Wiederholt & Bryant, 1992), ask the student to read passages aloud and then answer oral questions about the passages. On the Spache, the questions are purely oral and open-ended. On the GORT-3, the questions are multiple choice and are both shown to the student in print and simultaneously read aloud. The passages are, at most grade levels, longer than those on the K-TEA/NU or WIAT, but still not long enough to help answer questions about study skills and sustained reading comprehension. Some of the questions, especially on the Spache, have high "blind ratios." Students may be able to answer some of the questions without reading the passage, e.g., "What was the girl's name?" "Where was she going?" "What did she do when she saw the red light?" [Mary, school, stop].

Chall and Curtis (1990) observe that some students do not easily comprehend material that they have read aloud. Such students may need to read silently in order to understand what they have read. The Spache partially addresses this concern by having the student read aloud successively more difficult passages and answer oral questions until the student's oral reading errors exceed a specified criterion. After that criterion is reached, the student continues to read more difficult passages silently and answer oral questions after each one until the student misses a specified number of questions for a passage. However, a student whose comprehension was severely impaired by oral reading might fail more than the allowed number of comprehension questions before making the specified number of oral reading errors. That student would never have a chance to attempt silent reading comprehension.

On the GORT-3, the student earns separate scores for the rate of reading, the number of reading errors, and the comprehension questions. The two oral reading scores are combined into a "passage" score, which has a basal and ceiling separate from the basal and ceiling for the comprehension score. It would seem that comprehension could then, as on the Spache, be measured separately from oral reading once a ceiling for oral reading had been reached. However, no explicit provision is made in the manual for allowing the student to read silently on higher-level passages after reaching a ceiling for oral reading speed and accuracy.

Allowing a student to stop reading aloud would also raise another problem. Just as Chall and Curtis observe that some students do not comprehend well while reading aloud, other students do not read carefully **unless** they read aloud. The latter group of students naturally exhibit limited performance on silent reading comprehension tests. Students who are distractible, tired, bored, unmotivated, resistant, or discouraged may pay attention to what they are reading only when they read aloud. The prudent examiner will include measures of comprehension of material read silently and material read aloud when students exhibit difficulty with silent reading comprehension.

The Spache and the GORT-3 both offer two forms. These are composed of parallel sets of passages of increasing difficulty. The Spache passages are identified by specific grade levels, which seem to be reasonably accurate for criterion-referenced purposes, when viewed with some flexibility. The availability of two sets of parallel passages on the Spache allows the examiner to discover those situations in which a student's comprehension of material read silently is very different from the student's comprehension of material read aloud.

The GORT-3 offers "standard scores"[3] and percentile ranks for: reading rate, reading accuracy, combined rate-and-accuracy "passage score," comprehension, and total score. The passage and total scores are combined scores that I find difficult to interpret. The GORT-3 also offers grade equivalent scores. Since grade equivalent scores can be misleading, it is best to use only the percentile or standard scores.

The Diagnostic Assessments of Reading with Trial Teaching Strategies (DARTTS) (Roswell & Chall, 1992) completely separates comprehension from oral reading. Comprehension is assessed with orally presented questions about a set of reading passages that the student may choose to read either silently or aloud. Decoding accuracy is not scored on these passages since oral reading of text is assessed with a second set of passages without any comprehension questions. This is particularly helpful since some students become slow and inaccurate in their oral reading when they realize that they must prepare to be quizzed in comprehension as well.

---

[3] These would be called "scaled scores" on most tests, since they have a mean of ten and a standard deviation of three.

The DARTTS measures the student's success by specified criteria on each of a series of graded passages. Consequently, the examiner can report both that the student's **oral reading** was acceptable on passages written at or below a certain grade level and that the student's **comprehension** was acceptable on passages written at or below a certain, possibly different, grade level. This use of passages identified by the grade level of the content is a very useful way of reporting reading scores and is very different from statistically deriving a grade-equivalent score for a raw score on a test. With the Spache or the DARTTS, the examiner is reporting the highest grade level **of material** that the student could handle successfully. In contrast, tests yielding grade-equivalent scores provide only the **average grade placement of students** who obtained the same number of raw score points as this student, even though this student may have struggled and failed on some passages far below that grade level or easily succeeded on others far above it.

The Gates-MacGinitie Reading Tests (4th ed.) (MacGinitie & MacGinitie, 2000) and many other group tests offer a format of reading a passage and responding by marking answers to printed multiple-choice answers. The disadvantages of this format include the lack of interaction with the student and lack of any way to monitor the student's work until the tests are scored afterwards. The primary advantage is the length of the passages, usually longer than those for individual reading tests, and the total length of the test, which allows a better measure of the kind of sustained reading demanded by middle- and high-school courses. The large number of items and huge norming samples on group tests contribute to highly reliable scores, a virtue offset by the examiner's difficulty in monitoring the student's attention while taking the test.

Read and choose. The Peabody Individual Achievement Test-Revised (PIAT-R/NU) (Markwart, 1998) offers the unusual reading comprehension format of having the student read a sentence, turn a page, and, without looking back at the sentence, choose the one of four pictures that best illustrates the previously read sentence. This format requires the student to directly connect the printed language with meaning and avoids contamination by such factors as the student matching isolated words in multiple-choice answers with isolated words in the text. However, the PIAT-R/NU also clearly differs from other reading comprehension tests, and is not measuring the same skills. In addition, it puts a premium on memory. These differences imply that, although the PIAT-R/NU correlates well with other reading comprehension tests, it might yield different results with an individual student.

Cloze technique.   The Woodcock Reading Mastery Test-Revised (WRMT-R/NU) (Woodcock, 1998) and Woodcock-Johnson III (WJ III) (Woodcock, McGrew, & Mather, 2001) offer reading comprehension tests with a fill-in-the-blank format, e.g., "'Woof!' said the ____ before biting the hand that fed it." The student tells the examiner the one word needed to complete the sentence. Two-word phrases synonymous with the correct answers are not acceptable, and the student is again asked for a one-word answer. This cloze technique measures grammatical knowledge and word-finding as well as reading. Students with weak oral grammar are penalized, and students with strong oral grammar may earn inflated scores. There is one item for which the missing word is *such* in the phrase *such as*. Only the most grammatically sophisticated students pass that item since it is marked wrong when a student answers *like*.

In my opinion, there are so few reading comprehension items on the WJ III that, despite impressive standardization statistics, scores for individuals may be inflated or depressed by one or two lucky or unlucky guesses. Consequently, I am reluctant to use these reading tests.[4] Instead, when using the rest of the WJ III achievement battery, I substitute the WRMT-R/NU for the WJ III reading tests,

---

[4]Consider, for example, a student in the eighth month of grade five (5.8) whose actual reading comprehension ability, as measured by the WJ III form A test of naming the missing word in each passage, is precisely at grade 5.8, which is equivalent to a raw score of 32 points. If the student inattentively or impulsively misses two items, the grade equivalent drops a full year to 4.5, and the student's standard score falls from 100 (50th percentile) to 95 (36th percentile). If, instead, the student accidentally passes two additional items, the grade equivalent climbs almost two years to 7.7 for a standard score of 107 (67th percentile). The 68% confidence bands for the lucky and unlucky scores do not even overlap.

The WRMT-R/NU also reflects large changes in scores for small numbers of lucky or unlucky guesses, but the longer tests show less variability than the shorter WJ III tests. For example, on the WRMT-R/NU form G, the same student described above at grade 5.9 would drop from the 50th percentile to the 42nd percentile by missing two items, thus remaining in the 5th or average stanine. If the same student scored two lucky guesses on the WRMT-R/NU, the score would increase to the 58th percentile.

Clearly, examiners need to worry about the effects of random errors, even on longer tests. It is always wise to examine the norms tables of tests and perform thought experiments such as the one described above. In general, longer tests are to be preferred over very brief ones. Random errors on brief screening tests are not harmless, since they may precipitate unnecessary further testing or, worse, prevent further testing for a student who really needs it.

314

preserving the format of the WJ III tests, but substantially increasing the number of items.

The cognitive battery of the WJ III includes a listening comprehension test that is similar format to the Passage Comprehension. The student listens to a tape recording of sentences with missing words and tells the examiner the missing word. This would allow a very precise comparison between listening and reading comprehension with both tests normed on the same sample, except for one difference: the missing word on the listening comprehension test is always the last word in the sentence. There is still some value to the comparison, since both tests are normed on the same students, but the comparison is not perfect. When teachers are taught to construct their own examinations, they are urged to write fill-in-the-blank items with missing words only at the end of the sentence because missing words imbedded within sentences are much more confusing and difficult.

Informal reading inventories. Passage comprehension can also, of course, be assessed by examiner-made or published informal reading inventories (e.g., Ekwall, 1981). The scope of the assessment is the same as with published, standardized, normed tests. The examiner-made informal reading inventory has the advantages of containing the precise material and format that the examiner wishes to use. The examiner-made inventory can also use materials from, or materials similar to those used in, the student's classes, an important consideration as curriculum-based assessment becomes more popular.

The examiner-made or published informal reading inventory should include measures of comprehension of passages read aloud and passages read silently. It should extend low enough to include a student's level of solid comprehension and high enough to include the student's level of very limited comprehension. Ideally, it should include material similar to what the student will encounter in science, social studies, English, and other classes. It should include passages as long as the longer passages that the student is expected to read for classes. Except, perhaps, with very shy youngsters who could write answers better than they could explain them orally, the comprehension questions should ordinarily be oral so that reading the questions and writing the answers do not become confounding variables clouding the assessment of reading comprehension. The questions should require both factual information and understanding that exceeds recall. In addition, students should not be able to answer the questions without reading the passage.

It is best to avoid placing undue emphasis on memory. When designing an inventory, distinguish between questions the student can answer immediately, from memory, and those the student can answer after re-reading part of the passage. The inventory should include questions calling for recall or location of important, factual information, for inferences from information given, and for predictions. When creating an inventory, try it out on students who do not have reading difficulty, at various grade levels in the local school system. Even though materials were selected from the local curricula, there still could be questions that are much too easy or much too difficult for average readers.

The major limitation of examiner-made and published informal reading inventories is the lack of trustworthy norms. Such instruments may be thoroughly "standardized," that is, equipped with a standardized set of instructions so that they are always given precisely the same way under the same circumstances. However, they either are not "normed" at all or are normed without selecting a sufficiently stratified, random, national sample of students who form a microcosm of the United States student population.

If an evaluation/placement team is using precise, numerical scores as a cut-off to make important decisions about students—a practice I do not recommend—then precise norming becomes a paramount concern. For instance, one cannot compare reading results from an informal reading inventory to results from a normed intelligence test. However, in other situations, it may be far more useful to concentrate on information gleaned from an informal assessment. For example, it can be helpful to examine the social studies text that a student is expected to read; such a review could indicate that the text would present a problem for the student and require appropriate instruction.

VOCABULARY TESTED THROUGH READING

As discussed in Chapter 9, knowledge of word meanings is one of the essential foundations of reading. If a student has difficulty understanding a reading passage, one possible reason would be a limited reading vocabulary. In this instance, I am referring to understanding the meaning of printed words rather than the ability to decode words with or without understanding their meanings.

There are a great many kinds of reading vocabulary tests and a great many examples of each kind. As with the passage comprehension tests, each type of reading vocabulary test has advantages and disadvantages that the examiner must keep in mind when selecting, interpreting, and reporting results. Few characteristics of vocabulary tests are unconditionally poor, but any of them can render an assessment inappropriate or invalid for a particular student. The following discussion of vocabulary tests describes their features, some aspects of what they measure, and how their construction may influence findings.

Oral synonyms and antonyms. The Woodcock Reading Mastery Tests-Revised (WRMT-R/NU) (Woodcock, 1998) and the Woodcock-Johnson III (WJ III) (Woodcock, McGrew, & Mather, 2001) offer tests on which the student reads a word and states a synonym or antonym for the printed word. This is sometimes a useful technique, but it has its limitations. Thinking of synonyms and antonyms requires, besides knowledge of the meaning of the given word, specific types of verbal reasoning and also the ability to think of or "retrieve" a wanted word quickly. Problems with this "word-finding" ability are common among students identified as having specific learning disabilities (especially "language-based" specific learning disabilities) and speech/ language disabilities. As with the cloze technique discussed above, students with word-finding difficulties may understand the material on the test, but not be able to retrieve the single word needed for a correct answer. As on the cloze-technique tests, phrases are not acceptable for the WRMT-R/NU antonyms and synonyms tests. If the student complains, "I know the word, but I can't think of the answer," ask the student what the printed word means. If the student is able to define several of the words without being able to think of synonyms or antonyms for them, this test is not a valid measure of reading vocabulary for that student.

Some students also have difficulty shifting between the synonyms and antonyms subtests. These students may need an intervening activity and some warm-up before beginning the second subtest.

Multiple-choice synonyms and antonyms. Many of the group achievement tests, such as the Gates-MacGinitie Reading Tests (4th ed.) (MacGinitie & MacGinitie, 2000), offer multiple-choice tests asking for synonyms or antonyms for written words. These tests have the advantages of avoiding the word-finding problem and of providing a large number of words in a fairly narrow range of reading levels, since the group tests offer several different forms for different grade levels. They are also normed on vast numbers of students. However, the examiner has difficulty monitoring the student's care and attention, even if the test is administered individually.

Also, if the test is administered in a group, and if it has both synonym and antonym sections (as on the California Achievement Test), there is the danger of the student continuing to select synonyms when taking an antonym section. If the student's item analysis from a group test shows a much higher score for the first of two synonym and antonym sections, the student probably failed to make the change or failed to adhere to it.

Analogies. The WRMT-R/NU measures reading vocabulary with a test of completing printed analogies, e.g., pig:domestic::aardvark:____. Once again, this test is contaminated by verbal reasoning and by word-finding abilities, so that students with strong verbal reasoning abilities who do not have word-finding difficulty will earn inflated scores, higher than simple reading vocabulary knowledge, and students with weak verbal reasoning skills or with word-finding difficulties will earn scores lower than their simple reading vocabularies.

Verbal reasoning abilities are important for reading, and word-finding difficulties are often related to reading disabilities. It is valuable to know about a student's verbal reasoning and about any word-finding difficulties the student may have. However, it is also important not to let these issues confound measurement of reading vocabulary. The examiner must be clear about what is being measured and reported.

The WRMT-R/NU classifies each word in the reading vocabulary tests as General Reading, Science-Math, Social Studies, or Humanities. A numerical score is not offered for the number of items correctly responded to in each category, but the totals can be plotted on the Diagnostic Comprehension Profile on p. 15 of the WRMT-R/NU Test Record and compared visually to one another.[5]

Oral definitions. Many oral vocabulary tests use the straight-forward approach of simply presenting a word for the student to define orally. To the best of my knowledge, there are no silent reading vocabulary tests using this approach. The Test of Written Language (3rd ed.) (TOWL-3) (Hammill & Larsen, 1996) has a written vocabulary subtest on which the student writes definitions of printed words, but this method deliberately adds assessment of writing skills to assessment of reading vocabulary.

---

[5]If further information is desired, the scores could also be compared to the oral science, social studies, and humanities knowledge test on the Woodcock-Johnson III (WJ III) (Woodcock, McGraw, & Mather, 2001). The WJ III also offers oral tests of synonyms and antonyms and of completing analogies. It can be valuable to compare a student's performance on the written and oral versions of these tests. It can be very instructive to compare analogous measures of oral and reading vocabularies as well as comprehension.

Picture vocabulary tests. The lowest levels of some of the group reading tests, e.g., Gates-MacGinitie Reading Tests (4th ed.) (MacGinitie & MacGinitie, 2000), provide reading vocabulary tests on which students match a picture to one of several printed words in a multiple-choice format. To my knowledge, none of these tests extends this valuable format beyond early primary reading levels.

Informal reading vocabulary inventories. Here is an opportunity for an informal reading inventory to fill a gap in the offerings of existing normed tests. The examiner could take words from reading materials in the local curricula, present them in printed form, and ask the student what the words mean. Ambiguous responses should be questioned, neutrally—without "leading questions"—until the student's meaning is clear. General definitions that could apply to a great many words should also be questioned. The student should be given credit for any response that makes it clear that the student recognizes the printed word and knows what it means. If words were placed in separate lists from various curriculum materials, the examiner could estimate the student's highest grade level of solid reading vocabulary in each subject area.

Another approach involves follow-up questioning after informal passage comprehension inventories. The examiner can ask in general if the words were difficult and can specifically ask for the meanings of some of the more challenging words in the passages with which the student had difficulty. This approach would not yield a score, but might shed some light on the source of the student's difficulty with passage comprehension.

VOCABULARY TESTED ORALLY

In-depth assessment of oral meaning vocabulary is beyond the scope of this chapter, but it provides a means of measuring knowledge of word meanings when a student's decoding skills are too limited to permit vocabulary assessment through a reading measure. It is particularly important not to confuse a meaning deficit for a decoding weakness or vice versa since vocabulary knowledge is essential to successful reading, as discussed above in chapters 2 and 9. For example, some oral reading errors, such as "hyperbowl" for "hyperbole," make it clear that the student's problem is with meaning vocabulary, not with decoding. Complaints such as, "I don't know what these words mean," can be another indication of difficulty with meaning vocabulary. As suggested above, the examiner can also question the student about the meaning of key words in a difficult informal inventory reading passage. If the student cannot decode a word, the examiner can tell the student the word and again ask about the meaning.

If the examiner begins to suspect that limitations of oral meaning vocabulary are contributing to the student's reading difficulty, there must be further investigation. It would be futile to continue teaching higher-level decoding skills alone without also teaching the definitions of words whose meanings are unfamiliar.

The Diagnostic Assessments of Reading with Trial Teaching Strategies (DARTTS) (Roswell & Chall, 1992) includes a test of oral meaning vocabulary. Like most of the other parts of this assessment, the DARTTS oral vocabulary test is organized by grade levels, so that the examiner reports that the student correctly defined acceptable numbers of words up through a given grade level and not beyond it. The test is much less sophisticated than the oral vocabulary tests used in speech/language, educational, and psychological assessments, but it provides some indication of the student's oral vocabulary. It can suggest whether limitations of oral vocabulary interfere with the student's reading progress or whether a strength in oral vocabulary could be exploited to support reading instruction.

If there appears to be a problem with oral vocabulary, the student should have a thorough and accurate assessment of it and probably of other oral language abilities as well. Such assessments are usually performed by speech/language pathologists, specialists in the assessment of intellectual functioning, and psychologists. The findings of the additional assessment should be **integrated** with the reading assessment report to create a more comprehensive picture of the student's academic functioning rather than being presented simply as a separate package.

When present, limitations of oral language should be ameliorated through work on oral language as part of the student's reading instruction or Individualized Education Program. Such limitations must never be considered a valid reason for giving up on instruction in reading nor as an indication that the student is already reading at maximum capacity.

FLUENCY AND ACCURACY IN ORAL READING OF PASSAGES

Above, we discussed assessment of **comprehension** during oral reading of passages. This section discusses assessment of **decoding fluency and accuracy** during oral reading of passages. As described in Chapter 5, fluent decoding enables a student to engage more attentively in reading for meaning. The tests described below provide some means of measuring the extent that students have achieved the automaticity in decoding connected text that will let them shift attention to meaning.

Many reading tests include oral reading of connected material. Some, such as the DARTTS (Roswell & Chall, 1992), completely separate the oral reading from comprehension. Most, such as the Diagnostic Reading Scales (Spache, 1981) and the GORT-3 (Wiederholt & Bryant, 1991) ask comprehension questions about material read aloud. The Diagnostic Reading Scales also include comprehension questions on passages read silently above the student's highest level of successful oral reading. The criteria for successful oral reading of the passages are based on the ratio of errors ("deviations from print" on the GORT-3) to the total number of words in the passage.

Each test of oral reading of connected material offers its own system of recording errors on the examiner's copy of the reading passage. Examiners may wish to adopt or adapt one of these systems and use it for all oral reading tests rather than continually changing systems from instrument to instrument. As suggested below, it would be wise and necessary to record a personal notation system so that, if asked, the examiner could demonstrate that it contains all of the information covered by the system published with a particular test in use. A more important point is that the examiner absolutely must adhere to the penalty system used with each test. Some tests penalize a student for errors even if the student spontaneously corrects them. Others do not. Some tests penalize a student for repetition of a single word, some for repetitions of more than one word, and others do not penalize at all for simple repetitions. An examiner needs to review the penalty rules when switching among oral reading tests.

The examiner must make a verbatim transcript of the student's reading, at least according to the errors "counted" by the test. It is good to maintain an accurate and complete record and notes that would permit later reading of the passage aloud exactly the way the student did, including pauses, repetitions (whether scored or not), and intonation. General characteristics of the student's reading should be noted while or immediately after the student reads, before the examiner begins to forget, for example, whether the student read word-by-word or in phrases, whether the student acknowledged punctuation (I cross out and insert punctuation marks to show how the student read aloud), and how much expression the student gave to the reading (interrogation and exclamation points may help with recording expression).

Grade-level designations of passage difficulty.   The Diagnostic Assessments of Reading with Trial Teaching Strategies (DARTTS) (Roswell & Chall, 1992), Diagnostic Reading Scales (Spache, 1981), and published informal reading inventories identify each reading passage by its readability grade level and report a passing or non-passing performance for oral reading at each passage level. This is a useful way of looking at oral reading performance, so long as the examiner is careful to note situations in which a particular type of penalty rule depressed or inflated the student's reading score beyond reason.

The designation of the highest difficulty level of a passage read by a student is very different from a grade equivalent derived from the number of raw score points earned. The examiner is reporting that the student read satisfactorily from passages written up to a certain difficulty level, but not beyond that level. However, this designation still does not tell whether the student's performance was within, near, or far from the average range for the student's age or grade. Reading skills vary a good deal within any grade, so the successful reading of passages at levels one or two grades below or above grade placement may not deviate dramatically from the norm for that grade.

Within-group comparisons.   As noted earlier, the GORT-3 provides percentile ranks and standard scores for the rate (number of seconds to read the passage) and for the accuracy (number of "deviations from print") of the student's oral reading of a series of successively more difficult passages. There is also a "passage score" that combines the rate and accuracy measures in a mixture that I do not find useful.   The standard score tells how far away the student's score is from the average for the student's age group, and the percentile rank tells the percent of students in the same age group whose scores this student tied or exceeded. These scores do not tell the highest grade level at which the student demonstrated acceptable oral reading accuracy. The grade-equivalent score on the GORT-3 merely lists the average grade placement of other students who earned the same number of points for reading rate, reading accuracy, or the combined "passage" score. Grade-equivalent scores may differ dramatically from the grade level of reading material that the student can read aloud, and I recommend that grade equivalent scores **not** be used.

Informal inventories of oral reading. For the examiner who wishes to use them, there are published informal reading inventories that include measures of oral reading. Examiners can also make their own oral reading tests, using local curriculum materials (e.g. see Chapter 5, Appendix C, p. 168). A rigorous recording system should, of course, be employed as described above. Even in high school, oral reading of connected material can allow an examiner to determine whether work on oral reading fluency would help improve the student's overall reading skills and whether teachers should be encouraged to have the student read aloud in class or should be discouraged from doing so.

ORAL DECODING OF WORDS

Most reading tests include measures of oral reading of words. This valuable exercise helps the examiner assess a student's ability to decode a word without using cues from the context in which the word may appear. Reading in context is a much more "natural" process and a major portion of mature reading. However, in order to advance to the level of mature reading, the student must first be able to figure out what the words say. Chapters 4 and 5 discuss in depth the processes of learning to decode words. Assessment of reading of less skilled readers needs to include a measure of reading single words aloud.

Recording responses. When testing oral reading of words, examiners should record verbatim the student's preliminary attempts at reading a word, some indication of the length of time before starting to pronounce the word, the length of any pauses before the student finishes with the word, and the final pronunciation of the word. This can be accomplished by marking any mispronunciations on the examiner's sheet followed by "sc" (for self-correct) to indicate that the word was finally read accurately. The subsequent analysis of the transcript may be the most valuable aspect of this part of the assessment.

Untimed word lists. Many oral reading tests, such as those of the WJ III (Woodcock, McGrew, & Mather 2001), K-TEA/NU (Kaufman & Kaufman, 1998), and WIAT (Wechsler, 1992), ask the student to read words aloud from lists of unrelated, increasingly difficult words. The student is allowed to take the necessary time to attempt each word, and the student's final decision is accepted. These are "power" tests that permit the student to use recall of "sight" words as well as phonetic and structural analysis skills. The examiner's verbatim transcript, including latencies—time from initial encounter to final reading of a word—helps distinguish sight words from words that were analyzed.

Timed word lists. Other tests, such as the WRMT-R/NU (Woodcock, 1998), SORT-R (Slosson, 1991) and Diagnostic Reading Scales (Spache, 1981) put a time limit on the student's response to each word. These tests are designed to test "automaticity," or the student's immediate recall of sight vocabulary and instant application of decoding skills. Many examiners are comfortable using an untimed test and determining whether the student read most of the words quickly. Other examiners prefer to use both a timed and an untimed oral reading test. The disadvantage of the first approach is that the distinction between automatic and non-automatic words is determined subjectively and may not be accurate. The disadvantage of the second approach is that the norming samples of the different reading tests are radically different, and it is not always safe to compare scores on different reading tests. Schultz (1988) compared nine popular reading tests and reported extraordinarily different scores for the same level of skill. In one example, a six-year-old student who could name all letters, but not read any words on a test, would receive standard scores (mean = 100, standard deviation = 15) ranging from 65 to 98 on the various tests!

Timed oral reading tests should always be accompanied by untimed measures as well, since automatic reading of words is one important skill, but phonetic and structural analysis are also essential to comprehension of unfamiliar words and text.

Grade-level word lists. Many tests, such as the DARTTS and the SORT-R, group words into brief lists. Each list is composed of words at a difficulty level typically found at a particular grade level. The DARTTS reports performance in terms of the grade level of the highest list on which the student correctly read the requisite number of words.

Single word lists. Other tests, such as the K-TEA/NU, WIAT, and WRMT-R/NU use a single, increasingly difficult, list with a "ceiling rule" to determine when to stop testing the student after a certain number of errors. The raw score is the number of words read correctly plus any words not tested below the student's "basal" level (a certain number of words read correctly). This raw score is translated into a standard score and percentile rank. In some cases, a grade equivalent is also available, but I recommend that it is not used.

It would be most helpful to know both the grade level of the highest group of words that a student could read easily and also how that student's performance compared to the scores of other students in the same grade or of the same age. Decisions concerning whether to test both or one are often based on the time

324

available for assessment along with sensitivity to avoid wearing out the student with testing since few tests offer both kinds of information.

Nonsense words and word fragments. Several instruments, such as the Diagnostic Reading Scales and the DARTTS, provide tests of reading aloud parts of words, such as common syllables, vowels, consonants, digraphs, diphthongs, and blends. Such tests are usually criterion-referenced with, at most, a footnote indicating the grade level at which the particular skill is usually taught. There really is little need for normative data on these skills. If, for instance, a student can read most single consonants, some digraphs, and no blends, the instructional implications are clear, regardless of the student's age or grade placement or the performance of other students of the same age or grade. At this point in the assessment process, the question is no longer whether there is a reading problem, but what specific skills need instruction. That question does not require comparison with age or grade peers.

Some tests, such as the Goldman-Fristoe-Woodcock Auditory Skills Test Battery Sound-Symbol Tests (GFW) (Goldman, Fristoe, & Woodcock, 1974), the WJ III, and the WRMT-R/NU use lists of nonsense words, such as "blik" or "slopeck," to test phonetic word attack skills. The GFW also offers a test of written spelling of dictated nonsense words. The Diagnostic Reading Scales use nonsense words as carriers for the sounds being tested. For instance, short vowel sounds might be tested with the list, "bap, bep, bip, bop, bup." Nonsense words are appealing vehicles for testing phonetic word attack, since they eliminate any confusion with sight vocabulary. However, they must be used with great caution, since the process of reading a nonsense word is very different from that of reading a real word, and some students are confused or even upset by the idea of trying to read words that are not real. I usually use the word "fake" in my introductory discussion with the student before beginning testing, and I explain that the goal is to see how the student can sound out words that the student has never seen before.

The GFW and WRMT-R/NU nonsense word tests offer error inventories that allow the examiner to specify which sounds were read incorrectly. This is a useful analysis, but is not as direct and may not be as effective as the approach used by the DARTTS or Diagnostic Reading Scales of using specific word lists to test particular phonetic word attack skills.

Use of word decoding tests. The oral reading decoding tests have the purpose of analyzing the student's ability to decode individual words in isolation. Consequently, the examiner's verbatim transcriptions of errors and latencies are crucial. The examiner is attempting to determine the level of the student's reliable sight vocabulary, the phonetic and structural analysis skills that the student can apply reliably, and gaps in the student's reading skills that should become instructional goals. The Diagnostic Assessments of Reading with Trial Teaching Strategies (DARTTS) is unique in including a separate set of mini-lessons that the examiner can use with the student to assess the student's ability to learn the missing skills and to evaluate possible methods of instruction.

Informal inventories of word decoding. These goals can also be accomplished through informal inventories. If an oral reading score is going to be used as part of an official determination of need for remedial reading or special education, then a normed test would be necessary, although score cut-offs and formulae should not be used alone to determine eligibility for services. An examiner-made inventory could be tied very closely to reading materials such as reading series, literature, and content-area textbooks in the local school system. However, it is essential that the favored method or methods of reading instruction in the child's school **not** be allowed to limit the skills tested nor the reading methods and materials considered. No single system of reading instruction is going to be effective for all students at all times. There always will need to be exceptions, and one goal of the reading assessment is to identify those exceptions.

AUDITORY SKILLS AND PHONEMIC AWARENESS

If the student is experiencing serious difficulties with oral decoding of single words, it is probable that there is an even more basic weakness in auditory skills, phonemic awareness, or rapid automatized naming (RAN), as discussed in Chapters 3 and 5. The student may have difficulty hearing sounds correctly, discriminating between similar sounds, determining the order of sounds in a word, identifying the different sounds in a word, or even realizing that a word is made up of separate sounds; or the student may have difficulty quickly retrieving even well-known letter sounds and words from memory. Although these skills are essential foundations for reading, adequate assessment of them is specialized and beyond the scope of this chapter. Please see, for example, Wolf, Bowers & Biddle (2000).

A variety of tests may be used to assess phonemic skills (See Appendix E, p. 337.) For example, the GFW provides many tests of several aspects of auditory skills, which are easy to administer thanks to tape-recorded test materials. Norms are old and based on small, poorly defined samples. The WJ III includes briefer versions of some of these tests. The Lindamood Auditory Conceptualization Test (rev. ed.) (Lindamood & Lindamood, 1979) and the Comprehensive Test of

Phonological Processing (CTOPP) (Wagner, Torgesen, & Rashotte, 1999) are two examples of tests of phonemic awareness. The WJ III includes a wide range of phonemic tests that are taped and well-normed, but extremely brief. The WJ III includes one and the CTOPP four tests of rapid naming. The Test of Word Reading Efficiency (Torgesen, Wagner, & Rashotte, 1999) assesses speed of reading words and nonsense words aloud. Tests of reading and spelling nonsense words (e.g., GFW, WRMT-R/NU, WJ III) can often illuminate phonological difficulties. If the student's single-word or passage decoding skills suggest underlying auditory, phonological, or rapid-naming difficulties, it is imperative to assess these skills, if necessary by making a referral or seeking assistance. It is essential that the fundamental auditory skills be assessed thoroughly and precisely, if there are possible difficulties in this area, since remedial training is likely to be challenging, but effective.

Interactions with the Student

Introducing the assessment. The examiner's first contact with the student will help determine the value of the evaluation. The evaluation should be a pleasant or at least tolerable experience for the student. It should: leave the student with some accurate information about his or her reading skills, enhance or at least not impair the student's self-esteem, and yield recommendations that will be useful for the student's progress in reading.

When introducing the evaluation, it is important to displace the emphasis from the student's possible deficiencies onto the student's reading instructional program. I usually begin by asking what the student knows and suspects about the evaluation, including its purpose and nature. Then I offer a comment such as the following:

> Everyone is better at some things than at others, but it is different things for different people, of course. What I am trying to do is find out which are easier for you—which things you are best at—and which are hardest for you. If your teachers know more about what things you are best at and which you might need more help with, then they should be able to teach you better, so this is mostly to help them. However, to find out these things, I have to ask you to [brief description of planned activities]. Some of the things we do will be too easy. Please don't be insulted. Some of them will be too difficult. They are really for older students [I often specify a grade level well above the student's, roughly corresponding to the ceiling-level items the student will encounter]. We need those to make sure we don't miss anything you are especially good at. You may not be able to do those since you've not been in [grade X, high school, college, graduate school, etc.] yet. Just do the best you can. On most of the

things we do, I am not allowed to tell you if you are right or wrong or tell you the answers. Whenever I can, I will. Don't assume my little comments, like "umhm," mean you are right. I'm just thanking you for answering. If I don't say anything, it just means I didn't say anything. You can always change your answers. After we are all done, I will go over all the results with you. You will be the first to find out what happened. Later, I will [explanation of planned meetings and reports].

I never promise any particular format for reviewing the results. I do not want to promise, for example, numerical test scores and then discover to my horror that the student is reading much worse than I had suspected. Sometimes I do give the student numerical scores. Often I provide a table listing, for example, "Things You Were Best At" and "Things That Were More Difficult For You." I defer the decision on how to report the results until later in the assessment.

After the introduction, I solicit questions, concerns, and observations from the student. After my presentation, the student may have additional responses to my earlier question of what the student knows or suspects about the evaluation.

Examiners differ on how much time to spend introducing an evaluation and establishing rapport. Each examiner needs to find a comfortable style, but remain flexible in adapting it to each student. I find that most students usually remain worried until the testing actually begins and the tests evolve from abstractions into realities. Therefore, after the above introduction and discussion of the student's comments and questions, I generally move right into the first test. I find that additional conversation is more productive after the student has had an opportunity to experience some testing and to get to know me in that context.

During the testing, students often recall the introduction and ask me if a particular, difficult item is at the X grade level. I am usually inclined to agree that it is, since any item is within the broad range of abilities for any grade. I am not saying that the student is working at grade level X or even that the student passed an item at that level, since I am not telling the student whether the response was correct.

It is sometimes necessary to halt testing occasionally to answer further questions. This is usually time well spent, unless the student is making a serious effort to stall. In that case, it can be helpful to remind the student that the length of the evaluation is determined by the material to be covered, not by the time originally planned for the assessment.

The goals of these interactions with the student are to obtain the most valid possible samples of the student's reading and to build the student's legitimate self-confidence about reading. These goals cannot be accomplished mechanically. It is essential to clear your mind of the other pressures of the day and concentrate completely on building this brief, but important relationship as well as you can. You have an opportunity to do some good or a great deal of harm.

Sharing assessment findings with the student. Most tests do not allow feedback to the student during the exam, and that rule must be adhered to if the test norms are to be used. However, even though specific feedback about the correctness of responses is forbidden, most tests do allow general encouragement and allow more specific feedback between subtests. One of the obvious virtues of the DARTTS is that it permits much more encouragement of the student than do most standardized reading tests. The examiner would be wise to read the manuals for the DARTTS if for no other reason than to gain an idea of the kinds of encouragement that can be offered to the student. Throughout the assessment, it is important to remind the student of the purpose: finding more effective ways for the student to be taught reading skills. Even if a student obviously has a hopeless struggle with a subtest, the examiner can express satisfaction that the test helped clarify exactly what can be worked on.

It is very important to elicit from the student some idea of the student's own assessment of reading strengths and weaknesses and a detailed picture of the student's interests in and attitudes toward reading. The School Self-Rating Scale (SSRS) (RSEC Staff, 1993) is one vehicle for beginning this assessment of the student's own perceptions, attitudes, and interests.

The concluding interview ("debriefing") with the student should provide specific, concrete information about the student's test results. When results are not promised in any particular form, examiners are free to use a form most appropriate for the particular student and the results obtained. In some cases, I present a table of test scores in stanines. In others, I recall the discussion of "things you are best at and things that are most difficult for you" and give the student two such lists, always including more skills in the first than the second list. The debriefing should include reference to the self-perceptions, attitudes, and interests expressed by the student, and it should focus on the recommended instruction, without promising delivery of services that the examiner cannot guarantee. Above all, the debriefing should end on a truthfully optimistic note.

Some Rules for Testing Reading

Following are some basic testing rules developed from more than a quarter-century of mistakes I have made or witnessed in testing reading skills. Since my purpose is to summarize ideas elaborated earlier in this chapter, these rules are presented bluntly and with little explanation. The points are reiterated here to protect you, and therefore your students, from repeating these mistakes. I hope that a brief list will serve as a ready reference for future use.

1.   **Do not alter standardized tests**.   If the format of the test is uncomfortable for you or inappropriate for your student, do not use that test. **Do not use a norm-referenced, standardized test for informal testing**. This is the reason we have informal reading inventories. If you give a norm-referenced, standardized test, **administer it precisely as instructed**. Do not change the wording of directions at all, although you should read them in a natural, pleasant tone. Treat the directions like the lines in a play, delivered smoothly, naturally, and with expression, but absolutely verbatim.

Obey the basal and ceiling rules, and make sure you have them right, since they vary from test to test. Carefully observe time limits. If you are compelled to "test the limits" after standardized administration, for instance by allowing additional time for pronouncing words on the Slosson Oral Reading Test-Revised (SORT-R) (Slosson, 1991) or the Wide Range Achievement Test 3 (WRAT3) (Wilkinson, 1993), carefully and blatantly label the results everywhere they appear in your report. When reporting findings that occur with additional time or prompts, avoid giving a specific score, unless you put it in brackets, in Italics, and in the subjunctive mood. Each and every time the result is mentioned or listed, make it abundantly clear once more to your reader that these are not norm-based, but only your experiments. Otherwise, someone will eventually mistake your experiments for valid scores, with dire consequences when the student is re-evaluated. It would, however, be far better to substitute another test that does not require the unwanted constraints.

2.   **Never report test scores that are inaccurate or results that are invalid**. Simply report that you gave the test and obtained invalid results and explain the reason. **Do not specify the invalid results** because I promise you that someone will copy the number or classification onto a form where it will be used incorrectly for years to come.

3. **Pay attention to norming samples**. If an examiner cannot resist the unwise desire to use a poorly normed, standardized test instead of an informal test or a well-normed one for "diagnostic" purposes, the scores from the poorly normed test should not be reported under any circumstances.

4. If a skill is worth testing at all, **test with an adequate number of examples** so that random fluctuations in performance do not excessively inflate or depress assessment results. No matter what the published statistics suggest, check whether a single lucky or unlucky guess on a very brief test can dramatically change a score. Before considering the use of a brief reading test, look at the norms tables to see what would be the effect, for someone the age of your student, of raising or lowering a raw score by two points. If the effect is large, seek an alternative. Misleading data are worse than none at all.

5. **Record the student's oral reading and answers to questions verbatim**. Whenever the student reads aloud, use an expendable copy of the passage or word list that you can mark to reflect precisely the way the student read it, including: short, long, and very long pauses; misplaced stresses; repetitions of sounds, syllables, and words; insertions; omissions; substitutions; and words provided by the examiner. Various reading tests (e.g., Spache, 1981; Wiederholt & Bryant, 1992) offer such editing systems. Most examiners prefer to develop their own systems that they can use consistently on different tests. It would be well to record your own system so that it could be submitted along with the manuals for the tests used and the test record forms if raw data were subpoenaed for a legal action. The record would demonstrate that the personalized system included everything in the systems offered with the various tests used.

6. **When reporting numerical scores, limit the scoring systems used and include a clear explanation of each system** (Willis & Dumont, 1998, pp. 24-27). Nothing bewilders and antagonizes readers faster than a statistical Tower of Babel with age equivalents, grade equivalents, and age-based and grade-based standard scores, scaled scores, percentiles, percentile ranks, and quotients used apparently interchangeably and without explanation. If the examiner finds it difficult to translate a confusion of scores into a single statistical system, imagine how difficult it must be for many parents and many classroom teachers, who may not have recent, advanced training in mental-test statistics. When several examiners test the same student, the examiners should agree on a single statistical framework for the student's reports. Failing such utopian consensus, the team members should at least be punctilious in clearly and graphically defining each

statistic they use.   The alternative is confusion, misunderstanding, and poor decisions.

7. **Use nonsense words with caution**. I find them very useful for testing phonics skills, since they guarantee that the student will not be familiar with the test words, unless the student is given frequent re-evaluations with the same form of the same test. However, some students are disturbed by the concept of reading words that are not real words, and other students who can accept the idea still cannot resist substituting similar-sounding, real words. Furthermore, there is the danger of false generalizations. The process of sounding out a nonsense word in a list is not quite the same as that of decoding an unfamiliar, real word in a list and is very different from decoding an unfamiliar word in a meaningful reading passage.

8. When tests offer both grade and age norms, always **calculate scores compared to students of the same age *and* compared to students in the same grade**. If the scores are similar by both methods, you can report only one set, better the age-based ones, if other tests are used which offer only age-based scores. If scores are different by the two comparisons, then report both sets, since the complete truth is found in neither alone.

9. **Be cautious with fall-spring or fall-winter-spring norms**.   For younger students, the drop in scores overnight from one season to the next can be dramatic (Willis & Dumont, 1998, p. 72-73).

10. **Be wary of grade-equivalent or other potentially misleading test scores**. Tests which offer grade-equivalent scores corresponding to a number of points earned by a student can be very misleading, e.g., Willis & Dumont (1998, p. 223). The same number of points, and therefore the same grade equivalent, might be earned by three students, one of whom read through a sixth grade level very well, but could not read much of anything above that level, another of whom read well only through a third grade level, but accumulated additional points for partial successes to a ninth grade level, and yet another who read with moderate but inconsistent accuracy to an eighth grade level. Labeling all three students as sixth-grade-level readers would be seriously misleading. The International Reading Association (1982) has wisely recommended that grade equivalent scores NOT be used for reading tests.

Likewise, be aware that the "easy" and "difficult" grade-equivalent ratings on the Woodcock Reading Mastery Tests-Revised (WRMT-R/NU) and Woodcock-Johnson III are not based on actual passages at certain grade levels which the particular student read easily or with difficulty, but on confidence bands established with the norming sample. Instead of these scores, examiners should report only percentile or standard scores. A grade-level designation of material that a student reads easily, reads with difficulty, or cannot read at all is a different matter and can be very useful information. Tests such as DARTTS (Roswell & Chall, 1992) with graded passages which the student "passes" or "fails" attempt to offer this type of information.

11. **Examine responses carefully before deciding whether to report the interpretive categories developed for tests**. If a comprehension question labeled "inference" is missed by a student because the student simply could not decode most of the words in the passage, do not take this as evidence that the student has difficulty making inferences. Even if reading "synecdoche" as "sinnecdoch" is officially listed as a phonetic vowel miscue, report that the problem lies in oral vocabulary. Diagnostic interpretive systems can be very valuable, but they cannot substitute for an examiner's good judgment.

12. **Do not assume that a student's ability in one reading skill predicts a similar level of skill in others**. For example, the Wide Range Achievement Test 3 (WRAT3) (Wilkinson, 1993) Reading Test involves reading words aloud from an increasingly difficult list. The author's published intent is simply to measure the student's mastery of the reading code system and to ignore comprehension. In fact, the WRAT3 accomplishes even this limited purpose only in part, since the test includes only single, unrelated words and no decoding of connected text. Many examiners mistakenly assume that a student's success on the WRAT3 reading accurately predicts the student's ability in other aspects of reading, even comprehension. This mistaken assumption is not the intent of the authors of the test.

13. **Use tests that report different reading skills with separate, differentiated scores**. The ultimate goal of reading instruction is integration of all of the various reading skills into a coherent whole. The goal of reading assessment is the opposite. A thorough reading assessment requires analysis of the student's reading as separate skills so that strengths, weaknesses, and needs can be observed. Therefore, tests that report skills in a single score cause confusion.

For example, the Brief Form of the Kaufman Test of Educational Achievement (K-TEA/NU) (Kaufman & Kaufman, 1998) begins with oral reading from a word list and ends with comprehension questions for brief reading passages, providing a single "reading" score, which gives no information concerning specific areas in need of instruction. The Comprehensive Form of the same test (K-TEA/NU) more appropriately offers separate tests of oral reading from a word list and of reading comprehension.

The comprehension tests for both versions of the K-TEA/NU offer oral questions about reading passages and oral direction-following items similar to "Spin in your chair, then leap to your feet." The potential value of these comprehension questions is lost when reported as a combined score that includes performance on oral reading from a word list as happens with the Brief Form.

Similarly, the second edition of the Gray Oral Reading Tests (GORT-R) (Wiederholt & Bryant, 1986) combined oral reading speed and oral reading errors into a single "Passage" score which inextricably confused slow, accurate readers with fast, inaccurate readers and with moderately fast, moderately inaccurate readers. The GORT-3 (Wiederholt & Bryant, 1986) wisely remedied this error by providing separate scores for speed and for accuracy as well as the combined "Passage" score.

14. **Do not assume that comprehension of passages read aloud and of passages read silently are comparable**. Some students seem to need to hear themselves reading before they can make sense of a passage. Others can read aloud or understand, but not both at once. Although they implicitly make the unwarranted assumption that silent reading comprehension will always be as strong as or stronger than comprehension of passages read aloud, the Diagnostic Reading Scales-Revised (DRS-81) (Spache, 1981) have the virtue of including comprehension questions for passages read both silently and aloud. This is a necessary provision for any thorough reading assessment when silent reading comprehension is in question. The DARTTS (Roswell & Chall, 1992) completely separates oral reading from comprehension.

15. **Do not mistake limitations of oral vocabulary for weaknesses in word analysis skills**. If a student pronounces "hyperbole" to sound like a post-season football championship, the fault is not in phonetic and structural analysis. In fact, phonics generalizations were followed; the word and its meaning

are unknown. Limitations of oral meaning vocabulary essentially impose a ceiling on reading decoding. After students can decode most of the words that they know orally, further reading progress is enhanced more effectively by development of oral vocabulary along with instruction in advanced decoding skills as needed.

16. **Do not assume that all measures of reading comprehension are comparable**. In fact, assume the opposite. Among the common methods for testing reading comprehension are orally supplying missing words in printed sentences (cloze technique), orally completing printed analogies, and orally supplying synonyms and antonyms for printed words [e.g., Woodcock Reading Mastery Tests-Revised (WRMT-R/NU) (Woodcock, 1998)], multiple-choice tests of synonyms and multiple-choice questions about reading passages [e.g., Gates-MacGinitie Reading Tests, 4th. ed., (MacGinitie & MacGinitie, 2000)], oral questions about passages read silently or aloud [e.g., Diagnostic Reading Scales-Revised (Spache, 1981)], oral, multiple-choice questions about passages read aloud with the questions also presented in print [e.g., GORT-3 (Wiederholt & Bryant, 1992)], and choosing one of four pictures that best conforms to a sentence previously read silently [e.g., Peabody Individual Achievement Test-Revised (PIAT-R/NU) (Markwart, 1998)]. Although there are strong correlations among **groups** of students taking some of these tests, individual variation reveals differences in aspects of reading comprehension tested.

17. While it is important to evaluate everything that is relevant to the particular student's reading, **do not automatically test everything that could be tested**. If, for example, the student easily and accurately pronounces and correctly spells almost all words that are unfamiliar but phonetically regular, there is little need to test auditory discrimination. Even if the student's auditory discrimination is imperfect, the student is compensating successfully. Do not fall into the trap of testing for, finding, and recommending "remediation" of problems that do not exist or do not interfere with the student's reading.

18. Similarly, **it is generally best to test higher-order skills first**. Begin by having the student attempt to read aloud unfamiliar passages at or above the student's grade level and by having the student answer factual and inferential comprehension questions about grade-level or higher passages. This will quickly reveal how much, if any, testing is needed for more basic skills, such as auditory discrimination, phonological awareness, rapid naming, primary and advanced phonics skills, structural analysis, use of context cues, and sight vocabulary. In contrast, an assessment that begins with the more basic skills may take a long time in revealing that they did not need to be tested.

19. **Pay attention to referral questions and background information**. View the information with informed skepticism, but also keep it in mind. If, for example, one of the referral concerns is that the student seems to have a short span of attention, include an assessment of the student's comprehension of long reading passages. A test consisting of only brief passages would miss essential information. If, for another example, the referral cites special difficulty with reading comprehension in high school science and social studies courses, assess higher-level reading skills for technical material. You may ultimately determine that the background information or referral question is inaccurate—hence the need for skepticism—but always consider the information during the assessment.

20. **If they are not offered, solicit specific referral questions from teachers, the student and, at least for students who are not adults, parents**. Quote each question or concern in your report and reply to each one, even if it is only to say you do not know. Consistent application of this rule will eventually elicit better questions from your referral sources, will increase acceptance of your recommendations, and will ensure that you always pay attention to potentially valuable information.

21. **Pay attention to the student**. Find out how the student assesses her or his own reading ability. Find out how much the student enjoys various kinds of reading. Learn about the student's reading interests and other interests that might be exploited for reading. Solicit complaints about previous and current reading instruction. See if the student has any recommendations for reading instruction.

22. **Carefully consider the student's educational history**. For example, limited phonics skills have very different instructional implications for students who have been taught primarily in whole language programs than for students who have been given intensive instruction in phonics.

23. **Do not allow assessment results to be used as numbers to mask whether a student needs help**. Focus evaluation reports, team deliberations, recommendations, and instruction on the realities of the student's situation, not on the numerical scores. If reading difficulties are interfering with the student's education, then the student needs help with reading, whatever the numbers from an evaluation.

Conclusion

The process of assessing a student's reading requires much more thought than simply selecting and administering a test battery. At every step in the process, the examiner must exercise cautious judgment and pay close attention to what is really happening. It is not enough only to assess individual reading components. Cause-and-effect relationships among the components must also be examined. The entire process should be undertaken to achieve the goal of determining what needs to be taught and how it might best be taught.

None of the standardized, normed tests covers all the components that might need to be assessed for a particular student, and none of these tests is without limits. However, when parts of different tests are combined in one assessment, the examiner must also consider differences among test norms. Does the difference between two test scores reflect a real variation in the student's skills, or just the difference between norms on two different tests?

Informal reading inventories can be tailored specifically to the needs of the assessment of a particular student, but they provide no normative information. Furthermore, an informal inventory that is designed to match the local curricula poses the danger of restricting possible instructional approaches that might be recommended only to those currently in favor. This restriction would seriously penalize any student whose needs did not match the currently popular, local model.

In general, testing should proceed downward from the highest-level skills expected of the student, through more fundamental skills, until solid foundations are reached. At each stage, the examiner should be asking why the student is doing something well or why the student is having difficulty with something else. The *what*s are the beginning of the assessment. The real value lies in the *why*s.

Appendix E: A Few Tests Measuring Some Aspects of Phonemic Awareness and Rapid-Automatized-Naming
Melissa Farrall, PhD and John O. Willis, EdD

TESTS	rapid naming	word discri-mination	rhym-ing	segmen-tation	isola-tion	dele-tion	substi-tution	blend-ing	graph-emes
(Note: Several of the tests below also include subtests of skills that are not represented by this chart.)									
Test of Auditory-Perceptual Skills - Revised (TAPS-R) Gardner (1997). Auditory Word Discrimination Subtest: identifying whether two words spoken by examiner are SAME or DIFFERENT.		X							
Test of Phonological Awareness (TOPA) Torgesen & Bryant (1994). Marking pictures of orally presented words that are distinguished by the same/different sound in final position.					X				
Rosner Test of Auditory Analysis Skills (TAAS) (1999). Say "cowboy" without the "cow." Say "picnic" without the "pic." Say "cart" without the /t/. Say "blend" without the /bl/.						X			
Lindamood Auditory Conceptualization Test (LAC) (1979) Using colored blocks to represent differences or changes in sequences of speech-sounds.							X		
Woodcock-Johnson III (WJ III) (2001) Incomplete Words, Sound Blending, Auditory Attention, Auditory Working Memory, Rapid Picture Naming, Word Attack, Spelling of Sounds, Sound Awareness.	X	X	X	X	X	X	X	X	X
Goldman-Fristoe-Woodcock Auditory Skills Test Battery (GFW) (1974). Listening to words on tape that sound alike pointing to the matching picture, repeating specified sounds in taped words, reading & spelling nonsense words, choosing pictures matching taped words broken into speech-sounds.		X			X			X	X
Roswell-Chall Auditory Blending Test (1997). Blending sequences of sounds spoken by the examiner.								X	
The Phonological Awareness Test (PAT) Muter, Hulme, & Snowling (1997).	X		X			X			X
The Phonological Awareness Test (TPAT) Robertson & Salter (1997).			X	X	X	X	X	X	X
Comprehensive Test of Phonological Processing (CTOPP) Wagner, Torgesen, & Rashotte (1999). Includes memory tests and phoneme reversal.	X			X		X		X	
Dynamic Indicators of Basic Early Literacy Skills (DIBELS) Kaminsky & Good (1998). Repeated-measures battery. One-minute subtests of accuracy/speed.	X			X	X			X	X
Pre-Literacy Skills Screening (PLSS) Cumrine & Lonegan (1999). Fifteen-minute screening test.	X		X	X		X		X	

338

References

Altus, G.T. (1953). WISC patterns of a selective sample of bilingual school children. *The Pedagogical Seminary and Journal of Genetic Psychology. 83*, 241-248.

Brody, S. (1987). *Study skills: Teaching and learning strategies for mainstream and specialized classrooms.* Milford, NH: LARC Publishing.

Chall, J.S. & Curtis, M.E. (1990). Diagnostic achievement testing in reading. In C.R. Reynolds & R. Kamphaus (Eds.), *Handbook of Psychological and Educational Assessment of Children's Intelligence and Achievement.* NY: Guilford Press.

Cumrine, L., & Lonegan, H. (1999). *Pre-Literacy Skills Screening.* Chicago, IL: Applied Symbolix.

Ekwall, E.E. (1981). *Locating and correcting reading difficulties (3rd ed.).* Columbus, OH: Charles E. Merrill Publishing Co.

Fuller, R. (1983). *In search of the I.Q. correlation.* Stony Brook, NY: Ball-Stick-Bird Publications.

Gardner, M.F. (1997). *Test of Auditory-Perceptual Skills – Revised.* Austin, TX: Pro-Ed.

Goldman, R., Fristoe, M. & Woodcock, R.W. (1974). *Goldman-Fristoe-Woodcock Auditory Skills Test Battery.* Circle Pines, MN: American Guidance Service.

Hammill, D.D. & Larsen, S.C. (1996). *Test of Written Language (3rd ed.).* Austin, TX: Pro-Ed.

Hammill, D.D. & McNutt, G. (1981). *The correlates of reading: The consensus of thirty years of correlational research.* Austin, TX: Pro-Ed.

Hynd, G. & Cohen, M. (1983). *Dyslexia: Neuropsychological theory, research, and clinical differentiation.* Boston: Allyn and Bacon.

International Reading Association. (1982). Misuse of grade equivalents: Resolution passed by the Delegates Assembly of the International Reading Association, April, 1981, *Reading Teacher*, January, p. 464.

Kaminski, R., & Good, R.H. (1998). *Dynamic Indicators of Basic Early Literacy Skills.* Eugene, OR: University of Oregon.

Kaufman, A.S. & Kaufman, N.L. (1998). *Kaufman Test of Educational Achievement, Brief Form* and *Comprehensive Form, Normative Update.* Circle Pines, MN: American Guidance Service.

Lindamood, C.H., & Lindamood, P.C. (1979). *Lindamood Auditory Conceptualization Test (rev. ed.).* Austin, TX: Pro-Ed.

MacGinitie, W.H. & MacGinitie, R.K. (2000). *Gates-MacGinitie Reading Tests (4th ed.).* Chicago: Riverside Publishing Company.

Markwart, F.C., Jr. (1998). *Peabody Individual Achievement Test-Revised Normative Update.* Circle Pines, MN: American Guidance Service.

Muter, V., Hulme, C., & Snowling, M.J. (1997). *Phonological Abilities Test.* New York: Psychological Corporation.

Robertson, C., & Salter, W. (1997). *The Phonological Awareness Test.* East Moline, IL: Linguisystems, Inc.

Rosner, J. (1999). *Test of Auditory Analysis Skills (TAAS) test forms.* Novato, CA: Academic Therapy.

Roswell, F.G. & Chall, J.S. (1992). *Diagnostic Assessments of Reading with Trial Teaching Strategies.* Chicago: Riverside Publishing Company.

Roswell, F., & Chall, J.S. (1997). *Roswell-Chall Auditory Blending Test*. Cambridge, MA: Educators Publishing Service, Inc.

RSEC Staff (1983). *School Self-rating Scale*. Milford, NH: Regional Services and Education Center.

Schultz, M.K. (1988). A comparison of standard scores for commonly used tests of early reading. *Communiqué*, Newsletter of the National Association of School Psychologists, *17*(4), 13.

Siegel, L.S. (1989). IQ is irrelevant to the definition of learning disabilities. *Journal of Learning Disabilities*, 22(8), 469-478, 486.

Slosson, R.L. (1991). *Slosson Oral Reading Test-Revised*. East Aurora, NY: Slosson Educational Publications.

Spache, G.D. (1981). *Diagnostic Reading Scales-Revised*. Monterey, CA: CTB/McGraw-Hill.

Torgesen, J., & Bryant, B. (1994). *Test of Phonological Awareness (TOPA)*. Austin, TX: Pro-Ed.

Torgesen, J., Wagner, R., & Rashotte, C. (1999). *Test of Word Reading Efficiency*. Austin, TX: Pro-Ed.

Wagner, R., Torgesen, J., & Rashotte, C. (1999). *Comprehensive Test of Phonological Processing*. Austin, TX: Pro-Ed.

Wechsler, D. (1949). *Wechsler Intelligence Scale for Children*. New York: Psychological Corporation.

Wechsler, D. (1974). *Wechsler Intelligence Scale for Children-Revised*. New York: Psychological Corporation.

Wechsler, D. (1991). *Wechsler Intelligence Scale for Children-Third Edition*. San Antonio: Psychological Corporation.

Wechsler, D. (1992). *Wechsler Individual Achievement Test*. San Antonio: Psychological Corporation.

Wiederholt, J.L. & Bryant, B.R. (1986). *Gray Oral Reading Test-Revised*. Austin, TX: Pro-Ed.

Wiederholt, J.L. & Bryant, B.R. (1992). *Gray Oral Reading Test-3rd ed.* Austin, TX: Pro-Ed.

Wilkinson, G.S. (1993). *The Wide Range Achievement Test (3rd ed.)*. Wilmington, DE: Wide Range, Inc.

Willis, J.O. (1977). Overall achievement test—cumulative evaluation reflecting educational ability level. *NH Personnel and Guidance Journal*, 6(1), 9.

Willis, J.O. & Dumont, R.P. (1998). *Guide to identification of learning disabilities (1998 NY State ed.)*. Acton, MA: Copley. [Available at: http://alpha.fdu.edu/~dumont/]

Willis, U. (1971). Personal communication.

Wolf, M., Bowers, P.G., & Biddle, K. (2000). Naming-speed processes, timing, and reading: A conceptual review. *Journal of Learning Disabilities*, 33(4), 387-407.

Woodcock, R.W. (1998). *Woodcock Reading Mastery Tests-Revised Normative Update*. Circle Pines, MN: American Guidance Service.

Woodcock, R.W., McGrew, K.S., & Mather, N. (2001). *Woodcock-Johnson III*. Itasca, IL: Riverside.

Chapter 12. Program Planning: Forging a Link Between Assessment and Instruction

Generally, students are referred for reading assessment or for individualized instruction when someone perceives that their reading ability is lower than anticipated in comparison to the performance of their peers. Usually, assessment is recommended as a means of establishing the area(s) in which reading development is lagging as well as to determine the extent that developmentally earlier foundation skills are present to support further growth. In order for the assessment process to be useful, examiners and teachers need to translate assessment findings into instructional objectives that appropriately match the student's reading strengths and needs.

By planning and developing effective reading instruction through attentive use of initial and follow-up assessment findings, instructors can maximize their students' progress (Chall & Curtis, 1990; Curtis & Longo, 2000; Holzman, 1990; Honig, 1998; Moats, 2000/1999). This chapter explores the process of forging a link between assessed reading needs and effective instruction. The discussion reviews circumstances in which assessment data indicate that additional testing is needed and also illustrates the relationship between various reading abilities and specific instructional objectives. Table 12.1 (following page) presents a global summary of reading needs, assessments, and related instructional strategies in order to provide an overview of issues under discussion.

Table 12.1. Reading: Linking Needs, Assessment, and Instruction. This brief sketch suggests the sequential scope, but not the depth, of reading development, assessment, and relevant instruction.

Area in Need of Development	Type of Assessment	Reading Stage (Chall, 1983)	Focus of Teaching Strategies
receptive/expressive language inner language to direct own actions	Oral Language Hearing/Vision	0	See Chapter 2 read to child; talk with child; listen and respond to child's talk
segment spoken words into syllables/rimes/sounds blend spoken syllables, onset/rimes into words blend spoken phonemes into words remember and retell familiar stories enjoy listening to stories/making up stories	Phonemic Awareness (Auditory Perception) Oral Language Hearing/Vision	Transition 0 - 1	See Chapter 3 read aloud often; chant nursery rhymes/repeating songs/poems identify words/pictures/objects that begin/end with /x/ sound orally segment/blend words, syllables, phonemes discuss activities and memories, define unfamiliar words
correspond letters, and letter-clusters to sounds blend sounds to read words recognize 3- and 4-letter words in rhyme families recognize "glue" words such as "which, is, that" read stories written mostly in one-syllable words enjoy listening to and understanding stories with a variety of common story structures	Phonemic Awareness Word Decoding Hearing/Vision Rapid-naming Comprehension	1	See Chapters 4, 6 match letters/sounds: display pictures/ words with initial letter read aloud charts of CVC, blend, vowel-team word families read aloud stories and passages written with the word families dictate words and sentences incorporating the word families spell, write simple sentences with the word families and glue words read stories aloud often while student sounds along with the reader
read familiar, connected text with accuracy read with appropriate pace/intonation/pausing read polysyllabic words in connected text read without drawing attentional resources away from comprehension	Reading Fluency Rapid-naming Comprehension Stage 1 assessments as needed	2	See Chapters 5, 6 repeated reading of words, phrases, passages (oral, choral, silent) teacher tape short text; student reread with tape often learn/apply advanced decoding strategies (syllables/affixes) read familiar stories often; repeated reading/writing of longer words
expand knowledge of words and their meanings select among multiple meanings of a word recognize specialized meanings of words recognize words in varied contexts use many words in varied contexts in context, learn words for abstract concepts	Reading/Oral Vocabulary Comprehension Stage 1 & 2 assessments as needed	3 - 5	See Chapter 9 directly state/explain/demonstrate meanings, applications create opportunities for students to tell/explain/demonstrate retrieve/use target word to discuss relevant issues and contexts read/write target word embedded in sentences/paragraphs read widely and regularly
locate/state details when reading unfamiliar text identify central vs extraneous points in text synthesize details into main ideas attend to questions or problems that focus learning identify organizational schema of a passage summarize, extend, express learnings	Passage Comprehension Stage 1 & 2 assessments as needed	3 - 5	See Chapters 7, 8, 10 answer teacher/text questions; generate/answer own questions locate/classify details; sequence events develop crucial background concepts before/during reading identify organizational schema/summarize/discuss reading material apply and extend specialized or abstract concepts

HYPOTHESIS TESTING

As discussed in Chapter 11, reading assessment should typically begin with higher-level skills that are noticed to be lacking and then proceed downward until a foundation of more basic skills is established. Testing in this top-down fashion requires that the examiner make many judgments concerning whether reading difficulties revealed by particular assessments are, in fact, actual areas in need of instruction. Alternatively, are the assessments unveiling symptoms of difficulties at a more basic level of reading development?

An accurate answer to this question requires methodical and creative detective work (Budoff, 1972; Kaufman, 1979, 1994). Well-targeted instruction depends on an accurate assessment. As noted in Chapter 11, an accurate assessment need not test every underlying subskill of reading. However, it must be planned and guided by someone with a solid understanding of reading development in order to assure that specific subskills are tested adequately but not unduly. Selection of assessment instruments must also be guided by competency in recognizing the actual information yielded by various testing instruments in contrast to reliance on the name of the test, which may inaccurately suggest what it measures (Willis & Dumont, 1998).

With practice, attentive examiners increase their ability to stalk a reading problem through the steps of an assessment/instructional cycle:
   a) awareness of a difficulty;
   b) initial assessment;
   c) formation of tentative diagnostic hunches;
   d) further assessment if needed;
   e) initial instructional recommendations;
   f) confirmation, rejection, or adjustment of hypotheses and recommendations to reflect student's on-going progress;
   g) additional assessment if needed;
   h) formation of better informed hypotheses if needed; and,
   i) continuation of the cycle.

Competent examiners and teachers recognize that lack of anticipated progress in a carefully planned program does not indicate a student's failure but instead the need for analysis and adjustment of the program to fit the student's needs and abilities adequately (Brody, 1987).

CHAPTER ORGANIZATION AND SOME CAUTIONS

This chapter explores the sleuthing process of reading assessment and instruction by examining some common profiles of reading difficulty. These profiles are analyzed by considering strengths and needs presented during referral; types of assessments that document the nature of the specific profile; and related diagnostic findings. In addition, referral and assessment evidence are drawn on to develop recommendations for appropriate instruction.

The profiles selected for discussion are representative of reading difficulties commonly observed in schools. However, the profiles described here are by no means the only common reading difficulties found in schools, nor representative of all types of reading difficulties. It remains the responsibility and challenge of the skilled examiner/teacher to pursue whatever reading behaviors present themselves through a careful step-wise process in order to define the *actual* reading profile of a specific student.

Examiners and teachers are cautioned to avoid assiduously efforts to fit real, individual needs and strengths to prototypic patterns without regard for the nuances of each unique reader. And finally, when making recommendations and carrying out instruction, teachers are urged to help readers develop their strengths even while attending to remediation of weaknesses (Willis & Dumont, 1998).

With these cautions in mind, the following discussion examines differences among readers in their performance on specific types of reading tests along with the instructional implications of these differences. The discussion begins by considering variation in reading performance on passage comprehension tests and its reflection in several interesting reading profiles. Next, variation in performance on vocabulary meaning tests is considered. This is followed by a review of issues suggested by differing scoring patterns on oral reading fluency, rapid-naming, decoding, and phonemic awareness tests.

In each assessment area, several profiles are presented in order to illustrate that different instructional needs may underlie similar presenting symptoms. The variety of profiles may provide a sense of the diversity in reading development that appears in schools and the community. Table 12.2 (following pages) delineates each reading profile under review by briefly noting assessments used, performance level demonstrated, and instructional strategies recommended.

Table 12.2. **Profiles of Common Reading Difficulties: A Very Brief Summary.** (Read chapter 12 for necessary detail.)

Pro-file	Passage Comprehension: locate, classify sequence details & concepts; study strategies; application	Vocabulary: word meanings background breadth depth	Fluency: oral reading speed accuracy intonation pace rapid-naming	Word Decoding: letter-sound correspondence word analysis strategies	Phonemic Awareness: segment blend add delete syllables rimes phonemes	Diagnostic Hypotheses and Potential Recommendations
A	Low	OK	OK speed OK accuracy	OK	—	Passage comprehension is low but other areas adequate. Instruction in comprehension and organization skills.
B	Mixed	Mixed	OK speed OK accuracy	OK	—	Passage and vocabulary scores seem to vary in relation to topic familiarity. Basic comprehension skills seem ok. Decoding adequate. Develop background and vocabulary.
C	OK	Low Read High Oral	OK speed Low accuracy	OK short words Low long words	—	Oral vocabulary is high and decoding weak suggesting that comprehension is supported by great background. Decoding instruction is needed to realize potential.
D	Low	Low	OK speed OK accuracy	OK	—	Passage comprehension and vocabulary are low yet referral indicates basic organization and street-smart understanding is solid. Teach broad background concepts and word meanings.
E	Very Low	Very Low	OK speed OK accuracy	OK	—	Very low comprehension and vocabulary despite adequate decoding suggest limited language development. Intensive, concrete, direct teaching and practice with meanings, background concepts, and text study strategies.
F	Low	Low Read High Oral	Low speed OK accuracy OK rapid-naming	Accurate & Slow	—	High oral vocabulary and accurate, slow decoding, along with limited fluency, suggest an instructional need for practice of basic and advanced decoding patterns with repeated readings, timed readings, pleasure reading.
G	Low	Low Read High Oral	Low speed Low accuracy OK rapid-naming	Low	—	Oral vocabulary is high despite deficits in passage comprehension, fluency, and decoding. Provide instruction in decoding patterns and strategies with plenty of practice reading paragraphs and passages.

H	Low	Low Read Low Oral	Low speed Low accuracy Low rapid-naming	Accurate Slow	—	Reader needs to develop fluency through intensive, extensive, repeated readings of letter-cluster/sound patterns in words, phrases, passages along with much direct explanation of word meanings, background information, text formats, and genres.
I	Low	Low Read Low Oral	Low speed Low accuracy Low rapid-naming	Low and Slow	—	"Double-deficit" of low phonological skills and low rapid-naming with slow but steady reading progress. Base of phonemic awareness has developed. Continue systematic instruction in decoding with plenty of review and support for accuracy. Teach word meanings as well.
J	Low	Low Read High Oral	OK on Basic Low Advanced	OK Basics Low Infrequent	—	Oral vocabulary is high; reading is fluent on basic and intermediate passages; decoding is adequate for most words, but low for infrequent irregular words. Focus instruction on advanced word analysis strategies will decrease dysfluency, increase passage comprehension.
K	Low	Low Reading Low Oral		Low	OK	Comprehension, oral vocabulary, fluency, and decoding are weak. Phonemic awareness is intact from indirect environmental exposure. Needs direct teaching of unknown letter/cluster-sound patterns and word family rhymes practiced with lists, phrases, paragraphs.
L	Low	Low Reading Low Oral	Low speed Low accuracy OK rapid-naming	Low	OK	Profile similar to K but with solid phonemic awareness attributable to systematic home instruction. Offer intensive, prolonged teaching and practice of letter-sound correspondences, rhyming word groups, affixes, syllabic patterns.
M	Low	Low	Low speed Low accuracy OK rapid-naming	Low	Low	This young student exhibits weaknesses in all areas of reading. Systematic, intensive aural and print based phonemic awareness instruction is needed with follow-up assessment to determine whether cause is lack of exposure, learning disability, or other issues in order to appropriately pace later instruction.

Note: Emotional disability can inhibit reading progress. Instruction should focus on assessed reading needs; appropriate personnel should be involved to alleviate the emotional stress.

Reading Profiles and Related Recommendations

PASSAGE COMPREHENSION

This discussion of passage comprehension assessment and instruction will consider three profiles. Profile A, Arnold, scored low on passage comprehension by answering many items correctly early in the test, then missing a string of items beyond a clearly observable limit. Profile B, Bethany, also scored low on passage comprehension, but with performance that fluctuated depending on the content of the passage. And Craig scored appropriately for grade placement by comprehending passages written at and below grade level; yet Craig may need some short-term, reading intervention. These readers' specific profiles are discussed below in detail.

Profile A. An example of low comprehension and study skills coupled with strong vocabulary and decoding ability. The referral for Arnold indicates that he has difficulty answering questions or developing summaries related to assigned passages in science, social studies, and reading/language arts texts and trade books. It is noted that his vision and hearing were recently tested as normal.[1] In addition, the referral indicates that Arnold seems to possess a good meaning vocabulary relative to peers. Further, he seems to have had many home and school exposures to enriching experiences along with satisfying interactions and relationships with peers, teachers, and family.

Since reading assessment typically begins at the level at which difficulty is perceived, Arnold's assessment begins with tests of passage comprehension—the Kaufman Test of Educational Achievement-Comprehensive Form (K-TEA/NU) (Kaufman & Kaufman, 1998) and the Gates-MacGinitie Reading Tests, 4th edition (G-MRT) (MacGinitie & MacGinitie, 2000). If, as in Arnold's case, these tests suggest that passage comprehension is weak, additional testing is needed to determine the reading and language processes, as well as any other factors, that may be contributing to weak comprehension. Since Arnold's referral information suggests that vision, hearing, and emotional/social issues are unlikely to be contributing factors, his assessment will focus on reading and language processes that contribute to passage comprehension.

---

[1] It is necessary to check near point, far point, tracking, and binocular function to assure vision is not interfering with reading ability. The student who reads a wall chart at some 10 or 20 feet distance may need corrective lenses in order to read print at near point. In addition, complete hearing assessment requires impedance testing.

Measurement of knowledge of word meanings is a logical next step in assessment. Such information can indicate whether lack of word meanings and background concepts is making comprehension of passages difficult (Biemiller, 2000; Chall, 1987). In Arnold's case, this assessment is a useful follow-up to confirm referral information that suggests background is strong. A measure of Arnold's vocabulary, taken with the vocabulary subtest of the Gates-MacGinitie Reading Tests (G-MRT), indicates that word knowledge is similar to that of age and grade peers. Since this is a multiple-choice test, and consequently may not indicate any problems with retrieval of word meanings, word meanings are also assessed with the vocabulary subtest of the Woodcock Reading Mastery Tests-R (WRMT-R/NU) (Woodcock, 1998).

The WRMT-R/NU vocabulary subtest is used with caution since students often score low on it due to their difficulty with synonym, antonym, and analogy constructs, rather than with word meanings. However, Arnold performs well on this vocabulary measure. Together, the solid scores on the G-MRT and WRMT-R/NU provide some assurance that Arnold's passage comprehension difficulty is not an indication of lack of word meaning knowledge. The vocabulary scores also suggest that Arnold's low comprehension is probably not an indication of poor decoding skills since the words on the vocabulary test had to be deciphered in relative isolation.

When passage comprehension difficulties are noted, it is generally a good idea to test reading subskills at least to the level of decoding fluency on connected text. This is done to determine whether a lack of automaticity with the subskills of decoding and/or rapid-naming is drawing attentional resources away from the process of arranging and comprehending thoughts and concepts (Lovett, Steinbach, & Frijters, 2000; Lyon, 2000; Perfetti, 1985; Samuels, Schermer, & Reinking, 1992; Wolf, Bowers, & Biddle, 2000).

To check his reading fluency, Arnold is given the Gray Oral Reading Test-3 (GORT-3) (Wiederholt & Bryant, 1992). Arnold reads passages written at grade level without reversals, substitutions, inversions, or deletions, as well as with good pace, intonation, and pausing. In addition, he accurately answers questions concerning passages written several grades below current placement, but continues the pattern of weak comprehension of grade-level passages.

Since Arnold's reading fluency seems robust, and polysyllabic words within unfamiliar oral reading passages are read with ease and accuracy, further testing of isolated rapid-naming, decoding, or phonemic awareness skills may not be necessary. However, there remains some question concerning Arnold's ability to

348

decode fluently without requiring use of comprehension as an assist to word recognition. Therefore, the examiner takes a few minutes for an assessment of word decoding on isolated lists using the WRMT-R/NU. Such a test provides targeted evidence that Arnold does not need to rely on context to decode longer words.

With vision, hearing, emotional/social issues, word meaning knowledge, and decoding fluency eliminated as likely underlying factors, the referral and assessment evidence suggest that Arnold's reading comprehension difficulty probably lies in lack of skills such as locating, classifying, or sequencing information and ideas. To confirm this hypothesis, the examiner should study Arnold's errors and successes on the reading comprehension test items. If time permits, it would be instructive to help Arnold work through a few pages of his science textbook. If this is Arnold's difficulty, his comprehension will not be helped by further instruction in decoding or word meanings. Instead, he needs explicit instruction in comprehension techniques including: questioning, categorizing, outlining, and summarizing, both orally and in writing. These strategies need to be clearly explained and modeled during reading of content text (Call, 2000; Santa, Havens, & Harrison, 1989; Stotsky, 1986).

The examiner indicates that Arnold needs explicit instruction and modeling of comprehension techniques in order to enhance his ability to: pull information from the text, evaluate relevant and irrelevant details, and apply what is read to what else is under study concerning the topic. In addition, the examiner indicates that Arnold's reading assignments need to be supplemented with written study guides that ask specific questions, paragraph-by-paragraph and/or section-by-section, related to important concepts, details, and conclusions. These questions should be sequentially arranged to fill in a clear framework or outline that replicates the text's structure. At first, in addition to guiding Arnold's focus on the text, these questions will provide a model of how to pose relevant questions during reading of texts. As Arnold develops skill in self-generating appropriate questions, and as his comprehension improves, the frequency of the study guide questions for a particular assignment can be reduced. (See Chapters 7, 8, 10 for detailed descriptions of strategies appropriate for students whose reading difficulties lie in these areas.)

Profile B. An example of comprehension and vocabulary skill levels that vary with text familiarity, coupled with solid fluency and decoding skills. Bethany also has difficulty understanding the science text, but she seems to do better with social studies readings. As with Arnold, the referral indicates that Bethany has good vision and hearing and adequate social/emotional adjustment.

She performs below peers on the G-MRT and K-TEA/NU passage comprehension subtests. Unlike Arnold, Bethany's correct and erroneous responses are somewhat scattered.

Bethany answers several items correctly, then misses several, and next performs accurately on a few items that are more difficult. At several points in the testing, Bethany nearly meets the test's ceiling, then answers several advanced items correctly. Noticing this pattern, the examiner asks Bethany to describe the kinds of reading materials that seem easier to read and the kinds that seem more challenging. Bethany indicates that books on music, a hobby, are fun to read, but textbooks are challenging.

Again, with passage comprehension scores below expected levels, the examiner checks Bethany's vocabulary knowledge. Bethany's score on the G-MRT vocabulary subtest is somewhat low, but again with scatter showing greater vocabulary knowledge in some areas than others. To explore whether there is an easily defined pattern to the scatter, the examiner administers the WRMT-R/NU vocabulary subtest. The examiner's record booklet includes a grid to record the vocabulary items by subject area. Bethany's responses do not reflect a clear pattern of error related to science, social studies, or the humanities. Although such a pattern could give useful guidance, Bethany's lack of pattern directly related to an academic subject area in no way rules out the presence of splinter vocabulary knowledge.

To determine whether the vocabulary scatter might reflect splinter deficits in decoding skills rather than a lack of word meaning knowledge, the examiner administers the oral vocabulary subtest from the Diagnostic Assessment of Reading with Trial Teaching Strategies (DARTTS) (Roswell & Chall, 1992). When it is given to Bethany, the scatter again appears, suggesting that her splinter performance is not likely produced by limited decoding skills (since it does not require reading).

The examiner could have skipped the oral vocabulary test and stepped directly to a test of decoding fluency, which would also provide evidence concerning whether decoding deficits impede Bethany's comprehension. Either choice makes sense in Bethany's case since her ability to read and identify some difficult vocabulary words suggests that decoding is not interfering with her knowledge of word meanings. The scatter in her comprehension and vocabulary scores, with some correct responses in the upper range, also leads the examiner to suspect that scattered word meaning and general background knowledge are making passage comprehension difficult when the content area is unfamiliar, and that Bethany is not hampered by a lack of study skills or a weakness in decoding fluency.

Whether the oral vocabulary test is administered or not, decoding fluency should be checked. Such assessment provides evidence concerning potential gaps in decoding mastery and its influence on types of words that can be read and understood. Such assessment suggests whether a lack of decoding fluency is contributing to limited passage comprehension. In Bethany's case, the examiner finds that decoding is fluent since the student does not stumble when orally reading difficult passages. Further, the scatter that appeared in earlier passage comprehension tests surfaces again with passage comprehension items on the GORT-3.

After reviewing the referral and assessment information for Bethany, the examiner hypothesizes that mixed passage comprehension difficulties arise from gaps in knowledge of word meanings and background concepts. Further assessment could include a more comprehensive test of oral vocabulary, such as the Woodcock-Johnson III (WJ III) (Woodcock, McGrew, & Mather, 2001), and the WJ III oral test of science, social studies, and humanities knowledge. The examiner recommends that teachers introduce reading assignments by previewing vocabulary words and their meanings, and by preteaching any crucial background concepts that are prerequisite to understanding an assigned text. Recommendations for Bethany's instruction encourage exposure and practice with concepts, vocabulary, and applications in a broad array of areas since the gaps did not appear in selected content areas as measured by the WRMT-R/NU (Brody, 1993; National Reading Panel [NRP], 2000, Pressley, 2000). (See Chapters 8 and 9 for detailed discussion of vocabulary and background instruction.)

Profile C. An example of comprehension below potential in need of advanced decoding instruction. Craig is referred for reading assessment by a teacher who feels that this student is not performing to potential. The referral notes that the science text is written well above grade level and that Craig discusses the concepts competently but avoids reading in class and almost never completes written assignments. Vision and hearing are normal; Craig appears to have several friends; he seems very quick to brush aside any mention of academic difficulty.

When given the passage comprehension subtests of the K-TEA/NU and G-MRT, Craig scores similarly to average peers. In fact, he answers most items correctly on passages written at grade level and below; comprehension difficulty is apparent only on passages written above grade level.

When asked to reflect on his reading experiences, Craig gruffly indicates contentment with his current reading ability and expresses no desire for assessment or assistance. The examiner is tempted to attribute the referral to the difficulty of the school's science text since Craig scores firmly at grade level on passage comprehension, the goal of reading instruction. However, the entire class has not been referred for testing, and thus the examiner suspects a broader picture may be revealed through more detailed assessment.

In order to develop another perspective, the examiner administers the G-MRT vocabulary test of word meanings and finds low reading vocabulary scores that are incongruent with Craig's grade-level passage comprehension. The examiner recalls the articulate manner in which the youngster discussed the process of assessment. The examiner also considers the critical difference between reading words in isolation on a vocabulary test and reading words in context during passage comprehension testing (Curtis, 1987). Since Craig's reading vocabulary scores are much lower than his passage comprehension scores, the examiner begins to suspect that decoding deficits may be contributing to the low reading vocabulary scores.

It seems that Craig may be guessing from context to compensate for weak decoding when reading, even with grade level passages. To test this hypothesis, the examiner gives the DARTTS oral vocabulary subtest, (which does not require the student to read vocabulary items), and discovers that Craig scores extremely well. This suggests that Craig possesses a very broad and deep knowledge of word meanings and concepts that could support passage comprehension through the use of context clues until concepts become highly specialized.

Since Craig's oral vocabulary score is high, it is likely that he would be reading passages above grade level if decoding issues were not interfering with comprehension—the referral concern begins to make sense. To clarify the existence and nature of Craig's decoding difficulties, the examiner administers the GORT-3 to test decoding fluency. In addition, the word decoding subtests of the WRMT-R/NU are given to identify specific phonetic difficulties. Craig reads the GORT-3 passages with age-appropriate speed and intonation, but with many substitution errors, particularly on longer content words. Some of the substitutions tended to preserve meaning and Craig's GORT-3 passage comprehension performance is similar to that on the K-TEA/NU and G-MRT. Performance on the WRMT-R/NU word decoding subtests indicates that the student can read many one- and two-syllable words in isolation with accuracy, but that word analysis strategies are lacking for the decoding of less-familiar polysyllabic words (Brody, 2001).

The referral and assessment evidence suggest that Craig has been quite successful in compensating for his limited decoding strategies by using context clues and by memorizing words as logographic wholes. The referring teacher was correct to suspect that Craig could improve reading ability; the assessment evidence suggests that this is likely to occur if Craig learns phonological (letter-cluster/sound) patterns for decoding longer words. Craig's profile suggests that he can read passages at grade level with understanding. However, as his ability leads to interests in more specialized areas, it will be very difficult for Craig to keep up with reading that involves technical terms. Accurate reading of such material is difficult when relying only on context clues and the memorization of individual words as logographic wholes (Biemiller, 2000; Liberman, 1987; Moats, 2000).

Effective instruction needs to help Craig take time to learn advanced decoding strategies by providing him with direct, systematic instruction and practice in applying word analysis strategies to the decoding of longer words. In addition, teachers can help Craig practice decoding of longer words by presenting polysyllabic content words whole and in syllables to introduce vocabulary before assigning independent reading of text. (See Chapter 5 for a detailed description of advanced decoding strategies.)

Summary of passage comprehension profiles and recommendations. As seen in the profiles of Arnold, Bethany, and Craig, it would be misleading to assume that passage comprehension scores indicate simply the level of reading comprehension at which students should be taught. Instead, results of passage comprehension tests may represent a variety of underlying reading difficulties. Low passage comprehension scores may indicate difficulty with higher-level comprehension skills such as classifying, sequencing, and synthesizing; or, low scores may represent a lack of broad vocabulary and background knowledge; further, low scores could suggest a lack of decoding fluency (Armbruster, 1991; Brody, 1989; Curtis & Longo, 2000; Perfetti, 1984; Snow, Burns, & Griffin, 1998).

In addition, passage comprehension scores commensurate with peers cannot be assumed to represent proficient reading. Bright students who possess broad and deep vocabulary and background knowledge at times mask an underlying decoding difficulty by managing to compensate with context clues and logographic memorization of individual words. The masking through compensation can help very bright students hide their reading difficulties until they are in middle school or occasionally even beginning high school. At this point, the need to teach underlying decoding skills often is not understood. This may lead some students to seek help outside the school setting and others to abandon hope of developing reading proficiency commensurate with their intellectual ability.

READING/ORAL VOCABULARY

The following analysis considers the profiles of Daisy and Ernest, readers whose referrals indicate that vision and hearing are fine, passage comprehension scores are consistently low, and decoding fluency and word sounding skills are competent.   The discussion considers subtle differences in the assessment performances of Daisy and Ernest that suggest variation in the types of instruction needed to advance their acquisition of enhanced reading proficiency.

Profile D. An example of comprehension lowered by limited vocabulary and background. A solid base of fluent decoding is present. Daisy has difficulty comprehending texts and trade books written at grade level. Performance on the vocabulary subtest of the G-MRT places her at the bottom of the 2nd quartile—performing near the top of the bottom third of the class. Assessment with the fluency and word recognition subtests of the DARTTS suggests that decoding fluency and word recognition are solid. Daisy converses easily with the examiner concerning daily, familiar topics, but becomes an active listener when encouraged to discuss reactions to an international political event.

Referral information indicates that Daisy is well organized, tries hard, seeks clarification on assignments and directions, and reliably responds in a streetwise, competent manner to unexpected events in the classroom. Although Daisy's assignments are well organized and neat, their content often misses the mark. Referral information also indicates that Daisy bears much responsibility in the care of two younger siblings.

Daisy's referral and assessment data suggest that she seems to possess limited reading comprehension and vocabulary knowledge, although she demonstrates strong organization, sequencing, and synthesizing skills within familiar, non-academic contexts.   Daisy also demonstrates competent reading fluency and word decoding. Since Daisy's organizational and decoding skills seem strong, reading comprehension as well as vocabulary knowledge seem to lag due to lack of experiences and exposures (Biemiller, 2000; Snow, Burns, & Griffin, 1998; Stanovich, 1994). The WJ III vocabulary and knowledge tests would allow further exploration of this question.

Together, these factors suggest that Daisy's instructional plan should include direct, explicit instruction in meanings of unfamiliar words, along with direct explanation of unfamiliar background concepts. In addition, her school day should include many opportunities to develop reading vocabulary meanings and background knowledge through application of newly learned vocabulary during wide reading. In many ways, Daisy represents an ideal candidate for Title I services since her low comprehension skills appear attributable to a lack of instruction and exposure to broad and deep background experiences and language rather than to learning disabilities.

Profile E. Comprehension compromised by very limited vocabulary and background. Adequate decoding skills provide a base for growth. Ernest's assessment procedures and test results are similar to Daisy's except that both vocabulary and passage scores are lower—deep in the 1st quartile. Nevertheless, his decoding and fluency skills are solid. However, referral information suggests that Ernest lacks the organizational skills and streetwise knowledge demonstrated by Daisy.

Ernest's profile seems to reflect limited language development that is more pervasive than Daisy's limited vocabulary and background knowledge. Such a profile may appear whether the underlying difficulty is from lack of exposure, slower intellectual maturation, or a learning disability that affects language processing and facile assimilation of word meanings, syntax patterns, and textual organization. Ernest's apparent language limitations suggest that it would be wise to refer him for a psychoeducational and/or language evaluation.

Ernest needs extensive, intensive, concrete, direct, repeated instruction in the areas of vocabulary word meanings and background concepts. It is helpful to provide such instruction prior to the reading of stories, informational passages, and texts. Ernest needs many opportunities to engage in reading and being read to from challenging text while being guided through unfamiliar vocabulary and concepts with an explanatory discussion (Brody, 1993; Graves, Cooke, & Laberge, 1983; NRP, 2000). (Please see chapters 7, 8, 9, 10 for detailed suggestions related to vocabulary and background instruction.)

Summary of vocabulary profiles and recommendations. Students who lack word meaning and background concepts often score low on tests that measure vocabulary orally or in print. Clear, systematic vocabulary meaning instruction is crucial to students who do not extend their word meaning knowledge sufficiently through independent reading and the exposure of weekly class vocabulary tests. Intensive vocabulary instruction that is most useful begins with the teacher directly providing word meanings along with models of the word's use, followed by many opportunities for the student to define, use, and read the word in multiple contexts. Such instruction is particularly needed by students with learning disabilities, by students with limited cognitive abilities, and by students whose organizational skills and/or background knowledge have been limited by lack of experiential exposure to the academic language of school learning.

Not all students with limited language development have Ernest's and Daisy's advantage of early, systematic, and ample decoding instruction with sufficient practice to produce fluency. However, such instruction is particularly important for students with limited language development. Once decoding is mastered, reading can be used to provide visual (print) exposure to language, vocabulary, and word meanings. Print exposure can reinforce and augment auditory (talk) exposure that is not present in the community environment or that is not processed particularly well by students with learning disabilities (Carnine, 2000; Stanovich, 1986, 1994).

READING FLUENCY

This section presents five profiles related to difficulties with decoding fluency. The number of profiles in this section reflects the importance and complexity of this reading component as the gateway from beginning reading to advanced reading comprehension success (Adams, 1994; NRP, 2000; Perfetti, 1985; Wolf, Bowers, & Biddle, 2000). Since many adult illiterates were overcome by failure at this stage of reading development (Chall, 1996), examiners need to be particularly sensitive to assessment of reading fluency.

Published assessment instruments that measure fluency, such as the GORT-3, DARTTS, or Diagnostic Reading Scales-81 (DRS-81) (Spache, 1981), are very useful but somewhat cumbersome to administer. They require use of detailed coding of insertions, omissions, reversals, inversions, and repetitions, and some need timing of passage reading, and noting of intonation and attention to punctuation cues (Salvia & Ysseldyke, 2000). The Test of Word Reading Efficiency (TOWRE) (Torgesen, Wagner, & Rashotte, 1999) provides a very quick, superficial assessment of single-word reading fluency. Proficient and regular use of fluency tests is crucial since they give an examiner a wealth of diagnostic information concerning a critical juncture in reading development.

In addition, fluency assessment sometimes requires use of instruments such as the rapid-naming subtests of the Comprehensive Test of Phonological Processing Processing (CTOPP) (Wagner, Torgesen, & Rashotte, 1999). These instruments measure rapid-automatized-naming (RAN)—an ability that contributes to fluency.

Rapid-naming is measured with tasks that require timed naming of symbols such as colors, single letters, numbers, or pictures (of common objects such as a cat) that are presented visually on a list or grid. The task of naming the symbols on the list replicates the aspect of reading involved with quickly translating printed symbols into spoken words. However, naming common visual symbols does not require phonological (letter-cluster/sound) decoding skill. Therefore, rapid-naming tasks provide a means of testing speed of symbol-naming separately from accuracy and speed of phonological (letter-cluster/sound) decoding.

Since fluency appears to depend on both automatic phonological (letter-cluster/sound) decoding skill and automatic rapid-naming ability, when questions of fluency arise, both aspects need to be checked (Lovett, Steinbach, & Frijters, 2000; Wolf, Bowers, & Biddle, 2000). If a reader performs well on passage fluency tests such as the GORT-3, rapid-naming is likely to be fine. However, when passage fluency scores are low, rapid-naming testing, along with word-decoding testing, is needed to determine whether the difficulty lies in phonological decoding, rapid-naming, or both. This determination can translate into lesson plans that give more weight to teaching unfamiliar letter-cluster/sound patterns or to practice with previously learned patterns as needed. (See Chapter 5 for further detail on fluency.)

Profile F. An example of comprehension compromised by lack of decoding automaticity despite adequate rapid-naming skill, adequate decoding knowledge, and extensive oral vocabulary. Fiona illustrates the importance of decoding fluency tests in understanding reading disability. Fiona performs poorly on passage comprehension and reading vocabulary tests, but scores well on the DARTTS oral vocabulary subtest. This suggests to the examiner that Fiona's underlying reading difficulty may rest with decoding. Rather than taking the recommended step-wise progression and next testing reading fluency, the examiner hopes to lighten the testing load by skipping the cumbersome fluency tests and going directly to measures of word decoding.

Consequently, the next test administered is the WRMT-R/NU word decoding test. To the examiner's surprise, Fiona performs quite well, reading even unfamiliar polysyllabic words to grade level. The examiner notices that Fiona requires a great deal of **time** to read each word and that some items would have been failed if the test were strictly timed. The Wide Range Achievement Test-3 (WRAT3) (Wilkinson, 1993) and the Slosson Oral Reading Test-Revised (SORT-R) (Slosson, 1991) are timed for this purpose, and one could have been given for confirmation.

Since Fiona's difficulties remain a mystery, the examiner administers the GORT-3. The results are far below grade level in speed, but accuracy remains good. This suggests that either: 1) most of her attention is needed for accurate phonological (letter-cluster/sound) decoding, leaving little available for comprehension, or 2) her decoding skills are fine but her rapid-naming skills are weak. To determine whether one or both of these problems underlie Fiona's weak comprehension, the rapid-naming subtests of the CTOPP are given. Fiona scores in the normal range on these tasks. Considered together with the other test results, this suggests that it is lack of decoding speed that impedes Fiona's comprehension. If decoding were practiced to enhance automatic recognition of letter-sound correspondences and common syllable patterns, Fiona could then allocate more attention to understanding text concepts.

To test this hypothesis, the examiner administers the DARTTS subtests that measure reading fluency with and without accompanying comprehension questions. Fiona decodes accurately on both assessments, but with much greater speed when comprehension is not assessed. These findings suggest to the examiner that Fiona may attempt to sacrifice comprehension for speed (when not in a testing situation) in an effort to get through the reading of connected text—a habit that ultimately defeats its own purpose.

Since the referral information indicates no hearing, vision, or emotional issues, and also suggests that Fiona follows discussions of abstract concepts well in class, the examiner recommends lots of practice to develop decoding automaticity oral and silent reading and rereading of stories and paragraphs, interspersed with questions to check comprehension as speed increases. Recommendations include "warm-up" with repeated oral readings and repeated oral timed readings of words, syllables, prefixes, and suffixes that follow specific letter-cluster/sound patterns on lists of word and phrases. This is to be followed by oral reading of passages and/or stories that include the words under study. (Brody, 2001; Leslie & Allen, 1999; Samuels, Schermer, & Reinking, 1992; Wolf, Miller, & Donnelly, 2000).

Since Fiona's lack of decoding automaticity is mild and not intertwined with lack of phonological knowledge, these oral reading practice activities can occur in a reading circle, through choral reading in a whole class, or in a smaller setting with an aide or adult volunteer. In addition, Fiona, needs to be provided with multiple opportunities and rewards for independent, silent, pleasure reading in materials that were written at her mastery level. This would be facilitated by an interview to identify current and potential reading interests.

Frequent, informal follow-up testing through listening to Fiona's oral reading of passages along with checking her comprehension with questions concerning the material read, will indicate when her decoding becomes automatic and no longer draws attention away from comprehension. At that point, repeated practice on lists is no longer needed. Her fluency and comprehension are likely to be maintained so long as she continues to read extensively while answering questions, orally or in writing, about what she has read. (See Chapter 5 for detailed strategies to improve fluency.)

Profile G. An example of comprehension compromised by lack of decoding knowledge as well as lack of decoding automaticity. Oral vocabulary knowledge and rapid-naming skill are present to support comprehension. Referral information indicates that Gerald demonstrates articulate and focused verbal class participation. However, he seems unable or unwilling to read since he engages in distracting activities when directed to begin reading assignments, and routinely asks to leave the room when assigned a turn at oral reading. Notes from Gerald's cumulative folder indicate that he stumbled often during oral reading in earlier years. Vision and hearing are normal, and Gerald seems otherwise well adjusted.

The referral suggests to the examiner that Gerald's difficulties may lie in the basic decoding processes and that passage comprehension may be thwarted by his limited decoding abilities. The examiner administers the WRMT-R/NU passage comprehension subtest to record a base-line score against which to measure future instructional effects. Oral vocabulary, rather than reading vocabulary, is tested with the DARTTS and is strong, as anticipated by the referral.

Next, the examiner administers the GORT-3 and finds that Gerald reads very slowly and with many errors. Little time is taken up by the assessment since Gerald quickly reaches the ceiling on the passage comprehension and decoding fluency tests. Since Gerald shows dysfluency, the rapid-naming subtests of the CTOPP are given. Gerald performs well on these tasks. Now, the examiner focuses on measuring Gerald's skill in decoding of words in isolation. When administering both the real-word and phonetically regular non-word lists on the WRMT-R/NU, the examiner pencils in each nonstandard response (Willis & Dumont, 1998). Unlike Fiona, Gerald makes many decoding errors.

Based on the referral information and the assessment findings, the examiner stresses the need to teach decoding patterns and principles directly and systematically with patterned word lists, accompanied by multiple opportunities to practice reading those word patterns orally in sentences, paragraphs, and passages of text to provide reinforcement and speed transfer to broader text (Brody, 2001; Lyon, 2000; Stahl, Heuback, & Cramond, 1997; Wolf, Miller, & Donnelly, 2000).

Further, teachers are reminded that Gerald's strong oral vocabulary is an advantage that can foster continued development of background and concept knowledge at grade level. Teachers can facilitate such growth through lessons that teach content and measure understanding through oral means, along with reading and writing. These oral supports can be faded gradually as Gerald's decoding and fluency catch up with the potential demonstrated by grade-level oral vocabulary knowledge. If opportunities to learn and be evaluated orally on content knowledge are not provided, Gerald may give up and no longer maintain the intellectual competence that currently far exceeds his reading ability.

Profile H. An example of comprehension supported by solid knowledge of decoding strategies but compromised by slow rapid-naming skill and low vocabulary knowledge. In contrast to Fiona and Gerald, Heidi exhibits weak oral vocabulary knowledge in addition to limited reading fluency. The referral for Heidi indicates adequate vision, hearing, and emotional well-being. Heidi sometimes seems hesitant to express ideas in class. When pressed, she generally provides a reasonable response. Her teacher has a feeling that Heidi possesses greater potential than comes across in class but isn't sure how to tap it.

K-TEA/NU and G-MRT tests of passage comprehension, and DARTTS tests of oral vocabulary and reading fluency, bear out the difficulties predicted by the referral. However, a test of Heidi's decoding indicates adequate word recognition and knowledge of word analysis strategies. Consequently she is given the CTOPP rapid-naming subtests, on which she scores far below the norm.

The referral and assessment results suggest that Heidi needs extensive practice in order to develop her speed and ease of word-naming and word-meaning retrieval. Heidi's practice needs to include repeated and timed readings of words, phrases, sentences, and passages that follow specific letter-cluster/sound patterns, along with explicit instruction in unknown word meanings. Such practice seems to aid in improving adequacy, accuracy, and availability of word memories and and their retrieval processes to increase reading fluency (Lovett, Steinbach, & Frijters, 2000).

Because Heidi is weak in rapid-naming and vocabulary, her needs for practice are much greater, and of much longer duration, than Fiona's. The extensive practice needed in order for Heidi to automatize retrieval of many words and their meanings exceeds what generally is practicable during whole class

360

instruction—most students improve dysfluency that results from lack of practice with much less repetition than is needed in instances of rapid-naming difficulties.

Consequently, arrangements need to be made for Heidi to receive repeated, oral practice with a learning disabilities or language specialist, or an aide who is guided by a specialist, to match the level of repetition and practice to Heidi's needs. Heidi's ability to accurately, but slowly, sound out specific phonologic word patterns indicates that she does not need instruction in order to identify specific phonologic word patterns. In fact, Heidi may brush off initial instruction by showing the instructor that she can read the patterns under practice, albeit slowly. This demonstration must not deter the instructor from providing plenty of repeated practice toward *rapidly* reading words of those patterns on lists of words and phrases, and in passages (Brody, 2001; Wolf, Miller, & Donnelly, 2000).

In addition, unlike Fiona who exhibits strong oral vocabulary, Heidi needs to be given direct explanations of unfamiliar word meanings and background information along with fluency instruction. Heidi does not already possess broad and deep vocabulary and background knowledge with which to process living and reading experiences, nor does she recognize a variety of story and text plots. Until these are developed, Heidi needs direct teacher feedback to assure that fluency practice is done with accuracy since unfamiliar story content cannot predictably confirm whether material was decoded with accuracy. In addition, teachers need to prepare Heidi for independent reading by directly and explicitly previewing the vocabulary meanings of words in the assigned material as well as by previewing the gist of the material to be read (Biemiller, 2000; Brody, 1993; Graves, 1987; Graves et al., 1983; Stahl, Heubach, & Cramond, 1997).

In short, Heidi's program needs to provide sustained, long-term direct instruction in vocabulary meanings, explicit descriptions of literary language and conventions, along with extensive repeated reading practice in materials that exhibit the letter-cluster/sound patterns, vocabulary, and literary characteristics she is studying. Such instruction will enhance Heidi's fluency and background, and facilitate learning from a variety of text formats and genres. Through intensive instruction, Heidi can increase her familiarity with a wide range of concepts and, in turn, such familiarity can confirm accurate decoding during independent pleasure reading and fluency practice (Chomsky, 1978; NRP, 2000; Pressley, 2000).

Although Heidi shows weaknesses in both rapid-naming and vocabulary knowledge, her solid base of phonological decoding skills, developed through earlier systematic instruction, will make her reading progress more rapid than if she had not received that solid foundation.   (See Chapter 5 for detailed fluency strategies and chapters 8 and 9 for background and vocabulary development strategies.)

Profile I. An example of comprehension compromised by a "double-deficit"—limited decoding knowledge and inadequate rapid-naming skill. A base of phonemic awareness, developed through explicit, direct instruction, is present, although oral meaning vocabulary is weak. Ike is referred for end-of-year testing prior to his special education annual review. His teacher questions what direction to take with future instruction since Ike's progress is slow. After a year of intensive instruction, his reading is still well below grade level and filled with inconsistencies. Some days, Ike seems to read fairly smoothly, especially in text that follows the very patterns that he has been practicing. Other times, his reading is choppy and slow and he needs to be coaxed to "try." His teacher is concerned that it may be a waste of time to continue the laborious process of systematically teaching Ike to read since his progress is so slow and sometimes not apparent. She wonders if he will ever be able to read independently.

A K-TEA/NU passage comprehension subtest and DARTTS oral vocabulary subtest are given to compare with previous testing and note current progress for future comparison. Although Ike's scores are well below age and grade level, Ike has scored more correct responses compared to previous testing and shows small gains over prior years.

Aware that Ike exhibited difficulties in phonemic awareness, decoding, and rapid-naming during the prior end-of-year testing, the examiner is not surprised by concerns that fluency is still weak, but wants to see how much progress has been made toward building the base skills that can eventually support fluency. The examiner decides that it is important to measure for gains in these areas first, before giving fluency tests that may tire and discourage a student whose skills are quite low. The examiner also suspects that testing the subskills that underlie fluency first may "prime" Ike for better performance on fluency tests. The examiner notes the testing order, and its intent, in the written report.

First, Ike's phonemic awareness skills at the syllable, onset-rime, and phoneme levels are checked with the CTOPP. He is able to complete the syllable and onset-rime (word-family) tasks accurately and much less hesitantly than noted in the previous year's report. Segmenting words into individual phonemes shows less improvement. This is expected since awareness of syllables and onset-rime skills typically appear earlier, developmentally, than segmenting of individual phonemes. Since onset-rime segmenting skills are particularly predictive of later reading success (Goswami, 2000), Ike and his teachers can be pleased that much concentrated work on phonemic awareness through the use of print has reaped positive results.

Next, Ike's word decoding skills are tested with the WRMT-R/NU real-word and phonetically regular non-word lists. Again, though below grade level, Ike shows clear gains in the number and types of words that he can read. Next, rapid-naming subtests of the CTOPP are given and no significant gain is recorded. This is not surprising since Ike's instruction during the year was focused on reading words in lists, phrases, sentences, and paragraphs rather than naming symbols of objects, letters, and numbers in sequence. It appears that rapid-naming may need lots of practice to show modest gains when a "double-deficit" is present and that it is more likely to improve for specific items repeatedly practiced rather than for items not practiced (Lovett, Steinbach, & Frijters, 2000). It was a wise decision to have spent instruction time on reading and rereading words rather than isolated symbols since it is rapid reading of words that Ike will use in the future.

To complete Ike's assessment, the examiner gives the GORT-3 to determine whether any improvement has occurred in Ike's speed and accuracy in oral reading of passages. Again, although Ike scores well below grade level, he has made measurable gains over the prior year. He reads passages two levels higher than the previous year, with a little more speed and a little more accuracy. His responses to comprehension questions were minimal in the previous year. This time, he answers some correctly.

In making recommendations for Ike, the examiner stresses the need to continue with direct, systematic instruction in phonological (letter-cluster/sound) correspondences along with their repeated oral reading, untimed and timed, on lists of words and phrases following specific patterns, as well as in sentences and paragraphs written with those words. The examiner notes that the student and teacher should be pleased with the results since direct, systematic instruction with repeated oral practice has a slow but snowballing effect in improving "double-deficit" reading difficulties and the testing shows the beginning phases of such progress.

The examiner urges that the instructor use a comprehensive list of phonological patterns to select, teach, review, and note progress (see pp. 138-140 for a sample). Because the double-deficit makes learning to read "hard work" for student and teacher, it is especially important to chart progress, review, and celebrate each small step of accomplishment. To reduce loss of memory and retrieval speed for previously studied patterns, frequent review of patterns learned earlier (through reading on word and phrase lists as well as in sentences and paragraphs) needs to be built into lessons along with instruction in new material.

The examiner also recommends that oral reading instruction be paced carefully. When Ike is reading accurately, the lesson proceeds as planned. As soon as Ike begins to make mistakes, the instructor needs to name the misread word correctly and ask Ike to repeat it; and if another error occurs, do so again. If errors seem to be building, scaffold Ike to read one last word correctly, in order to end with a success experience, then change to a different task.

Part of the process of improving reading speed and accuracy involves building strong, clear memories of words, along with developing subconscious neurobiological pathways that retrieve those word-memories. Consequently, it is crucial that Ike practices reading the words accurately rather than inaccurately. Inaccurate practice will make muddy and confused memories of the words and the pathways to the words. Therefore, if a run of errors is about to occur, stop oral reading, take a breather, and come back later to the task. Begin first with accurate review, follow with direct instruction in newer material, then practice on the newer material, and finally practice with the review and newer material combined (Brody, 2001; Wolf, Miller, & Donnelly, 2000).

Unlike, Fiona, Gerald, and Heidi, Ike's "double-deficit" dysfluency will require much more intensive and prolonged teaching, practice, reteaching, and review. Although the work required for learning to read is great, students who begin their schooling with weak phonological and rapid-naming skills can learn to read with accuracy and understanding, provided they receive sufficient instruction (Bradley & Bryant, 1983; Goswami, 2000; Lyon, 2000). The rewards and opportunities that open with reading ability are worth the effort.

Profile J. An example of comprehension compromised on unfamiliar material by lack of knowledge and automaticity with advanced decoding skills. A base of adequate rapid-naming ability and strong oral vocabulary knowledge will support rapid learning with direct instruction. Jeb was referred for testing due to somewhat lower than average performance on written responses to class reading assignments. This difficulty contrasts sharply with Jeb's apparent understanding during class discussion and his willing and fluent reading of simple notes and stories. Vision and hearing are reported normal as is his emotional well-being.

Jeb demonstrates a common pattern on the passage comprehension tests with nearly 100 percent accuracy on K-TEA/NU and G-MRT lower-level passages, mixed accuracy on intermediate passages, and failure on advanced passages. The overall pattern and scores suggest a low-average reader—no cause for concern except that oral class performance is reported as at or above average.

The reading vocabulary subtest of the G-MRT reveals scores slightly below grade level, with most of the early and middle items answered correctly and only the more difficult items missed. These scores are commensurate with passage comprehension and, again, unremarkable until the examiner decides to follow a hunch and check oral vocabulary knowledge with the DARTTS. On this test, Jeb scores well at all levels, suggesting that some kind of decoding deficit may be lowering reading comprehension and reading vocabulary performance.

When administered the GORT-3, Jeb reads the beginning passages without error and the middle passages with very few errors—completing the beginning passages with good speed and the middle passages more slowly. When advanced passages are attempted, Jeb's reading speed decreases considerably, and errors on longer words creep into the profile along with substitutions, reversals, and omissions of short "function" words such as *a, the, then*. The rapid-naming subtests of the CTOPP are given and scores are normal. The WRMT-R/NU decoding subtests are administered next; they suggest that Jeb has a good grasp of basic decoding strategies but lacks knowledge for decoding longer polysyllabic words that follow infrequent patterns.

Synthesizing the referral and assessment evidence, the examiner hypothesizes that decoding automaticity is not an entrenched problem since Jeb performs well on simple text. Instead, similar to Craig, fluency seems to break down when attempted with unfamiliar, technical words for which Jeb lacks effective word analysis strategies. The examiner recommends that Jeb's reading comprehension be encouraged through direct, systematic instruction in word analysis strategies for advanced and atypical word patterns. (See Chapter 5 for advanced decoding strategies.)

The report notes that many adult readers are hampered in their otherwise competent reading by lack of these advanced decoding strategies (Chall, 1994; Strucker, 2000). The examiner recommends that teachers support Jeb's practice of unfamiliar letter-cluster/sound patterns during independent reading in the following way. When assigning independent reading, give Jeb a list of unfamiliar technical words that will appear in the passage. List these words whole in one column and separated by spaces, into syllables, in a parallel column. Read the list of words orally to Jeb. Ask Jeb to read the lists back orally, first reading a word in syllables, then whole. Since Jeb's vocabulary is very strong, he often will not need to be taught the meaning of these words—but do tell the meaning if he asks. As Jeb becomes familiar with letter-cluster patterns, begin asking Jeb to give the first reading of the words—starting by reading the syllables, then blending them into the word.

Summary of fluency profiles and recommendations. Lack of decoding fluency can compromise passage comprehension even when readers possess extensive background and vocabulary knowledge. An adequate reading assessment must determine whether students have developed sufficient fluency to engage fully in reading comprehension. Underdeveloped fluency may arise from an absence of word-decoding instruction and/or from insufficient oral reading practice in earlier grades. Fluency can also be compromised by weak rapid-naming skill.

Sometimes reading dysfluency is attributable to a curriculum that is deficient in direct, systematic decoding instruction supplemented by plenty of oral reading practice. Other times, it reflects that a student's learning difficulty requires **intensive** practice with letter-cluster patterns to improve decoding skills and/or to enhance rapid-naming of words in print. When dysfluency is entrenched, instruction must extend well beyond the duration typically provided to teach letter-sound correspondences, word families, and advanced word analysis strategies to elementary-grade students.

WORD DECODING

We have already considered several profiles in which word decoding is the underlying factor contributing to reading difficulty. Craig, Gerald, and Jeb are representative of the difficulties experienced by readers who have difficulty with decoding despite **strong oral vocabularies and rich experiential backgrounds**. The two profiles considered below illustrate the nature of decoding difficulties and instruction among students who, unlike Craig, Gerald, and Jeb, exhibit **limited oral vocabulary and experiential background**.

Profile K. An example of comprehension impeded by lack of knowledge and automaticity with basic decoding skills. A base of adequate rapid-naming ability and phonemic awareness is present. Kelly's referral indicates that she exhibits halting and inaccurate oral reading, confusions concerning several letter-sound correspondences, and a lack of familiarity with many of the terms that the teacher uses during instruction. Kelly's vision and hearing are adequate. Based on performance in class discussions, activities, and field trips, the teacher suspects that Kelly comes to school with limited exposure to literary language and thought structures.

The examiner quickly takes a baseline passage comprehension measure using the K-TEA/NU Comprehensive Form. Since it is suspected that problems lie in the more basic processes, the examiner selects the K-TEA/NU, which exposes the student only to those items needed to establish a baseline, record performance, and reach a ceiling. This approach may decrease testing stress for Kelly by avoiding the many items that must be perused to complete the G-MRT.

Since the referral indicates that Kelly has difficulty with decoding, the examiner measures oral vocabulary word meanings with the DARTTS oral vocabulary test. As expected, the results are low. Next, the GORT-3 is administered to establish an oral reading fluency baseline; the results are low as expected, but the testing is useful since the examiner records the errors verbatim for later use in instructional planning.

The examiner tests word decoding using only the real-word subtest of the WRMT-R/NU. Again errors are recorded verbatim rather than only correct/incorrect in order to provide useful instructional planning data. The examiner now tests rapid-naming with the appropriate subtests from the CTOPP, followed by administration of several phonemic awareness measures from the same test. Results indicate that Kelly's rapid-naming is fine and that she is able to segment and blend syllables, onset-rime, and individual phonemes.

Since Kelly's phonemic awareness and rapid-naming seem to be intact, the referral and assessment evidence suggests that Kelly's weak decoding and fluency skills are the result of insufficient instruction and practice with decoding a wide range of phonological (letter-cluster/sound) patterns. Although Kelly has limited vocabulary in the realms of academic and literary language, a foundation of phonemic awareness is present to facilitate successful mastery of decoding knowledge through direct instruction (Blachman, 2000; Honig, 1998; Goswami, 2000; Rath, 1990).

The examiner recommends that Kelly receive instruction in letter-sound correspondences that are not yet mastered, in word-family rhyme patterns that are not yet known, and in word analysis strategies such as recognition of common affixes and syllabic patterns (Juel & Minden-Cupp, 2000; NRP, 2000). In addition, the recommendation also stresses the need to accompany instruction with exposure to literary language through peer reading, reading books accompanied by tapes, and being read to by the teacher, an aide, or a school volunteer (Chomsky, 1978; Leslie & Allen, 1999; Snow, Burns, & Griffin, 1998).

Profile L.   An example of comprehension lowered by lack of knowledge and automaticity with basic decoding skills. A base of adequate rapid-naming ability and phonemic awareness developed through explicit intensive instruction is present. The reading behaviors of Len are very similar to those of Kelly. Again, class performance suggests that Len has little background exposure to literary language and broad experiences. However, the examiner's contact with the parent contradicts this perception by indicating that the child is read to often and participates in a variety of family outings and experiences. Further, it is learned that the parents interact extensively with the child in language activities linked with written words. These activities include the repetition of rhymes, the playing of word-sounding games such as forming an onset sound and guessing a word that follows, and forming word families with plastic, magnetic letters by changing the initial, medial, or final consonant.

The examiner conducts Len's assessment using the same routine followed with Kelly. The evidence gathered from Len's assessment is the same as that for Kelly. Similar to Kelly, Len needs instruction in unfamiliar letter-sound correspondences and unknown word family patterns. However, the examiner suggests a small but crucial difference in recommendations for instruction. Len needs much more intensive and repeated practice in phonological (letter-cluster/sound) decoding since Len's difficulties seem to stem from a learning disability rather than from limited instruction and practice with reading. While Kelly does not appear to have a learning disability since phonemic awareness skills were developed through limited home and school exposure, Len's progress likely would be much further behind if he had not received direct phonemic awareness coaching in the home setting.

Summary of word decoding profiles and recommendations. Readers may exhibit a lack of decoding skill as a result of insufficient instruction or inadequate opportunities for practice. Decoding instruction is typically provided during the elementary school years. When basic decoding instruction is required beyond that time, the need reflects that sufficient instruction was not provided at an earlier, more developmentally appropriate time, or that a learning disability is prolonging the period of time needed to master decoding skills. No matter what the student's age, if decoding instruction is needed, direct, systematic instruction in unfamiliar phonological (letter-cluster/sound) patterns is needed to develop the prerequisite base for independent reading. (See Chapters 4 through 6 for detailed descriptions of decoding instruction techniques.)

Timely, clear instruction in decoding skills is particularly important for students whose backgrounds and out-of-school experiences provide only limited

368

exposure to language and literacy activities and experiences. Research shows that these students are at particular jeopardy since it is only through mastery of the code that they will be able to competently access the world of books as a means of gathering rich literacy experiences independently. This risk is greatly reduced when schools offer ample, clear instruction in letter-sound correspondences, word-family rhymes, and word-analysis elements such as common affixes and syllabic patterns (Blachman, 1991, 2000; Carnine, 2000; NRP, 2000; Rath, 1990).

Instruction in the code is equally important for students with learning disabilities. For these students, mastery of decoding can lead to better understanding of language, since reading offers exposure and reinforcement of language through print. This is particularly important for students with learning disabilities, when learning through listening is inefficient (Stanovich, 1986, 1994; Lerner, 2000). Effective decoding instruction includes direct explanation and demonstration of letter cluster patterns *and* opportunities to apply the target patterns to connected text. Such instruction enhances fluency, transfer, and motivation.

Teachers are sometimes tempted to abandon reading instruction and revert to a purely oral language approach when students need intensive decoding instruction. Although oral instruction is helpful in providing temporary assistance to foster learning in math, science, and social studies classes, it must be accompanied by decoding practice since learning through reading is particularly important for the very students who may need additional, intensive instruction to master decoding. As students develop adequate decoding fluency and word identification skills, reading begins to augment their development of language ability.

PHONEMIC AWARENESS

Phonemic awareness typically develops during the preschool and kindergarten years. However, insufficient environmental exposure and support, the presence of a learning disability, or a history of intermittent hearing loss, can contribute to phonemic awareness developing more slowly (Boucher, 1986; Willis, 1998). Students who lack adequate phonemic awareness, whether from lack of exposure, learning disability, or hearing loss, exhibit difficulty in learning letter-sound correspondences and in learning to sound and blend letters into words (Blachman, 2000; Liberman, 1987; Lyon, 1998; Rath, 1990).

Profile M. An example of comprehension lowered by lack of knowledge and automaticity with basic decoding skills. Phonemic awareness, but not rapid-naming, is underdeveloped. Mattie has been participating in choral reading, student authoring with invented spelling, and peer reading experiences in first grade over the past several months. Each time that the teacher takes an opportunity to hear Mattie read, letter-sound correspondence misunderstandings that arise in the reading are explored within the context of the word, sentence, and story. In early spring, the teacher refers Mattie for assessment since she does not seem to remember the three-letter words introduced through repetitive use in shared stories, consistently misreads "function" words such as *the* and *if*, and persists in misassociations between the letters she writes and the sounds of the words they are meant to represent. Referral information indicates that vision and hearing are normal.

The examiner follows the procedure used with Kelly and Len and establishes that Mattie's passage comprehension, vocabulary knowledge, and reading fluency are very low. Performance on the WRMT-R/NU decoding and letter recognition subtests and supplemental letter checklist indicates that Mattie cannot read many common three-letter words nor basic "function" words such as *is, the, when*. In addition, Mattie does not consistently recognize all the letters of the alphabet nor their sounds. Further, results of the CTOPP suggest that Mattie lacks phonemic awareness—the ability to segment and blend the sounds of syllables, onset-rime, and letters in words. However, her rapid-naming skills are intact.

The examiner recommends systematic, daily instruction in phonemic awareness tasks, both aural and with letters used to represent the sound patterns under study. The examiner also suggests that Mattie's situation be reviewed within a few months to determine her rate of progress with intensive instruction. If Mattie's progress is rapid, it would appear that the initial difficulties arise from a lack of sufficient exposure to phonemic awareness and decoding tasks as well as inconsistent instruction through the school's first-grade curriculum. Rapid progress would also suggest that the newly recommended instruction is providing sufficient intensity and practice. In addition, the examiner can use the review as another opportunity to stress the value of practice in phonemic awareness and decoding.

In contrast, if Mattie's progress is slow, it would appear that she may have a learning or language disability in addition to limited exposure and instruction. This would suggest that she may need involvement of the speech-language pathologist along with the learning disabilities specialist to adjust the content, pace, and frequency of her instruction to match her specialized needs. The review will offer a mechanism to check whether further testing is needed. Whatever the finding, the check-up will help to ensure that further instruction is paced appropriately for Mattie's rate of learning.

Summary of phonemic awareness profile and recommendations. Some students who exhibit weak phonemic awareness make good progress and catch up with their peers when given early, timely, and intensive instruction in phonemic awareness and decoding strategies. Others seem to have a specific processing difficulty that interferes with language development at the phoneme level; these students need much prolonged phonemic awareness instruction, both aurally and with print. Instruction with print letter-cluster/sound correspondences seems to facilitate phonemic awareness development for students.

Students with phonemic awareness difficulties that do not respond in good time to direct instruction often exhibit poor language skills in general. It is crucial to bring these students to the attention of the speech and language pathologist for further recommendations concerning language instruction as well as language deficits and their influence on reading ability and school learning in general. (See Chapters 2 and 3 for detail concerning language development and strategies for teaching phonemic awareness.)

EMOTIONAL ISSUES

During earlier days of remedial reading development, it was believed that emotional issues lay at the base of most reading difficulties (Bettelheim & Zelin, 1981; Dahlberg, Roswell, & Chall, 1952). Although this belief is no longer held, it is recognized that emotional issues can, at times, inhibit reading development. Emotional issues that interfere with expected reading progress may lead to performance that mirrors closely any one of the profiles, A - M, described above. Such reading difficulties may be induced or prolonged by an underlying fear of reading success or an underlying emotional distraction that draws attentional resources away from the project of learning to read. Careful information gathering, through interviews and observation during the referral stage, may highlight the existence of these issues.

Whether reading difficulties arise from emotional issues or not, reading instruction must focus on teaching the reading skills that exhibit a deficit (Dahlberg et al., 1952). However, when an underlying emotional issue exists, instruction must also include a component that focuses on alleviating the emotional stress. Within the instructional setting, teachers can use reading materials in which characters overcome difficulties similar to those that the student is encountering. Or, teachers can use materials that sow and cultivate a spark of interest in an unfamiliar area that promises hope for satisfying engagement and productivity. In addition, appropriate sources should be consulted to assure that adequate psychological treatment and support are provided by qualified personnel.

Conclusion

Linking reading assessment with program planning is a detective activity that attempts to clarify areas of weakness and strength while proposing instructional approaches appropriate to hypothesized needs. Well-designed and implemented assessments can suggest what components contribute to reading weaknesses and strengths. Such assessments can indicate whether it would be more helpful to provide instruction that targets one specific component or more useful to teach several subskills.

Examiners and teachers can check the accuracy and effectiveness of their diagnostic hypotheses by reviewing their students' progress under recommended instruction. When students do not make expected progress, diagnostic hypotheses need to be reconsidered and revised in light of this further evidence.

The assessment and instruction of reading are challenging, involving, and rewarding. Answers to the puzzles that present themselves, along with effective and appropriate instructional programs, can transform readers' lives. Knowledgeable, committed teachers remain the essence that links effective assessment and instruction. The expertise and dedication of good teachers enable learners to enter a world of knowledge, concepts, and experiences that would be unavailable without the joy and skill of well-developed reading ability.

References

Adams, M.J. (1994). *Beginning to read: Thinking and learning about print*. Cambridge, MA: MIT Press.

Armbruster, B.B. (1991). Framing: A technique for improving learning from science texts. In C.M. Santa & D.E. Alverman (Eds.), *Science learning: Process and applications*. Newark, DE: IRA.

Bettelheim, B. & Zelin, K. (1981). *On Learning to read: The child's fascination with meaning*. New York: Knopf.

Biemiller, A. (2000). Vocabulary: The missing link between phonics and comprehension. *Perspectives*, 26(4), 26-30.

Blachman, B.A. (1991). Getting ready to read: Learning how print maps to speech. In J.F. Kavanagh (Ed.), *The language continuum: From infancy to literacy*. Parkton, MD: York Press.

Blachman, B.A. (2000). Phonological awareness. In M.L. Kamil, P.B. Mosenthal, P.D. Pearson, & R. Barr (Eds.), *Handbook of reading research*. Mahwah, NJ: Lawrence Erlbaum Associates.

Bradley, L. & Bryant, P.E. (1983). Categorising sounds and learning to read: A causal connection. *Nature*, 310, 419-421.

Boucher, J.P. (1986). An investigation of the relationship between middle ear dysfunction and school difficulty in young children. *Dissertation Abstracts International, 47*, 6, 2115-A.

Brody, S. (1987). *Study skills: Teaching and learning strategies for mainstream and specialized classrooms*. Milford, NH: LARC Publishing.

Brody, S. (1989). Elements of effective instruction. Unpublished Qualifying Paper, Harvard Graduate School of Education, Cambridge: MA.

Brody, S. (1993). Developing background knowledge: A context enrichment strategy that may provide more consistent results than activation of prior knowledge. In D. Wray (Ed.), *Proceedings: 1992 United Kingdom Reading Association Annual Conference*, Exeter, England: UKRA.

Brody, S. (2001). *The Brody reading manual: An implementation guide for teachers (2nd ed.)*. Milford, NH: LARC Publishing.

Budoff, M. (1972). Measuring learning potential: An alternative to the traditional intelligence test. In G.R. Gredler (Ed.), *Ethical and legal factors in the practice of school psychology*. Proceedings of the First Annual Conference in School Psychology. Philadelphia: Temple University.

Call, P.E. (2000). Reflective questioning: A strategy to review notes. *Journal of Adolescent and Adult Literacy*, 43(5), 487-488.

Carnine, D. (2000). *Why education experts resist effective practices*. Washington, DC: Thomas Fordham Foundation. [available at http://www.edexcellence.net].

Chall, J.S. (1987). Two vocabularies for reading: Recognition and meaning. In M.G. McKeown & M.E. Curtis (Eds.), *The nature of vocabulary acquisition*. Hillsdale, NJ: Lawrence Erlbaum Assoc.

Chall, J.S. (1996). *Stages of reading development (2nd ed.)*. Orlando, FL: Harcourt Brace

Chall, J.S. & Curtis, M.E. (1990). Diagnostic achievement testing in reading. In C.R. Reynolds & R. Kamphaus (Eds.), *Handbook of Psychological and Educational Assessment of Children's Intelligence and Achievement*. NY: Guilford Press.

Chomsky, C. (1978). When you still can't read in third grade: After decoding what? In S.J. Samuels (Ed.), *What research has to say about reading instruction*. Newark, DE: International Reading Association.

Curtis, M.E. (1987). Vocabulary testing and vocabulary instruction. In M.G. McKeown & M.E. Curtis (Eds.), *The nature of vocabulary acquisition*. Hillsdale, NJ: Erlbaum.

Curtis, M.E. & Longo, A.M. (2000.). Teaching adolescents with reading difficulties: Lessons learned from Jeanne S. Chall. *Perspectives*, 26(4), 49-50.

Dahlberg, M.D., Roswell, F., & Chall, J.S. (1952). Psychotherapeutic principles as applied to remedial reading. *The Elementary School Journal*, December.

Goswami, U. (2000). Phonological and lexical processes. In M.L. Kamil, P.B. Mosenthal, P.D. Pearson, & R. Barr (Eds.), *Handbook of reading research*. Mahwah, NJ: Lawrence Erlbaum Associates.

Graves, M.F. (1987). The roles of instruction in fostering vocabulary development. In M.G. McKeown & M.E. Curtis, (Eds.), *The nature of vocabulary acquisition*. Hillsdale, NJ: Lawrence Erlbaum Assoc.

Graves, M.F., Cooke, C.L., & Laberge, M.J. (1983). Effects of previewing difficult short stories on low ability junior high school students' comprehension, recall, and attitudes. *Reading Research Quarterly*. 18(3), 262-276.

Honig, B. (1998). Preventing failure in early reading programs: A summary of research and instructional best practices. In W.M. Evers (Ed.), *What's gone wrong in America's classrooms?* Stanford, CA: Hoover Institution Press.

Holzman, S. I. (1990). The use of medical-educational test reports in schools. Unpublished doctoral dissertation. Harvard Graduate School of Education, Cambridge, MA.

Juel, C. & Minden-Cupp, C. (2000). One down and 80,000 to go: Word recognition instruction in the primary grades. *The Reading Teacher*, 53(4), 332-335.

Kaufman, A.S. (1979). *Intelligent testing with the WISC-R*. NY: John Wiley & Sons.

Kaufman, A.S. (1994). *Intelligent testing with the WISC-III*. New York: Wiley Interscience.

Kaufman, A.S. & Kaufman, N.L. (1998). *Kaufman Test of Educational Achievement, Brief Form* and *Comprehensive Form Normative Update*. Circle Pines, MN: American Guidance Service.

Lerner, J. (2000). *Learning disabilities: Theories, diagnoses, and teaching strategies (8th ed.)*. Boston: Houghton Mifflin.

Leslie, L. & Allen, L. (1999). Factors that predict success in an early literacy intervention project. *Reading Research Quarterly*, 34(4), 404-424.

Liberman, I. (1987). Language and literacy: The obligation of the schools of education. In *Intimacy with language: A forgotten basic in teacher education. Conference proceedings*. Baltimore, MD: The Orton Dyslexia Society.

Lovett, M.W., Steinbach, K.A., & Frijters, J.C. (2000). Remediating the core deficits of developmental reading disability: A double-deficit perspective. *Journal of Learning Disabilities*, 33(4), 334-358.

Lyon, G.R. (1998). Why reading is not a natural process. *Educational Leadership,* 55(6), 14-18.

Lyon, G.R. (2000). Learning to read: A call from research to action. *NEBIDA Newsletter,* Spring/Summer 15-18.

MacGinitie, W.H. & MacGinitie, R.K. (2000). *Gates-MacGinitie Reading Tests (4th ed.)*. Chicago: Riverside Publishing Company.

Moats, L.C. (2000/1999). Teaching reading is rocket science: What expert teachers of reading should know and be able to do. *NEBIDA Newsletter,* Spring/Summer, 10-12. [Original work published in 1999.]

Moats, L.C. (2000). *Whole language lives on: The illusion of "balanced" reading instruction*. Washington, DC: Thomas Fordham Fooundation. [Available at http://www.edexcellence.net/.]

National Reading Panel [NRP]. (2000). *Report of the National Reading Panel: Teaching children to read.* Washington, DC: National Institute of Child Health and Human Development. [Available at http://www.nichd.nih.gov/publications/nrp.]

Perfetti, C.A. (1984). Reading acquisition and beyond: Decoding includes cognition. *American Journal of Education.* November, 40 - 60.

Perfetti, C.A. (1985). *Reading ability.* New York: Oxford Press.

Pressley, M. (2000). What should comprehension instruction be the instruction of? In M.L. Kamil, P.B. Mosenthal, P.D. Pearson, & R. Barr (Eds.), *Handbook of reading research.* Mahwah, NJ: Lawrence Erlbaum Associates.

Rath, L.K. (1990). Phonemic awareness: Its role in reading development. Unpublished Qualifying Paper, Harvard Graduate School of Education, Cambridge, MA.

Roswell, F.G. & Chall, J.S. (1992). *Diagnostic Assessments of Reading with Trial Teaching Strategies.* Chicago: Riverside Publishing Company.

Reutzel, D.R., & Cooter, R.B. (1992). *Teaching children to read: From basals to books.* NY: Merrill.

Salvia, J. & Ysseldyke, J.E. (2000). *Assessment.* Boston: Houghton Mifflin.

Samuels, S.J., Schermer, N., & Reinking, D. (1992). Reading fluency: Techniques for making decoding automatic. In S.J. Samuels & A.E. Farstrup (Eds.), *What research has to say about reading instruction (2nd ed.).* Newark, DE: International Reading Association.

Santa, C., Havens, L., & Harrison, S. (1989). Teaching secondary science through reading, writing, studying, and problem solving. In D. Lapp, J. Flood, N. Farnam, (Eds.), *Content area reading and learning: Instructional strategies.* Englewood Cliffs, NJ: Prentice Hall.

Slosson, R.L. (1991). *Slosson Oral Reading Test-Revised.* East Aurora, NY: Slosson Educational Publications.

Snow, C.E., Burns, M.S., & Griffin, P. (Eds.) (1998). *Preventing reading difficulties in young children.* Washington, DC: National Academy Press.

Spache, G.D. (1981). *Diagnostic Reading Scales-Revised.* Monterey, CA: CTB/McGraw-Hill.

Stahl, S.A., Heubach, K., & Cramond, B. (1997). *Fluency-oriented Reading Instruction. Reading Research Report #79.* Athens, GA: National Reading Research Center.

Stanovich, K.E. (1986). Matthew effects in reading: Some consequences of individual differences in the acquisition of literacy. *Reading Research Quarterly,* 21(4), 360-406.

Stanovich, K.E. (1994). Romance and reality. *Reading Teacher.* 47(4), 280-291.

Stotsky, S. (1986). Asking questions about ideas: A critical component in critical thinking. *The Leaflet,* Fall, 39-47.

Strucker, J. (2000). Jeanne Chall and adult literacy. *Perspectives,* 26(4), 45-47.

Torgesen, J., Wagner, R., & Rashotte, C. (1999). *Test of Word Reading Efficiency.* Austin, TX: Pro-Ed.

Wagner, R., Torgesen, J., & Rashotte, C. (1999). *Comprehensive Test of Phonological Processing.* Austin, TX: Pro-Ed.

Wiederholt, J.L. & Bryant, B.R. (1992). *Gray Oral Reading Test-3rd ed.* Austin, TX: Pro-Ed.

Wilkinson, G.S. (1993). *Wide Range Achievement Test-3rd ed.* Wilmington, DE: Wide Range, Inc.

Willis, J.O. (1998). Post otitis auditory dysfunction. *NHASP Protocol*, Newsletter of the NH Assoc. of School Psychologists, *17*(1), 6, 7, 9. Reprinted 1999 in *The School Psychologist*, NY Assoc. of School Psychologists, *XVII*(2), 10, 27.

Willis, J.O. & Dumont, R.P. (1998). *Guide to identification of learning disabilities (1998 NY State ed.).* Acton, MA: Copley. [Available at: http://alpha.fdu.edu/~dumont/]

Wolf, M., Bowers, P.G., & Biddle, K. (2000). Naming-speed processes, timing, and reading: A conceptual review. *Journal of Learning Disabilities*, *33*(4), 388-407.

Wolf, M., Miller, L., & Donnelly, K. (2000). Retrieval, automaticity, vocabulary elaboration, orthography (RAVE-O): A comprehensive, fluency-based reading intervention program. *Journal of Learning Disabilities*, *33*(4), 375-386.

Woodcock, R.W. (1998). *Woodcock Reading Mastery Tests-Revised Normative Update.* Circle Pines, MN: American Guidance Service.

Woodcock, R.W., McGrew, K.S., & Mather, N. (2001). *Woodcock-Johnson III.* Itasca, IL: Riverside.

Glossary

ABILITY In educational testing, "ability" usually refers to performance, attainments, or scores on tests, or other measures, that are used to assess intelligence or basic processes.

ACADEMIC In educational jargon, the term has come to mean "relating to skills formally taught in school," so that "academic testing" is likely to mean testing of reading, writing, and arithmetic skills in contrast to scholarly or impractical testing.

ACHIEVEMENT In educational testing, "achievement" usually refers to performance, attainments, or test scores in school subjects.

AGE EQUIVALENT The average age of students who earned the same number of Raw Score points on a test as did the student being tested. Usually written with a hyphen: 10-3 would be ten years and three months. Potentially a very misleading score. See MENTAL AGE and GRADE EQUIVALENT

AUTOMATICITY Successfully performing a task without conscious attention.

BACKGROUND KNOWLEDGE Information related to a topic under study. May be known or unknown by the reader. See also PRIOR KNOWLEDGE.

BACK VOWEL OR CONSONANT Set of sounds made in the back of the mouth such as /h/.

BOTTOM A sufficient number of easy items on a test to allow accurate measurement of the achievement or abilities of students who are weakest in the skills being tested. See TOP.

CHRONOLOGICAL AGE For children who were born prematurely, it is often best to calculate a "due date age" based on the due date instead of the birth date. Writers must be very clear concerning which is used.

CLOZE A technique of testing reading comprehension by asking the student to supply missing words.

CODE Any system of symbols used to transmit information.

COGNITION Thinking.

COGNITIVE PROCESS Any mental process.

COMPONENT A subskill, facet, or aspect of the reading process that contributes to overall reading ability.

CONNECTED TEXT Material written in phrases and sentences to convey meaning, rather than single words or lists of single words.

CONTEXT CLUES A strategy for reading unfamiliar words by inference from the rest of the passage.

CONTINUANT A speech sound such as /m/ that may be prolonged without distortion.

CRITERION-REFERENCED Generally, criterion referenced testing is evaluation in which the student's performance is compared to a set criterion rather than to the scores of other students. Test criteria include, for example, a certain percentage correct or passing an item designed to test a certain skill.

DECODE To transform a printed letter, or group of letters, to its corresponding sound. The process of recognizing words; print-to-sound mapping. Decoding involves pronouncing written words correctly, but not necessarily knowing their meanings.

DIRECT INSTRUCTION Teaching through explicit teacher explanation, demonstration, description direction, etc.

DYSLEXIA A disorder affecting ability to read and/or spell despite good instruction, adequate intelligence, sufficient physical and emotional health, and supportive environmental background.

DYSPEDAGOGIA A failure of teaching. A didagenic disorder.

ENCODING Spelling; matching sounds with their corresponding letters; sound-to-print mapping.

FRONT VOWEL OR CONSONANT Sounds made in the front of the mouth with the blade of the tongue, such as /t/.

GLUE WORDS Common words that are often taught as logographic wholes, such as *and, then, is*.

GRADE EQUIVALENT The average grade placement of students who earned the same number of Raw Score points on a test as did the students being tested. Usually written with a decimal point (3.2 would be the second tenth of third grade or 36 to 53 school days into third grade.)

GRAPHEME The smallest unit in the writing system of a language; letter symbols.

GRAPHIC CODES Neurological codes that process printed symbols for speech.

IQ Intelligence quotient. Originally the ratio of Mental Age (MA) to chronological age (CA), multiplied by 100. The ratio IQ is a very poor score because of the problems with Mental Ages and because the same IQ means different things at different ages. Most IQs today are deviation IQs, simply a form of Standard Score, usually with a Mean of 100 and a Standard Deviation of 15 or 16 points.

INTONATION Variation in pitch from one part of an utterance to another.

LANGUAGE-BASED Based in language, as in a language-based learning disability that reflects deficits in skills requiring the use of language.

LATENCY In testing or research jargon, the time elapsed between display of a test item and initiation of response.

LEXICAL ACCESS Connecting to the lexicon during cognitive activities that make use of language.

LEXICAL CODES Neurological codes that process meaning.

LEXICON Mental dictionary.

LINGUISTICALLY-BASED Information or processes involving language, conveying language, or conveyed by language.

LOGOGRAPH symbol (picture, icon) used to represent a word in a system of writing, such as Chinese, in which words are written in symbols that represent their meaning rather than by symbols that represent their sounds.

MENTAL AGE The average age of students who earned the same number of Raw Score points on a test as did the student being tested. Potentially a very misleading score.

METACOGNITION Attentiveness to one's own thinking during the process of thinking.

METALINGUISTIC AWARENESS Attentiveness to one's own language processing during the process of using language.

MODEL or MODELING In education jargon, to teach by demonstrating the skill, process, or activity under study.

NEURAL CODES In reading jargon, linguistically-based messages carried by nerve cells.

NORMED or NORM-REFERENCED A test is normed if it is administered to a selected sample of people whose scores are then used as a yardstick for assessing the performance of persons who subsequently take the test. To do this, the test must first be standardized.

ORTHOGRAPHY Spelling system.

PHONEME A representation of the smallest sound unit in a language. For example, the phoneme /f/ represents the sound of *f* or the sound of *ph*.

PHONEMIC AWARENESS Ability to segment and blend the sounds of language.

PHONICS A method of teaching reading that is based on decoding words using letter-sound relationships; direct instruction in the spelling and decoding of printed letters.

PHONOLOGICAL CODES Neural codes that process sound stimuli.

POLYSEMOUS Multiple meanings.

PRIOR KNOWLEDGE A reader's knowledge related to a text under study. See also BACKGROUND KNOWLEDGE.

RAPID-AUTOMATIZED-NAMING (RAN) An automatic process that contributes to reading fluency. It is assessed by asking readers to quickly say the names of a series of common symbols (such as numerals, pictures, or single letters) that are presented in printed lists or rows. Rapid naming involves recalling and saying the names of visually presented symbols and is independent of phonological decoding of the spelled names of these symbols.

RAW SCORE The simple number of points or items correct on a test.

RELIABILITY In statistics, reliability refers only to the consistency of a test. A test that consistently gives the same, wrong, score to the same person would be considered very reliable. Head size used to be considered a reliable and valid measure of intelligence during the era when most psychologists were men, who tend to have larger skulls than women.

SCAFFOLD A support provided to help a student perform a challenging task that could not be done independently.

SCALED SCORE A form of Standard Score, variously defined by different authors. Wechsler (1939, 1974, 1991) uses Standard Scores with a Mean of 100 and a Standard Deviation of 15 for his broad scales and "Scaled Scores" with a Mean of 10 and a Standard Deviation of 3 for his individual tests. Hammill (1985; Hammill & Larsen, 1988) reverse this usage, much to the confusion of report writers and readers.

SCHEMA, SCHEMATA *(plural)* In reading comprehension jargon, the term refers to a reader's understanding of a text. The reader constructs a schema, or understanding, of a text. Readers construct schemata in their minds as they read texts. Schemata are also constructed during the use of oral language. In this case, a schema is the speaker's, or listener's, understanding of what was said.

SEVERE Extreme or very serious in the opinion of the person using the term.

SEQUENCING Perceiving, understanding, or remembering things in a particular order.

SIGHT WORDS *See* GLUE WORDS

STANDARDIZED A test is standardized if the content and the rules for administering and scoring it are set down in a prescribed manner that is followed by each examiner. A standardized test is not necessarily normed, but a normed test must be standardized.

STANDARD DEVIATION (s, s.d., or S.D.) In a normal distribution, a yardstick that can be used to mark off units. The distance from one Standard Deviation below the Mean to one Standard Deviation above the Mean includes about the middle two-thirds of all the scores in the Normal Distribution. The distance from two Standard Deviations below the Mean to two Standard Deviations above the Mean includes approximately the middle 95% of all the scores in the Normal Distribution. Wechsler IQs use a Standard Deviation with 15 points and a Mean of 100; consequently, approximately two-thirds of the possible scores fall between 85 and 115. Binet IQs use a Standard Deviation of 16 points, with the middle two-thirds of scores falling between 84 and 116.

STANDARD ERROR OF MEASUREMENT SE_M The Standard Deviation of all the scores that a hypothetical student might receive in retaking a test an infinite number of times.

STANDARD SCORE A score defined by the number of Standard Deviation units that it lies away from the Mean of the distribution of scores.

STANINE STAndard NINEs, a nine-point, ascending scale for reporting test scores. Stanines have a Mean of 5 and a Standard Deviation of 1.96. Except for stanines one and nine, which theoretically stretch out infinitely, each Stanine is one-half Standard Deviation in width. Stanine 5 is centered on the Mean.

STREPHOSYMBOLIA A term used by Samuel Orton to describe learning disabilities—literally, twisted symbols.

STRUCTURAL ANALYSIS Decoding words by breaking them into syllables or affixes and base words for easier and more effective phonetic word attack.

TOP Sufficient number of difficult items on a test to allow accurate measurement of the achievement or abilities of students who have strong abilities in the areas the test assesses.

VALIDITY In statistics, validity is the accuracy with which a test measures that which it is supposed to be measuring. The test must, of course, be reliable, but determination of validity requires additional information concerning how accurately it predicts the information it purports to measure.

Z-SCORE A score defined by the number of Standard Deviation units it lies away from the Mean. A Z-Score of -1.00 is exactly one Standard Deviation below the Mean.

Index